MAN FOR ALL SEASONS

By the same author

Out in the Cold: Pacifists and Conscientious Objectors in New Zealand During World War Two

On A Roll: A History of Gambling and Lotteries in New Zealand

Bulls, Bears and Elephants: A History of the New Zealand Stock Exchange

Three Over Two on Goodtime Sugar: The New Zealand TAB Turns 50

Thoroughbreds, Trainers, Toffs and Tic Tac Men: A Cartoon History of Horse Racing in New Zealand

Those Who Can Teach: A History of Secondary Education in New Zealand from the Union Perspective

A Question of Faith: A History of the Christian Pacifist Society

The Big Blue: Snapshots of the 1951 Waterfront Lockout

Drivers, Dongas and Divots: The Story of the Titahi Golf Club 1958–2008

Field Punishment No 1: Archibald Baxter, Mark Briggs and New Zealand's Anti-Militarist Tradition

Jagged Seas: The Story of the New Zealand Seamen's/Seafarers' Union 1879–2003 (in press)

The Dream Team: The Greatest Players to Wear the All Black Jersey (with Maurice Bennett, in press)

MAN FOR ALL SEASONS

The life and times of Ken Douglas

DAVID GRANT

RANDOM HOUSE
NEW ZEALAND

A RANDOM HOUSE BOOK published by Random House New Zealand
18 Poland Road, Glenfield, Auckland, New Zealand

For more information about our titles go to www.randomhouse.co.nz
A catalogue record for this book is available from the National Library of New Zealand

Random House New Zealand is part of the Random House Group
New York London Sydney Auckland Delhi Johannesburg

First published 2010

ISBN 978 1 86979 389 0

Cover design: Pieta Brenton
Cover image: Ian Mackley, *Dominion Post* Collection, Alexander Turnbull Library, Wellington, New Zealand.
Text design: Saskia Nicol

Printed in New Zealand by Printlink

FSC
Mixed Sources
Product group from well-managed forests, controlled sources and recycled wood or fibre
Cert no. SGS-COC-005088
www.fsc.org
© 1996 Forest Stewardship Council

CONTENTS

Introduction

Rarely does mention of the name Ken Douglas engender a neutral response. Some are dismissive; a few cringe in anger; more are guardedly respectful; others are enthusiastic and suggest a study of the man and his work would be illuminating and educational. Many, purporting to be informed students of history and politics, point to an enigmatic quality in the man. They wonder about a perceptible political swing from 'hard left' to 'apparent right' whereby Douglas has counted communist union leaders Chip Bailey and Bill Andersen alongside former journalist turned lobbyist Dick Griffin and National Party politician Philip Burdon as close friends. Yet these reactions reflect an emotional response, and as such are often superficial, relying on little more than a perception of the man who was responsible — or not responsible enough, as some have argued — for leading the New Zealand trade union movement through its most challenging time.

As a young adult Ken Douglas — the confrontational son of an alcoholic, often-absent mother — was a large, physically imposing man, with a rough, pockmarked face and unkempt hair, all of which seemed indicative of a tough, no-nonsense union leader to come. His relatively early and very public membership of the Communist Party, and later the Socialist Unity Party — which he helped to establish — further stereotyped him as a union 'heavy' out to smash the forces of capitalism for his own ideological ends. In Douglas's case the truth is much more complex.

Evoking images is easy. To get to the heart of the man is more difficult. A beguiling and extensive list of adjectives can be employed to explain the multi-faceted personality traits that have determined Douglas's life and work — charming, intelligent, larger than life, diligent, single-minded, busy, far-sighted, adroit, brusque, controversial, quick-witted, temperamental, determined, opinionated, energetic, thick-skinned, gregarious, impatient, stubborn, unapologetic, unpunctual and obsessively tidy come to mind. In themselves, these traits do not fit into an easily discernible whole and collectively they reflect a set of paradoxes.

Douglas has lived a life full of contradictions — the truck driver who has parleyed with heads of state, the failed student who now holds an honorary doctorate, the lifelong Marxist who now sits on boards with admiring capitalists, the crumpled-cardigan-wearing, coarse-tongued trade unionist who in 1999 collected, in well-tailored suit, both the Order of New Zealand, the country's highest honour, awarded to only 20 living New Zealanders, and an honorary Doctor of Literature from Victoria University of Wellington. Needless to say, these contradictions do not marry easily into a logical and cohesive whole. That there were and remain different and apparently competing tangents to his life and work has made the research for this biography even more intriguing, just as it has made explaining why this was the case so challenging and contentious. This concerned me until I discovered that some scholars have argued that 'contradiction and ambiguity are central to the construction of meaning'. Yet the debate over the apparent incongruities that permeate Douglas's life and work will continue long after this book's publication.

Researching the biography of a living person has both advantages and disadvantages. The big advantage, of course, is that I was able to get to know Douglas and talk with him at length — both formally and informally. I was also able to talk with family members, friends, unionists, political allies and antagonists — and he has plenty of all of these — to obtain the most comprehensive picture I could. These discussions were both fascinating and illuminating. Ken Douglas is sharp, companionable and has a prodigious memory. Acutely aware, however, that developing too close a relationship could lead towards hagiography, I was determined to keep a certain distance from him. To be as fully informed and discerning as possible, I needed to gather and assess all fact and opinion and arrive at conclusions that could stand up to the most rigorous scrutiny.

Douglas himself wanted me to be absolutely honest — to write a 'warts and all' biography — and he made no demands for expurgation of any kind. He made a promise to himself that he would answer all my questions with complete honesty; nothing was to be off the table. While he read every word in the text, there were no censorious reflections, just the intermittent drawing of my attention to some further potential area of research, or the provision of an occasional anecdote.

I could not have wished for more. For this first-time biographer such unfettered access was both a huge advantage and a welcome relief. I found honesty to be one of Douglas's most admirable traits. In all the discussions I and others have had with him, alongside the others I conducted with both 'friend' and 'foe', there has never been any hint that he has suffered from self-delusion or self-aggrandisement. As with many people who have achieved prominence, Ken Douglas's confidence and outspokenness hide a certain insecurity, the origins of which can be seen in his upbringing.

This book had its genesis late in 2004, when historical researcher David Filer contacted me on behalf of documentary-maker Vincent Burke, to see if I was interested in writing a biography to accompany a television documentary that Burke's company, Top Shelf Productions, was making on the life and work of Ken Douglas. He hoped to have the documentary ready for screening within 12 months. My initial response was guarded as I was busy with other projects and the timing would be a problem. On reflection, however, I reasoned it was too good an opportunity to turn down. I would be able to explore the life and work of one of New Zealand's most prominent and controversial trade union leaders, a man who was in charge of the movement during this country's most tumultuous period of political and industrial change, the speed and all-embracing nature of which has been unmatched in the Western world before or since.[1]

Given its significance, I demurred at executing a quick and superficial assessment of the man and his work. That, I reasoned, would be an injustice both to his achievements and to my integrity as a professional historian. Burke, who knew Douglas personally, and Tom Beran, then publisher at Random House New Zealand, agreed with my proposal that the book needed to be a thoroughly researched and comprehensive biography of Ken Douglas, trade union leader, in the context of his time.

Taking time out from other responsibilities, I began the project over four months in 2005 and recommenced it for periods in 2007 and 2008 with the assistance of a generous New Zealand History Trust Fund Award from the Ministry for Culture and Heritage and a scattering of funds from other sources. Other writing projects and teaching responsibilities intervened, and, as a consequence, the draft was not completed until May 2010.

The early chapters of the book are unapologetically wide-ranging, and are critical to understanding Douglas's working-class roots. They recall both the strength of kinship ties within this poor family and the real problems of, at worst, spousal abuse, alcoholism and early death. Into this environment, Douglas was born in November 1935. Distant during his early life, sadly, was his mother, who abandoned the young Douglas and his sister for a party life in the city and was later ravaged by long-term alcoholism. In her place, his father's mother Carrie Douglas, his principal caregiver from the age of six, imparted both love and the personal values that he would hold dear in his adult life. His mother's father, George Farrow, willingly shared his working-class principles and, within those, the ethics of responsible and assertive trade union practice.

Douglas left high school an academic failure and worked variously in a wool store, as an asphalt labourer, and on the wharves before joining his father as a truck driver. At drivers' union meetings, where he was usually the youngest, he was outspoken from the start, and was noticed with a mixture of awe and admiration by the older drivers. Helped by his family connections, before long he became an executive member, then an organiser, and soon afterwards president — the youngest ever in all these positions — of the Wellington Drivers' Union as it sought reaffiliation with the Federation of Labour after the travails of the 1951 lockout. In 1963, Douglas became the union's secretary — at 27 the youngest in the country — and was appointed to the national council of the umbrella New Zealand Drivers' Federation.

Thereafter he cut his industrial teeth in two contentious and long-running industrial disputes in Wellington. His reputation enhanced, Douglas became one of the most prominent union officials in the country — along with Bill Andersen in Auckland — in part because the drivers' awards were among the first to be fought and settled every year. By this time, like Andersen, Douglas had become a student of Karl Marx and was a card-carrying and forthright member of the New Zealand Communist Party; three years later he took a leading role in the establishment of the Russian-aligned Socialist Unity Party, and he led its Wellington branch until the party's demise in 1995.

Despite his growing reputation as an assertive, no-nonsense and analytical trade union leader, his politics for seven years denied him a place on the Federation of Labour's executive. Once successful in 1977, his ascent was rapid. The following year, he became FOL secretary after Jim Knox took over the presidency on Tom Skinner's retirement. He faced off against Robert Muldoon, at the same time winning momentous industrial battles at Kinleith and later Kawerau.

From 1984, Knox and Douglas went head to head with Roger Douglas's deregulatory economic reforms, which along with ever-increasing technological advances devastated traditional New Zealand industry. In 1987 he was at the forefront of the merger of the private and state unions, overseeing as its first president a Council of Trade Unions that initially represented more than 650,000 workers and was by far the largest organisation in the country. By this time he had developed a negotiation and conciliation thesis and an ethos of adaptability which he believed would help workers cope with new worlds of work. The alternative was facing unemployment with or without redundancy.

Despite the signals, however, he did not anticipate the radical extent of Bill Birch's 1991 Employment Contracts Bill, which turned industrial relations in New Zealand on its head, destroying the 'historic consensus' between capital and labour which had been the cornerstone of industrial relations in this country for close to 100 years. He raged against the Bill, but he also understood that with National's huge majority and some of the outdatedness of the 'compulsion' elements in the existing law it would not be overturned.

Instead, working with unions, business and the government, he sought to 'humanise' the Bill, searching for a new consensus where unions would not only return to a meaningful role in wage and condition negotiations but also play a proactive role in New Zealand's economic development, as had occurred briefly in 1990 when the CTU had signed a 'compact' with Mike Moore. This stance alienated Douglas from a significant number of traditional unionists who wanted the Bill to be overturned with no conditions, and resulted in a bitterness which has lasted to this day.

Increasingly through the 1990s Douglas took leading roles in international trade unionism, garnering respect from union leaders in the Pacific, Asia and Europe through the International Labour Organisation. 'Retirement' in 1999 turned out to be a misnomer as he found outlets for his considerable energy in extensive involvement in local body politics, sports administration and myriad boards, both capitalist and altruistic. His colleagues on those boards universally praise his world view, strategic thinking, integrity, honesty, and concern for humanitarian ideals. This admiration disconcerts Douglas. In 2010, his politics remain communist and he brings the same values to his tasks as he did when he was a young leader of the Wellington Drivers' Union.

This book could not have been written without the assistance of many people. Random House's publishing director Nicola Legat was an enthusiast for the project from the beginning and I thrived in the company of her expertise, professionalism and willingness, always, to go the extra mile. Other Random House personnel — in particular Sarah Thornton, publicity manager, Karen Ferns, managing director and Stuart Lipshaw, editorial assistant — lent their collective expertise to its successful publication. Publicist Lorraine Steel handled the public relations with aplomb. Nicola van Aardt managed the project, which included organising and processing the illustrations and their captions, and Diane Lowther was responsible for devising the index. Editor Susan Brierley expertly tiptoed through the script with gentle precision rather than the stomp of a heavy jackboot, and for that I am most grateful.

I thank also the following for assistance and support in many ways great and small: John Allen, Kathleen Angel, Terree Barrymore, Matthew Beattie, Roger Blakeley, Peter Bromhead, Bob Brockie, Philip Burdon, Ron Burgess, Doug Catley, David Colquhoun and his colleagues in the Manuscripts and Archives Section of the Alexander Turnbull Library, Jane Douglas, Hannah Douglas, Helen Douglas, John Douglas, Peter Douglas, Anthony Ellison, Kieran Elvy, Gerald Dowthwaite, Brian Fitzwater, Gary Fitzwater, Roger Fowler, Richie Gillespie, Richard Griffin, Peter Harris, Nicky and Jock Hobbs, June Hoskin, Cathy Marr, Jim Hubbard, John McCormick, John Miller, Marian Minson, Rosanne Meo, Grant Morgan, Paddianne Neely, Therese O'Connell, Monique Oomen, John Palmer, Dean Parker,

Len Parker, Susan Richards, Glwadys Robson, Tom Scott, Jackie and Alan Thomas, Steve Tew, Paul Tolich, Marilyn Tucker, Christine Turner, Pat Walsh, Betty Walton and Ross Wilson. Most of all I thank Ken Douglas, who answered all my questions with alacrity and has stimulated my intellect in areas which I had not thought possible. There is one key name missing from this list. Angela Foulkes, who worked closely with Douglas, first as vice-president then as secretary of the Council of Trade Unions between 1987 and 1999, declined to be involved with the project.

It is unfortunate and extremely disappointing that the Security Intelligence Service has declined three times to release to Ken Douglas the information it has on him in its files, despite a 2008 acknowledgement from the SIS that he was not of current security interest. Indeed, it was only in 2008 that Dr Warren Tucker, director of the SIS, acknowledged that his organisation *had* a file on Douglas. In 2005 Tucker's predecessor, Richard Woods, nonsensically refused even to 'confirm or deny' that it had any information on him — despite the well-known fact that he had been a frequently condemned leader of the Russian-aligned Socialist Unity Party for 30 years. The core of Douglas's argument is that the cold war is long over, communism has disappeared, and the Socialist Unity Party has been inactive since 1995. Today Douglas is a member of the Labour Party, sits on many boards, and holds, and has held, the confidence of the current and previous prime minister and Cabinet ministers.[2]

In March 2008 and July 2009, Tucker argued in letters to Douglas's lawyer, Hazel Armstrong, that for 'security and privacy' reasons much security reporting from the cold-war period could not yet be made public. He noted that 'operational methods', for example, were still in use and needed to be protected, and that where information had been provided from abroad the originator must authorise its release. Moreover, he noted, there were security issues that concerned the roles of foreign powers in New Zealand. Douglas was not interested in overseas information, but rather material on his activities in New Zealand that pertained to the SUP and its predecessor the New Zealand

Communist Party, to which he belonged for six years during the early 1960s.

In subsequent conversation with Douglas and Armstrong, Tucker has called separating such material from overseas information 'inappropriate'; no information will be released. Douglas is appealing to Privacy Commissioner Marie Shroff, asking the Commission to seek an investigation into Tucker's decision.[3]

David Grant
Wellington
May 2010

CHAPTER 1

Working-class son

On 14 September 1946, when Ken Douglas's grandfather George died suddenly, his son Bryce rushed from the prostrate body sprawled on the bedroom floor into the kitchen, uplifted his father's treasured framed photograph of Winston Churchill from the shelf above the coal range, and smashed it into a hundred pieces over the coal bucket. 'I've been wanting to do that for fucking years!' he shouted. Bryce's anger was a manifestation of his family's decades-long struggle to find economic security and relief for their mother Carrie, who had carried an enormous personal burden in trying to bring up and educate her large family. When talk around the dinner table became heated and the loud socialist argument left George more and more isolated, he would grab the Churchill photograph and thrust it back and forwards in front of him in a pitiable gesture of defiance.

For Bryce and his brothers, it was irrelevant that Churchill still basked in an appreciative glow in the vast majority of New Zealand households for having inspired mother England and its Commonwealth to smash the might of German Nazism. This was a class issue. Churchill, the Tory, represented the forces of the haves. The Douglas family, like the Farrows from whose family Ken's mother Madge originated, were staunchly working class, sustained by the dignity of their labour to make the world a better place for their families to live in. As children, the Douglas brothers wore hand-me-downs and went to school barefoot. There was only money for the youngest of them, Lyndsay, born in 1923, to be sent to secondary school. The Farrows of the same generation all left school at 12, or earlier. George Farrow, Ken's maternal grandfather, went to no school, leaving home with a group of itinerant sheep herders in Victoria, Australia, at the tender age of seven so he would be less of a burden on his poverty-stricken mother. He learned to read and write around an outback campfire.

Among those in the immediate family, only George Douglas was not dyed-in-the-wool Labour. His personal politics were obscure but he was an Empire-loving imperialist, an allegiance best highlighted by the overt visibility of the Churchill photograph. He persistently refused to remove it, despite the remonstrations of members of his family who would, like many other working families of the time, have preferred to have assembled underneath the benign countenance of the venerated Joe Savage. (Bryce in particular would incite the old man's ire by rising while his father was sitting at the head of the table during a meal, his back to the image, and turning it back to front.) In contrast, Carrie and her sons, who still lived at home even as adults, were socialist Labourites, their political views hewn through the tough years of the 1930s Depression.[4] All of the family, including George, had been unemployed and hungry for various lengths of time, and had suffered the indignity of having furniture and personal belongings cast out onto the street by a rapacious landlord when they could not pay the rent.

When Ken Douglas went to live with his father's parents in this Northland, Wellington, home in 1941 at the age of six, George was not the most senior resident. That honour belonged to Carrie's father, Henry Dowthwaite, a Yorkshireman by birth, and by then a widower who would outlive his wife Emma Jane by 11 years. Born in 1854, Henry was barely a teen when he skipped school and ran away to sea as a ship's boy. For close to 30 years he lived a tough, adventurous life as a seafarer, the scars on his back the legacy of whippings by brutal masters. Shipwrecked three times, he was the only survivor on one occasion. He came ashore in Wellington in the late 1870s and worked on scows, coasters and trans-Tasman vessels. Whether he had jumped ship or emigrated legally is not certain. One family anecdote recalls Henry burying — and later uplifting — a cask of rum stolen from a ship wrecked on the Patea bar. What *is* known is that Henry lived a rumbustious life. Fisticuffs, drinking, gambling, whoring and carousing were part and parcel of seafarers' lives and Henry was no exception.

He settled down somewhat after he met and married servant-housekeeper Bridget Lilly, a feisty colleen of Irish extraction, on 11 July 1882. The couple settled in Patea, where Henry joined a bridge-building gang, though the family later moved to Wellington. Henry was 28 and Bridget 22 when they married. She was Roman Catholic. Henry was not, and he insisted that his new wife change her name from Bridget to Emma Jane to conceal her Irish-Catholic heritage. Changing faiths meant estrangement from her closest relatives but in fact she never forsook her Catholicism, sneaking out behind Henry's back, or in his absence, to attend Sunday Mass. But Henry had the last word. When, on her deathbed, Emma Jane called for a priest, an Anglican minister arrived instead.[5]

After their move to Wellington, Henry built a cottage at 3 Hanover Street, Wadestown, for Emma Jane and their eight children, who came in quick succession. His pride and joy was the huge two-acre garden he established, which stretched down to the fish-laden Kaiwharawhara Stream at the edge of the property. He also built a hothouse in which he grew grapes and tomatoes. When most of the children had left home, Emma Jane and Henry sold this house and bought a smaller cottage at Trentham, very close to the racecourse, where he established another large garden.

Henry continued to pursue his less salubrious habits. He loved his ale, much more than he should have. After one late-night appearance at home from a drinking session with yet another lame excuse, Emma Jane let fly with a saucepan. Henry just managed to close the door in time as the pan slammed into it. Opening it, he exclaimed triumphantly, 'Ya missed me, woman!' just as a second pan struck him hard on the bridge of his nose. 'Damned Fenian witch!' was his oft-heard response in such situations.[6]

Work hard, play hard, was Henry's philosophy. Gambling was an associated passion; poker and three-card-loo were favourite pastimes, as was placing bets with bookmakers or at the tote during his frequent journeys to race meetings all over the southern half of the North Island. Once, in the 1920s, the most fussy of his daughters, Hilda, happily married and settled in Wanganui, would not let her father in the house at the end of a local race meeting because he was staggeringly drunk and might damage her pristine carpets and polished furniture, quite apart from the bad influence he might have on her four children. He spent the night down the road in a run-down boarding house.[7]

Hilda's son, Colin Browne, recalled Henry as a 'rough old cuss who gave Mum a hard time'. In many families at this time, such behaviour was par for the course. Conversely, Henry's granddaughter Gwladys Robson — from another part of the family — remembers Emma Jane as being a tough biddy in her own right. 'I remember once when she was brushing my hair when I was a child. If she struggled with the tangles and I squealed in pain she would strike the back of my head with the back of the brush, which was ivory. She also added soda to glasses of milk she gave to us. It was undrinkable but our remonstrations got nowhere. Maybe it was an old Irish habit.'[8]

In Wellington, Henry became a stevedore on the wharves, working for Scotland and Gannaways, the city's biggest firm. While not a member of the watersiders' union during the 1913 strike, he marched and attended protest rallies in sympathy with the watersiders, on one occasion being transported home by cart after being injured by a wallop from a police baton. Henry had no peer as a worker. Over the years he became highly sought after by shipping companies and ships' captains for his expertise in ensuring that cargo was safely stowed before vessels sailed or steamed from the harbour, his many years at sea having taught him the utmost importance of safe stowage.

It is not known exactly when Henry moved into 111 Northland Road, but it would have been some time after Emma Jane's death in October 1931.[9] It was tough for Henry with no spouse. Regularly he would walk, in tears, to the Karori Cemetery, carrying flowers from the Northland home to place on her grave. His grandson Maurice Fitzwater recalled that he and his Douglas cousins would delight in teasing Henry about his loyalty to Britain. If the Americans, or any other race, were mentioned, Henry would thump his chest and declare 'British, me!'[10]

To his great-grandson Ken — born in 1935 and living at 111 Northland Road from March 1941 — Henry was a grizzled old sea dog, stocky and bald with a craggy face, white bushy beard and the outsized red nose indicative of a life of hard work and much drink. Dressed in a ship's blazer, he often wore a marker's shade — somewhat like a sun visor — and a polka-dot kerchief attached around his neck. To the amusement of his grandchildren, he would drop eggs into his mouth to eat, shell and all, and he would rub his arms to produce flakes of sea-salt which floated up from the pores. By his ninth decade, Henry spent much of his time in bed, or at least in his bedroom, and it was Ken's chore as a boy to empty the piss-pot that stood under his bed and fetch him from this room for dinner in the evenings. He would struggle out in his pyjamas, with an old jersey or favourite multi-striped blazer pulled over the top.

Once a month, Henry traipsed off — resplendent in blazer and kerchief — into the city to collect his pension and then to chew the fat with old seafaring mates in the Pier Hotel opposite the Public Trust in Lambton Quay, or the Western Park in Tinakori Road where he had his own 'corner' near the fireplace. He always caught the 6.30pm tram home, though once or twice he did not make it from the tram stop to the front door. One evening, some children knocked on the door to inform the family that old Mr Douglas had collapsed drunk in the gutter down the road and was in need of assistance. Henry's son-in-law George Douglas, who answered the door, took umbrage at the do-gooders, exclaiming that his bloody name was Dowthwaite, not Douglas!

Henry had a reputation for being generous. Years earlier, when the last penny was paid on his Hanover Street house, he shouted all his mates in the hotel by throwing down a bunch of gold sovereigns on the bar and exclaiming, 'Cut that out, boys.' When one of his bachelor friends, a retired sea captain, died, he left Henry his Newtown cottage. Henry was well loved despite his intemperate habits and mourned deeply after he died on 22 October 1942, aged 88.[11]

Henry and Emma-Jane's eldest son, Henry Alfred — called 'George' by his family — was born in November 1882, left school at 10, and became a butcher boy, road worker and then a harbour board worker in Wellington. He sailed for France as a private in the 19th Reinforcements on 15 November 1916, just two months after marrying factory worker Mabel Hunter. After joining B Company, Wellington Infantry Battalion, he was killed in action at Messines on 31 July 1917.[12] Little seems to be known of the second son, Robert. After a sickly childhood he became a conductor on trams in Wellington and Wanganui before succumbing to emphysema, exacerbated by a severe bout of pneumonia, in November 1917. Aged 32, he left behind two small children, Mawby and Phyllis, from his 1914 marriage to Eliza Penn.[13]

The oldest of the boys' sisters, Annie, was a short, pert and controlling woman who left school early and worked as a housekeeper in Patea before marrying Charles Carey, a foreman carpenter in the local freezing works. Charles came from a strict Church of England home, and he and Annie inherited some ascribed social standing from his father, Matthew, a long-term local body politician and 'grand old man' of the town.[14]

Hilda, next in line, married Walter Browne, a master baker in Wanganui who was 19 years her senior, on 9 November 1908. Among the sisters, Hilda was closest in years to Ken's grandmother Carrie and they were close friends all their lives. Hilda was a tall, regal woman, orderly and disciplined, who expected high standards of behaviour from her family. She had trained as a seamstress and was a fastidious housewife.

The home was spotless. 'If it moved, she polished it,' was Ken's sister Terree's sardonic memory. She did have pretensions. She referred to Madge Farrow, who became Ken and Terree's mother, as a woman of 'not much class'. Her sister Ivy considered Hilda a 'snob'.[15]

Carrie's younger sister, Lillian, married Ted Favell, a policeman, on 11 November 1915. He enlisted in the infantry the following year and sailed for France in the 25th Reinforcements on 26 April 1917. A private in C Company of the Canterbury Infantry Battalion, he was killed in action on 8 November 1917 and buried at Polygon Wood in Belgium. He never knew his son James, who was born after his departure. After his death, pregnant and isolated in her Plimmerton home, Lillian became delusional, believing spies were watching her everywhere. Her mental health deteriorated, and she suffered a severe nervous breakdown from which she never recovered. She spent the rest of her days as a patient in Porirua and later Lake Alice and Kingseat psychiatric hospitals, under brutal regimes of strict regimentation, locked doors and electric shock treatment.[16]

Henry and Emma-Jane's youngest daughter, Ivy, kept house for Annie in Patea after leaving school. At the age of 17 she married Fred Fitzwater, a freezing worker and later a baker who worked in a shop on the main street. Annie took umbrage at this liaison and there was little communication between the two families for the rest of the sisters' lives. Fred's mother, Sarah Fitzwater, was a hard-nosed and fiery boarding-house keeper whose infelicitous outbursts against all and sundry made her unpopular in the town. Annie felt Ivy had married beneath her station, certainly below that of the high-church Careys.

Ivy was an overstretched housewife and mother to six boys (Maurice, Keith, Bert, John, Robert and Noel) and two girls (Lillian and Cynthia). She was on her own much of the time. Despite being an impressive athlete and rugby player — he captained Patea's senior team for a period — Fred drank a lot, was a heavy smoker and an even heavier gambler, both of which addictions became more pronounced as he got older. His business collapsed during the Depression and he secretly mortgaged the family home — financed by his mother Sarah — to feed his gambling habit. With his health failing, and in debt, Fred and Ivy shifted in 1942 to a rented house in Hastings. Fred died in 1951, Ivy in 1984. Their third son Bert was killed in a motorbike accident in 1937. The other boys, particularly Noel, were distinguished boxers. After a successful amateur career Noel won the New Zealand professional welterweight title on 29 October 1951, defeating Auckland's Tommy Rudolph on points. He remained undefeated, relinquishing the title in January 1953.[17]

The youngest Dowthwaite, Albert (Bert), was born in December 1903. At 13 he became a telegram boy for the Post Office. In 1917, not yet 15, he was faced with the unenviable task of bringing the news of the death of his uncle, Ted Favell, to the family in Northland. He later worked as a labourer and truck driver before finding employment as a grader driver for VA Draper and the Ministry of Works, clearing land for state houses in the Hutt Valley and the Porirua basin. He married Mary McDonald, a dour Scottish woman, and bought a house in Standen Street, Karori, adjacent to the cemetery, where Mary worked in the office.[18]

Joining the 2nd New Zealand Expeditionary Force early, Bert was batman for an army captain in camp in Britain but lost this posting after going absent without leave after a drinking binge in Tunbridge Wells. As a private in 22 Battalion, he served in the Greek campaign. He was promoted to lance corporal and saw action in Crete before being captured near Maleme Aerodrome in May 1941 and spending the following four and a half years as a POW, first in Italy and later in Lamsdorf Prison Camp, Stalag VIIIB (later Stalag 344) in Silesia, in eastern Germany. He tried more than once, unsuccessfully, to escape, and on one occasion lost teeth in an altercation with a German guard. Towards the end of the war he survived a 12-week 'death march' from Lamsdorf west through Czechoslovakia to a collection point at Stalag XIIIC, near Himmelburg, before being forced to march again, this time south towards Nuremberg. He was eventually liberated by advancing American forces in Bavaria.[19]

After the war Bert dug graves in the Karori Cemetery. He would steal black and purple ribbons from the wreaths and give them to his seven-year-old great-niece Terree Douglas, who used to plait them into her hair. By the late 1940s Bert had resumed work as a truck driver — on a horse and cart for the Milk Department at first — and was active in the Wellington Drivers' Union, along with his nephews Attie, Bryce and Laurie Douglas. Mary and Bert had two children, George and Gerald, but later the marriage failed and he married Joyce — volatile and gregarious like himself — who was a caretaker in the Kirkcaldies' Department Store building on Lambton Quay before shifting to Auckland. Bert followed her, and they lived in Takapuna where he drove graders for the local borough council and was a delegate for the Northern Drivers' Union before he retired in 1964. He died in 1972.

Contrasting images of Bert Dowthwaite run through the extended family. His niece Gwladys Robson remembered him as being 'full of fun', a great leg-puller and story-teller. Ken's cousin, June Hoskin, recalls him as a smiley character, 'always pleasant to us kids'. He was known widely to his nieces and nephews as 'Uncle Boy', as some of his sisters referred to their much younger brother 'affectionately' as 'Boy'. Ken Douglas recalls Bert as a 'harum-scarum character'. That comes closer to the truth. Bert's dark side was largely hidden from the wider world, but his nephew Brian Fitzwater, who knew him after the war, recalled him as stubborn, selfish in his relationship with Mary, and like many in the wider Douglas/Dowthwaite family, one who drank more than was good for him. Bert's surviving son, Gerald, goes much further. In May 2005, he described his father as a 'drunken, gambling, obnoxious wife- and child-beating bully who physically and mentally abused my mother for years, so much that in the end she had a nervous breakdown and spent time in Wellington Hospital'. They divorced soon afterwards, and when Bert moved to Auckland to be with Joyce he became persona non grata to Mary and Gerald, who cut off all contact with him.[20]

Little is known of the Douglas family beyond George Douglas, who was born in Australia and left Sydney for Wellington as a young man some time around the turn of the 20th century. In Wellington he met Carrie Dowthwaite, whom he married in 1904. George was a latter-day remittance man; the black sheep in a prosperous Sydney family whose patriarch sent him to New Zealand on a one-way ticket. The nature of his rebellion is not known. What is known is that he was born in 1880 and attended Sydney Grammar School which, as a paying school, was only accessible to the sons of the well-to-do.[21]

In New Zealand, George and Carrie rented poky semi-detached flats in Wadestown and Aro Valley before settling in the working-class suburb of Northland, renting a small cottage on Wireless Hill. It had been built on a damp, scrubby hillside facing south, and, consequently, was cold, damp and draughty, with double-hung sliding windows that rattled in the wind.[22] When George's mother visited Wellington she was horrified at the state of George and Carrie's house on Wireless Hill and loaned them enough money to put a deposit on a house of their own — at 109 Northland Road. Other finance was arranged through Joseph Selig, a Wellington money-lender. This place, like Wireless Hill, was a 'shotgun' house, so-called because you could fire a gun from the front door down the hallway and the bullet would penetrate the back door. Later, when the family began to grow and Carrie started to drag other members of the family and assorted waifs into her home, George's parents helped her to purchase a bigger house at 113 Northland Road. A few years later this place was sold, and the even larger house next door at 111 Northland Road was purchased. Money was always short, and while the interest was slowly paid off the mortgage, the principal owed was never touched. This would cause a crisis in later years.

The house at 111 Northland Road sat below the road and was on two levels as rooms were added to accommodate all the residents. There were four bedrooms, two sun-porches which were turned into extra bedrooms, a guest room, a small kitchen with a coal range, a dining room, and a sitting room where people also slept. Often a curtain hung down the middle of the bigger bedrooms, separating them into two sleeping spaces. There was no garage or workshop and on occasion the front room resembled a motor garage as Bryce and Laurie worked on their truck engines, laying out the pieces on the floor. In the 1940s and 1950s there could be up to 13 or 14 people staying at one time. There was Henry Dowthwaite (until he died in 1942), his son Bert, Carrie and George, and their grandchild Terree, who slept in their room. As boys Carrie's sons Laurie and Ken had shared a room until Ken's death, and later Laurie slept in the same room as Attie and his son Ken — with a division signalled by a blanket hung down the middle — taking it over when Attie left for war in 1944. Lyndsay and later Hannah, and their first daughter Marilyn, shared another room, while Bryce, his wife Betty and their children Raymond and Earland were squeezed into a fourth bedroom. Others such as David, the little boy Bryce and Betty adopted, also lived there for a period, while visitors and waifs from the wider family, as well as friends, also came to stay for periods of time.[23]

As a young girl Terree resented being pushed out of her Nana's bed when relatives — notably Carrie's sisters, Hilda, Annie or Ivy — came to stay; she would be removed to a camp stretcher in the corner of the room.

Downstairs there was a basement laundry where huge flop-bins of dirty workers' clothes awaited Carrie's all-day Monday vigil over the wringer. A rusting corrugated-iron outhouse served as the property's only toilet until the mid-1950s. Beyond, there was a fish-pond complete with goldfish and water lilies, and a central fountain presided over by two dwarves. There was just enough space for Raymond and Earland to ride around the pond in their pedal-cars. Beyond that, a sloping lawn was dominated by a ngaio tree and an area in the southwest corner where Ken as a boy grew dahlias and gladioli which he entered in local flower competitions, one gladioli being good enough to become a North Island champion for growers in his age group.[24]

George's working life took many twists and turns. As a young man, before the First World War, he worked as a butcher in Tills Butchery on Lambton Quay opposite the Occidental Hotel. School-lad Bernard Freyberg, later one of New Zealand's greatest military leaders, spent some time as his 'boy', helping George deliver meat on a cart to their customers. Later George worked as a cook on construction jobs around the North Island and would be away for periods of time. In his final career he kept books for the Gear Meat Company before moving to the

Wellington waterfront where he worked for many years as a tally clerk for the Union Steamship Company. George was a dapper man, and his aspirations toward respectability were discernible most prominently in his working attire — pinstriped suit, waistcoat adorned with time-piece and medal, Homburg hat and shiny black shoes that glistened in the sunlight.[25]

George was also stocky, shortish at around 5 foot 8 inches (1.73 metres), thick-set and big-chested — a Douglas characteristic. He had dark eyes and olive skin, similar to Carrie — both traits being inherited by his daughter Minnie and eldest son Laurie — in contrast to his younger sons, Attie and Bryce, who were leaner and had blue eyes and fairer complexions. George smoked heavily, preferring 'roll-your-owns' which he prepared each night, storing them in his Capstan tin to take to work the next day, a ritual he repeated every 24 hours. Smoking had an adverse reaction on his throat, and, according to Ken, his grandfather 'could hoick like a master — when he began making that unmistakable sound of dredging phlegm from his gut, others in the house were forewarned and left the room'. Like his father-in-law Henry, George loved his tipple, whisky being a favourite, and was a keen gambler, poker preferably. Sitting round the kitchen table close to the coal range holding forth in a card school with his mates and his sons was his most-favoured activity on cold nights. He tolerated rather than embraced Carrie's humanitarianism towards life's down-and-outers. At one time during the 1930s Depression he rushed to the front gate with a bucket and brush to scrub out an identification mark drawn upon it by tramps to indicate that a 'sucker' lived there.[26]

The Douglas family was well known in the Northland community. It was hard to miss the Munt Cottrell trucks, driven by George and Carrie's sons, Laurie, Bryce and later Lyndsay, parked in line outside the house and along the street. The wider family was the essence of Carrie's being, and 113 and especially the much bigger 111 Northland Road were her turangawaewae. After Carrie and George fell behind in their mortgage repayments on No. 111 Carrie entered an arrangement with a man named Lambert to purchase it, with Lambert leaving money in the house, in effect acting as principal mortgagor. It was the beginning of the Depression, and with her elder sons struggling to find work and even George unemployed for a period, the family fell further behind in their repayments. Moreover, by refusing to sell the family piano — the only item of worth they ever owned — Carrie upset the petty bureaucrat from the Social Welfare Department who insisted it must be sold as an 'unessential' item before she received any family support payment. With this, Lambert took steps to have all of the family's furniture removed and dumped on the street — effectively nullifying their part-stake in the house.[27]

After some heated words, and with a substantial police presence, Carrie forfeited the remaining equity and Lambert allowed the family to move back into the house — but only as tenants. Carrie continued to rent the house until her death in 1958. Ken Douglas believes that the landlord's unilateral action in kicking the family out into the street in 1931 was the first step in the politicisation of his father Attie and Attie's brothers Laurie, Bryce and Lyndsay.

Carrie had been born in June 1886, the third child of Henry and Emma-Jane Dowthwaite. She was raised in Hanover Street, Wadestown, and received a rudimentary primary education before going into service as a housemaid, although her employers are unknown. She was 18 when she met and married George Douglas. Her first child, Minnie, was born in 1906, then followed a succession of boys — Laurie, Attie and Ken before the First World War, and Bryce and Lyndsay after it.

Carrie was Slavic in appearance, short and stumpy, with a dark complexion and a round face projecting a kindly countenance. Outside the house she always wore a scarf and stumpy black hat. While Carrie was benevolent and loving — demonstrating particular tenderness towards the children — she showed scant regard for domestic democracy. She was very much in charge and brooked no nonsense, organising the running of the house like clockwork — she was a stickler for routine. It was Carrie's responsibility to make ends meet, which was not easy during long periods of unemployment among the sons, especially during the Depression. They eked out an existence. All the sons — three of whom lived in the house until well into adulthood (and one of these, Bryce, with spouse and two children in tow) — gave their weekly pay packets to Carrie. After she had purloined her share for household expenses and food she divided the remainder into 'spending tins' for each individual to use as pocket money. When Ken, after his first day at work as a 'seagull' (a non-union worker) on the Wellington wharf while still at high school, gave her his first weekly pay packet of £9 she burst into tears, explaining that he did not have to.

Carrie was the fulcrum around which the extended Douglas family revolved. At times there were up to 14 family members and a succession of other waifs and strays camped in bedrooms and hallways, squeezed in like sardines. While Carrie organised the house, it was within the accepted gender parameters of the days. When her husband, sons and assorted friends were arguing politics or playing cards and drinking whisky around the kitchen table of an evening she uncomplainingly kept them supplied with alcohol, scones, cake and cups of tea for supper.

She also possessed a quick and puckish sense of humour. With a friend, Mrs Catanach, it was her habit to go to the pictures once a month, catching the tram in Glenmore Street after a walk down Military Track. One evening a flasher dressed in just an overcoat jumped out from behind the bushes at the terminal and exposed himself. Quick as a flash Carrie instructed him, 'Put it away, you silly little man, I've got a much better one than that at home,' at which point the flasher burst into tears. She missed both the tram and the movie as she consoled the devastated reprobate.

After George died Carrie became the driving force behind the card nights at 111 Northland Road. These took place every Sunday night, drawing in not only all the family but many of the neighbours as well. They played 500, euchre, loo and poker. Her sons also ran 'crown and anchor' nights. The game was illegal but that did not stop profits often finding their way into Labour Party coffers. Many in the family, particularly Attie, Bryce and Lyndsay, were keen punters on the horses, losing money to local bookmakers or on the tote at Trentham Racecourse. Going to race meetings was a treasured and important social occasion for many New Zealanders at that time. This was very true for Carrie and her sisters, who delighted in dressing up in their finery for the big day out.

Carrie's leadership was not restricted to her home. She worked as a relief cleaner at Northland School, over the road from her house, and she was also a prime mover in organising card evenings at St Anne's Church supper room at the top of Randwick Road to raise money for the Labour Party through, most commonly, 500 and cribbage. The evenings were popular, with up to 100 players and more on occasion. From about the age of 10 it was Ken's responsibility to put on the urn and help make the sandwiches for supper. Occasionally when they were short he'd be 'roped in' to make up a four. It was serious business; there was money at stake. One woman clipped his ear when he trumped a trick that she had already won — such were the dangers of being his grandmother's trusted helper. Peter and Janet Fraser, who lived in the prime ministerial residence in nearby Harbour View Road, also attended these evenings when they could, and were also occasional, albeit very welcome, visitors to 111 Northland Road for Carrie's well-known 'high teas'. Unlike all the others in the house who smoked and drank prolifically, Carrie did neither.

Carrie was loved and respected by all who knew her and benefited from her bounteousness. Hannah Douglas remembers her mother-in-law with much affection. 'She was a lovely caring woman who looked after all of us with endless patience and tolerance. She very much ran the house, but not in a bossy way.' She would brook no nonsense, but this was leavened by an irrepressible sense of humour and an unflappability when things got tough or hectic. According to Gwladys Robson, who described Carrie as her favourite relative, she was a wonderful and tolerant person who worked like a galley-slave. 'She spent as much time as she could with the young ones, trying her hand at riding horses and bikes, falling off and laughing uproariously. Terree and I teased her by sewing up the bottom of her nightdress and putting hairbrushes in her bed. She always took it in good spirit.'[28]

Nonetheless, it was a hierarchical household, with Carrie as 'Queen

Bee'. She dished out the big stick, metaphorically, not only to the children when need be, but also to her adult sons. Rightly, she understood that without discipline the large household could not function as efficiently as it needed to. For all family members in this milieu, it was a fight to make yourself heard and seen. For Ken this meant having to stick up for himself, aggressively if need be. For his assertive sister Terree it meant demanding that the whole family sit down and watch her one-person drama and dance performances while she was at primary school. With her cousin June Hoskin, Terree would often entertain neighbours on the weekends with dance routines on the six- by three-foot area of lawn by the steps that led to the front door.[29]

While George, as befitting his earlier experience as a chef, was usually responsible for the midday Sunday roasts which were de rigueur in the household, it was Carrie who orchestrated high-teas later in the day. Commonly up to 15 to 20 people — relatives, friends (including school friends of Ken and Terree, who in their primary school days sat at a little table of their own) and workmates — attended these events. If he was home, Laurie did the baking. Carrie's daughter-in-law Betty made the salads, 'works of art' in their own right, Terree remembered. Lettuce, radishes, carrots, tomatoes, beans, snowpeas, sprouts and much else would be gathered from the garden and local greengrocer and delicately arranged. Carrie supervised, moved furniture around and laid the table — often with assistance from Terree and June — and determined the seating arrangements. On offer would be cold meat — left over from the midday roast — the salads, baked potatoes, rock cakes, scones (date and plain) and slabs of dark fruit cake purchased from Ward's Bakery on Woburn Road. For dessert, a huge bowl of fruit salad would appear, as did jellies, trifles, sponges and cream served in large glass bowls. Ice cream was a special treat, especially for the children, as were mallow puffs which were placed on the sitting room pedestal. The men drank beer or whisky, the women brandy and gin — and there was tea and hickory essence for the abstemious.

Carrie also had an interest in the occult, and while not identifying herself as a spiritualist or a medium, after tea she would predict the future by reading her guests' tea leaves. She used 'special' cups, not household ones, and reading the leaves and how they fell at the bottom of the cup became one of Carrie's favourite party tricks; her fascinated guests were spellbound by her predictions, and some of them later swore that they had come true. She was superstitious to the point that she would refuse to do this for any members of her family. Nonetheless, it was these early incidences that first set Terree on the path to fashioning a career as one of New Zealand's first media-savvy mystics in the 1970s.

During the mid-1950s Carrie contracted cervical cancer. She fought it, had treatment, and it went into remission for three years, but it re-emerged in 1958. This time she refused hospital treatment, insisting that she was all right, but finally, as her condition worsened, she was admitted to hospital. Ken, married by then and living in Hobson Street, recalled a bitter-sweet moment during a visit to see her in hospital. She was upset. 'You know he's seen all my parts — and he's Chinese,' she exclaimed. 'He [the doctor] is the only person to have done that since your grandfather! The trouble is,' she continued, 'he really is a nice man.' Carrie died on 9 December 1958, aged 72.

The children of Carrie and George Douglas were all strong personalities. Minnie, born in 1906, was the only child born to Carrie and George while they lived in the Wireless Hill Cottage. As she grew, she resembled her mother in looks and temperament — short, dark, energetic, lively and intelligent. She was fond of music and after marrying purchased a piano decorated in black lacquer, a fashion of the time. But her life was tinged with difficulty. She had osteomyelitis in her legs as a young child, and as a consequence spent a considerable time in hospital and had to wear calipers as one leg was shorter than the other. After receiving some rudimentary schooling Minnie stayed home and helped Carrie with the housework and cooking for her father, brothers and the myriad visitors who came to the house. Later she met and began living with a divorcee, Selwyn Marryatt. He had been both a draughtsman and a mechanic, but after he and Minnie began living together they purchased and ran a boarding house in Wellington's Kent Terrace. In 1940 Minnie became pregnant, giving birth to a son, Kevin, who was followed a short time later by a daughter, June, born on 30 June 1942.

Four days after June's birth, Minnie died of septicaemia. Minnie was a much-loved daughter and sister, and there was deep sadness in the Douglas household at the tragedy of her early death at just 36. In later years the family would go misty-eyed listening to 'Robyn's Return', her favourite tune, in the Sunday request session on the radio. Ken's mother, Madge, had a different response. 'Oh, the sainted Minnie,' she exclaimed with irony and frost whenever her name was raised. She was often 'off-side' with the Douglas clan.[30]

For Selwyn Marryatt, mourning the loss of his wife, there was also the difficulty of having two very young children. There were few solo fathers in 1942, and the fact that it was wartime aggravated the difficulties. Moreover, Selwyn still had responsibilities towards his four sons from an earlier marriage. In the short term, Kevin and the baby June were taken in by Carrie, but as she already had a full house June soon went to live with Edna and Percy MacMillan, who lived in nearby Harbour View Road. Edna, who was one of Carrie's best friends, had offered to help out and later formally adopted June. Kevin was adopted and raised by Selwyn's younger sister Marjorie and her husband Alan Annas, who lived in Christchurch. Later in the war Selwyn went to the Pacific Islands as a mechanic servicing American war planes. In 1957, at the age of 54, he died tragically when a trench collapsed on him in Arney Road, Remuera, when he was working for the Auckland City Council.[31]

Laurie, Attie, Bryce, Lyndsay and later Ken all had chores around the house, supervised by Carrie. Attie, the most skilled among the handymen, would lead the gang in building additions at the back and underneath the house. Terree recalled the house as 'elastic-sided': 'Carrie was a great one for constantly shifting furniture around to try to find some extra space.' The men brought home free coal and wood, especially car carcasses, on their trucks — with their perennial lack of funds, members of the family were expert scavengers.

Laurie, born in 1908, lived at Northland Road all his life, apart from periods working as a fireman and living in fire stations. At other times, like his brothers, he drove trucks for Munt Cottrell, coal merchants whose yard was situated in George Street, off Tinakori Road in Thorndon, and later in Aotea Quay. He was active in the Drivers' Union, and helped to organise the union's protest against the government and the Federation of Labour in support of the deregistered watersiders during the 1951 lockout. After his mother died, Laurie continued to live at 111 Northland Road with Attie and Bryce. He was still working as a driver — and living in Northland — when he died in April 1964.

Quietly spoken and broad-shouldered, Laurie never married. There was an effeminacy in his make-up and his brothers called him 'Pansy'. He was a flamboyant dresser, best illustrated by one photograph of him leaning over a rail at the zoo, hair slicked back with Brylcreem, dressed in a shiny coat and long white silk scarf, and clasping a clutch bag. His appearance and his single status led to covert accusations that he was homosexual. If he was, he was never 'outed' and he hid it well. Ken remembers Laurie having a longtime girlfriend who worked at the Western Park Hotel, and Terree recalls a dalliance he had with the music mistress at Wellington Girls' College. Like his brothers, Laurie liked a beer — he carried around a latch-locked bowls' case, which normally carried four lawn bowls, but Laurie discovered that two half-gallon flagons were a perfect fit.[32]

Laurie's brother Ken was born in December 1911, but died tragically at the age of four after he was struck by a cricket ball and his bruised leg became infected. Bryce was born much later, in 1920. Unusually for a Douglas, he was tall and lean. After leaving school at 13 he worked first as a message boy, then from his late teens as a truck driver. This brother, who among all of them would have the most to do with their young nephew Ken, married Betty Howe when he was 22 and she was just 17.

Betty's life was permeated by tragedy from the beginning. When she was just three her father was imprisoned for sly grogging, and Betty and her younger brother were placed in a state-run orphanage in Miramar while her mother and older sister 'disappeared', not to re-emerge until much later in her life. At the age of eight she was fostered to a family called Holcombe in the Hutt Valley, upright Christian folk whose way of disciplining Betty for misdemeanours, real and imagined, was to tie her up and thrash her. She 'escaped' to a girls' home in Thorndon at 13, only to be bullied by bigger and older girls who used stand-over tactics to force the diminutive Betty to do their bidding.

By then she was working for Stewart Printers in Manners Street, collating and stapling together programmes and booklets. When the manager tried to sexually harass her she left and started working in a downtown tea rooms. While boarding with a Northland family called Hutchinson — who lived in Harbour View Road right next door to Carrie's friends Edna and Percy Macmillan — she met Bryce, who did deliveries to the house. When she became pregnant they married, first moving into a draughty one-bedroom flat in Highbury before joining the rest of the Douglas family in the Northland Road home. It was there that their two children, Raymond and Earland, were born. (Bryce's life as a truck driver, wood and coal merchant, prominent unionist and Labour Party activist is described in Chapter 3.)[33]

Betty was welcomed by Carrie into the Northland Road home where she was worked hard, becoming Carrie's 'right-hand woman' in the roles of housekeeper, cook and bottle-washer. As well as that she was the primary care-giver to her own children, and provided much of the same service to Ken and Terree, who were older, taking them out to the pictures or to visit relatives. Terree remembers her as a tense and nervy woman who was rarely allowed to express her own opinion. Bryce was very controlling, refusing to let her wear lipstick, for example. Nonetheless, Carrie was the first woman in Betty's life to treat her with respect. 'She was my first real Mum,' Betty recalled in 2005. 'That's what I called her. We just clicked like that.'[34]

Bryce was an oddball in the sense that, unlike the other members of the family, he became religious later in his life, converting to Jehovah's Witness. Betty, however, stayed well clear, unable to cope with the public proselytising. Among the wider family there was an interesting religious mix. Carrie and George were Church of England, both irregular attenders at St Anne's Church in Northland. Ken himself had been christened a Catholic as his mother was Catholic, but he would carry nothing of its liturgy into adolescence or beyond. Carrie sent Terree to a Catholic primary school in Northland for a brief time in recognition of her mother's faith, but that ended suddenly when the two of them observed the nuns brutally punishing their young charges.[35]

Bryce and his family lived at 111 Northland Road until Bryce died suddenly of a heart attack on 21 August 1959, aged just 43. For a while Betty stayed on in the house with her teenage sons, but the remaining brothers — Attie and Laurie — expected her to carry on as before, cooking, cleaning, washing and ironing for all of them, as well as looking after the children. She wanted more from life, and she seemed to have found it when she met Stan Hullah, a cook in a Paekakariki tea rooms. They ran off to Christchurch, married, and set up a coffee bar together. But Hullah was an out-of-control drinker and gambler who stole money from the till to feed his habits, and the business collapsed. He then drove trucks for Amberley Transport, but was killed when his vehicle was buried when a section of road collapsed. Betty, who by then was working as a machinist in the Kaiapoi Woollen Mills, was not yet 40. She subsequently met and married Frank Reeves, a crane-driver on the Lyttelton waterfront. Reeves was an alcoholic and died in his early fifties of a heart attack. They had been married just two years.

By this time, both her sons had also died. Raymond, a Petone-domiciled truck driver, died of a heart attack, while Earland, her favourite son, suffered a cerebral haemorrhage on a Christchurch bus on the way home from work. Both boys were in their thirties. After Reeves died, Betty found employment as a 'dogsbody' in Christchurch's Lancaster Park Hotel. There she met her last husband, truck driver Leslie Joseph, and until his death in 1995 they spent happy years together sharing a love of fishing and travelling with their caravan. Before her death in August 2007, Betty lived in a Christchurch rest home, active, effervescent and addicted to 'roll-your-owns'.[36]

Lyndsay, Carrie and George's youngest son, who was born in 1922, was the only child in the family to receive a secondary education. While at primary school he fell down a bank and broke his ankle; an infection set in which could not be stemmed, and his leg was amputated below the knee. It was the first electric-knife amputation carried out at Wellington Hospital. Nicknamed 'Hoppy', Lyndsay did not allow his handicap to affect him, and he became a good swimmer in his adolescence. He also joined the air force as soon as he could after the war began, though with his missing leg he should not have — such was his determination to join the air force and serve overseas that he persuaded a sympathetic doctor to 'turn the other way' when his name was called. He subsequently saw service as a machine operator in the Pacific, including Fiji, New Caledonia and Guadalcanal in the Solomon Islands where he drove fuel trucks at air bases.

He stayed in the air force after the war, serving at Ohakea. By this time he had met Hannah Allcock, who was working as a hotel waitress in Wanganui. After Lyndsay left the air force in 1947 she moved to Wellington with him and stayed at 111 Northland Road for a period when he was back driving for Munt Cottrell. Hannah worked as a machinist in a Wellington clothing factory before they both returned to Wanganui, where they married and had the first of their three children. After the first-born, Marilyn, became sick and needed specialist medical treatment the family returned to Northland Road and Lyndsay to Munt Cottrell.

They moved to Mangakino when Hannah's sister, who was already living there, wrote enthusiastically about work prospects for Lyndsay on the new hydroelectric dams then under construction on the Waikato River. Lyndsay found employment driving the fuel tankers that serviced the Euclids, trucks, graders and other machinery at the dam sites at Mangakino, Whakamaru and Atiamuri, and later 'shot-blasting' — cleaning the cast iron and steel before it went into the dam construction. For many years he was secretary of the Workers' Union in Mangakino, which covered the bulk of the workers labouring at these sites. After the dams were finished, and refusing to relocate to Twizel, Lyndsay found work as a maintenance man on the Lands and Survey Department farms. He and Hannah had two more children, Neil and Carol, and Hannah also worked in the local TAB for a number of years before following her brother-in-law Attie as caretaker of the local primary school. Lyndsay died in May 1987, aged 64, of a burst aorta.

Ken's father, John Atholwood (Attie) Douglas, the third of Carrie and George's children, was born on 28 February 1910. After leaving Northland Primary School he began a Cabinet-making apprenticeship, but once he had completed it he found only sporadic work, making wooden coat-hangers on a production line in a Petone factory for a period. He then took on a series of temporary jobs, first as a garage hand at Lambton Garage in Thorndon, then as an itinerant labourer round the North Island, at times boarding with his cousins the Fitzwaters in Patea. In 1930, Attie obtained intermittent work driving trucks for HW Thomas, the carriers, in Northland's Creswick Terrace. He knew the family, having attended Northland Primary School with Ken Thomas, son of the founder Harold. Nonetheless, this was the beginning of the Depression and he was forced to remain a casual, having to sit on a form outside Harold Thomas's window waiting for his name to be called after the men in the queue ahead of him. Even if he arrived at 5am there was no guarantee of work, and when there was no work, there was no income. He remained a casual for four years before securing a permanent job with the firm. This experience, among others, made him a strong Labour supporter and unionist, and he later became a Wellington Drivers' Union delegate and executive member. On 27 December 1934, Attie married 24-year-old seamstress Marjorie (Madge) Farrow whom he had met at a Labour Party dance.

Ken Douglas's forebears on his mother's side can be traced back to his great-great-grandfather John Farrow, who emigrated from Norfolk to Victoria, Australia, as a young man in 1833. In 1838, John married a 22-year-old Tasmanian woman, Eliner Corker. They had a family of four, the third of whom, George Farrow, Ken's great-grandfather, was born in 1845. George became an itinerant labourer round the state of Victoria, and on 9 May 1877, in Wangaratta, he married Eleanor Byrnes. Eleanor, a dressmaker, was born in 1851 and raised in a 'poor but decent' family in the Beechworth district of Victoria. Family legend has it that one of Eleanor's earlier boyfriends was Ned Kelly — they were raised in adjacent districts and Ned, at a few years older than Eleanor, would have been more than eligible — however, in the absence of hard evidence this connection needs to be treated with suspicion.

George and Eleanor Farrow had six children, the first of whom, George Frederick Farrow, was born at Morrisons, Victoria, on 8 September 1878. This young man, Ken's grandfather, had a rugged upbringing. During his childhood his father held dubious title to a 'selection' of Victoria's poorer land, from which the family tried to eke out a living. But it was not enough. To keep his family fed, George Farrow senior became an itinerant stockman, driving cattle from the Northern Territory to South Australia and Victoria. At other times he cut sugar cane in Queensland.

In September 1885, his father having been gone for months, young George, aged just seven, spotted a flock of sheep being herded past their property, skipped home and joined the drive. Reasoning that his absence would make one less burden on his poverty-stricken mother, and wary of his father's anger, George did not return home for another eight years. Instead he worked at the same itinerant rural lifestyle as his father from boyhood to adolescence.

George junior received his education on the road, teaching himself to read and write, and becoming a voracious reader for the rest of his life. He became an expert horseman — part of his work on the road was to break-in brumbies. When work dried up in Australia he preceded a large number of other semi- or unskilled Victorians — future political and union leaders Joe Savage, Bob Semple, Pat Hickey and Paddy Webb among them — in crossing the Tasman to look for employment. He worked around Wellington and the Manawatu as an itinerant rural labourer and as a slaughterman in various meatworks. Returning to Australia, George married 19-year-old Eleanor Malligan at Wangaratta in 1906.[37]

George brought Eleanor to New Zealand permanently soon after they married. He laboured on a farm near Nelson initially before finding work as a surfaceman on the Rimutaka Incline railway project north of Wellington, during which time they lived in the workers' settlement at Cross Creek. He then worked on a dairy farm near Gracefield, a rural community hugging the eastern Hutt Valley hills, where his responsibilities included a milk run from the farm down the eastern side of Wellington Harbour to Day's Bay and Eastbourne. He developed and expanded the milk run, later buying it, and also had an opportunity to buy the farm. However, Eleanor, now stuck at home with five children — Ellenor (Nell), born 1907; Eileen, 1908; Lillian, 1909; Madge (Ken Douglas's mother), 1910, and George, 1918 — and developing an unhealthy passion for excess alcohol, was keen to move closer to the city. A second son, Terry, would be born in 1923.

In 1919, George sold the milk run to two returned World War I servicemen and bought a dairy in John Street, Newtown, which he ran for the next 10 years before the family shifted to a bigger two-storeyed house at 287A Cuba Street which took in boarders. George found employment at the Wellington Municipal Milk Department where he operated a bottling machine — and helped establish a union for the workers. During the 1930s Depression he and Eleanor took a number of unemployed men into their house, providing them with food, accommodation and solace. Effectively their home became a boarding house for the dispossessed, and it continued that way for many years, through to the early 1950s. George also kept his links with the land, purchasing a small plot at Raumati where he grew potatoes for family, friends, and the Labour Party. It was while working with George at this plot that Ken Douglas, as a young man, really got to know his maternal grandfather well. He developed a huge respect for him, attracted to his humanitarianism and belief in the dignity of work, especially hard physical labour. Indeed, George never 'retired' and was still working as a cleaner and 'lunch-boy' at Peterson's Chemical Factory in Vivian Street on the day, in August 1959, that he entered hospital with bowel cancer. He died soon afterwards, aged 81.

George's tough early years had prepared him well for Labour politics, which dominated his non-working life. A foundation member of the New Zealand Labour Party, he was a long-time president of the Wellington Central Branch, a member of Peter Fraser's electorate committee every year from 1919, and Fraser's campaign manager during his last 20 years in office. Fraser was a frequent visitor to the Cuba Street house, using George as a confidant, particularly on local issues. Their politics were analogous. Later in life, Fraser was conservative, as was George, who had a distaste for the communist 'radicalism' that was then a potent force among some on the fringes of Labour politics and in the trade union movement. Fraser wanted to appoint him a Labour member in the Legislative Council but George refused, being suspicious of MPs and their 'operations', and expressing a particular aversion for Parliament's confrontational politicking. He had a specific dislike of Jim Collins, the 'numbers man' for the Labour Party who secured the trade union votes. He believed politics was a personal issue and distrusted coercion of any type. His long-term loyalty to the party never wavered, but he preferred to work behind the scenes. Eleanor was a key support, and their home was open to all Labour people.

There were more strings to George Farrow's bow. He was a gambler, liking nothing more than celebrating a winning hand at poker or, dressed in his only suit, coming home beaming from the race-track flush with a wad of notes — or with very empty pockets. He also operated a book — making, and losing, more than a little money — with slips, coins and notes being kept in a series of tins hidden in high cupboards. Before and during race meetings the telephone rang constantly day and night.

Because of their work ethic George had a particular respect for Wellington's Chinese, whose lives were largely confined to an area in and around Haining Street, off Taranaki Street, which George passed through every day as he walked to his work at the milk station in Tory Street. The Chinese also loved to gamble, their two favourite games being fantan — a speedily played dice game — and pakapoo, an indigenous Chinese game roughly akin to the present-day Lotto.[38]

George was a Justice of the Peace, and he used his position to help the Chinese. When police from the nearby Mt Cook Street Station applied to him to sign a warrant for a raid on the Chinese gambling houses and adjacent opium dens, George would sign the warrant as was his duty, but then warn his friends in the community to 'shut up shop' until the danger had passed. Not unnaturally, he and his family benefited, receiving free gifts such as vegetables from the Chinese market gardens or hand-made trinkets and paper lanterns for Eleanor and the children. Donors never identified themselves, simply leaving the baskets at his front door.

Eleanor was a large, generous-spirited woman. Their marriage was frequently difficult, with George often away on work or political business and 'bossy' when he was home. Befitting the mores of the time, Eleanor washed, ironed, cooked and cleaned, as well as looking after the lodgers she took into their Cuba Street home. She was both an empathetic hostess — having a continuous 'soup pot' bubbling away on the coal range into which all manner of food items were deposited and fed to family, lodgers and visitors — and the owner of a fiery temper which, her youngest son Terry recalled, resulted in periodic scoldings, beatings and 'pots being hurled through the air'. She never lost her Roman Catholic faith, unlike her husband who cared little for church of any kind, being one of the first to use the term 'God-botherers' in reference to Christians. 'Never met one yet,' he once told his grandson, 'who has done any bloody good for any bugger.' Nonetheless, when he died a priest administered the last rites and his funeral was held at St Mary of the Angels on Boulcott Street.[39]

Although the knowledge was kept from others, Eleanor had a problem with alcohol. Later in her life she was often in bed 'with the flu', as George described it, sipping gin from a hot water bottle. When the house was later pulled down, scores of empty spirit bottles were discovered, surreptitiously hidden away by Eleanor over the years. Terry Farrow recalled ruefully in 1997 that 'she had taken to worshipping the shrine of Bacchus'. She died in 1953, her body ravaged by alcoholism.

The eldest of George and Eleanor's six children, Ellenor (Nell), married Jack Fage in 1927 and had two children, John and Lesley. They lived in Garrett Street, off Cuba Street. Nell was very much the matriarch of the family and for many years ran the watersiders' cafeteria at the Wellington wharf, having earlier worked in the kitchen at Wellington Hospital. They were a gregarious family and generous hosts, filling a similar role, though to a lesser extent, to Carrie and her brood in Northland Road. Jack Fage was a painter and paper-hanger. He was an asthmatic and a heavy smoker, and died of lung cancer in 1957.

George and Eleanor's second daughter, Eileen, died tragically young in 1923. She had been a champion Irish dancer, winning medals in Gaelic competitions — sometimes with her sister Madge. Lillian, the third-born, married Frank Southee, a rugged, gruff outdoorsman who trapped and skinned possums in Rimutaka Forest. It was an inconsistent living for the family of six, the income dependent both on the availability of skins and the price that Frank was able to obtain for them — prices which fluctuated widely. Lillian was a cheerful, compassionate woman who despite suffering under the constraints of 'too many kids and not enough money' was gregarious and generous to family, friends and neighbours.[40]

The eldest son, George, was born in October 1918. He served as a soldier in the Pacific Islands in the latter days of the Second World War and developed a severe skin rash which bothered him for the rest of his life. Sun seemed to be beneficial and he developed a penchant for nude bathing in a secluded spot in the bush above Oriental Bay. After the war George secured a night job cleaning trams at the council depot. Rejecting Catholicism, he embraced communism for a period, writing out the whole of Karl Marx's *Das Kapital* by hand as a way of trying to learn and understand it. It was a monumental task. George never married, but he did have a long-term de facto relationship with Mavis West and supported her children, including Phillip Soraya, an illegitimate grandson born to Mavis's daughter Regina and fathered by an American soldier.[41]

George spent many years living with his parents in Cuba Street. After their deaths he bought a cottage in Duppa Street, Berhampore, where he lived as something of a recluse. He died in 2000. The youngest son, Terry, born in 1923, became both a strong influence on Ken Douglas and a close friend. His life is discussed in detail on page 78.

Marjorie Alice (Madge) Farrow, Ken Douglas's mother, was born in Featherston on 12 May 1910, when her father George was working on the railways and the family lived at Cross Creek. She had a lively spirit and loved to dance, a passion she shared with her older sister Eileen. On leaving primary school, Madge worked in a woollen mill in Petone, later training as a tailoress, then expanding her skills to seamstressing and dressmaking. She met Attie Douglas at a Labour Party dance organised by her father in November 1933, and married him at St Joseph's Church, Buckle Street, Wellington, on 27 December 1934. On 15 November 1935 their first child, Kenneth George, was born, named after Attie's late brother. Four years later, on 24 October 1939, Madge gave birth to a daughter, Terree Ellenor.

Attie and Madge initially moved in with her parents at 287A Cuba Street, but after Terree was born the family was allocated a small state house in Homebush Road, Khandallah. While it was in a prime position with stunning views of Wellington Harbour, Madge hated it. It was too far from the city. With two small children and little social contact she suffered from what sociologists would later call 'suburban neurosis'. There was only one workers' bus to town, where she loved to go. Catching the bus involved a long trek down the hill, with Terree in the pram, to the Bellwood Bitumen factory on Hutt Road. They would have to catch the same bus at four in the afternoon for the return journey. Madge enjoyed dancing, drinking, party life and 'roll-your-own' Silver Ferns. Being stuck at home with two small children, her husband working long days driving his truck, was akin to a death sentence.

Attie was content in the house in Homebush Road, and inevitably, it seemed, the marriage collapsed. Early in 1941, Madge abandoned the family home and moved back in with her parents in town, where she was closer to the generosity of American servicemen. Attie went to live with his parents in Northland Road with the two young children in tow.

At the insistence of their grandmother Carrie — who refused to take sides in the marriage break-up — the children visited their mother most weekends, although there was more enthusiasm for the visits from Carrie and from Madge's parents, George and Eleanor, than from Madge herself. Madge returned to seamstressing — manpowered to stitch sheets and pillow cases to be used in hospitals for wounded servicemen. She also did piece-work on a sewing machine at the back of John Moran's drapery opposite her parents' house in Cuba Street. After weekends with Madge, the young Ken was particularly popular at school, handing out to his mates chewing gum given to him by his mother's American friends.

Early in 1942, Madge gave birth to a third child, a boy, who was immediately adopted by a family named Gordon and raised in the Waikato. In 1992 the Douglas family made contact with John Gordon and his wife Molly and they have since become part of the extended family. Late in 1944, Madge became pregnant to a Norwegian seaman — or so the birth certificate recorded — and a daughter named Patricia was born on 28 July 1945. Patricia was adopted by a family named Richards, became Susan, and was raised in Nelson. Today Susan Richards is a mother of two, grandmother of three and lives in Whakamaru. According to Ken's cousin Nell Elvy, who had been doing research on the family before her death in 2004, the companionable Madge might have had even more children out of wedlock during the wartime period or soon afterwards. It was probable that the father of one of these children was a steward on the *Dominion Monarch*.[42]

Madge loved the party life — jazz, chocolates, uniforms. At parties she drank gin and beer to excess, danced on tables and rolled her own cigarettes. In a time of sartorial restraint she stood out, having a penchant for brightly coloured garments, vivid lipstick and red high-heeled shoes. Black humour reverberates through her daughter Terree's 2005 reflections. 'As we all know,' she said, 'at that time red shoes were only worn by children and prostitutes. Well, Madge was not a professional, but she was a very enthusiastic amateur!'

In July 1942, Attie was conscripted into the army. After training at Trentham, Linton and Waiouru military camps he was called for overseas service in February 1945 as part of the 15th Reinforcements. He set sail for Italy the following month to join the 2nd Divisional Postal Unit, a division of the New Zealand Engineers, leaving his 10-year-old son and six-year-old daughter in Carrie's capable hands. Promoted to corporal, he later volunteered for J-Force, sailing from Naples to the port of Kuri in Japan on 21 February 1946. He served in the Postal Unit until September 1946, returning to New Zealand just four days before his father died.[43]

He returned to live at 111 Northland Road, reuniting with his mother and children — Ken now aged 11, Terree aged seven — and his brothers. Just prior to going overseas Attie had left Thomas's, where driving work was short, and had been driving for JM Middleton Carriers, a small company with a yard and office in Hanson Street. On his return from Japan he drove for Thomas's before rejoining Middleton's, where the work was full-time. He was still with the firm during the 1951 waterfront lockout when, with the Wellington Drivers' Union striking in support of the watersiders, he was given 'off-wharf' work. Soon after, the Master Carriers' Association brought down a heavy hand, banning all carriers from allowing their employees such options.

As a consequence, Attie, active within the union, refused to work and was sacked. Banned from driving, he returned to carpentry, working on the Wharenui Flats construction project opposite the Botanic Gardens in Glenmore Street. With that completed, and itinerant by nature, he went to live in Levin where he helped build a new hospital. When Ken completed his compulsory military training at Waiouru in 1954, Attie was working as a carpenter on the Kings Chamber project in Palmerston North. In between construction projects he returned to the family home in Northland Road, and driving for Thomas's. For some of this time, and up to his retirement in the early 1970s, the firm took advantage of his carpentry expertise as he designed and built trays for their new flat-top and tip truck chassis.

At some time in the late 1940s Madge shifted to Nelson, where she worked in a hotel and met and married barman Harry Johnson. For a period, she found contentment and much-needed stability. They later returned to Wellington where Johnson was head barman at the Forrester's Arms in Ghuznee Street, while Madge found employment as a postwoman. After Johnson died, she returned to live with her now-elderly parents in Cuba Street, cooking and cleaning for them in lieu of rent. But she was a lost and tortured soul whose inability to cope with the real and perceived pressures in her life found an all too ready outlet in alcohol. Her drinking became uncontrollable and she would disappear for days or even up to a week or two at a time. Her father George and son Ken would search for her, usually finding her in one hotel or another. She would be taken home drunk — unkempt often, unfed, and talking gibberish. As her alcoholism became more extreme her brother George became less tolerant of her presence in the family home and insisted she leave. She did, for periods, bunking down with friends until the 'crisis' was over, after which she would return to her long-suffering and ever-supportive parents.[44]

Some episodes were more serious than others. One evening, when her addiction was close to its worst and she had been missing for four days, her father took Ken to a house where they found Madge with a young fellow, equally drunk, with whom she had slept for beer money — an unwelcome pattern of behaviour she had fallen into. There was both vomit and excrement spread throughout the bed in which they had been rolling around. Ken was outraged, and says he would have 'killed the bastard' had his Pop not been there. The two men wrapped her in a blanket and carried her back to Cuba Street, where Ken held her in a bath while his aunt Nell Fage bathed and cleaned her up. It was a very low moment in all of their lives.

The family was told that Madge needed to be committed to Porirua Hospital to receive treatment for her addiction. In denial, she refused to go voluntarily, so Ken admitted her. It was the move of a desperate son, but she took a long time to forgive him. It was August 1959. Madge was 49 years old. She stayed in Porirua for seven months, emerging nearly clear of the disease that had wracked her, and her family's lives for the past 10 years. There had been hypocrisy in Madge's alcoholism. Earlier in her life, at around six in the evening she would sit with her mother, Eleanor, also a heavy drinker, at an upstairs window in the Cuba Street house, giggling and making snide comments about the drunken men lurching unsteadily out of nearby hotels. Terree, who was sometimes present as a child, winces at the memory.[45]

After her parents died, Madge purchased a small property at 131 Apu Crescent, Lyall Bay. Ken and his wife Lesley lived with her for a time, paying rent of £5 a week. Some time before she was admitted to Porirua she had developed a romantic liaison with a barman, Jack McGilligan. When he became ill with the H-bug, Ken and Lesley invited him to live with them and be cared for. This included nursing him, with frequent changes of dressing, a task which fell mainly to Lesley. When his health deteriorated McGilligan moved to Wellington Hospital, where he died.

Following her release from hospital, Madge returned to live with Lesley and Ken. While not completely cured of her alcoholism she was a lot better, keeping her addiction under control with the help of doctors for long periods of time. But she could not return to her job as a postwoman, so Ken arranged for her to be 'medically retired' and she received a sickness benefit. By this time her former husband Attie had come to the rescue, using his considerable carpentry skills to build Madge a bach at the back of the Apu Crescent property. Attie, who never remarried, retained a very strong affection for Madge for the rest of his life.[46]

It was difficult for Ken and Lesley in the house with a bitter Madge close by, and late in 1961 — now with their first baby, Jane, and with Lesley pregnant after earlier suffering two miscarriages — they moved to a small house in Titahi Bay. With money saved from holiday jobs and with help from Carrie, as a schoolboy Ken had bought a section from a fireman mate of his Uncle Laurie's in Horokiwi Street, Newlands, for £500. He now sold that to buy the Titahi Bay house. Madge was repentant, pleading with them to return to live in Apu Crescent, but to no avail.

As she overcame her alcoholism, the mother-son relationship improved markedly. Ken continued to work on the Apu Crescent house for her, painting, building a fence and doing general maintenance in the house and around the property. Later in her life, her alcoholism licked, Madge took over the responsibility, with her brother George, of raising Phillip Soraya. They formed a mutually beneficial bond — Madge needed Phillip as much as he needed her.

Ken Douglas's feelings of resentment towards his mother emanated from her long absences during his childhood. Madge had failed as a mother when the children were young, and Ken's sense of abandonment ran deep. 'I respected her for being my mother, but I didn't love her.' Much of the work Attie and Ken later did for her was little appreciated at the time, her mind being clouded by the effects of her long-term alcoholism.

Madge became close to Ken and Lesley's children, especially Jane and Peter who remember her with deep affection. Sadly, she tried to buy their love with the promise of presents (rarely delivered), being unable to be truly loving and caring toward those closest to her, a condition exacerbated by her drinking. Ken recalled a conversation he had with her not long before her death in November 1985: 'I don't want anything. You never gave me anything. You're my mother and that's it. Stop trying to buy my kids' affections. Earn love from them because of who you are. Love them; don't bribe them!'

Madge's desire, or perceived desire, to be close to her grandchildren, was of course part of the sublimation of the guilt she felt towards Ken and Terree. She felt she never received the appreciation she craved from any adult, disguising her hurt with an overt focus on her grandchildren, and on Phillip Soraya, because, unlike the grown-ups in her later years, they were never in a position to reject her. The final straw for Ken and Terree (in particular) was learning that Madge had cut them out of her will altogether in favour of Phillip. This slight led to a bitterly contested court case, in which the judge directed that Madge's assets be divided three ways: one-third to Phillip, one-third to Terree and her children, and one-third to Ken's children.

There was, however, another side to the older Madge Johnson. She was respected and liked by her postie mates, becoming particularly friendly with Gwen Winter, whose daughter Lesley would become Ken's wife. She was a good worker despite her affliction, and became an enthusiastic union member, taking a full part, for example, in the 'Surf' strike of July 1963 when Lever Brothers attempted to use posties to market their product in little packets delivered to private homes. Later

Madge returned to dressmaking, at which she had considerable skill.

In her earlier days she had been a happy drunk, enjoying singing and dancing in hotels, and this did not change when she became sober. She would regularly visit hotels with two or three close friends, drink sarsaparilla, and dance and sing with the same pleasure as she had before. She remained gregarious and generous to her friends. Her biggest victory was when she realised that the hotel had now become a safe meeting place where she could entertain herself, and others, without needing to touch one drop of alcohol. At home she kept alcohol close to her bed — knowing it was there stopped her indulging in it, the pangs returning when she knew it was not readily accessible. She loved dressing up and going to the races, having a flutter on the horses — and staying sober. When she learned the value and necessity of constraint on her hitherto drunken excesses she became a much happier person, and this newfound and unencumbered joy spread to those closest to her. Moreover, in raising Phillip she had found a belated sense of self-worth.

She also enjoyed social functions held by the Wellington Drivers' Union, the Socialist Unity Party and, later, the Federation of Labour, and was often to be found in the kitchen preparing the food and washing the dishes. This was reflected glory; a manifestation of a newly discovered pride in her son's success as a respected trade union leader rather than any expression of political activism. The subliminal status she attained through Ken's achievements allowed her to become, in Terree's words, a kind of respectable 'dowager duchess' in her older years — no longer the tortured soul of earlier days. This allowed her comfort and peace of mind, as did a belated return to worship in the Catholic Church.[47]

Ken Douglas had a similarly sporadic relationship with his father, although without the anxiety that Madge's alcoholism had brought him. Like Madge, Attie flitted in and out of Ken's life. He was most at home with his mates, enjoying the camaraderie, the shared 'blokey' sense of humour, as well as the comfort and sense of security that these associations engendered. He was proud of his wartime service and wore his J-Force beret both when working and in the pub, complete with navy blue overalls and work boots. Though he never became addicted like Madge, Attie loved his beer, wiling away many Saturday hours in the pub, or with his driving mates after work; story-telling, gambling, laughing — often at his own misfortune — playing cards and darts, participating irrepressibly in the six o'clock stagger. He was a keen student of horse racing. The latest edition of *Best Bets* hung from his back pocket and he spent much time, and money, at the TAB, with bookmakers, and at the totalisator at Trentham and Hutt Park on race days.

He drove a Humber Super Snipe later in life and, as had been his habit in his truck, he was fond of waving or yelling enthusiastically out the window or tooting his horn at people he recognised on the street — sometimes to the detriment of his driving. He also had a particular habit of flicking mates across the ear to get their attention. He loved to tease people, performed practical jokes on them, told tall tales, continually 'wisecracked' and, according to Jackie Thomas, Alan's wife, was always 'full of cheek'. He was a 'real rascal', she recalled. 'He tormented my life when I was young,' she added, tongue firmly in cheek.[48]

As a boy and young man he had enjoyed the outdoors, and rabbiting had been a favoured pursuit. Aged 17, he accidentally shot his school friend Tom Wilkinson in the backside while he was climbing through a fence. Wilkinson was less than amused, and scolded Attie: 'Ya shot me, ya bastard; you'll hang for this!' Attie was so frightened about what he had done that he scarpered into the bush, not emerging for two days. The injury proved to be serious enough for Wilkinson, later a successful asphalt contractor, to walk with a permanent limp.

Attie shied away from confrontation, and after he fell out with a rebellious Terree when she was 17, it was years before they resumed a loving father-daughter relationship. He would not attend her marriage to Peter Kilmore in 1959 — she had to leave the papers for him to sign on the kitchen table at Northland Road.[49]

After his mother's death in 1958, and with Ken married and Terree having left home, he rented a flat in Randwick Road, Northland, for a time. He had purchased Bryce's business in the owner-driver cooperative QED, but early in the 1960s he sold QED and moved to Mangakino where his younger brother Lyndsay lived, becoming caretaker at the local primary school. He rented a little cottage at 3 Matai Street which he modernised, and performed a number of charitable acts in the community such as gardening and doing up flats and houses for old people, sometimes working with Lyndsay. The two brothers got on well, and Attie also enjoyed the company of Lyndsay's wife Hannah and their three children.

He fitted in well in his new community, the locals responding positively to his cheery presence. He enjoyed the open-air lifestyle Mangakino had to offer, and he could indulge his passion for fishing. He played and gambled on cards incessantly and went to race meetings at Rotorua, Te Awamutu, Te Rapa, Te Aroha, Cambridge and Tauranga. He had his own telephone account at the TAB and participated in a betting syndicate with other locals. Hannah, who worked at the TAB, recalls him as a 'thoroughly good, happy-go-lucky joker' who would do anything for anyone.

In 1977 Attie suffered a stroke which incapacitated him to a degree. Disappointed that Ken did not come to see him one long weekend when he was ill, he seemed to regress. Ken fetched him back to Wellington but he died after suffering a second stroke on Labour Day 1978. He was 68 years old.

While there were painful gaps in his childhood, with his mother gone from an early age and his father 'on the road', Ken Douglas compensated for that through the unconditional love and care of his grandmother Carrie and the role models the other adults in the house provided. Nonetheless, the experience of fighting for recognition in the volatile and often crowded household made him independent from an early age, and tough. He learned never to take a backward step from anybody and at the same time, with Carrie's words ringing in his ears, always to be honest and true to himself and loyal to others. He recalled in 2005 that his 'in and out' relationship with both his mother and his father had benefits in his later life, although this was not apparent at the time.

'When Attie took us to his mother after the family split up it was just an extension of what had always happened in the Douglas family. Carrie aggregated all of the relatives to her bosom in good times and bad. I was raised in this "culture of connectedness".' In more ways than one, this background experience would serve him well in his later career.

CHAPTER 2

'Doony loved school more than school loved Doony'

Kenneth George Douglas was born in the Harris Maternity Home on the corner of Buller and Ghuznee Streets in central Wellington on 15 November 1935. The home was a private birthing unit used as 'overflow' by Wellington Hospital during the baby-boom of the post-Depression years. At that time, Madge and Attie were living with her parents at 287A Cuba Street. Soon afterwards, they rented a small cottage in Plimmerton so that Attie, truck driving for HW Thomas, could be closer to his work carting sand, shingle, chip and gravel from Plimmerton's Hongoeka Quarry to the military camp that was being built at MacKay's Crossing. Before Ken reached school age the family shifted again to a seaside bach at Golden Gate, between Paremata and Pauatahanui.

He began primary school at the Catholic St Mary of the Angels in

Aro Street while his parents were staying temporarily, once again, at the Farrow home in Cuba Street while they searched for a home to rent. He recalls with affection his slightly older cousin Lesley Fage taking him in hand on the way to and from St Mary's. His sister Terree was born before the year was out, and soon afterwards the family moved to Homebush Road. Ken attended nearby Cashmere Primary for just on a year. After Madge decamped for the bright lights, Attie and the children found sanctuary in the Douglas family home in Northland Road, where his grandmother enrolled an unwilling Ken in the local school over the street. It was April 1942. Northland Primary was his third school, and he was not yet seven.[50]

Ken was a flaxen-haired child; the hair, while short, veered towards curly and was often greasy and unkempt. He had a pale complexion and freckled face, and in his earliest years was of average height and weight. Reflecting the family's poverty, his clothes were hand-me-downs or op-shop purchases. Adventurous children of the time spent their unstructured leisure time outdoors, and the perpetually grubby Ken spent many hours fossicking, either with his mates or on his own, around or in the Wilton Creek that skirted the bottom edges of the suburb, or in the council tip in the gully between Northland and Karori. He revelled in the rough and tumble of playtime at school among the boys, occasionally indulging in more serious fist fights or wrestling matches. During his early primary years he acquired the nickname 'Doon' or 'Doony' — the circumstances and the origin of the name are obscure, although Terree believes it originated from *Lorna Doone*, a popular children's novel of the time.

At home, while there was lots of love — particularly from his grandmother Carrie — he had to work hard to assert himself as a personality in his own right and 'find a place' among all of the residents in the big household. His aunt Hannah Douglas, who married his youngest uncle Lyndsay, recalls Ken as a 'tearaway as a kid, bouncing on tables' and one whom his grandmother could not control at times. Carrie told Ken that if he did not eat his vegetables he would 'turn black', and one day when he spied an African-American sailor on a city-bound tram he exclaimed to the accompanying Betty Douglas, 'Jesus bloody Christ Aunty Betty, will I look like him if I don't eat my food?' Betty recalled that she wished a hole would open up in the tram and she could have slid through it, dragging the lad with her. His cousin June Hoskin remembers his mates Don Baker and Brian Coomber, and his uncles, teasing Ken when he was older about his acne — forcing him to eat sulphur and treacle, one of his grandmother's 'cures'.[51]

School life at Northland Primary started inauspiciously. On his very first day Ken was told to stand up, because he was not sitting up straight. As he slouched sheepishly over the desk he was told, with three others, that he was being shifted to another class. Although he did not understand it at the time he was being demoted, with the excuse that this class had too many pupils and was cramped. His memories of the school are vague. There was headmaster EG Thomas, a remote figure, and Miss Rowe, a strict disciplinarian who taught him for one year. Miss Simpson is recalled for a very different reason. She was young and attractive, catching the eye of a number of the American servicemen camped in Western Park, who used to come courting, even to the school, where they were teased for their boldness by Ken and his mates. More prurient was his delight in spying on certain 'extra-curricular' activities that occurred in the closed-off air raid shelters that the Home Guard had dug into the hills surrounding the school.

Prime Minister Peter Fraser was an occasional visitor. He lived nearby and would arrive, unannounced usually, and converse with both teachers and children as he strolled around the playground at lunchtime. Through his association with both the Douglas and Farrow families he knew young Ken, and always proffered a friendly greeting. So too did Donald (Dan) McLeod, secretary of the New Zealand Federated Seamen's Union — and for many years chairman of the Northland Home and School Association — who knew Ken through his association with George Douglas on the wharf. For years McLeod gave the same Anzac Day address at the school, but the children never understood a word of it, so thick was his Scottish Hebridean accent.[52]

It was wartime, and Ken recalls the excitement of the evacuation drills, climbing into the trenches dug on the school's boundaries and eating the apples and pears that were stored there. In wintertime the students drank cocoa supplied by the school. Otherwise, school life itself was uneventful. These were the days when the instruction was teacher-led, often by repetition or rote to which the pupils listened intently for fear of being scolded, or strapped for more obvious misdemeanours such as talking out of turn.

In the 1940s, Northland was a mixed suburb of older-style private housing, rental property of varying degrees of comfort and a growing state house development towards Wilton. It was an 'in-between' suburb, not as distinctly middle class as 'city-end' Karori, its neighbour across the gully which acted both as a metaphorical and a literal gulf between the two areas, nor as working class as Thorndon down the hill towards the city's centre. It was a self-contained community. The village, through which the tram ran up to the terminus near the corner of Northland and Woburn Roads, opposite Woods for Goods grocery, contained a large general store, J Russell and Sons, which sold groceries, drapery and hardware; another grocery at the other, western end of the village; an engineering workshop; a Methodist church; a hairdressing salon; Syd Ward's greengrocery; a butchery; a Post Office; a police station-house; a pharmacy; a dairy at the city end of the village; a fire station, and Bob Goslin — both bootmaker and bookmaker — into whose premises many men in the district retreated on a Saturday afternoon to listen to horse races on the radiogram, and exchange pounds, shillings and pence on the consequences. This is a far cry from the Northland village of 2010, where the seven remaining shops include three pizzerias, a fish and chip shop and a burger bar — the fast-food hub of Wellington's western suburbs.[53]

Children's pleasures focused on the outdoors. Northland lads went mushrooming in the open spaces towards Wilton, rabbiting in the nearby hills and eeling in the streams. Ken and his friends mounted expeditions on foot into the bush- and scrub-covered hills, sometimes as far as Makara on the southern coast, which could take a whole weekend. Closer to home was the landfill in the gully between

Northland and Karori in which the boys fossicked for hours. The tip was like a goldmine to Ken and his mates and had the added advantage of being close to home. Terree recalls a time when she was in the back bedroom and heard a 'clanging and bashing' coming from the vicinity of the back steps. On investigating, she spied her brother dragging into the house a whole bunch of ex-army paraphernalia — gas masks, water bottles, thick khaki belts — all 'recycled' from the landfill.

At other times they dragged home discarded bike and pram frames and hubs which led, with the addition of some small pieces of wood, some bars and a crude steering device, to the construction of unsophisticated racing carts on top of which the boys would take off, brake-less, down the hill from the Northland shops into Glenmore Street and Tinakori Road, trying to avoid being tipped off. At the bottom, the cart would be abandoned and the lads would walk home up the hill. On other days, after school the same boys would gather around the local policeman, Constable O'Callaghan, who made a habit of standing outside Benefields Store on the corner of Farm and Northland roads dishing out good advice and a friendly smile in return, unbeknown to the kids, for any information on happenings in the neighbourhood. This was also where the *Evening Post* was dropped off by van for local lads to deliver.

In his senior years at Northland Primary Ken played rugby — at fullback — for the school team, competing against other schools at Kelburn Park on Wednesday afternoons. In 1948 the school team came under the aegis of the Athletic Rugby Club and was coached by club members. In return, schoolboys played for the club in the Saturday morning competition. There were local hockey and softball clubs based at Northland Park, and later at Western Park as they grew in size. Ken played both sports, in one memorable softball match facing a team from the Berhampore Rugby Club which included his uncle Terry Farrow. Terry was none too pleased when his nephew caught him in the outfield without gloves! The Northland team owned just four pairs. In his latter years at Northland the Methodist Church started up a harrier club as an offshoot of the Scottish Harriers Club. It was run by Fred Silver and his wife from their home in Harbour View Road, Fred being a former New Zealand titleholder. Ken, like many of the others, enjoyed the competition but was even more attracted to the biscuits, cakes and hot chocolate Mrs Silver prepared for her young charges at the end of each run.[54]

As in many communities, church was a focus. Not only did the young Ken attend Sunday school and Bible class at St Anne's, but he also frequented the church's boys' club on a Friday night where he played handball, table tennis and even undertook elocution lessons with Lottie Comber, the mother of his future groomsman. During his high school years he attended the Methodist Easter Camp, and it was there that he first met Lesley Winter, a young lass from Masterton, who would later become his wife. While at high school he also attended Bible-class dances in the church hall, as well as the Saturday-night dances on the first floor of the Northland Fire Station, which were well attended by the young and not-so-young.[55]

For some years, Ken subsidised the family income and earned himself some hard-won pence by working after school at the grocery at the top of Woburn Road. The business was initially owned by Vern Brooky, but when he retired it was taken over by Ivan Woods and became the first premises of the 'Woods for Goods' conglomerate, which later included two other shops in Manners Street and Courtenay Place. Much of the bulk produce such as flour and rice came to the store in large sacks. With his friend Don Baker, Ken's main task was to weigh up this produce and redistribute it into much smaller bags for sale or delivery. Most of the purchasing was done on credit by telephone, with customers squaring off their grocery bill on payday. The boys' other important task was to organise the goods for delivery to individual households in the little Morris van driven by Woods or his adult store assistant. Woods paid the boys a pittance, but there was a 'black market' operating, in which the boys nicked small items of food — Woods acquiesced in this practice, provided it was within reason, knowing he could not stop it.

TERREE BARRYMORE — 'MISS ELLEN'

Terree Barrymore, Ken Douglas's only sibling, has had a remarkable life in her own right. Born on 24 October 1939, she was just two when her parents separated and she went with her father and brother to live with her grandparents Carrie and George — and the extended family — at 111 Northland Road.

The precocious Terree was raised, like her brother, by her grandmother Carrie and to a lesser extent her Aunty Betty. In this very busy household Terree, the youngest, fought hard to gain attention by attempting to make herself indispensable — setting the table, running errands to the shop, operating the musical entertainment during party evenings by changing the records over at the appropriate times. She often made a space for herself under the kitchen table during meetings, drinking sessions and/or card games, there to listen or read a book. At primary school she became a star of the stage, excelling in school performances, sometimes writing her own plays to be performed, with or without other actors, in front of her classmates and before the family at home. Her cousin Colin Browne recalls visiting the house in 1947 and being intrigued by the pretty little girl and her passion for dancing, as she performed pirouettes for her uncle and his wife.

But a career as a professional thespian or dancer had little appeal and in 1955, after three undistinguished years at Wellington Girls' College, Terree joined the Willis Street firm of Brahms and MacPherson, furriers, as a salesgirl, receptionist and house model. She loved the sense of display that modelling engendered — besides, it paid £5 a night, about the same as she was getting for the rest of the week working on the shop floor. This was the first of some 60 'careers' that Terree would pursue over the following 45 years.

Rock 'n' roll was coming into its heyday at this time and Terree could not get enough of it, dancing six nights a week at various cabarets around Wellington. At 17 she met Peter Kilmore, a young printer who was also a keen rock 'n' roller, and soon they were hitting the floor together. When impresario Milton Mitchell organised a 24-hour dance competition at the Majestic Cabaret, Terree entered, danced non-stop for 28 hours and five minutes, won, and collected a princely £10 for her efforts. By this time she was training to be a psychiatric nurse.

Over Elvis Presley's 'Love Me Tender', Kilmore proposed on the dance floor. She accepted. He handed her a ring. He took it back to pawn because he needed money to gamble. It was not an auspicious beginning. They were married in Wellington's Basilica — in silence because the organist failed to show. Terree was 18. She paid for the reception at the family's Northland Road home, the rooms brightened by the display of a truck-load of jonquils brought by Bryce. Two children were born within 13 months, by which time the family was renting a tiny flat above Wadestown Road, accessible only by a steep dirt path. With no washing machine, refrigerator or clothes drier, boiling the copper was a daily chore, as was hanging wet, hand-washed nappies in Wellington's wind to freeze.

By December 1960, however, before the birth of their second child, Peter Kilmore decided he was too young to be a father so he left the pregnant Terree for a redhead 'with an 18-inch waist and gorgeous'. Living alone with her children, with no child support from her husband and a token amount from the state, Terree became deeply depressed, and her mother Madge tried to persuade her to put the children up for adoption. She refused. However, she did hand them over to her mother — and paid her a steep fee to look after them — while she arranged a live-in barmaid's job at Stallards Hotel in Lambton Quay. To survive, she shoplifted and stole garden vegetables at night.

At Stallards she met Raymond Pratt, a porter, and was attracted by his dancing skill and sense of humour. They started to go out together, and some time later Terree offered him a deal — in exchange for his agreeing to care for her kids she would raise the money to purchase a tattooing business for him. They married and moved to Hamilton. Only the third professional tattooist in New Zealand, Pratt was talented and the business thrived. Terree became manageress of the Copper Kettle restaurant. They also had a child — his first, her third.

After they moved to Cambridge to be close to Raymond's parents, who were farm labourers, Terree learnt about animal husbandry from library books and became a share-milker. Later they went to Kawerau and Mangakino, where Terree's father Attie and uncle Lyndsay were living, but by now the marriage was in trouble, and Pratt returned to Hamilton. It was at this time that Terree changed her surname by deed poll to the more 'exotic' Barrymore.

Terree remained in Mangakino with the children for four years, cleaning the local primary school, working as a barmaid in the house bar of the town's hotel, and later becoming editor and chief reporter of the local newspaper and a stringer for National Radio. Finally returning to Wellington, she worked as a postie before leaving for London to study at the British College of Astrological Sciences. After completing what was normally a three-year course in one year, she returned to Wellington and established herself as one of New Zealand's first spiritualists, mediums and tarot card readers. It took a while to become established as 'Miss Ellen', and to support her children, who were now at high school, she returned to psychiatric nursing at Porirua Hospital. The astrology business took off after she opened a studio in Manners Street and won a regular spot on Radio Windy. Later she opened equally successful studios in Auckland and Sydney.

Ever keen to explore new directions, after a chance encounter with a Lebanese businessman in Sydney, she trained in Christchurch to become an artificial inseminator of sheep. Her intention was to travel to Lebanon to teach stock yields improvement which would mean a gradual phase-out of the ancient and unproductive local breed. She stayed there for nine months but it was hard to persuade the villagers to change their ways. Moreover, Lebanon's civil war had resumed with considerable intensity. At the same time her Lebanese financier in Sydney had been convicted of fraud and sent to jail. The project came to a sudden end. Borrowing money from her son, she flew home.

She resumed life as 'Miss Ellen' in Auckland, before moving to Melbourne, where her daughter was working as a journalist. Here, Terree came into conflict with a group of religious fundamentalists and drug dealers. Following a physical confrontation in which she struck the 'leader' with a sewing machine, the police advised her to leave Melbourne until after his trial. She moved to Ballarat, to be near her former daughter-in-law and grandchildren. Today Terree still lives in Ballarat gardening, minding grandchildren and studying philosophy.

At the age of 13, Douglas left Northland Primary and a community with an easy-going familiarity, and travelled on the tram across town to Wellington College. The Kenneth George Douglas story at this school is not one of achievement and glory. There were no heroics in the 1st XV or 1st XI. He never made, nor progressed close to, either team although he was very keen on both rugby and cricket. There were no formal leadership roles on offer and his academic record was dismal. He received no accolades, not even a class prize for effort, in the five years he attended the school. His one claim to fame was that he was a member of the inter-collegiate cross-country team in 1953, and in the same year, his last, he won the senior handicap mile at the school's athletic sports.

He achieved prominence in other, less salubrious, ways. His first day at Wellington College was traumatic. More than 200 wide-eyed youngsters had been herded into the school's quadrangle to listen to deputy principal James Cuddie read out lists of names in alphabetical order for dissemination into different groups. Each group, accompanied by a master, then moved off to be assigned to a particular class. Douglas found himself in a group of close to 60, sitting at a desk and being lectured by a big, brawny fellow on what the procedures were.

Suddenly, the master started bellowing, ordering a boy at the back of the room to stand up. Nobody moved. The group quietened. The master repeated his order. Nothing. Those assembled sensed a clash of wills developing. The master headed for the back of the room, stood adjacent to Douglas, and repeated his command.

'But I wasn't talking, Sir.'

'You were, boy. On your feet.'

'I wasn't talking.'

'Come on. Get up. I don't like liars.'

'Don't call me a fucking liar!'

The tension in the classroom was palpable. Nobody moved a muscle. The master was taken aback. His face began to redden.

'Can't have this.' He glowered at Douglas. 'Outside!'

In the corridor, the master stood close, peering over the boy. He smiled weakly. In the absence of others, voices were lowered.

'You were talking, weren't you, son?'

'No, Sir, I absolutely wasn't.'

With that, the master, EMP 'Fanny' Flaws, whacked Douglas six times on the hand as hard as he could with a long strap. Back inside the classroom, Douglas moved slowly back to his desk, wringing his hand although not so obviously as to draw attention to himself, wanting, as 'tough' boys do, to remain staunch. The other boys, barely recovered from the shock of his effrontery, whispered nervously to each other.

'He's mad', murmured one, in Douglas's earshot.

Flaws was not finished.

'Now stand up, Douglas,' he ordered, having learned the name of his antagonist, 'and apologise to the class.'

'No, I'm not apologising,' his tormentor replied. 'I wasn't talking. If I was, I would have told you.'

'You're still a liar.'

'You've got no right to call me a liar, Sir, and I'm still not apologising.'

Flaws' hackles rose again. He was in a no-win situation. To save face, further retribution was the only option. 'Outside,' he barked, following up with another six on the same hand. Twelve in all; it hurt. Then he sent Douglas to the headmaster, EN Hogben. After standing outside for some time he was called into the office.

'I'm told you refused to apologise,' was the head's first comment to the recalcitrant first-dayer.

'Yes, that's right.' Douglas explained his side of the story matter-of-factly, burying within himself the deep sense of injustice he felt. At the end of the conversation he sensed that Flaws had not told Hogben about the swearing.

'You what?' was Hogben's reaction when he heard that piece of news. 'I think you should return to Mr Flaws and apologise straight away. Otherwise he should punish you again.'[56]

Returning to the classroom was anti-climactic. A stalemate ensued. There was no apology but nor was there a sense of victory. Douglas retreated to his desk and there was no further mention of the incident by either party. It was as if nothing had happened. Later Flaws, who came to sense underlying qualities of leadership in his adversary, developed a friendship with Douglas that lasted throughout his school days. 'He called me Doony after that,' was Ken's wry memory.

Among the boys, Douglas became an immediate cause célèbre, to the extent that some of the older boys decided to take him down a peg. Traditionally, initiation for Wellington College third-formers involved the older boys grabbing the newcomers, cutting the threads round the waists of their pants and pulling them out so that they fell down around the boys' ankles. Cutting the bob off the new cap was also common. Some of the smaller boys were frightened and tearful about this unwelcome attention; Douglas grabbed two of the perpetrators and dealt to them. His new-found fame as an 'upstart trouble-maker' led to six or seven of the fourth- and fifth-form boys taking Douglas behind the fives courts and giving him, in his words, one hell of a hiding. When he returned home that night, his grandmother took umbrage, not at the fighting, but at the fact that the new school uniform she had purchased (the first new clothes he had ever worn) was in tatters, and she gave him a wallop as well. As he recounted ruefully, he had 'gotten it from both ends'.

His beating behind the fives courts was Douglas's first introduction to the injustice of the mob mentality. It would not be his last. His anger ran deep over the incident and he was determined on revenge, but under his own conditions. Patiently, over the next 18 months he fronted all of the boys who had taken part in the incident and, one at a time, extracted a personal apology from each of them — sometimes after physical retribution had been exacted. For those who had done damage to his frightened classmates on the first day, he insisted that they apologise to those boys as well.

Some called Douglas a bully. Others understood that he was exacting revenge on real bullies the only way he knew how. This side of his personality had an interesting sequel. His reputation as both a scrapper and a pupil who had by now become proud of his school led others to persuade him that he should become their 'main man' in the weekly altercation that took place between some of the more macho of the fifth formers and their counterparts from neighbouring Wellington Technical College. This confrontation took place on neutral ground between the two schools — a large gravel area inside the south gate of the Basin Reserve. Up to 300 boys from each school would gather to watch and cheer on their protagonists as they did battle in these gladiatorial contests.

Douglas recounts, 'For quite a time I was the college gorilla who would fight their "champion". It was no-holds-barred stuff — punching, kicking, throwing — I was no good as a boxer in the college competitions but I knew how to scrap. I'd had some experience.'

There were no prizes — just bruises, ripped clothing and the occasional broken digit or two. Prefects from either school might come to break up the fight, but only if their fellow was losing. For decades, when single-sex education was predominant, fighting — often ritualistic — was commonplace at boys' schools during interval and lunch times, although organised clashes between schools were rarer.

In his third-form year, and having paid very little attention to his books at primary school, Douglas was streamed into 3 Remove, the bottom class, in the strictly regimented and streamed system of pupil ability which was then the norm. The origin of the term 3 Remove is clouded in the mists of history, although wags had long suggested that the name indicated that pupils therein could not be removed any further down. Three Remove was Douglas's most successful academic year at the school. Under form master 'Slug' Cameron he persistently scored in the top half of the class in tests, even topping science for the second half of the year. He improved from tenth in the class of 32 in the first half-year to fifth in the second half-year, and this occasioned his promotion to the next class up, 4 Special, in 1950.

This year saw Douglas's first attempts to become an entrepreneur. As a bonus, Ivan Woods of Woods for Goods, for whom he still worked after school, sold him condoms for one shilling a packet, as opposed to the usual price of 1/6d. Ken would open the packet of three and on-sell them at school for ninepence each. Word got around and nervous boys sought him out at the back of the fives courts where they surreptitiously purchased the wares, more likely for the fun of it rather than with any intention of using them for their proper purpose. The business was not a long-term success, lasting only a few months because most boys either did not have enough money or 'chickened out' at the last moment. Douglas may have realised then that business was not his calling, unlike sometime classmate Ron Brierley who sold stamps in their hundreds at the school and went on to become a multi-millionaire.[57]

Douglas's promotion to 4 Special was a doubtful call. Academically, it proved dismal. In science, which had held so much promise in 1949, he fell to 28th place out of 34 in the first half-year, and 33rd out of 35 in the second half-year. This was a familiar pattern. He was 28th out of 35 for English even though he loved reading; 32nd out of 34 for French, even though he loved French and in this subject would score his highest School Certificate mark in a year's time. Yet his overall position in class — 32nd out of 34 for the first half-year and 31st out of 35 for the second half-year — was just enough to prevent him being demoted. 'Could do better' was the clipped, blunt message on his report cards. Ken felt it was understated.

He entered 5 Special under form master GC Rowe in 1951. There was a marginal improvement, with a top-10 placing in French for the first half of the year, and Douglas recalls a rare classroom highlight when he came third in a commercial practice test, scoring higher than Brierley, who came 9th. He ended the year 24th-equal overall out of 30, and with a miserable result in the School Certificate examinations, scoring 65 per cent in French but failing everything else. This meant, as it did for most boys in 5 Special, a repeat year in the fifth form.

Upper 5th Special was his home in 1952. Under the guidance of OS 'Sam' Meads, on whose brother's farm near Feilding he cut scrub and dagged sheep over three summer breaks — and who was a popular and accessible figure around the school in his role as the hands-on head of the boarding establishment, Firth House — he worked harder and achieved class positions above halfway in both half-years. But that meant little in the long term. Passing School Certificate was his ambition. It went unfulfilled. While most of his marks improved, they fell well short of the necessary average of 50 per cent per subject; nor did he achieve the minimum 30 per cent required in English. He reached a nadir in mathematics — scoring just 4 per cent, a drop from 12 per cent the previous year.

Undeterred, and despite the obvious disappointment of his grandmother and his father Attie, who like most working-class parents of the day sent his son to school to obtain academic qualifications so he would not be stuck in unskilled or semi-skilled labouring jobs, as he had been, Ken returned for a fifth year. As his aunt Hannah Douglas put it, 'Doony loved school much more than it loved him.' He stuck out 6 Remove for nine months, achieving poorly — 19th out of 22 in the class — before leaving to train as a wool-classer, a job negotiated for him by his uncle Bryce.[58]

Hannah Douglas's remarks were prophetic. Ken Douglas enjoyed his days at Wellington College. He revelled in the tradition, the high columns, the grandeur of the hall, the stained glass windows. He gazed repeatedly at the long lists of old boys who had fallen in war. He enjoyed age-old rituals. Veins popped in his neck when he ripped into the school haka. He took pleasure in participating in the cadet corps. He liked the order, the sense of discipline, the working together. He became a junior under-officer in the school battalion during his last year at college and for a short time was keen to follow a career in the army. There was even a promise from Flaws that if he passed School Certificate in his second year the school would accredit him University Entrance the following year so he could enter the Royal Military College at Duntroon near Canberra to train as an officer. It was a pipe-dream.

He enjoyed the mateship and the camaraderie which developed in class. He formed a particularly close bond with three of his classmates, boys of varying backgrounds who would go on to forge very different futures — John McCormick, a Firth House boarder with a National Party background; Paul Henare, a part-Maori who would later father a controversial politician, and club-footed George Janis, who was of Greek origin and would later develop his father's hairdressing business into the largest in Wellington. In 2005, McCormick, who was in the same class as Douglas for four years, recalled their time together at Wellington College:

> Doony was not only the class 'hard case', he was also the school 'hard case'. Every boy either knew him, wanted to know him, or liked to tell others how much they liked him. Part of his popularity was because he was always so cheerful and funny. 'Moron' was a common word at the time for being admonished. One time after

an English lesson on figures of speech somebody crossed him and he replied, quick as a wink, 'You bloody oxymoron.'

He had a flat-footed, defiant gait. It was as though he was trying to draw attention to himself. If it was, it worked. He was easy to talk to; he spoke to anybody, and did so in the same respectful tone to master and pupil alike. He might have been cheeky but it was intended to be funny. He was a character. I wasn't. He was a magnet and I was so proud that he should want to befriend me.[59]

Douglas got on particularly well with many of the Firth House boarders who, like McCormick, offered him insights into a different way of life. His schooldays gave him the opportunity to associate with types of people he had not encountered before, giving him a confidence which, when transferred to the union movement in his adult life, would be of enormous benefit.

Through his charm, and his growing mana within the school, Douglas developed close relationships with several of the masters. This was partly the result of the close informal contact the boys had with their sports coaches. Alongside Flaws and Meads, Douglas felt a particular affinity for the dignified Frank Crist, a long-term teacher and rugby coach at the school, and 'Micky' Michael who taught him the joys of French translation, at which, unlike his other class work, he excelled. Another who he held in high regard was James Cuddie — short, bald, precise. He had begun teaching at the school in 1916, and by Douglas's time was deputy principal.

Douglas remembers the unique way Cuddie addressed the school assembly. 'Gentlemen of Wellington College,' he would intone. In response, the hall would hush immediately, become respectful, proud. The most extraordinary of Cuddie's qualities, in the days when it was common to admonish boys even for minor offences with a quick swish of a cane or whoosh of a strap, was that in close to 40 years at the college he never resorted to corporal punishment. In 1967, college historian HA 'Fish' Heron put it this way: 'He had the special gift of being able, by the force of his verbal admonitions aided by his own sincerity, to achieve more in correction than is normally attainable by conventional punishment. Assembly was at his feet.' Heron was headmaster of Wellington College between 1951 and 1962 and Cuddie worked under him until he retired in 1954.[60]

The most remarkable tale involving the masters concerned Douglas's first-day tormentor, Fanny Flaws. It was 1951, the year of the 151-day waterfront lockout. Flaws took 5 Special for a double period of English on Friday mornings, and for the duration of the dispute he ran projects based on what was happening on the wharf, including debates for and against the actions of the watersiders' union, and the responses of the government and the opposing Federation of Labour. One of Douglas's mates in the class was Tim Ord whose father was a watersider. During their discussions Ord — a real 'scone-doer', according to Douglas — would heatedly defend the union, as would Douglas, although with more circumspection.

But it was not as easy as that. Flaws arranged the debates so that these two had to argue for the government's position, and that of the Federation of Labour (which vigorously opposed the lockout). At the same time, others in the class whose parents regarded the watersiders, and their union, as ne'er-do-wells who were ruining the country had to present arguments in support of their stand. Douglas recalls this as a magnificent learning experience, teaching him the value of teamwork, hard research and an awareness that by taking an opposition standpoint your own point can become much clearer. 'Fanny's debates were a real crucible of passion, politics and philosophy,' he recalled in 2005.

Both Ord and Douglas brought illegal watersiders' pamphlets to school to help justify their arguments. Flaws would then take these to the staffroom, where they were popular among his colleagues mostly because they were clandestine and there was a 'black market' trade in them. At the time, Douglas's Uncle Laurie was on the executive of the Wellington Drivers' Union which was supporting the watersiders in their fight. At Laurie's suggestion, Douglas took up a collection in his class for the lockout fund, gathering up to 12 or 15 shillings a week on occasion, including more than a bob or two from Firth House boys who were predominantly farmers' sons. Flaws did not teach Douglas after 1951, but when he learned late in 1953 that Douglas was leaving school he sought him out. 'Shame you're going, lad,' he said. 'I've got a class now. Otherwise we could have popped down to the Callie for a beer.'[61]

Apart from Flaws' classes, politics rarely entered Douglas's life at school. The only exception was when the Governor General, Sir Bernard Freyberg, called in for a visit. Freyberg, who had lived next door in Northland, was universally lauded as New Zealand's greatest wartime soldier. Not in the Douglas household, however. There he was a persona non grata. In 1913 he had been one of Massey's Cossacks, batoning striking watersiders along Featherston Quay. Ken was warned by his family not to go anywhere near Freyberg during his Wellington College stopovers. Once a turncoat, always a turncoat.

Sport featured strongly in Douglas's life, and he entered as many events as he could in the school's athletic sports every March. Throwing the cricket ball was a particular passion. In his last year of school he surprised even himself when, with a start of 30 yards, he won the senior handicap mile. That year he was also in the senior cross-country team which won the inter-collegiate title, a win that gave him considerable pleasure. He also boxed in the school competitions and received, in his words, 'some terrible hidings' — ironic in view of his corporeal exploits in other areas.

Throughout his school life he played both rugby and cricket in lower-grade teams, and he would later return as a young adult to coach the sort of run-of-the-mill teams he used to play in. In his second-to-last year at school, a bone in his foot snapped when an opposing forward, John Maguire (a later 1st XV captain), came down heavily on it during a lineout in the trials to select the first and second fifteens. That was the end of his trial, and the foot was encased in a cast. Desperately disappointed, but keen to play sport nonetheless, he heard that the second hockey XI was short of a goal-keeper. Douglas volunteered, cast notwithstanding. From the beginning, he did a phenomenal job. The 1952 second hockey XI triumphed in its grade, winning 10 of 11 matches and scoring a massive 72 goals, with Ken letting in just five. It was his one and only excursion into hockey, but a fitting finale to his sporting career at high school.[62]

A Friday night ritual was to attend dances at Lawrence Mackie's studio in Willis Street, which gave the boys a chance to try out the skills they had learned at dance classes with the girls from Wellington East. A routine developed for these evenings, with both boys and girls rendezvousing at the Adams Bruce ice-cream shop for a milk shake, then over the road to the dance floor. Douglas was popular with the girls, who found his confidence and quick wit attractive. He also had size and a kind of rough magnetism that contrasted slightly with his grace as he tripped the light fantastic dressed in a striped blazer and trailing a knitted silk scarf. Helen Young, a Queen Margaret's girl, and Jill Morrieson from Wellington Girls were especially favoured dancing partners and close friends. Terree recalled, admiringly, that on the dance floor he swept the girls off their feet, so delicate and finely tuned were his movements. He also attended Labour Party and Bible-class dances where, again according to Terree, overstating the case, if a girl danced the foxtrot with Doony then 'her night was made'.

From Douglas's perspective, Wellington College was egalitarian rather than elitist in its roots and philosophies. He felt no sense of envy towards the boys in the top stream; neither did his classmates. Most were barely aware of the others surrounding them — the classroom satisfied their social needs if not always their academic ones. The pupils in 3 Remove realised they were as good as if not better then the boys in 3A if they were victorious over them during inter-class sports competitions, giving them a healthy sense of achievement. Within the wider school, Jew, Chinese, Indian, Maori, Pacific Islander (although all in very small numbers) were accepted without question as an integral and important component of the school population. Each year, he cheered on the 1st XV during their club and inter-collegiate matches with a sense of honour, sentiments that were at one with the great bulk of his fellows. He even revelled in the fact that in his last year — as a member of the 3rd XV — he could pack down in training against the school's top scrum and be used by them, in his words, 'as a sort of punching bag'. Needless to say, when Wellington College won the inter-school quadrangular rugby tournament with Christ's College, Wanganui Collegiate and Nelson

College, his heart swelled with pride.

Later, he returned to the school to coach lower-grade rugby teams. In 1963 he coached team 2D, who were in the second-to-top size bracket but assessed as being 'down the scale' in ability. Team member Sam Perry, a sixth former in 1963, remembered Douglas, by now broad of shoulder, with coal dust oozing out of his pores, climbing out of his truck at four o'clock every Tuesday and Thursday afternoon. Strolling purposefully to the practice ground in dirty work boots, grey shorts — sometimes ripped — and checked shirt with sleeves rolled up, balls in hand, he would dispense firmly, but not too seriously, his considerable knowledge to the team. According to Perry he was always on time, in contrast to some of the master-coaches, despite the fact that Douglas, in his work paid by the hour, was sacrificing earnings for his love of the game.[63]

It had become clear by 1953 that scholarly success was beyond his reach. Attie had become frustrated at his son's lack of academic attainments and was no longer prepared to provide the funding from his limited pay packet to keep him there. He proffered the view that Ken was now 'big and ugly enough to go out and look after himself'. He should leave school, find work and contribute to the family.

Carrie's attitude was that it was Ken's decision. Her values were more abstract. 'It does not matter what you do,' she would say, 'as long as you always remember who you are and what you represent. Nobody will respect you if you don't respect yourself.' This mantra encapsulated the key principles in her own life, and she hoped that they would be inculcated into Ken's.

Through all his school days, his mother, Madge, had been missing in action. He had had sporadic contact with her when she lived in Cuba Street with her parents, but for much of the time that he was in college she lived in Nelson with Harry Johnson. In his last year at school, Ken travelled there as part of the Wellington College team for the inter-collegiate tournament held that year at Nelson College. She was not there — she and Johnson had moved to Arrowtown to work for a short period — but Ken did visit the Panama Hotel where she worked as a barmaid, and talked to some of her workmates.

In October 1953, Ken Douglas, now big and burly, dispensed with his tight shorts and worn-out shoes and left Wellington College to train as a wool-classer at Wright Stephensons' woolstore in 47 Shed on Fryatt Quay. There he worked under foreman Jim Mather, who in turn answered to head classer Eric Williams. The job consisted of gathering the roughly sorted fleeces from the bales of wool that came into the shed, and spreading them out on the sorting table for the classer to remove unacceptable pieces and then classify them into grades preparatory to being auctioned. Douglas then had to gather up each fleece and put it in the appropriate bin or bale to be pressed ready for sale.

After all the wool had been classed, the wool pressers would begin their work in the evenings. Two men worked the press, one compressing the wool in the bale, the other sewing it up using an oversized needle and twine. At the time business was booming. The Korean War had created an insatiable demand for New Zealand wool, used in the manufacture of military garments worn by United Nations troops during the Korean winter. There was never enough, and prices — at more than £1 per pound for the best lines — were the best New Zealand sheep farmers have ever received, before or since. There was also a shortage of wool pressers. Douglas had a mate on the press, Freddy Stokes, who lived in a boarding house across the road from his grandparents in Cuba Street. In his very first week as a trainee wool-classer, Stokes asked him if he would like to relieve on his gang at nights. Of course he would — he was young and fit, and hard-working pressers made good money on contract.

The upshot of this was that feathers flew when he handed his first week's wages to his grandmother, as was the custom in the Douglas household. When Attie saw that his son's pay, at £19.19.10, was more than twice what he had earned as a truck driver that week — £9.11.0 — he hit the roof. 'What's bloody wrong with the world when I've been working my arse off driving trucks for 25 years and get less than half what you do in your first week at work!' Ken's reaction was to laugh nervously. Carrie's was to burst into tears — not about the pay disparity but because 'her boy' was now a man, out in the world, working hard and earning a crust so that he could be independent.

But Douglas's budding wool-classing career soon came to a crashing halt. Eric Williams loved to play cricket. The Wright Stephenson wool warehouse was now housed in the Winter Show Building, and at lunchtime when the weather was fine most of the 30 employees would take the field or pad up on the grass area outside. Williams liked to bat, and the workers soon learned that if lunch hour was to be extended he should stay in for as long as possible facing 'lollipops' from the other end. If he was out, it was back to work immediately.

In the holidays, schoolboys came to work in the warehouse to help clear the backlog, and play cricket. The young lads were mostly employed working through the ends of the fleeces which were often rife with dags and smelled oppressively of the fatty lanolin, which permeated both clothes and skin. To try to rid the boys of this stench, Williams turned a hose on them. One particularly small lad from St Patrick's College was frightened of this process and burst into tears as Williams began to douse him. Douglas, walking past pulling a cart of bales, noticed the lad's misery and asked Williams to leave him alone. The boy was clearly distressed.

'What's it got to do with you?' was Williams' terse response, as he continued to hose the boy.

'You're not my boss. Can't you see the lad has really had enough?' Douglas replied.

Indeed, Williams was not his boss. Mather was. Douglas had been employed by Head Office, not by Williams, whose sole responsibility was to run the warehouse.

Williams was irritated. Douglas was angry. He snatched Williams, threw him in the wool, grabbed the still-running hose and turned it on him, soaking him within seconds. The foreman exploded in anger. 'That's it! You're sacked, ya bastard!' he screamed as rivulets of water poured off his hair, face and clothes. An audience quickly gathered; some laughed; a few giggled nervously; others stood silent, mouths agape, gobsmacked at Douglas's gall.

Williams dispatched him to Cliff Plimmer, Wright Stephensons' general manager. Plimmer was fatherly. Perusing Douglas's work record, he commented on how well he had done at the firm, praising his initiative in enrolling at Massey University to study extramurally for a diploma in wool classing. But he made it clear that Douglas would need to offer contrition to Williams and mend the fence. When the headstrong Douglas was adamant that he would not apologise, Plimmer told him that he would have to go. 'We can't have the two of you at loggerheads and he's more important to us than you are.' Douglas left, unobtrusively. There was no argument. He had learned the very important lesson that everybody has their value in life.[64]

By this time Ken had acquired his first car, a Ford 10 found abandoned on the road between Levin and Palmerston North with a broken 'big end'. The car belonged to Joe Williams, a big-time Palmerston North gambler who had installed two dummy battery boxes in the floor of the back seat to hide his winnings from opportunist robbers. After the car was spotted by one of Ken's uncles, Williams offered it to Douglas 'as is, where is' for £5. Attie towed it back to Wellington and helped him repair it on the street outside 111 Northland Road.

Douglas was not unemployed for long. Tom Wilkinson, a concrete and asphalt contractor, took him on to help reseal tennis courts. He enjoyed the physicality of the work but lasted only six months before he was called up to do his compulsory military training. This involved a three-month-long camp in his first year and fortnightly camps for the next three years. The training provided a more sophisticated and exciting extension to his time in the school cadet corps and he thoroughly enjoyed it. He was assigned to the New Zealand Scottish Regiment, and travelled to Waiouru on 16 September 1954 to join the Royal New Zealand Armoured Corps with the rank of trooper. This meant driving tanks and playing 'war games' in the uplands beneath the Kaimanawa Ranges. He won high praise from the top brass who assessed his progress at various times, and was described as reliable and industrious, high-spirited, smart on parade, clean, with 'qualities of leadership developing', good enough, it was recorded, for the still-teenage Douglas to be considered officer potential. Douglas recalls that he was paid £7 a week to enjoy himself. During his third year he got married, and instantly his army pay more than trebled, to £23 a week. He was good at playing soldiers, and by the end of his first stretch in the army he was a corporal. He remained in the Territorials until 1965, attaining the rank of acting regimental sergeant-major.[65]

Having finished his time with Wilkinson, and after completing his first stint in the army, Douglas was again out of a job. By this time he was developing a friendship with his mother's youngest brother, Terry Farrow, who was 12 years his senior. Farrow had been a watersider on the Wellington wharf since 1949 and had tussled with police and struggled to keep his family fed during the 1951 lockout. On the back of the wool boom, the economy was burgeoning and men were needed on the wharf. Farrow persuaded Ken to apply for a job there.

TERRY FARROW

From adolescence to middle age, Terry Farrow, his mother Madge's youngest brother, was a giant in Ken Douglas's life. At Farrow's funeral in 1999, Douglas spoke of having tried to live his uncle's dream. Conversely, Terry Farrow was more proud of his nephew Ken's achievements as a trade union leader than any other person.

The youngest son of George and Eleanor Farrow, Terry was born on 9 November 1923. As a boy of 10, he watched with horror from the verandah of his Cuba Street home as mounted police chased fleeing men, women and children during a Depression riot. In 1937, at the age of 13, Terry left the Marist school in Newtown for a job delivering meat on a bicycle for Frank Mooney Butchers. After suffering bouts of pleurisy and pneumonia, he floated between a number of labouring jobs, lacking direction and having minor brushes with the law, until March 1942 when he was drafted into the army. By this time he had met Thelma Hutchinson — it was love at first sight and they would later marry. Based at Wigram but missing Thelma, Terry went AWOL, scarpering to Wellington, where he was caught and jailed for desertion.

Sent to Fort Dorset in Seatoun, he escaped again to see Thelma, was caught again, and had his clothes removed. This was no deterrent. He escaped a third time, wrapping his naked body in an army blanket. At Thelma's place he slipped into some women's shorts and an ill-fitting jersey, then at his brother George's he borrowed some 'gents'' clothes. He was caught again but avoided further prison time through the intervention of a friendly officer at the camp, promising he would not misbehave again. He and Thelma were married on 22 March 1944 at St Joseph's Church in Wellington. Terry returned to camp and was sent to Italy in June that year, serving until the war ended. Returning home on board the *Stirling Castle*, the highlight, he recorded, 'was winning a lot of money on crown-and-anchor and losing most of it on two-up'.

Nonetheless, he arrived home in January 1946 flush with more than £100 in his back pocket, delighted to be back with his beloved wife and his infant daughter. Back home Terry took a variety of labouring jobs — cellarman in the Grand Hotel; carpenter's labourer building state houses in Nelson, Naenae and Porirua, and from 1949 as a watersider on the Wellington wharf. Initially, Thelma and Terry lived at his parents' place in Cuba Street. After the birth of their second child in December 1947 they shifted into their own flat at the back of a butcher's shop in nearby Tonks Avenue.

The 1951 waterfront lockout began as Thelma was expecting their fourth child. With the emergency regulations banning watersiders and their families from being fed, and with no income, it was a tough 151 days. Fortunately there was strong family support — Terry's sister Madge paid the rent; his brother George brought vegetables, and his mate Jock Imlach supplied groper throats. After the lockout Terry stayed on the wharf, where he was an integral member of 'Red Square', the café area where communist watersiders ate their lunch. In his words, he slowly 'educated' the scabs who had remained; they would have 'jumped in the water if their bosses had told them to', he recalled. 'Fight them when you're out, educate them when you're back. There was one old joker I used to talk to and I remember someone saying to me, "He scabbed in 1913. But he stood loyal in '51", so there you are.' It was a big day for Terry Farrow and his family when they moved into their first state house in Dimock Street, Titahi Bay, in December 1953. They had been waiting for that moment for seven years.

Terry worked on the waterfront for 32 years, remaining active in the union except for a break for a few years in the late 1970s when he left to work for Ashley Wallpapers. Like his nephew Ken he was a keen rugby-player, and he became a foundation member of the Titahi Bay Rugby Club, playing and later coaching many age-grade teams. For more than four decades he was not only captain and coach but also administrator, cook, cleaner, taxi driver, raffle organiser and supporter. He even paid the subs and bought boots for less fortunate players — especially children. He was also a foundation member, player, coach and administrator at the Titahi Bay Softball Club. When the Titahi Bay and Porirua rugby and softball clubs later evolved into the Norths' Rugby Club and Porirua United Softball Club respectively, he was honoured with life membership of both clubs.

Much earlier, he had been active in the 'No Maoris — No Tour' movement, and protested against the 1981 Springbok tour. At the Titahi Bay Rugby Club he moved a motion, seconded by his son-in-law Murray Dick, condemning the NZRFU for inviting a racially selected rugby team to tour New Zealand. The members passed it, the only rugby club in New Zealand to pass such a motion. Terry's last job was as a cleaner on the waterfront, and he retired in 1988.

Terry Farrow died on 5 January 1999 after a year-long battle with cancer of the oesophagus. The local church was too small for his funeral, so hundreds turned out to farewell him at the Norths' Rugby Club number one ground, the casket under the goalposts. In farewell, he was honoured with a karakia led by local kaumatua Pikau Arthur. A recording of Paul Robeson singing 'Joe Hill' and 'The Internationale' was played, and then the assembled mourners belted out 'The Red Flag' and 'Solidarity Forever'. For years Farrow had been Ken Douglas's 'best friend' and mentor. In a tribute Ken wrote, 'As long as I can remember you were the compass of my life, work and play. Thank you Terry for being what you were and what you have given.'

Farrow had an ulterior motive in encouraging his nephew to join him on the waterfront. Trade unionism on the wharf was dysfunctional. As a consequence of the lockout, two unions operated — Kingsley Bell's 'scab' union, the Wellington Maritime Cargo Workers' Union, now led by a man called Rowlands, and the old union sustained by lockout leaders Tommy Wells and Ted Thompson who, unlike their counterparts in Auckland, had not lost their employment in the aftermath of the conflict, although both had been blacklisted by ship-owners and had to win appeals under a government-established tribunal to win their jobs back.[66]

The men worked in separate gangs, and ate and socialised apart. Friends before the lockout had become bitter enemies after it. Bos Murphy, the New Zealand champion middleweight boxer, joined the new Wellington union after the lockout. Billy Hedberg, his friend and trainer, was a pre-lockout watersider and remained loyal to the old union. Now, when Hedberg passed Murphy on the wharf he cursed loudly and spat at his feet. By this time there were wiser heads — Thompson chief among them — working towards an amalgamation of the two unions. For this to happen more newcomers were needed to join the scab union, to boost numbers for the 'yes' vote in the forthcoming merger plebiscite.[67]

To join the new union Douglas had to undergo an interview with the Waterfront Industry Commission, where it was necessary to indulge in truth-stretching exercises since through family association and personal sentiment he was sympathetic to the locked-out men. Schooled by Wells and Farrow, he denied that he knew anybody on the wharf or that he had ever worked there. (He had — as a seagull on Friday nights and Saturday mornings at times from his senior school days onwards. Moreover, he had other family on the wharf aside from Farrow. His cousin John Fage worked for the Waterfront Industry Commission as an accountant, and Fage's mother Nell ran the wharfies' cafeteria.)

Nevertheless, he won the job, attained a waterfront bureau number, and entry to the new union. He courted controversy immediately. The first job he was allocated was on the *Hororata*, a New Zealand Shipping Company vessel that had caught fire soon after its arrival in Wellington from Liverpool in March 1955. The fire had started in the boiler room then spread to the number-three hold, where it damaged the cargo of inflammable textiles and motor vehicles before it was extinguished. Although Douglas did not know it at the time, salvage work was regarded as a plum job because the urgency of the work meant plenty of overtime and a substantial pay packet. Fourteen men gathered in the hold to be divided up into two gangs of seven. Douglas knew none of the other men. As a lad of 19 he was the youngest by far. He had barely arrived when he was confronted by a Polish labourer of substantial proportions, who demanded to know how Douglas had secured this job as a beginner, while his mate, who was much more experienced, had missed out. Douglas felt a dreaded sense of déjà vu but remained calm, professing ignorance. His antagonist's anger was not assuaged and he took a swing at Ken with a wool-hook. A punch-up ensued. After the combatants had been pulled apart a bruised Douglas stormed off the boat, muttering that he 'didn't bloody need this'. He returned to the waterfront office, where the foreman questioned his presence. 'I'm not going back there,' he barked. 'They're fucking mad.'[68]

At lunch time he joined Terry Farrow who was parked in the cafeteria's 'Red Square', the set of tables around which Communist Party watersiders ate their lunch. Farrow and his mates were incredulous at his behaviour. 'You're a bloody idiot. Christ, a job like that's a goldmine!' Douglas returned to the bureau, where he was accused of being 'soft' by a man named Hughes, who he remembers as a 'big, ugly thug'. 'What do you think this is, son, Billy Butlin's holiday camp?' Hughes demanded. Nevertheless he did not receive any penalty, which he had been told was likely, nor any recrimination, just abuse from some workmates for mixing it with those 'bastards from Red Square'. It was the first time he had heard the term.

Work on the waterfront was arduous, heavy, often dirty and sometimes dangerous — the crowbar and the wool-hook being the men's only friends. In this time of economic prosperity men regularly worked 12 hours a day, or 60 to 80 hours a week, interrupted only by their practice from the late 1940s onwards of taking well-earned rests — called 'spelling' — most commonly one hour on, half an hour off. Because they had one of the highest injury rates among all manual workers, insurance companies charged watersiders a premium; the only occupational group who paid more for insurance were jockeys. In the cold temperatures of refrigerated holds, gangs of six or eight had to keep up with the crane or steam-winch slinging in nets of meat. With just crowbars for assistance, they lifted and stowed frozen slabs of beef or lamb and mutton carcasses — often above their heads, at times having to clamber over other carcasses to reach the corners. Loading bags of coal, soda ash and bales of wool was equally back-breaking. Least favoured of all was the unloading of lamp-black, an unpleasant fine-grained soot used in the manufacture of tyres. It left the watersiders covered in a black gunge which stuck to their skin and clothes.[69]

Ken Douglas worked on the Wellington waterfront for close to 10 months, during which time the ballot for union amalgamation was held and passed, being enacted later that year. It was a magnificent learning experience for the raw teenager. In later years he would often say that he learned far more 'of importance' in his months on the wharf than in five years at Wellington College. Farrow would later refer to the wharf and the union as 'my Eton, my Oxford', and his nephew experienced the same thing, in miniature. There were many teachers. Veteran watersider and old sea-dog Ned Fitzgerald was one. He was a wiry Irishman, close to 70 years old at that time, who wore a suit coat to work, with a matching timepiece, topped by a tam-o'-shanter on his head and an old oak pipe stuck in his mouth.

Douglas first worked with Fitzgerald in a gang of two, loading quarters of beef on the *Dominion Monarch*. Each of the four gangs in the hold was responsible for loading the carcasses in one corner. When the first 300-lb (140-kg) slab of beef came their way from above, Douglas, aware of Ned's advancing years and the weight of the carcass, instructed, 'You stay there, Mr Fitzgerald.' He reached for the beef off the sling and immediately lost his balance, the carcass falling one way and Douglas the other. He then had enormous difficulty uplifting and moving it across the floor. Ned watched, unperturbed, pipe puffing voluminously, then drawled, 'Are ye fin'shed yet, laddie?' He cocked his eye at Douglas and grinned. ''Ere, I'll show ye 'ow to do it.' With that, using a series of adroit balancing manoeuvres, Ned 'kind of walked the carcass on its own into where it was supposed to go'. 'It's na' ab'ut brawn, matey, it's ab'ut brain,' counselled the old man, pointing to his forehead.[70]

There was an eclectic mix among the men working on the wharf: debarred lawyers, defrocked priests, displaced migrants who spoke little English, ex-cons of all descriptions — each commanding various degrees of trustworthiness — and the openly effeminate Gladys, the first gay man Douglas had known. Gladys was a union delegate, effective and popular with his colleagues. He was also fiercely protected. More than once when Gladys was insulted because of his sexuality the perpetrator felt the hard end of a watersider's fist.

Douglas found he enjoyed working on the wharf. He luxuriated in the spontaneity of working-class humour; the quick wit, the bawdy reminiscence. He agreed with the 'spelling' system, which resulted in a more productive, fresher workforce and a speedier turnaround of ships. Moreover, the work could be dangerous when there was a full gang in a hold with two derricks working above. However, the night work, of which there was plenty, began to interfere savagely with his rugby training. (He was propping the Wellington College Old Boys second division scrum at this time.) Moreover, during their time off many watersiders went straight to the pub. With alcohol a problem among many in his family, Douglas did not want to be faced with the same temptation.

It was while working on the Wellington waterfront that Douglas came face-to-face with effective union practice for the first time. He developed huge respect for Ted Thompson in particular, who along with Chip Bailey, with whom he would work closely soon afterwards, was the most effective delegate he saw in action. The small, square-faced Thompson, who was by this time the union's full-time walking delegate (disputes officer), never raised his voice but was always resolute, analytical and well-informed in negotiation. He commanded respect from employer and worker alike. Whereas others who were to follow, like Tom Skinner, were 'dealers', an easy role, Thompson was a true negotiator, calm in hand-to-hand industrial combat, with a quick sense of humour which he often used to his advantage. Thompson and the union he worked for provided Douglas with a foundation of preparedness and determination, traits that would serve him well in later battles.[71]

It was during these years, when Douglas was in his late teens, that Lesley Winter began to supplant other paramours in his affections and there was talk of a more serious commitment. They had been friends for a long time, having met when Ken was in his early years at high school. Lesley had grown up in Masterton but shifted to Wellington to begin training as a primary school teacher at Wellington Teachers' College. She was an intelligent, attractive young woman with curly brunette hair and an olive complexion. Like Ken, she was interested in reading, politics and the Maori language; later, in 1959, they both became active participants in the 'No Maoris — No Tour' protest movement.

Lesley's sister Marion had been boarding at George and Eleanor Farrow's house in Cuba Street. George had recently acquired his section at Raumati, and he and members of the family spent time at the weekends clearing scrub and grass, tilling the soil and planting potatoes. Ken would spend much of his Sunday there, labouring on the land, absorbing political 'lessons' from his grandfather at the same time. Sometimes he took his mates and girlfriends with him. Lesley, meanwhile, visited Raumati periodically with her mother and sister, and it was there that their friendship deepened into something more significant. Later, Lesley taught at Eastbourne School, flatting with Marion and two other friends in Old Bullock Road, Highbury. Douglas's army exercising, wharf work and rugby training had made him fit, and on a good night he could run the three kilometres between Lesley's flat in Old Bullock Road and his Northland home in just 12 minutes.

Lesley attended Wesley Methodist Church in Taranaki Street, and was a keen member of its Bible class. It was here that she and Ken were married, on 18 August 1956. He was young, just three months shy of his 21st birthday. Lesley was the same age. Ken displayed some anxiety before the service because 18 August was also the day of the third rugby test between the All Blacks and the Springboks at Lancaster Park. The wedding was originally set down for two o'clock but Ken and some of his male relatives prevailed upon the minister, the Reverend David Storkey, to delay the service until 4.30pm so that they could all — the guests, family, and Ken and Lesley — listen to Winston McCarthy's commentary on the radio. Douglas knew Storkey, as he had been the padre of the Armoured Corps at Waiouru, the unit Ken was attached to during his military training. The service itself was traditional, enlivened by the singing of the church's Samoan choir. Don Baker and Brian Coomber, friends from both primary and high school, were best man and groomsman respectively.[72]

The reception, held in a hall in Sydney Street East, was a rumbustious affair. The band played; the Samoan contingent swayed and sang with panache; and Lesley's mother Gwen, Madge and their Post Office mates cavorted with huge enthusiasm. Likewise, Carrie, Ken's uncles, his school- and workmates, his rugby chums and the Irish Catholic relatives from the Farrow side of the family all helped to drink the kegs dry, polish off the corned beef sandwiches, lamingtons and wedding cake in style, engage in loud banter, sing out of tune and boogie around the dance floor with varying degrees of adeptness. Jack O'Halloran, mine host of the Panama Hotel, shouted Ken and Lesley their first night together in his establishment, after which Ken, in a newly acquired Morris Series E motor car, drove Lesley to Hastings to stay with her sister Marion, now living there with her husband. Neither Lesley nor Ken had experienced the kind of opulence that surrounded them at Turangi's Bridge Lodge, where the honeymoon proper began. They soaked it up for three days before the return drive to Wellington and their respective jobs — Ken driving trucks for HW Thomas Ltd and Lesley at Eastbourne Primary School. Ken left his grandmother's house — where he had lived since he was six — and he and Lesley rented a bed-sit in Hobson Street. There was an accommodation shortage at the time, and their exploitative landlord Jack Travers charged them a steep £5 for a small double room. They shared a kitchen with the occupants of the whole house, and a bathroom and toilet with the others on the ground floor.[73]

Douglas had started working as a driver for Harold Thomas on 26 October 1955, within two days of leaving the wharf, thereby joining his father Attie in the trucking business. Attie must have wondered why he and Carrie had bothered sending Ken to high school for five years, but within days Ken had attended his first drivers' union meeting and found himself being asked to stand for the local executive — partly because he was the first of the next generation of the Douglas family to attend such a gathering. He did not know it then, but this would be the first step in the career that would dominate his working life. He was not yet 20 years old.

CHAPTER 3

Captain of a ship on a bitumen sea

Harold (Harry) Thomas founded his trucking firm, HW Thomas Ltd, on 25 October 1924. A former railway worker, he financed the company by raising a nominal share capital of £3000. This bought him an open-sided cart, two ageing horses and a rented yard and stables at 52A Creswick Terrace, Northland, on top of which he built a flat for his family of five to live in. At first, he delivered groceries and hardware from local shops to customers in Northland and adjacent communities. Hard work, long hours and a reputation for reliability soon saw Thomas expand his business, forsaking the horses and carts for his first truck in 1926 and employing two drivers and a yardman. By 1929, the firm had expanded to seven trucks. Part of the reason for its success was Thomas's acumen as a businessman. Around the traps he became known as 'Hungry Harry' for his ability to rush to a job and secure a contract before his competitors, an especially useful trait when cartage work diminished during the 1930s Depression.

The business thrived during the later 1930s and the 1940s, and in 1950 Thomas purchased a property adjoining Haining Street and St Martin's Square, close to Wellington's central business district. In the expanded area he designed and constructed a purpose-built yard. There were dockway entrances from each street, with offices in between the two dockways on the lower level, a garage with a lube bay, petrol and diesel pumps, and an open area behind in which he stored bulk raw material. Adjacent was a smoko room where his drivers and yardmen ate tomato and peanut butter sandwiches, mutton pies and slabs of cake, and drank chest-stored tea or chicory in stained cups or mugs that had seen better days.[74]

Harold Thomas was a grim, tough, no-nonsense taskmaster, who expected hard work from his employees. Every morning, with head cocked forwards and hands clasped behind his back, he surveyed his domain from his office window — the master of all he could see. Yet behind the gruff exterior beat a benevolent heart. During the 1940s and early 1950s, hundreds of workers and their families were relocating out of slum-filled inner-city districts such as Aro Valley and Thorndon into state houses in the Hutt Valley and the Porirua basin. Thomas would loan his drivers up to £500 so that they could outfit their new homes with carpets, furnishings, drapes and linoleum, on the basis that they would pay it back, at no interest, at a rate of £1 a week. (The downside to this arrangement, Ken Douglas recalls, was that he found it very difficult to sack ineffectual workers if they still owed him money.) His paternalistic attitude took other forms too, chief among them bestowing extra cash on his workers if their children were sick and needed medical attention, or for any other family crisis. This practice was carried on by his son Ken when he took over the firm in 1957, and by his grandson Alan who succeeded Ken in 1975.

Although in business as a general carrier, HW Thomas specialised in carting builders' products — sand, gravel, cement, lime, stone, iron, chip, steel, timber, plaster additives, mesh and builders' mix. Home-handymen building driveways, paths or patios comprised up to one third of the firm's business. Builders' mix was made up according to the customers' instructions. On the way home from building sites in the suburbs, the trucks would be back-filled with sand from Lyall Bay beach, or gravel and chip from quarries in Owhiro Bay, Horokiwi or Mabey Road in Upper Hutt.

The work was hard. The sand at Lyall Bay was shovelled by hand onto the truck, and Harold and later Ken Thomas paid the men an extra halfpenny for every yard shovelled. If a strong southerly sprang up, the truck had to dump some of its load so that it was light enough to be driven off the beach. The shovelling began again once the wind had died down. During the building booms of the 1950s and 1960s, one Thomas truck followed another to Lyall Bay. A second driver, waiting at the bay in a custodian's shed, would work as a labourer, helping to load the truck.[75]

The Lyall Bay sand was soft and ideal for builders' mix. Sometimes it was taken straight to a building site, at other times to the Haining Street yard where it was stored. In these days of strict regulation, every trucking firm was required to charge the same price for an equivalent amount of raw material. Thomas's managed to maintain a competitive edge through efficient, quick service and by providing a good product. When Ken Douglas joined the firm in 1955, it had 14 Ford, Bedford and International flat-top and tip trucks, and one articulated truck. Smaller trucks were 'three-yarders' — designed to carry three yards of sand or other bulk material; bigger, 14-tonne, six-tyre trucks carried six yards. The tip trucks carried 14 yards, while the 10-tyred articulated truck carried more again. If the sand or gravel was wet the trucks carried more, irrespective of the regulations. The articulated truck driver was Doug Scotson, a former serviceman and the Wellington Drivers' Union site delegate, and also, as we shall see, the leader of a campaign in the early 1960s to rid the union of its communist secretary, Chip Bailey.

Wellington transport firms were only allowed to work within a 20-mile radius of the central Post Office — a hangover from the days of horses and carts, when working within such distances was the usual practice. The bureaucracy had not kept pace with the rate of change in the trucking industry, and by the time Douglas joined Thomas's the firm needed a special licence from the Ministry of Transport to cart material to and from the Dunlop tyre factory in Upper Hutt, one of its customers. The Ministry did issue 'blanket' licences to cover this regulation, but it would be years before this nonsensical rule was liberalised.

Thomas's had other specific long-term contracts which were not only lucrative but also allowed for significant social activities. From the late 1930s through to the 1970s, for example, they transported all of the wool from Terawhiti and Te Mamara sheep stations at South Makara to the railhead or cargo vessels at Wellington Wharf, and back-loaded household and farm supplies, hay, building materials for the farm, and fertiliser for the topdressing planes at Te Mamara airstrip. Thomas employees often played rugby and cricket against farmhands and shearers from the stations in friendly matches characterised by dubious decision-making and rule-breaking, the participants sustained by never-ending supplies of Pat Smith's rugged home-brew. Smith, the larger-than-life farm manager at Terawhiti, became a personal friend of both Harold and Ken Thomas, often participating in drinking sessions with them, and sometimes staying overnight in the Thomas home in Karori.

Ken Douglas's first job with the firm was shovelling sand at Lyall Bay beach. Harold Thomas instructed his new employee to go upstairs into the storeroom and choose a shovel. Douglas was immediately on edge, perceiving that this was some kind of test. He knew little about shovel sizes and before him was a whole range, varying in size from a No. 9 'square-mouth', a huge implement used for moving large quantities of light material such as coke at one time, down to a No. 1 'round-mouth', a thin shovel used to dig narrow trenches for wires or small pipes. He tried to remember what his father used. In the end, he picked up a 'middle of the road' No. 3 round-mouth, estimating it was about the size he could handle for shovelling sand at the beach. He tentatively showed it to Harold. It turned out to be a fortuitous choice. 'If you had brought down a bigger one,' Harold informed him, 'you wouldn't have got a start because you would never have mastered it. If you had grabbed a smaller one you wouldn't have got a start because you would not have been producing enough!'[76]

The relieved newcomer revelled in the camaraderie of his new working environment, and Alan Thomas, who was also driving at the time, recalled Doony quickly becoming one of the boys. Douglas spent his first week loading sand onto the succession of Thomas trucks, arriving at the beach first thing in the morning and departing last thing at night. It was hard graft. The driver loaded his side of the truck around to the centre of the tail-gate at the rear. The harder he shovelled, the harder the labourer had to work on the other side to avoid having to fill in the centre by himself. 'The productivity was startling,' Douglas recalls. 'The constant threat of a southerly buster made you work even harder.' He learned how to 'read' the sand so that trucks would not get stuck, realising that they did not travel near the soft, shiny patches — where water was close to the surface — but rather just below the high tide mark as the tide, whether coming in or going out, compacted the sand. He was fit and revelled in the physicality of the work, but it was an exhausting day's labour. Some months after he had started with Thomas's, the firm purchased its first front-end loader specifically to work the Lyall Bay sand. The drivers rejoiced.

Following his stint at Lyall Bay, Douglas drove Thomas's cement truck, hand-loading 112-lb cement bags from the wharf onto his truck to be carted to the Francis Home Store in Taranaki Street, where Wellington builders purchased their cement. The bags were shipped to Wellington from Golden Bay and stowed on trolleys for storage in 16 or 18 Shed on Jervois Quay — or straight to Douglas's truck parked outside the shed's double doors. The watersiders stacked the bags five-high, with a sixth bag on the top for Ken to take, then he would methodically stack them six-high on the tray of his truck. It was his job 'to keep the wharfies moving'. He would complete nine loads in an eight-hour day to and from the shed and the Francis Home Store, which was just eight minutes away. At that end he unloaded the bags, two at a time, onto another trolley, then either he or the warehouse storeman would back-stack them using a graduated staircase to 'make a mountain of cement bags' against a wall. The bags were slippery, and leather or rubber gloves were needed to handle them.[77]

Following Attie, he also worked the Terawhiti Station route, carting hay and farm supplies, and back-loading wool from the station to the wharf. It was a potentially treacherous drive on the station's narrow roads; a minor error of judgement could result in one of the back wheels revolving uselessly over the edge, the valley floor hundreds of metres below. Using a series of techniques involving leverage, balance, weight transference and knowledge of fulcrum and pulley strategies, veteran driver Bill Mallard taught Douglas how to load bales of wool three-high on the tray of his truck, single-handedly, and how to stack haybales correctly, with the 'mountain' moving towards the middle to leave triangular gaps between each bale. Mallard also instructed him on how to load and unload 44-gallon drums of oil. Douglas's first instinct was to lean over and try to pull the drum towards him on its rim. His mentor showed him how to put his toe against the bottom edge of the drum, push it hard so that the liquid slopped to the other side, and when it returned pull the drum quickly to get it up on its rim on a point of balance, after which it could be safely and effortlessly wheeled.

Tapping into the huge amount of knowledge possessed by experienced drivers such as Thomas, Mallard, and his father, Douglas absorbed other tricks of the trade. For longer trips he learned that the first 'extra' he carried was a silk stocking in case the fan belt snapped. A knotted stocking running around the pulley sufficed until the truck returned to base. He learned how to make a noose-hook and to splice a rope, and to tie down a load safely with these ropes. Drivers were vigilant about looking after their gear. Public safety as well as their own pride and job satisfaction were inextricably tied up with safely stowed loads. Good drivers insisted on using their own ropes if they were on another truck, fearing that others would not look after them properly. If they had to change a tyre, three-tonne jacks could not lift heavy, fully loaded rigs, so drivers learned to shift the load away from the offending tyre so that the jack could take the weight. If this was impossible, they would stuff punctured tyres with grass so they could crawl back to the depot.

One of the great attractions of truck driving, Douglas recalls, was that after leaving the depot you were required to make '110 decisions every day'— decisions which, in other circumstances, managers on three times the pay or more would be expected to make. 'You were the captain of the ship. Driving gave you a marvellous sense of freedom and pride in a job well done.' There was also an element of 'showing off' in the way drivers demonstrated their expertise. Doug Scotson, according to Douglas, was 'the typical embodiment of a dexterous truck driver'. Having learned his skill in the army, Scotson took pride in backing his articulated rig into narrow streets and driveways to load or discharge cargo, and, later in the day, demonstrating to 'going-home' audiences how he could safely negotiate his big rig to within inches of a footpath or the side of a building. Other drivers did the same. Their skilfulness was an indelible component of their work practice. Moreover, the more adept they were, the easier the job was. For many years, drivers demonstrated their skills in inter-district driving competitions organised by the unions, and later continued by the New Zealand Carriers' Association. For a time Douglas helped to organise these competitions.

WH Thomas held a lucrative contract with Winstone Building Supplies, carting building material from their supply depot in Ghuznee Street to building sites, or to home handymen in Wellington, the Hutt Valley and the Porirua basin. Initially, Alan Thomas worked the Winstone contract in a smaller, two-tonne truck, but as business increased Douglas became Winstone's second driver, operating a three-tonne Bedford. This was his first experience of working with the building industry, and he loaded, carted and unloaded a wide range of material — timber, corrugated iron, gib-board, bags of cement and builders' mix, and bulk bags of nails, screws and other items. Strictly speaking, a driver's responsibility for the product ended when he arrived at his destination. More often than not, drivers helped the men at the building site to unload the material. Just as often, there would be nobody there and drivers would unload on their own — sometimes uphill — because 'it was part of the customer service'. Some drivers grizzled at this extra work but Douglas never had a problem with it.

Over time, technology has made the lives of truck drivers less strenuous. When Douglas became a driver, those around him were well-muscled to cope with the physical demands of the job. Off-road, the great bulk of the drivers' work was loading and unloading by shovel, trolley or hand. In more recent years the use of front-end loaders, forklifts, containerisation and bulk transportation has meant that drivers have not needed the same physical attributes. Today such labour comprises less than 10 per cent of the workload, physical work being restricted to hooking up pipes and brake-lines, and securing ready-made straps to protect the load. On the other hand, the biggest truck on the road in the 1950s and early 1960s weighed 18 gross tonnes. Today combination rigs weigh 60 tonnes or more.

Douglas only had one significant accident, and its status has become elevated over time. Morrie Deterte and Bruce Oliver, rugby-playing mates with Wellington College Old Boys, had purchased a property on the corner of Haining and Frederick Streets to develop commercially. They rented the next-door section, on which 'most' of a house still stood, and where they stored bags of cement. In the back of this house lived an elderly Chinese gentleman, one of the last survivors of Wellington's historic 'Chinatown'. Douglas was backing into the property delivering a load of cement when a front wheel struck the gutter. Surging the accelerator to get over the gutter he momentarily lost control, and with cement dust clouding the back window and sun glaring in his eyes he sped towards the building, which had no front, and demolished it. The house, or what remained of it, was condemned and the Chinaman was evicted. Six of Thomas's trucks carted away the rubble. Douglas was later accused of damaging the house for his mates to get the old man evicted, but that was a fabrication. A momentary lapse in concentration caused the accident but for months afterwards he suffered ribbing from both his rugby mates and fellow drivers, acquiring the nickname 'Crash'.[78]

In the mid- to late 1950s, the regular consumption of alcohol was a 'normal' concomitant to the working lives of truck drivers. In between loads, drivers often stopped for a jug of beer or two. Trucks were parked

ABOVE LEFT Ken Douglas's great grandparents Henry and Emma Jane Dowthwaite with their family, c. 1894. *From left*: Henry (known as George), Annie, Carolyn (in front), Hilda and Robert. Lillian, Ivy and Albert were yet to be born. (*Kathleen Angel*)

ABOVE RIGHT Henry Dowthwaite with his grandson Lyndsay Douglas at 111 Northland Rd, Wellington, c. 1938. Lyndsay had his leg amputated after a childhood accident. (*Brian Fitzwater*)

BELOW Ken Douglas's grandparents George and Carrie Douglas with three of their five children, *from left*: Minnie, Laurie and Attie (Ken's father), c. 1924. (*Kathleen Angel*)

ABOVE LEFT Ken Douglas's grandfather George Douglas (right) in Wellington with his cousin Charlie Carey from Wanganui, c. 1937. (*Douglas family*)
ABOVE RIGHT Ken Douglas's great-grandfather Henry Dowthwaite on Lambton Quay, Wellington, later in life. (*Douglas family*)
BELOW Ken Douglas's maternal grandfather George Farrow (holding phone) with Prime Minister Peter Fraser and George Matthews (far right) in Fraser's Wellington Central committee rooms on election night 27 November 1946. The other people in the photograph are not identified. Farrow had been a member of Fraser's electorate committee since 1919 and was his campaign manager for five general elections. (*Douglas family*)

LEFT Ken Douglas's maternal grandparents George and Eleanor Farrow, May 1949. (*Douglas family*)

CENTRE Ken Douglas's parents, Madge Farrow and Attie Douglas, on their wedding day at St Joseph's Church, Buckle Street, Wellington, December 1934. *From left at back:* Lillian Southee, George Farrow (junior), Attie and Madge, George Farrow (senior), Laurie Douglas, Doreen Reynolds. John Fage is the page boy. The flower girl is not identified. (*Douglas family*)

LEFT Carolyn (Carrie) Douglas with her son Lyndsay, early 1950s. Carrie was Ken's principal caregiver as a child and adolescent. (*Douglas family*)

RIGHT Ken Douglas's father, Private John Atholwood Douglas (right) J-Force, Japan, July 1946. (*Douglas family*)

CENTRE Ken Douglas's mother Madge, later in life when she worked as a postie. With her is fellow postie and good friend Gwen Winter, the mother of Ken Douglas's first wife, Lesley. (*Douglas family*)

RIGHT Madge Douglas enjoying Mayday celebrations with Ken's uncle Terry Farrow, 1 May 1965. (*Douglas family*)

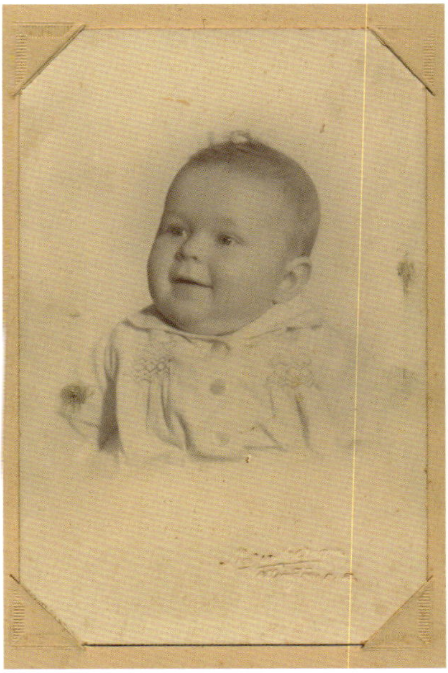

ABOVE LEFT Kenneth George Douglas, aged eight months, 1936. (*Douglas family*)

ABOVE RIGHT Ken aged eight with his sister Terree (right) holding the hand of their cousin Raymond Douglas, who lived with them at 111 Northland Road. (*Douglas family*)

LEFT Madge with Ken and Terree outside 278A Cuba Street, Wellington, September 1946. (*Douglas family*)

RIGHT A rare formal photograph of Ken and Terree, aged nine and five respectively. (*Douglas family*)

CENTRE Standards One and Two, Northland School, 1942. The 'perpetually grubby' Ken Douglas faces the photographer on the far right in the second row. (*Douglas family*)

RIGHT Ken, aged 11, at a Wellington Drivers' Union picnic at Maidstone Park, Upper Hutt, in 1946. He is leaning against his uncle Terry Farrow, not long returned from the war. His grandfather George Farrow is on his right. (*Douglas family*)

LEFT 'Four Special', Wellington College, 1950. Ken Douglas is third from the left in the third row from the front. (*Wellington College*)

CENTRE 'Upper Fifth Special', Wellington College, 1952. Ken Douglas is fifth from the left in the back row. Paul Henare is fourth from the left in the second row. John McCormick is fourth from the left in the front row, seated next to form master Sam Meads. (*John McCormick*)

LEFT One of Douglas's few sporting highlights at Wellington College was winning the senior handicap mile during the school's athletic sports in February 1953. Peter Millar, on his left, was second. (*Douglas family*)

ABOVE LEFT A street photographer catches Douglas in Manners Street, Wellington, on the day after his second attempt at School Certificate mathematics in November 1952. He scored four per cent. (*Douglas family*)

ABOVE RIGHT Douglas, standing at right, at a Bible Class dance circa early 1950s. (*Douglas family*)

BELOW Private Ken Douglas (centre) undergoing compulsory military training with the Royal New Zealand Army Corps at Waiouru Camp in October 1954. On his right is Bob Binning, who later became a New Zealand fencing representative, and to his left is Charlie Kennedy, who subsequently joined the merchant marine. Douglas loved school cadets and his time in the army. He had aspirations to attend Duntroon Royal Military College near Canberra to train as an army officer but academic failure at high school stymied that ambition. He stayed in the Territorials until 1965, attaining the rank of regimental Sergeant-Major. (*Douglas family*)

outside Wellington hotels stretching from Newtown to Thorndon, sometimes two and three deep. Alan Thomas recalls up to six Thomas trucks being double-parked outside the Waterloo opposite the Wellington Railway Station during the day, and one well-known City Council traffic officer, Anspatch by name, coming into the bar yelling for the Thomas drivers to 'shift those bloody trucks pronto because they're holding up the traffic!' Truck driving was physical work and drivers needed to replenish their salts as well as satisfy their thirst. Moreover, alongside the beer, public bars also offered cheap counter lunches, charging patrons sixpence for a plate of runny stew with two slices of white bread to wipe up the gravy. At that time no truck travelled faster than 40 miles an hour. There was much less traffic on the roads, and it all moved slowly. This, combined with ignorance about the potential dangers of drinking and driving, meant it was never seen as an issue. And because drivers spent much of the day by themselves, the opportunity to catch up with their mates at lunch times and after work was much treasured.

During the 1950s, Thomas's employees formed three distinct after-work drinking groups. The older drivers, which included Attie Douglas, Bill Mallard, Les Lord and Spud Holes, drank at the Panama; younger drivers including Alan's younger brother Trevor and Chook Fowler, among others, drank at the Royal Tiger. There was a third, smaller group of drivers who had scabbed during the 1951 lockout. Staunch unionists such as Mallard and Attie Douglas remained hostile towards these men, and while they worked together on occasion there remained an underlying tension between them. Wisely, these men, who included long-time employees Ted Alexander and Bluey Bruce, drank at a third pub, the Tramway in Adelaide Road.

When Douglas arrived he joined his father in the Panama set. He was soon holding his own in the drinking and bawdy joke department. All freely participated in the six o'clock swill — sometimes arriving at union meetings in the Trades Hall at the end of their session the worse for wear. At night or on weekends it was common for further gatherings round a keg or two, or a dozen 'Red Band', to take place in one or other's house. Like his father before him, Ken Thomas occasionally joined in these sessions, just as, also like his father before him and his son, Alan, after him, he lent his labour to the physical work when they were short-handed.

While the union was accepted at Thomas's, the management recognising its importance and worth for the drivers, it had a minimal presence because everybody was expected to pull their weight. When Douglas arrived the company did not have a site delegate so he assumed the role by default. Within the firm, which at its peak employed 18 drivers — compared with rival Munt Cottrell, which at its peak employed over 60 — the occasional lazy employee was easily identified and spoken to, and chastised by both management and, if appropriate, the other drivers who had to pick up the slack. Yard-based arguments sporadically resulted in fist fights although these were rarely serious. On the whole, Thomas's was a congenial workplace and conflict between management and worker, and between worker and worker, was rare. It was a 'family firm' in the widest sense of the word.[79]

For many years through the late 1930s, 1940s and early 1950s, Ken Douglas's uncle Bryce had driven for Munt Cottrell, Wellington's biggest transport firm. In 1952, a group of Munt Cottrell drivers, including Bryce Douglas, broke away from the parent organisation and established an owner-driver cooperative called QED.[80] Bryce needed a carrier's licence to operate as an independent, which he purchased from Ted Brooks, a truck driver who lived behind the Douglas's Northland Road home, in Woburn Road, in Wellington's western suburbs.

The licence had a coal permit attached, which was important because QED had just succeeded in a bid to undercut the Munt Cottrell price to transport West Coast coal from the wharf to the gasworks. Bryce did not want the coal business, but agreed to run it for a short time as the income would help him to get on his feet. Moreover, arranging credit through the banks was very difficult within the tight regulatory mechanisms in place at the time.

At this time Ken Douglas was still working as a trainee wool-classer, and Bryce enlisted his help, as well as that of other family members, to make the home deliveries that formed much of the coal business. Most of this work was done at night. As part of his QED contract, and using his Munt Cottrell truck, Bryce carted the coal from Aotea Wharf to the gasworks, but the last 15-tonne load was taken home to 111 Northland Road. Here, Attie, Ken, Bryce and anybody else who was available — including Bryce's wife Betty on occasion — unloaded and bagged the coal, then took it down the road to Catley's Garage in Kaihuia Street, which was rented as storage space. By hand, this took three to four hours. In between the berthing of colliers from the West Coast, Bryce and his family also unloaded open-cast coal that was brought from Taupiri in the Waikato on railway wagons. Most coal companies had mechanical loaders and tip trucks to undertake this process, but the fledgling Douglas operation could not afford such luxuries and the work was laboriously undertaken by shovel, irrespective of the weather. On nights when they were not unloading from ship or train, the bags of coal were home delivered around Wellington's western suburbs.

Slowly, however, Bryce built up other businesses as part of QED. Among others, he secured lucrative contracts with Nestlé, transporting imported raw materials such as cocoa from the wharf to their warehouse in Ghuznee Street, and another similar contract for Woolworths, where his cousin Jim Favell worked as produce manager. Bryce was tall and thin, with a long back, and while he was a hard worker he was not really suited to the physical demands of long-term coal cartage. Indeed, the strenuous labour was a factor in his early death in June 1959 when he suffered a heart attack while hand-loading a stack of wet timber. He finished the task, in pain, drove home and collapsed on the front doorstep. He died in Wellington Hospital later that night, aged just 43.

Not long before his death, Bryce had leased a cheap section in Cheshire Street, Wilton — a boggy waste area in between a new housing development. Attie, Bryce and Ken dug drains and installed pipes to draw off the water; they also bought big slabs of concrete from service stations that were replacing their bulk tanks, levered these into trenches on the section, rammed them down as hard as possible and back-filled the trench to secure them. Eventually the section had a central drive where trucks could back in between two tray-height loading/unloading bays. Here the coal was unloaded, bagged and stored for home delivery. Today, every time he passes the former coal-yard — now a residential home — Douglas winces at the memory of standing in the pouring rain, 'crying with rage', trying his damnedest to level the heavy concrete slabs. It was 'tough yakka', but he was fit, and the achievement of completing the task was immensely satisfying, as was the close family interaction during the process.

Ken took over responsibility for the coal in 1957, while he was working at Thomas's. He continued to work at night, and during the day in winter, when the bulk of the coal was purchased and delivered — taking time out from his driving duties at Thomas's. Long past its use-by date, he sold the 1937 Bedford truck he inherited from Bryce and bought a newer 3-tonne Bedford from the prison service. Only after the purchase had been completed did he discover that prisoners had dealt to it by putting shingle in the petrol tank. The truck ground to a halt after a few hours and cost a fortune to repair.

The home deliveries involved 112-lb bags of coal and 85-lb bags of coke; Douglas would throw the coal over his right shoulder and the coke over his left. He traipsed up and down paths to the coal-box, usually near the back door and often a long way from the front gate. After emptying each sack he would leave it folded by the customer's back door so that when the task was complete, and payment due, there could be no debate as to what quantity had been delivered. Trading as 'Douglas Coal', he could not afford to advertise on his truck although, as required by law, he had the title stamped on his petrol tank along with the tonne weight, registration and licence numbers. In the evenings and at weekends Lesley would accompany him, going to the front door with the invoice while he carried the coal around the back. Others would help as well, if and when they could. He did a deal with his chums from the Wellington College Old Boys Rugby Club, most of whom did not own cars: he would transport them on the back of his truck to the games in the afternoon provided they helped him with his Saturday morning deliveries. These helpful lads were easily identifiable in the shower after the game, when rings of black coal dust became visible.

But home delivery of coal was a struggling industry. The small capacity of Douglas's truck was a barrier to expansion and the work was seasonal. By 1958, when he was no longer working at Thomas's, he needed full-time work to free his debt and improve his cashflow. The prison truck was having mechanical problems and he went to Wright Stephensons to arrange to buy a new vehicle. The manager took one look at his financial statements and refused him a loan. It was not until the following year that the Labour government introduced legislation which allowed business people and farmers to secure loans irrespective of seasonal debt as long as processes were in place to pay off the debt during the good times.

State Coal, the biggest merchant of them all, then restricted its deliveries to a roadside end-point. This annoyed Douglas because it meant people had to move piles of coal dropped in their driveways or outside their front gates to the coal-boxes or stacks around the back of their homes themselves — or in the case of older or less fit people, pay for others to do it for them. For the first and only time in his life Douglas advertised, promising in a large flyer posted up in the window of the Woods for Goods store in Northland that he would continue personal coal-box deliveries. As one of the very few to make this promise, he was inundated with business and for some weeks was rushed off his feet. But it could not last. Smaller, part-time coal-delivery firms were falling by the wayside, and bigger merchants were taking bigger slices of a diminishing market as electricity and gas increasingly replaced coal for domestic heating and cooking. The transformation was dramatic. There had been 38 mostly family-run coal businesses covering the greater Wellington-Hutt Valley-Porirua basin when Douglas took over responsibility for the family coal business early in 1957. Some 18 months later, in November 1958, just nine remained.

With the savage reduction in work, and the approach of summer, Ken and Lesley decided to shut down the business. The situation was not helped by the reluctance of some of his bigger customers to pay their bills. Douglas recalls that workers and elderly people always paid — even if it was their last penny for the week. He explained it as class loyalty and community understanding. 'They understood it was tough for me. I knew they sometimes found squaring their account was equally tough,' he recalled. The goodwill was huge and implicit on both sides. Towards the end, these customers were particularly appreciative that he had continued his coal-box deliveries, greeting him with smiles, cups of tea and home-made date scones with lashings of butter and jam.

In contrast, Douglas remembers a particular bank manager in Northland who always refused to pay. He was an important customer — purchasing a tonne of coal every month — but was full of excuses when it came to settle the account (and Douglas was generous with his credit), persistently complaining about cashflow problems and 'other expenses'. Yet he had sufficient money to buy huge amounts of food in bulk which he kept in a shed and a freezer close to the coal-box.

After months of frustration and anger, Douglas began helping himself to some of these 'sponsors' products', such as tins of salmon — very expensive at the time — and cuts of meat from the freezer. When reimbursement was still not forthcoming, he began delivering 18 sacks instead of the 20 that made up the tonne, taking two empty sacks with him to leave with the others at the back door. Not long before Douglas gave up the business, the banker ordered two tonnes of coal; when after three months he had not squared his account Douglas went to see him, to be met with the response that 'it is not a priority for you or me, Mr Douglas, now that you're out of business'. In angry response Ken heaved two of his coal-weights through one of his windows. When the upset bank manager threatened to call the police, Douglas encouraged him to do so. The banker changed his mind. The police were not called; Douglas was never paid. It was of little financial consequence. By this time, he was working full-time for the Wellington Drivers' Union.

CHAPTER 4

Union man

The forerunner of the Wellington Drivers' Union, the Wellington Road Transport and Motor and Horse Drivers' and their Assistants' Industrial Union of Workers, was founded among 40 'drivers of drays' in the Trocadero Restaurant and Hotel in Willis Street, on 20 July 1899. In 1904, Andrew Parlane became president of the union, and in 1911 he began his 29-year tenure as the union's secretary.[81]

It was essentially a conservative body, remaining affiliated to the Trades and Labour Council in the period up to the 1913 general strike, as well as the Liberal-Labour Federation, and supporting compulsory arbitration. The union did not affiliate to the original Federation of Labour in 1908, and would not do so until 1917. It was not until late in the strike, on 14 November 1913, that the union officially sanctioned its support. Some striking drivers participated in the street skirmishes, which led to a handful being batoned by Massey's Cossacks. Others set up levies to raise funds for the strikers and their dependants. Still more, at their own cost, transported food and other essentials for the strikers and their families. A hard core of activists kept the union going through the First World War, with many drivers either volunteering or being conscripted into the armed forces. In 1917 the union joined a new Transport Advisory Board, which gave it closer contact with employers' groups and other transport unions such as Tramway Drivers and Seamen. It was also affiliated to the Drivers' Federation, which had been established in 1910 as an umbrella body — a collective and conduit to carry out the wishes of its constituent unions and their members to formulate and coordinate policy and represent them in outside bodies such as the Employers' Association and the government.

Through the 1920s, under Parlane's leadership, the union remained moderate, explicitly maintaining its trust in the arbitration system despite its parsimony towards drivers' claims. As drivers began to lose their jobs from 1928 onwards as the country went into recession, the union became more closely aligned with the Labour Party. The 1930s Depression took its toll, with many drivers being sacked. In some industries they were among the first to go. Those who remained were powerless to stop a 10 per cent decrease in wage rates from April 1932.

In the later 1930s there was a resurgence of drivers' union activity and a growth in membership as work opportunities grew along with the economy. Compulsory unionism, introduced by the new Labour government in 1936, boosted membership still further. The union was in on the ground floor at the establishment of the new Federation of Labour the following year, and by the outbreak of war in September 1939 it had a membership of over 1400 drivers and associated workers. In 1940 the union, by now commonly referred to as the Wellington Drivers' Union, purchased its first car, a Ford 10, and employed its first travelling organiser, Tom Magee.

In the late 1940s, Attie, Bryce and Laurie Douglas became Wellington Drivers' Union activists. On 23 September 1947, Bryce, then driving for

Munt Cottrell, was elected to the union executive. In February 1948 he topped the poll for reselection to the executive, and in December that year he was elected unopposed as vice-president. He resigned from this position before the 1951 watersiders' lockout, but would be re-elected to the vice-presidency in September 1951 for a two-year stint, standing down in December 1953 in favour of Chip Bailey. On 28 September 1948, his older brother Attie had been elected onto the same body although he lost his place, briefly, in a vote at the annual general meeting on 22 March 1949. When Clarence Reid resigned from the executive on 28 June, Attie was reselected in his place. In March 1951, Bryce stood for the union's presidency but was ruled ineligible because of 'insufficient time' spent on the executive. At this time also, the oldest of the Douglas brothers, Laurie, replaced Attie on the executive, and in April he became the union's treasurer. In November 1952 he would become its organiser — and, as such, chiefly responsible for elucidating union policy and enrolling new members throughout the district. The union's main man now was Tom Magee. He had become secretary in October 1945 and would lead the union through the turbulent events to come.[82]

In the days immediately prior to the lockout the union pursued a wary path. In February 1950 it opposed the expulsion of the Watersiders' Union from the Federation of Labour, but voted in favour of the watersiders' suspension. However, in July, following the walkout of several unions from the 1950 FOL conference, the membership resolved by secret ballot to disaffiliate from the FOL and join the newly formed Trade Union Congress along with the watersiders, carpenters and joiners, freezing workers, painters, biscuit workers and a raft of labourers, miners and other drivers' unions.[83]

This straightaway signalled a militant change in direction for the Wellington union. Immediately the emergency broke out, on 6 February, its executive issued a directive to members not to do any work normally carried out by watersiders. The bulk of the nation's exports and imports were transported by road from the wharf and drivers had the power on their own to paralyse this trade. At a meeting on 5 March a majority of members promised not to touch any goods on the wharf handled by 'free' (scab) labour or the armed services. The Douglas brothers had no doubts as to where their politics lay. They operated a Gestetner duplicator in a room under the family home in Northland, composing and printing drivers' union pamphlets highlighting the watersiders' cause. Under the Emergency Regulations this was highly illegal — the literature was 'seditious' — but they were never caught.

But not all drivers were in favour of tying themselves too closely to the watersiders, and in particular Jock Barnes, whom a minority considered a demagogue and rabble-rouser. At the meeting on 5 March, 183 members had opposed supporting the watersiders. The union's leaders realised that its members' conflicting attitudes towards the lockout could be used by the government and the FOL as an effective lever to split the union apart. As a precaution against the possibility of deregistration the union appointed Laurie Douglas, now on the executive, one of three trustees to take control of the union's assets and property.

At a subsequent meeting, members voted narrowly, 273 to 257, not to rescind the original motion banning drivers from working with scab labour on the wharves. This vote, close as it was, was the straw that broke the camel's back for the government; within 48 hours the Wellington Drivers' Union had been deregistered. In the vacuum, a group of disaffected Wellington drivers met to form a 'scab' union, the Wellington Motor-Truck and Horse Drivers' Society. Employers feeling the economic pinch as a result of their inability to transport goods to and from the wharf — for many, a crucial source of income — bent over backwards to welcome them, offering their yards as meeting places. But they were a motley lot. The scab union's initial executive included a driver employed by his father-in-law, a company shareholder and part-time driver, a bankrupt, and a renegade anti-union driver. The Drivers' Union, which had 'loaned' most of its funds out to prevent the state confiscating them, faced action from the Public Trustee who now attempted to remove what was left. But when his men descended on the union's office, Magee refused to allow them access to the records and the petty cash that remained. These visits became rituals, continuing for days on end until finally, on 2 May, Magee was arrested under new emergency regulations and fined £50.

Magee's arrest swung driver sentiment back towards militancy. A meeting of 300 resolved to down tools altogether if Magee was sent to prison, a stance that may have helped persuade the magistrate against taking such a course. Then Minister of Labour 'Big' Bill Sullivan stamped his foot, recancelled the registration of the old union, this time under the Trade Union Act, and threatened drivers that they would be forced to join the scab union as soon as it obtained an award from the Arbitration Court.

Magee and his executive continued to operate, clandestinely, while the scab union struggled to attract members. The Drivers' Federation refused to affiliate the new organisation. However, after a series of sometimes unruly meetings it became clear that to regain strength the majority of drivers wanted the two unions to amalgamate. By this time, July 1951, the waterfront lockout was over. The old union's executive, with help from the Leader of the Opposition, Walter Nash, was looking to regain registration, making a plea for scab members to come along with them. The writing was on the wall for the interlopers when, after a 'consensus' meeting between the leaders of both unions, Bryce Douglas was elected vice-president for a second term, defeating N Cottingham, a member of the scab union, by 36 votes to 10. Tom Magee was elected secretary by a similar margin. The new executive comprised men who had, without exception, remained loyal to the old union. This included Bryce and his brother Laurie, who became treasurer. In similar fashion, loyalist Charlie Jane was elected unopposed as the new president.[84]

It was a weakened organisation, however. Much energy post-lockout was expended trying to bring non-union or 'scab' drivers back into the fold, enforcing membership where it had lapsed and improving the dire financial state of the union which had been exacerbated by the state seizure of its 'non-hidden' funds after deregistration. It was not until March 1954 that the union was able to extract the £880 owed to it by the Public Trustee, who had seized it in 1951.[85]

In 1955, the union faced a major crisis. While Magee was representing the Drivers' Federation — of which he was national president — on a tour to celebrate May Day in China as a guest of the Chinese Trade Union Federation, Reginald 'Chip' Bailey, the union's city organiser and now acting secretary, discovered Magee had been filching union funds. The executive suspended Magee on his return from China. Rather than create a fuss, and in implicit recognition of his guilt, Magee resigned on 16 June. The wider membership was shocked; there was anger that Magee had betrayed their trust but there was also a strong feeling that he had been a capable secretary who had served the union well during a very difficult period in its history. Some members felt he had been victimised, while others pressed the executive to have him arrested and put on trial.[86]

The executive pursued a middle ground, ordering that Magee make restitution for the stolen money. He refused, as he did again later when Bailey called at his house. Following a threat to bring in lawyers, Magee began repayments. It was later ascertained that over £1000 was missing, the defalcations having begun in 1946. Included in this was some 'Loyalty Badge' money, funds put aside to pay for the manufacture of badges to be handed out to those drivers who had remained steadfast in support of watersiders throughout the 1951 lockout. This was a nasty kick in the guts for the union, and particularly for the men involved.[87]

On 3 August, Chip Bailey defeated Charlie Jane and Albert Small in the race to become the new secretary. Bailey and Jane, the new organiser, established a new job-delegate system of representation for members at work sites which until then had been operating haphazardly at best. Many employers treated job delegates with disdain, ensuring that they were, in Ken Douglas's words, the boss's son or the 'idiot employee'.[88]

Bailey and Jane also set about democratising union processes, re-establishing regular meetings at which the rank and file could be heard; this was particularly important in the country districts, within many of which the union had had minimal presence since 1951. Job and area meetings now became the focus of organisation. From here, the election of job delegates followed with more regularity. As a result of these changes the union enrolled close to 600 new members before the end of the year, the most ever in its history. The new cohort of delegates set about trying to enforce, at the very least, minimum award conditions, hitherto ignored by mostly small firms, particularly in country areas. On 28 April 1956 the union appointed its first country organiser, Felix Harvey, a dour, fastidious, well-organised Scotsman. He had held a similar position with the New Zealand Workers' Union, from which he had already gained experience in organising workers in rural areas. However, he faced a tough job, with, in his words, 'abusive language and threats from employers' being part of his everyday work. He faced extra flak in that he was a card-carrying member of the New Zealand Communist Party, a fact he never hid from employer or driver alike.[89]

Six months earlier, on 26 October 1955, Ken Douglas had joined the Wellington Drivers' Union — the same day that he had joined his father as a truck driver working for HW Thomas. Within days, the union had its annual general meeting. Ken had planned to attend a cricket practice to try out for the Wellington College Old Boys senior division team, but Attie told him in no uncertain terms that he was a unionist truck driver now and would be attending the meeting.

Some 140 Wellington truck drivers gathered that evening in the Wellington Trades Hall just after 6pm. Many were drunk — or nearly so — and animated, having lurched out of neighbouring hotels — the Panama, Royal Tiger and Foresters' Arms — at six o'clock. Douglas was grumpy about having to be there, unwillingly inhaling the thick cigarette smoke and alcohol fumes that permeated the air. President Reg Parkin noticed his scowl. 'I see we have the next generation of Douglases here. Anything you want to say, young man? We don't often get young fellas coming to our meetings . . .'

'Well I'm not that impressed actually,' replied Douglas. 'I'm used to a real union like the wharfies' union.' To a man, the attention of those in the room was quickly focused on the upstart. 'Instead of bragging about who drives the biggest truck or who carries the most valuable cargo,' Douglas continued, 'what about doing something for the pay and conditions of work for the drivers?'

Attie was furious, threatening to give him his comeuppance once they got out of there. More thoughtful heads, however, were interested in what the young man had to say, and when the election of officers came up later in the evening, Ken was asked whether he would stand for the executive. He was aware he was ineligible as he had not been a member for the previous 12 months, as required under the constitution. That he had scanned this document won him further kudos among the attendees and a debate ensued as to whether that requirement could be waived in this case.

Bailey suggested a compromise whereby Douglas would become the union delegate at his workplace. This won unanimous support. Until that time HW Thomas had not had an official delegate attached to it, although Attie had acted de facto in this capacity at times. At some trucking companies, union delegation was not taken seriously by the owners. In smaller firms, in particular, drivers had a close relationship with their employers, who considered the union and union matters either a nuisance or a waste of time. Moreover, the trucking industry was highly regulated and union's influence on improving wages and conditions was restricted as a result. Douglas saw union weakness in such places very quickly. He wanted to increase the standing of union delegates, not only at Thomas's but also among all of Wellington's transport companies.

By this time Ken's father and uncles no longer held leadership roles — Laurie being the last to do so, working as the union's city organiser until 1954. All three brothers, however, continued to be regular attenders and sometimes outspoken speakers at union meetings. This heritage gave young Ken a huge advantage over other potential office-holders. For one so young he demonstrated a confidence that surprised many drivers. His outspokenness made him even more attractive to the rank and file. The union needed new, younger drivers to enter the ageing ranks of its leadership, and Douglas came across as a keen, sharp and energetic young man who possessed a faultless pedigree — he fitted the bill ideally for who did not feel threatened by his assertive presence. But others were less sure. They felt he needed to 'do his time' in the union before being considered for higher office. His candour annoyed some of the older men, who were used to things as they were, and uncomfortable with the thought of radical change. Union organisations were inherently conservative. These drivers believed there was a hierarchy to climb, and Douglas needed to find his rightful place within that hierarchy, where seniority was more important than ability.

But these members were in a minority, and promotion was not long in coming. On 21 November 1956, having completed his compulsory year's membership, Ken Douglas was nominated both for the executive of the Wellington Drivers' Union, which had four vacancies, and for its presidency. By 210 votes to 146 he missed out in the presidential race to the incumbent Reg Parkin, but he was the second highest polling candidate, behind Charlie Jane, in a field of 11 for the executive. This was a remarkable result considering his youth and inexperience. Ken Douglas's trade union career had begun in earnest. He had just turned 21.[90]

Following the end of the 1951 lockout the Federation of Labour was bent not on revenge but on reconciliation. At the same time, it wanted to fashion a 'new-look' drivers' union after its own image. The FOL's plan was clear, not only for the Wellington Drivers' Union, but for all others of similar size: to persuade them to gather under its wing so that there would be a sole national industrial organisation embracing all blue-collar workers outside of the public service. It was also likely that as economic conditions improved still further through the 1950s, on the back, initially, of the 1951–52 wool boom, these unions, including the Wellington Drivers' Union, would grow stronger and more influential.

But the drivers themselves were in no rush to regather under the FOL umbrella. Many, including a majority on the executive, were scathing about what they believed to be the undemocratic nature of the FOL, and the seeming impossibility of reforming it into a progressive movement capable of fighting for improvements for the trade union movement as a whole. This was the essence of a remit passed at the union's 1955 annual general meeting. Implicit in this criticism was extreme wariness of the perceived, and later proven, demagoguery of Fintan Patrick

Walsh, the FOL's powerful, hard-nosed president. Moreover, Walsh's bitter antagonism toward, and opposition to, the leaders of the old watersiders' union, Jock Barnes in particular, and their allies was still fresh in the minds of Drivers' Union leaders like Tom Magee, Charlie Jane and the Douglas brothers, who had remained staunch through the devastations of 1951. They wanted no bar of Walsh. Like his father and uncles, Ken's antagonism towards Walsh remained intense. As far as he was concerned Walsh was still a scab — a dog — 'and because of the 1951 lockout the drivers believed if you lay down with dogs you get up with fleas'.[91]

Change came slowly. In 1956, union meetings throughout the district overwhelmingly rejected FOL affiliation. At the same time, executive members Chip Bailey (a communist and clandestine underground activist for the 1951 watersiders), Reg Parkin and Felix Harvey spoke firmly in support of affiliation, Harvey explaining to sceptics that the union needed to be part of a wider centralised movement to increase influence and boost membership. On the other hand, the rest of the executive, led by city organiser Charlie Jane, Attie Douglas (now back on the executive) and Ken Douglas (who would be elected onto it the following year), remained opposed, Ken referring to the FOL as nothing but a 'cancerous growth' on the trade union movement. 'We can improve the lot of our members better by remaining outside the FOL,' he told one meeting. 'Gains made through the award did not result in an immediate raising of costs as was the case with general wage orders.'[92]

During award negotiations in 1957, the Wellington union faced a torrid time in the wake of the larger and more outspoken Northern Drivers' Union undertaking more aggressive pay negotiations with its employers. Some local drivers accused their union of being 'gutless' by comparison, and this sentiment intensified pressure to affiliate with the FOL to, as Parkin put it, 'strengthen our bargaining position'.[93] A majority of the executive was now in favour — not because they trusted Walsh or his lackeys but because they felt the union needed wider and more powerful representation than the Drivers' Federation was able to provide, including more clout in arbitration negotiations, which were then stalled. But the wider vote to affiliate was lost, largely in the wake of a raft of negative votes from the Hutt Valley and the Wairarapa.[94]

This was more a reflection of continuing antagonism towards Walsh than a rational assessment of the benefits of broadening the base of the union's strength and solidarity. In the interim, the union had faced another potential crisis as Bill Sullivan, Minister of Labour in the Holland government, threatened to deregister both it and the Northern Drivers' Union after a prolonged stalemate during award talks. Employers were experiencing a profit squeeze as the country went through a minor recession but both unions — with the support of the Drivers' Federation and the Auckland Trades Council — remained firm and won a victory, with Sullivan agreeing eventually to a compulsory resumption of conciliation. As a result, the unions called off their planned stopwork meetings. This predicament was a heady introduction to the national maelstrom of trade union politics for Ken Douglas, just months into his first term on the union executive.[95]

In the meantime, the debate over whether the Wellington union should rejoin the FOL continued unabated. In September 1958, its executive closely analysed the FOL constitution in the presence of FOL secretary Ken Baxter — who addressed the meeting — and council member Fred Fenton. This was a new step, with the union taking a more pragmatic approach. There was a swing towards affiliation, although Ken Douglas held out, believing that such a move was premature. Instead, he considered, the union needed to focus its main effort on strengthening the Drivers' Federation.

Douglas toured the branches advocating non-affiliation but it proved a minority opinion. The executive recommended to the rank and file that the drivers affiliate to the FOL; in a December 1958 plebiscite they voted 454 to 251 in favour. On 17 March 1959, the FOL officially accepted the Wellington Drivers' Union into the fold. While the frosty relationship between the union and Walsh would take longer to thaw, two union delegates, Bailey and Charlie Jane, attended the 1959 FOL conference.[96]

Walsh was having his own troubles. Within the FOL, he was trapped in a bitter power struggle with union leaders Peter Butler and Tony Neary, Roman Catholic anti-communist moderates who were bitterly opposed to him. Walsh desperately needed support and was bending over backwards to seek a rapprochement with those 'militant' unions whom he had earlier castigated and despised — such as the Wellington Drivers' — and others which had joined the breakaway Trade Union Congress, now defunct in all but name. As the power of those more militant unions grew, both within and outside the FOL, their leaders assumed positions of strength. Chip Bailey, for example, was immediately elected onto the committee of the Wellington Trades Council.[97]

Moreover, Labour's election win in 1957 had proved no panacea for trade unionists despite the party's heritage. It did not, as had been urged, repeal the stiff penalty provisions imposed by the National government in a 1954 amendment to the Industrial Conciliation and Arbitration Act, and had continued to follow National's procedure of using the Labour Department to prosecute striking workers individually, making them liable for a substantial fine.

It got worse. In July 1958, in Arnold Nordmeyer's infamous 'Black Budget', the government significantly increased the tax on petrol, boosting costs for carrying firms. A few laid off drivers; many more cut overtime. Moreover, none of the extra tax was tagged for ploughing back into roading expenditure; it was dumped into the consolidated fund. Many roads were in a dire condition. Primary roads were riddled with axle-breaking potholes, and many secondary roads needed strengthening and metalling to cope with trucks that were getting bigger and carrying heavier loads. Protests against the tax from employers, the Drivers' Federation and the unions fell on deaf ears. Employers took their frustrations out on the drivers, their national body arguing that their employees should receive no further wage rises. It was this, and other acts, notably the government's decision to send an all-white All Black rugby team to South Africa in 1960, that later led Douglas to turn his back on Labour and join the Communist Party, as he saw it the only other and more potent 'left' alternative.[98]

In 1958 serious internal dissension within the union developed. The tension began with a letter from Charlie Jane criticising the inability of Chip Bailey and Felix Harvey to enrol taxi drivers in the union. Bailey had been a taxi driver, and this was meant, on the surface, as a personal censure. But the whole thing was a cover. The real reason was the growing disquiet at the increasing communist influence in the union — notably from Bailey and Harvey. The 'other side' was led by Jane, an uncompromising anti-communist, aided by Andy Thomsen, a 'moderate' executive member who was prominent in union politics for many years. In October 1958, Jane and Thomsen introduced a motion of no-confidence in Bailey on the taxi driver issue. The motion failed, but only on the casting vote of president Reg Parkin.[99]

The issue rebounded on Jane, however. Changing tack, the ever-inconsistent Wellington executive then resolved to sack him — voting 10 to 5 — for an 'unfair' and 'ill-conducted' campaign against Bailey. But a majority of the rank and file remained unconvinced. At a January 1959 stopwork meeting the Wellington members voted overwhelmingly against Jane's removal, a pattern repeated at further meetings of Hutt Valley and country members. Jane distributed pamphlets at all of these meetings, and they seemed to have worked. His easy 426- to 300-vote victory over Bailey for the union's secretaryship represented a telling victory for those who believed that Bailey's very visible communism was damaging his union's cause, irrespective of his widely admired organising abilities.

The controversy worked in Ken Douglas's favour. Indeed, 1959 would prove to be a highly significant year for him. In February he unseated the incumbent Parkin for the presidency, 339 votes to 283. Not yet 24, he had become the youngest president of a major trade union in the country's history. The union had earlier appointed him as its city organiser after Jane relinquished this position; Douglas agreed to take it on for a year.[100] He had already had his first taste of industrial negotiation the month before, when he had become involved in a pay dispute between drivers and their employer, the Wellington City Council. The drivers had been unhappy with Jane's representations on their behalf and after three weeks of stalemate Douglas, as city organiser, had stepped into the breach to help negotiate a satisfactory outcome of an extra 3d an hour. Douglas brought a new aggression to the negotiating table, albeit a considered one. One unionist driver later recalled that he was 'bloody glad' that Douglas was on his side. 'It would have been horrific to have to face the "big bastard" if he was against you.'

At this time, Douglas's beloved grandfather, George Farrow, lay dying in Wellington Hospital. Between driving jobs Ken visited him, every day, to engage in rigorous discussion about family, life and politics. He gloated about his success with the city council, but George, who had once been prominent in similar agitation for pay increases for railway workers on the Rimutaka Incline project, was less than impressed. From his bed, he lectured his grandson.

'When you can come and tell me that you've negotiated a change of ownership and in the means of production, distribution and exchange, then I'll tell you that you've been a good advocate. At the moment you're just the mouthpiece. It's the workers and their lives that are important. You're just the custodian of all their previous knowledge and experiences gained on the shop floor. So, stop poncing around, making fine speeches and winning the fights that have already been won!'

It was a good lesson his grandson never forgot. 'He took a chainsaw to my ego,' Douglas recalls. He felt a sense of tragedy, of injustice and frustration. It was characteristic of the way all his political convictions were subsequently forged — out of emotional kicks in the gut rather than out of theoretical treatise and intellectual altruism. It was the 'school of hard knocks, university-of-life stuff' that his lack of formal education allowed him to understand. Meanwhile as he sat, head bowed, on Farrow's hospital bed, the old man, eyes sparkling, reached over, grasped him on the shoulder and shook it. 'I'm still proud of you, son. You've done a damn good job.'[101]

CHAPTER 5

Stamping his mark

The same meeting that saw Ken Douglas become president of the Wellington Drivers' Union also processed the postal ballot that affirmed the executive's recommendation to reaffiliate with the FOL by 454 votes to 251. Two delegates, Douglas and Chip Bailey, attended the 1959 FOL conference on behalf of Wellington's drivers, their first representation for 11 years. While the Wellington Drivers' Union was now back in the fold, it is worth noting that it was one of just five provincial drivers' unions which reaffiliated, the other seven preferring to remain outside. But the Federation did now represent the vast majority of blue-collar unions, with the Carpenters' and Freezing Workers' Unions — the latter one of the largest in the country — having also reaffiliated at this conference.[102] For the Wellington union, reaffiliation to the FOL also meant immediate entitlement to representation on three local trades councils — in Wellington, Wairarapa and the Manawatu. Douglas, Bailey, Charlie Jane and Bill Reardon became the union's delegates on the Wellington Trades Council. Within a year Bailey had been elected onto its committee.[103]

Bailey's troubles did not end with his being dumped as secretary. Rumours floated around that he had been taking money from the union — allegations that he hotly denied. By March 1959 a new 'rank and file' commission, established to investigate these allegations, had also examined an unaccounted £8 allegedly misused by Charlie Jane. On Douglas's casting vote this commission now found against Jane, who proffered no explanation and within a month had resigned as secretary — returning to driving and later becoming a Porirua city councillor representing Titahi Bay. Bailey, his nemesis, was returned to the secretaryship pending elections.

The whole business was messy, with the contentious issue of ideological difference sublimated or side-stepped. To achieve a closer harmony and to try to streamline union processes in the wake of this affair, the union established a 'secretariat' comprising the secretary, president, vice-president and organisers, which met monthly to formulate business for and carry out the instructions of the wider council. But it did not address the wider philosophical divergences which still festered within the union — and had spilled over into personal attacks — and which, as its leaders understood, damaged its reputation in the eyes of its members and the public, as well as weakening its effectiveness in award negotiations. This boil would burst even more messily in 1962.[104]

Encouraged by Chip Bailey, who was both friend and mentor, Douglas showed the kind of leadership for which he would gain the respect of the drivers and later the wider trade union movement. In the early 1960s he initiated a new structure within the union to make organisers more accountable to the rank and file. He did this by beefing up the delegate system and organising the first regional- and national-delegate conferences for all drivers' unions. In February 1962 he expressed concern at the ability of drivers' union assessors to do their jobs properly, and urged that the secretary act as assessor at all future award hearings, with rank and file members as witnesses and observers. While this proposal was not taken up at the time, it was at the next meeting. His chief task as the union's 'temporary' city organiser was to enrol drivers in the union. While unionism was compulsory by law, it was up to each individual union to physically check that all drivers were members of the union. This meant Douglas had to travel to each driver's yard or work site and demand to see each employee's union card — often very early in the morning to avoid the ire of the bosses. It was a time-consuming task and less than pleasant when having to dealing with drivers who were either reluctant unionists — some of whom had scabbed during the 1951 lockout — or dilatory in paying their dues. Douglas recalled cornering one driver by Shed 37 on Pipitea Wharf:

> I jumped on the running board, opened the door and introduced myself. He said: 'I know who you are, you Communist bastard', slammed the door shut and proceeded to drive off in a hurry to the next shed. But I stuck with him. He looked pretty impressed with my athletic ability and after some further sharp words, paid up, most reluctantly. What he did not know was that my coat was caught in his door and I had no choice but to hang in there with him.[105]

Drivers without a union card were required, on the spot, to fill out an application form which was then processed in the union office and sent to the employer. The union then sent an account to the worker. (Periodically the union would have a 'Card Day' during which officials checked lines of drivers at depots to make sure their cards were current. Such days boosted union coffers by hundreds of pounds.) The problem was that the annual union fee, which at the time was £5/12/6d, was half or more than half of a drivers' average weekly wage of around £11 and it was a tough call to have to pay it in one hit. To overcome this barrier, the union introduced a deduction system. Some unions prosecuted non-paying workers in civil court, but Douglas believed this was too harsh. Conversely, some employers charged, or tried to charge, unions commission for enforcing union fees, seeing it as an easy earner, but the Wellington Drivers' Union scorned this tactic.[106]

Generally, there was negotiated agreement between employer and union, not only over facilitating the payment of union fees but also holding stopwork meetings. Douglas helped to negotiate an agreement in which employers paid their drivers for two hours for any stopwork meeting on a Thursday — traditionally the quietest day for road and rail transport — with the drivers themselves paying for any subsequent time, on condition that an employer could hold onto a union-approved driver for urgent work. Effectively, under this agreement the employer was sharing the management of his operation with his workers. There was lots of engagement between owner and driver, which led to better industrial relations and increased productivity. Later this conviviality led to the establishment of a Wellington Ruling Rate which put Wellington truckies on more advantageous rates of pay than those elsewhere.

Douglas had become interested in and influenced by the workings of international labour organisations, being particularly impressed with the work of Teamsters' Union boss Jimmy Hoffa. In 1937, Hoffa negotiated a path-breaking 'over the road' agreement for drivers in midwestern states whereby they were paid according to both how much they carried and the distance they travelled. As rigs became bigger and the technology more sophisticated, guaranteed payments for drivers under this scheme sky-rocketed and many of them became very wealthy. The agreement stayed in place for nearly 60 years. Negotiation of the Wellington rate was militancy at its sharpest but the economy was strong and transport companies were doing well. Douglas and his union wanted drivers to share in the largesse.[107]

Under this agreement the concept was that drivers were rewarded for the skill they possessed rather than the size of the truck they drove. The union negotiated for local drivers to receive an amount 1/9d above the award rate. Some employers objected, and the union lowered the claim (but still kept it higher than the national rate), in Douglas's words, 'to stop us terrorising you' for a higher wage. There was particular antagonism in these negotiations with Jack O'Brien, president of the Wellington Carriers' Association and managing director of O'Brien and

Sons, Carriers — subsequently Freightways Ltd. Like Douglas, the squat, pug-nosed O'Brien was well-known for his 'knuckle-ups'. During one negotiating session O'Brien swore at Douglas, who replied that he (the union) wanted industrial peace but that if O'Brien wanted a fight — both literally and figuratively — he could have it. At this point O'Brien began to clamber over the negotiation table promising to 'punch his lights out'. Sensible voices and quick restraining hands eased the tension although union executive member Richie Gillespie recalled the two antagonists continuing to glare at each other 'like front-row forwards before the scrum went down'.[108]

Douglas did use his fists at times to settle disputes, or scores. In 1968, in one such incident, Wellington's *Dominion* and its sister newspaper *The Sunday Times* were hit by a printers' strike that turned nasty. Other unions provided solidarity and a round-the-clock picket was established outside the *Dominion* building in Mercer Street. Keith Hancox, the solidly built political editor of the *Dominion*, pushed his way through the line and in the process had a confrontation with a unionist whom he knocked to the ground. When Douglas, then secretary of the Wellington Drivers' Union, was told of the incident he saw red because the victim was his friend, the diminutive Pat Kelly, then the union's assistant secretary. Kelly was cut and had his glasses broken in the fracas. Douglas, who knew his way around the *Dominion* building, marched in through a back entrance and took a lift to the editorial offices on the fifth floor, where he bumped into editor Jack Kelleher. When asked where he could find Hancox, Kelleher, who knew Douglas, motioned to an office down the corridor. Douglas strode in and bellowed at the startled Hancox, 'If you want to play that game, how about this,' and whacked him hard in the face.[109]

Late in 1962, a widespread industrial dispute involving both the drivers and a number of other unions exploded. The Cable dispute, as it came to be called, sorely tested the drivers' resolve and nearly brought the union to its knees. It both exposed the government's antagonism to 'militant' unions and sharpened the ideological dissension within the union itself. After the Arbitration Court awarded workers a general wage order of 2.5 per cent in July that year it became apparent that some firms that had been paying above-award margins did not intend to pass on the rise to their employees. The engineering firm William Cable & Co. was one of these, and at the end of August engineers, fitters, electricians, shipwrights, moulders, slip workers and drivers at its Kaiwharawhara plant imposed an overtime ban in support of their claim for the 2.5 per cent.[110]

In response, Cable sacked two of these men and warned that more would follow if the ban was not lifted. Negotiation proved fruitless and the dispute spread. Both the Employers' Association and the government, in the form of its Minister of Labour Tom Shand, threw their weight behind Cable. In response, the unions involved brought in the Federation of Labour. From the FOL's viewpoint it was tactically astute to 'sort out' one firm — even a large one like Cable — and then persuade other recalcitrant employers to fall into line. FOL president Fintan Patrick Walsh quickly identified Cliff Plimmer — Ken Douglas's old employer and a Cable director — as one of the major agents behind the company's refusal to pass on the wage increase. Plimmer was outspoken, calling for 'tough government action, even deregistration' to stop Cable's dispute spreading into an 'industrial conflagration', and drawing attention to the communist influence in the FOL. On Plimmer's coat-tails, Shand followed with an even more devastating punch. 'This is not,' he proclaimed, 'a struggle by workers for justice or fair play but a deliberate attempt, organised and led by the Communist Party, to disrupt and destroy the economy of our country.'[111]

Shand focused specifically on the FOL's communist 'troublemakers' — Chip Bailey, who sat next to Walsh in the negotiations, and his drivers' union deputy Ken Douglas. The right-wing *New Zealand Truth* (of which Cliff Plimmer was a major shareholder) picked up the cudgels when it claimed that the communists had found a suitable pretext for plunging New Zealand into industrial strife. It singled Bailey out for special censure — 'he's off to China next week', it intoned; 'It would be a great thing for this country if he stayed there.'[112]

Bailey's trip gave its antagonists another metaphorical stick to beat the union around the head with, but it was Shand and the *Truth* that were exacerbating the tensions, not the 'communists'. The unions and the FOL were hard at work at the negotiation table — Bailey and Douglas were there as representatives of the Wellington Drivers' Union, which had members tied up in the dispute. The central issue of Cable workers missing out on the general wage order was now in danger of being lost in ideological sideshows.[113]

The dispute continued. Cable laid off more workers. The drivers' union banned the transport of Cable's products. The dispute escalated further when seamen refused to sail with a cargo which included Cable-made materials that watersiders had unwittingly loaded on the coaster *Storm* bound for Bluff. In response, the Employers' Association instructed its members not to employ men laid off from Cable. By 20 September, Cable had sacked 22 men. Five days later it was 47. The Cable plant, previously crippled, was now completely idle.[114]

Pressure was mounting on the drivers' union, and a few drivers under threat of dismissal ignored the ban. Others were sacked for remaining loyal to the union. Meanwhile the FOL was having its own troubles. Early in September Tony Neary led the North Island Electrical Workers out after a series of disagreements with the 'militants', who included not only Bailey and Douglas but also Walsh, who was increasingly looking for their help to combat a growing Catholic-based campaign against his leadership of the FOL. Walsh fought fire with fire. The following day he called on all workers at both of Cable's plants to resign when they reported for work after the weekend. Apart from the electrical workers and engineers, they all did. With other engineering firms coming in behind Cable, finishing projects on their behalf — with strike-breaking drivers transporting materials from one firm to another (and with the government cutting off all unemployment pay to the striking men) the conflict was heading towards the country's most serious industrial dispute since the 1951 waterfront lockout.[115]

The FOL was the first to break. On 25 September, in a surprising move, Walsh asked AJ Neale, the secretary of the New Zealand Engineers'

Union — which had recently withdrawn from the FOL — to act as an intermediary between him and the Cable management. Cable, now operating through the Employers' Association — Plimmer being prominent — agreed to bring in an independent mediator to look for a solution. Adding to the Federation's woes was a no-confidence petition signed by 90 Wellington drivers against its own union, angry at what they called the 'pervasive communist influence' in the union's leadership.[116]

The arbitrator, Wellington solicitor Walter Kemp, was asked to decide whether there had been, as the unions claimed, a tacit agreement dating from 1947 that Cable would pass on general wage order increases to all its members. According to the FOL, if Kemp found there was such an agreement, then Cable would have to agree to reinstate the sacked men with 'no victimisation or discrimination', and pass on the 2.5 per cent. Cable denied that there was any such agreement, and even before Kemp had made a decision, a majority of the sacked men had returned to work. As it was, the gist of Kemp's decision was never made public — nor is it recorded in the Wellington Drivers' Union archives — although it was later determined, importantly, that wage orders would no longer be restricted to the 40-hour-week rate. What is known is that by 4 October, after more than a week's discussion, all the men had returned to work and the dispute was over. For the Wellington Drivers' Union, the FOL and the wider trade union movement, it was an important victory.[117]

In the middle of the Cable dispute the Wellington Drivers' Union faced its biggest internal crisis in years. Many drivers who had long been concerned at the communist influence among the union hierarchy felt that during this dispute the union was being unfairly singled out and punished simply because some of its leading members — notably Bailey, and to a lesser extent Douglas and Felix Harvey — were communists. On 22 September 1962, Wellington's *Sports Post* claimed that a group of Palmerston North dissidents comprising some 40 to 50 drivers planned to 'get rid of the Commo element in the Drivers' Union'.

Chip Bailey was an able, well respected, active, and committed trade unionist. But the driving motivator of his leadership — and Ken Douglas's later on — was his belief in, and the security and purpose he gained from, his communist ideology which, as he interpreted it, was egalitarian, fair and humane. The Communist Party, while agreeing with FOL policy during this dispute, was careful never to publicly identify itself in union matters. It did not want, as Bailey expressed it, 'to contaminate the importance of the struggle'. Douglas was similarly careful not to let publicity about his political beliefs intrude into the way in which he operated in his union life.

In 1962 Bailey was the key paid official of the Wellington Drivers' Union — widely respected for his efficiency, clear-headedness and pragmatism. Yet for a minority of disaffected 'moderate' unionists, targetting him as a scapegoat was easy. The Palmerston North drivers, alongside some others who were mostly from rural areas and a few from Wellington, organised two petitions late in September. The first called for a vote of no-confidence in the executive and the second was formulated to try to oust all Communist Party members from the union itself.

But the whole business was a damp squib. Out of a membership of more than 500, just 63 drivers signed the 'anti-communism' petition and 26 the 'no-confidence' petition. Furthermore, of these 89 signatories, only 49 were financial members of the union, six had paid some part of their current subscription, 19 owed dues and 11 others never paid. In Palmerston North, 86 drivers signed the anti-communist petition. That, too, was a farce as less than half, 37, were financial members of the union. Of the rest, 39 were unfinancial and 10 had never been members. The problem for the union, however, was that antagonism from an unsympathetic press, exacerbated by goading from the Employers' Association and the government, could set public opinion against it.[118]

The executive agreed to consider these petitions after consulting the wider membership, and after Chip Bailey had returned from China. In the meantime, messages of support for the union — and for its actions throughout the Cable dispute — rolled in from drivers who believed in the executive and who were annoyed that a 'rump of renegades' was trying to remove it for no reason other than their own selfish ends and a philosophy which had nothing to do with the practice of sound trade unionism. 'United We Stand — Divided We Fall' was the signature at the foot of a letter from 14 drivers employed by Certified Concrete in support of the executive. None of them was communist.

As they were entitled to do under the union rules, the dissenters requested a special union meeting. Held on 28 October, a Sunday morning, it attracted 149 members. Ken Douglas was calm, explaining that the key point was that employers were skilled at taking advantage of internal differences within the union, and such differences were damaging. The attack on Bailey, he said, was in reality a challenge to the policy of the union, which was one of activity and struggle. FOL secretary Ken Baxter told the men that the Cable dispute, negotiated by the union's 'communist' leadership, had been conducted in accordance with the wishes of the men on the job, including the drivers — as well as the unions involved and the FOL's national executive. 'The issue of the two and a half per cent wage order, involved more than just the men at Cables.'[119]

Unmoved by the explanations offered by Douglas and Baxter, the dissidents proceeded with their resolutions: that the secretary (Bailey) and the two organisers (Douglas and Harvey) be removed because their allegiance to the Communist Party precluded them from acting in the union's best interests; that Bailey and Douglas imposed a ban on the drivers connected with the Cable dispute without having ascertained the opinion of the union; and that they so directed the union's affairs that a number of members faced dismissal from their employment without having first obtained the views of the members of the union who were likely to have been affected by such dismissal.

Unbeknown to the dissenters, Bailey, returned from China, was sitting quietly at the back of the hall. The mover of the motion to dismiss him, Doug Scotson, Douglas's former workmate at HW Thomas, either aware of Bailey's presence in the room, or at the very least sensing it, began to see that the mood of the meeting was shifting against him. He and the other dissenters had already suffered a trouncing at meetings in Palmerston North and Masterton, where the motion suffered heavy defeats and the petitions were thrown out. Scotson now declined to speak to his motion, and after a short debate, he withdrew it, stating he had been 'misunderstood', and that he had learned a lot from the meeting. He had lost further credibility when it was revealed that his lawyer had provided him with advice gratis and had arranged for a truck to be driven around the streets of Wellington canvassing for signatures for the petitions. The meeting's final act, a motion 'that this meeting has full confidence in the paid officials, officers and executive council of the union', was passed by 149 votes (including Scotson and his seconder WT Ward) to none, thus putting the whole matter firmly to bed.[120]

Bailey was vindicated. By this time he was also making a mark among the FOL hierarchy, both as a result of his key negotiating role in the Cable dispute, and as someone whose expertise and clear thinking Fintan Patrick Walsh was increasingly coming to rely upon, despite his deep antipathy towards communists. By this time Walsh was fighting back — engaged in a bitter internecine row with Tony Neary and Peter Butler, who not only espoused policies of moderation within the FOL but whose squabbles were also as much personal as ideological. Bailey played a key role in this conflict — he was often at Walsh's side during major disputes — and the young Douglas found himself, enjoyably, becoming a kind of conduit between his union and the FOL leadership.

Tragically, Chip Bailey would not see plans for the progress of the Wellington Drivers' Union come to fruition. He had been unwell for some time. One day early in 1963, Bailey — a fastidious dresser — told Douglas he had had real difficulty doing up his tie that morning. Hospital visits confirmed that a malignant tumour was affecting the reasoning part of his brain, but despite his obvious ill-health he refused to slow down. Early in April, he collapsed at a Drivers' Federation conference in Dunedin. Within days he was operated on to remove the tumour but he did not recover. He died on the 25th of April, just 42 years old.[121]

Bailey's loss was a severe one. A union member since January 1948, he was elected to the executive within a year and remained there, despite challenges. He became organiser in 1953, vice-president in 1954, and secretary (and treasurer) in 1955, retaining that position, save for a brief period in 1959, until his death. He had played a key role in reorganising the deregistered union after the 1951 lockout and led major arguments for better conditions and wages for all drivers through the 1950s when the union was at a low ebb. When he was organiser he introduced the site-delegate system which went a long way towards making the union more democratic. He was also responsible for abolishing the overly oligarchic central executive and giving more power to an enlarged executive council. Since 1955, he had represented the Wellington Union on both the management committee of the Wellington Trades Council and the Drivers' Federation Council, and from October 1960 had been the FOL delegate to the Wellington Free Ambulance Board. An astute organiser, tireless negotiator and devastating debater, Bailey's untimely death robbed not only the Wellington Drivers' Union but also the wider trade union movement of one of its most able leaders.[122]

Ken Douglas had been acting as secretary since Bailey's first spell in hospital, in Wellington, on 18 April. He was in line for the permanent job but Harvey, the industrious country organiser, was also keen for it — and he was supported by a number of branches of the Communist Party. Unlike the confident Harvey, Douglas had strong doubts about his ability to take on the role permanently, not believing he was ready for the enormity and responsibilities of the task. He quickly came to miss Bailey's wise counsel. But he had friends within the union — and within the party — who believed that he was the most capable candidate.

Douglas had other advantages. By this time his year as acting city organiser was up and he decided to carry on, defeating Kevin Grimshaw, a Hutt Valley driver, in a ballot to hold onto the position. As Bailey's confidant he had accompanied him to FOL meetings and had played a key behind-the-scenes role in the negotiations around the union's readmittance. Bailey had also advocated for Douglas's appointment as the Wellington Trades Council representative on the 'No Maoris — No Tour' campaign. Not only was Douglas already a Wellington College Old Boys Rugby Club delegate on the Wellington Rugby Football Union, he and Lesley also spent hours on Friday nights behind a 'No Maoris

— No Tour' petition table in Chews Lane, in downtown Wellington. By this time he also sat on the Wellington Trades Council management committee, and he would soon be elected as its delegate to the Free Ambulance Board.[123]

Douglas also understood that the heart of influence in truck-driver unionism lay within the umbrella Drivers' Federation, and becoming secretary of the Wellington union would gain him automatic entry to the federation's key decision-making body — its national council. With these thoughts in mind, Douglas finally agreed to stand for the Wellington secretaryship. When Harvey realised he did not have enough party support to contest the position with Douglas, he stood aside. On 21 May 1963, Douglas was appointed to the position permanently, his being the only nomination. He was 27 years old, the youngest secretary of any trade union in New Zealand.[124]

At this time, the Wellington Drivers' Union membership was 2460 — comprising 1530 in the Wellington City/ Hutt Valley/Porirua basin region, 562 in Manawatu and 368 in the Wairarapa. In the broader Wellington area there were 55 site and area delegates covering 46 employers, including transport companies, local bodies (city and borough councils), taxi companies, bakers, brewers and the Wellington Free Ambulance.[125]

Wisely following Bailey's lead in making changes to the union structure, in November 1963 Douglas convened a job delegates' conference to discuss a new round of award negotiations. He continued and expanded another Bailey initiative, job meetings, where union policy and wage negotiations were discussed. Their success saw them established for decades. Not everything worked. In July 1964, the union abandoned its 'secretariat', although paid officials continued to meet on an ad hoc basis to review progress made on executive decisions. Membership continued to grow, and in September 1964 the union appointed a third organiser, Danny Crowley, a Palmerston North-based executive councillor. The other two organisers were both men who would become prominent in the wider union movement: Pat Kelly, who had replaced Douglas as organiser when the latter became secretary, looked after Wellington and Wairarapa drivers, while Hutt Valley members were Tom Poata's responsibility.

With his elevation, Ken Douglas now became a key functionary within the Drivers' Federation, whose most important function was to negotiate wages and conditions of work on drivers' behalf through the Arbitration Court. Unions nominated prominent members for the key positions of secretary — which became full-time from 1946 — and president. All unions were represented by two members on the federation's council. Annual conferences debated remits that came from each of the unions and through these formulated and coordinated policies on wages, conditions of work, and workplace practices. They also covered general social and political issues such as, during the 1950s and 1960s, opposition to nuclear weapons, opposition to the Vietnam War, opposition to apartheid-based rugby tours, opposition to the raising of Lake Manapouri to feed Bluff's new aluminium smelter, support for a New Zealand-owned shipping line and support for CARP (the Campaign Against Rising Prices). By this time, the Drivers' Federation had a high profile above and beyond union matters.[126]

Mostly the relationship between the unions and the federation was an agreeable one. For decades the officers of both the Federation Drivers' Federation and the Wellington Driver's Union worked close to each other in offices in the Trades Hall in Vivian Street. Besides negotiating their national agreements, the federation gave the driver unions clout and a vehicle for easier access to politicians, the state and big business while receiving loyalty — plus income, in the form of capitation fees based on membership numbers in each union — from their constituent bodies. By March 1968, there were 18,370 drivers from 12 unions affiliated to the Federation. The Northern Drivers' Union — covering Northland, Auckland and Waikato — was dominant, with 7003 members. Canterbury followed with 2900; then Wellington with 2587; Otago 1643, with smaller numbers in branches covering Poverty Bay, Hawke's Bay, Taranaki, Wanganui, Blenheim, Nelson, Westland and Southland.[127]

When Douglas first became a federation councillor in April 1963 he moved cautiously, understanding that anxiety over his communism could put him quickly offside with other, predominantly conservative, councillors; like the FOL, there was a strong Catholic presence spearheaded by national president Mick Sullivan, an oil-company driver from Taranaki, in industrial labour, political labour and in business circles. These synergies created a very powerful opposition to communist and socialist influences in the unions and, as Douglas saw it, were a barrier to reform. Many unions, including provincial drivers' unions, were not democratic. To maintain 'stability', their secretaries refused to hold elections, fearing they would undermine their power bases. They were aided by inadequate constitutions which did not include compulsory elections.

Douglas was intrigued when he arrived on the federation council, wondering how long this abrogation of democracy would be allowed to continue. He wanted closer contact with the drivers to ascertain their views, but this would take a long time. He had to work his way slowly up the ladder. Along with Sullivan, he became a federation trustee in 1966, a member of the editorial board of its publication *Wheels*, and was on the four-person award subcommittee from 1967. In April 1969, he was elected vice-president of the federation. His wider dream was to turn the federation into a national drivers' union with a streamlined nine-member executive which would be totally democratic and have more clout in dealing with employers, their federation and the government. This proposal was continually rejected, partly because of disagreements over the voting system, which was based on each union's numerical strength, as well as provincial fear of the major unions — Northern, Wellington and Canterbury — 'getting together' and dominating others whose membership was stagnant or declining.[128]

Nonetheless, Douglas and Bill Andersen, the secretary of the Northern Drivers' Union, continued to agitate for a more militant and activist federation. Sullivan, the national president, was decent and respected by the rank and file. Bill Welsh, the federation's long-time secretary, had been a driver in Nelson and on the executive of the union there before relinquishing both roles to take up the secretaryship after the 1951 dispute. Welsh was steady and uncomplaining, and many drivers and provincial union leaders saw him as a necessary force for stability in the federation. His position was secure — almost, it seemed, in perpetuity — and he became lazy, trapped among a coterie of union officials in Trades Hall who took two-hour lunches in the back bar of the nearby Terminus Hotel and, rather than returning to work 'half-tanked', took the afternoon off. Douglas resented that, and he, Andersen and a few others determined to create circumstances whereby Welsh had to respond. Replacing 'familiarity' with 'capability' in the union movement, difficult even to this day, became a primary focus. It was too difficult in this case. Loyalties remained strong, and Welsh remained federation secretary until he retired in July 1972.[129]

Douglas gained a wider union perspective with his elevation to the executive of the Drivers' Federation — and with his union's 1959 readmittance to the FOL — and it is from this early time that Douglas began to develop his temperate perspective of industrial relations. It was a perspective that would only modulate, but philosophically not change, until his retirement 30 years later. He was keen for solidarity and for the movement not to repeat the mistakes of 1951, when the watersiders and their union were isolated from the rest. There was pressure after that hiatus on astute trade unionists to be more inclusive. Leading the way on the waterfront was Ted Thompson, who realised that watersiders needed to collaborate as much as possible, not only with other unions but also with management, to reach favourable outcomes for all. Only when negotiations had completely broken down should there be resort to direct industrial action.

When Douglas came on the federation executive he was instrumental in the resurrection of a central committee of waterfront unions. As he saw it, this was a stimulus for unionists to be more responsible. 'Freezing workers going out at the height of the killing season is not going to win them any public support,' he believed. 'Drivers stuck with stock-in-transit in their trucks having to return them to farmers merely exacerbates the antagonism. It's muddled thinking. The natural unhappiness is worsened by the arrogance of one group saying, "Stuff you, we're milking the cow today." Union strategies needed changing. Workers acting selfishly are rightly accused of trying to assume a monopoly of control that they accuse the forces of capital of seizing. Union protest action always has to be measured against the bar of public opinion. This does not mean that we have to give in to conservative forces. It just sharpens the argument.'[130]

There were always other ways for unionists to frustrate unfair employers or unsympathetic politicians. Assessors were appointed by unions or the federation to carry out negotiation and conciliation in the arbitration process. Traditionally, appointees tended to be senior or favoured officials who may, or may not, have had a deep understanding of the problems workers faced. In his union, Douglas introduced a policy whereby assessors had to be experienced drivers. This caused tension in the Drivers' Federation, where for decades Welsh had often acted as union advocate — or ensured that the assessors he and the federation appointed were those who could be relied on not to rock the boat too much. Douglas's argument was that the rank and file needed to take more ownership of the process. It affected their livelihoods, after all, not the officials'. At the very least the workers needed to be able to ratify — or not ratify — the agreements reached.

When Douglas was secretary, assessors for local awards were chosen from a principal of the union, workplace delegates and a number of 'specialists' — if truck drivers' awards were under negotiation then there would be a group of rank-and-file truck drivers; for bus, van, ambulance and taxi drivers, a similarly chosen group would participate. The union would always seek to have additional delegates present as spectators or 'breathers', as they came to be known. Later, the drivers' union developed an 'oooh's and aah's' game. When the employers claimed something outrageous the delegates would exclaim 'oooh' in unison. Conversely, when the union scored a point, the same men would expire a resounding 'aah!' These humorous interludes served as a pressure release in the serious and often tense formal negotiation process and could also break the concentration of unwary employers. Conciliators could do little except request that the 'breathers' tone down their volume.

The conciliation process was argumentative by nature. Assessors ritualistically 'played games' — pushing forward an extreme argument, expecting compromise to follow. These were sometimes accompanied by jest or the assumption of the position of devil's advocate. Others allowed for little compromise and could leave a bitter taste in collective mouths as consensus was not reached or employers remained intransigent. Douglas recalls in his early days as secretary being present in the room as a union 'breather' when Fred Bognuda, the employer's advocate — and a strike-breaking truck driver in 1951 — offered a halfpenny an hour increase to the drivers. From the floor Douglas mocked him. 'Ah Freddy, are you sure you can afford it?'

'If farthings were still legal tender,' Bognuda yelled in reply, 'then you'd have got a bloody farthing! Be bloody satisfied, ya bastard!'[131]

In mid-1965, Douglas faced his biggest challenge yet as secretary of the Wellington Drivers' Union. It began as an innocuous dispute, but it spread to bring the union to the brink of deregistration. On Monday 19 July 1965, drivers employed by the Curtis group of companies stopped work. The union, as part of a campaign to raise drivers' wages, was undertaking job action for improvements on a broad front, including the payment of bonuses which were distributed to employers to be passed on to the drivers themselves. But not among the Curtis Group — Wellington's largest and most powerful transport conglomerate, comprising Munt Cottrell Carrying, JJ Curtis, Inter-Island Freight and Curtis Johnston. Their 66 drivers were on the award wage with bonus payments ranging from 31/- to 61/- a week. When the application of the 10/- increase obtained through award negotiations came up for payment, the Curtis Group passed on the hourly rate increase to its drivers, but deducted the bonus payments from their wages.[132]

The Curtis drivers were angry that the company was giving with one hand and taking away with the other. The company rectified the payments after the drivers complained but the business left a lingering dissatisfaction, and later in the year Douglas led the union in trying to persuade the company to incorporate maximum bonus payments into the hourly rate. This would have led to an increase in the award rate from 7/8¾d and 7/11½d to 9/3d and 9/6d for drivers of trucks and articulated trucks respectively.

When these negotiations broke down Curtis passed the dispute over to the Master Carriers' Association, which fanned the flames by issuing a press statement to the effect that the drivers' stoppage 'threatened to tie up the whole of the transport industry in Wellington'. The employers' own union, the Carriers' Association, promised that all companies would take a united stand to combat these 'illegal tactics'. When the Drivers' Union delegates went to meet the Master Carriers, as had been previously arranged, they were told that unless they returned to work immediately they would be sacked and other carriers would supply drivers to do Curtis's work. Faced with this pressure, and scaremongering in the following morning's *Dominion* newspaper, the Curtis drivers returned to work but resolved to stay staunch in their negotiations.

On the face of it, the employers held all the cards. Curtis showed no signs of compromising; the Master Carriers' Association stood firm in its support for Curtis, and on 7 August Tom Shand, the Minister of Labour (who had been having continual spats with the Wellington Drivers' Union since the Cable dispute three years earlier) leapt into the fray with threats of immediate deregistration for the drivers if they even considered strike action.[133]

Shand's comments raised temperatures all round. The New Zealand Seamen's Union, the Wellington Freezing Workers' Union Council and the Central Committee of the Combined Waterfront Unions all came out in public support of the drivers and their union, while the Wellington Trades Council kept a sympathetic watching brief. Even more importantly, driver support for the local union and the Curtis workers poured in from around the country. More than 600 drivers from far and near braved Shand's wrath by meeting on 11 August and vowing to support their colleagues at Curtis. Wisely, given the prevailing climate, they declined to take any further collective action — which included not placing a black ban on dealing with the Curtis

Group, as some had suggested. Notwithstanding, 300 of the drivers who attended this meeting were sacked when they returned to their own places of work. But the whole business proved to be of little consequence because after the big meeting the Curtis drivers gathered and decided to return to work. There was no strike fund; the men were losing wages and families were struggling financially.

They'd not given in, however, and when the dispute showed no sign of resolution it was handed over to the Federation of Labour. The Curtis men's decision to return to work proved a masterstroke. With the Carriers' Association still adamantly refusing to incorporate above-award payments into basic rates for the calculation of overtime payments, the Drivers' Union was now able to take the fight directly to Shand, asking him to prosecute the companies that had sacked drivers, charging them with wrongful dismissal, and claiming that this action had constituted a deliberate lockout. Shand refused — his mind was still set on deregistration, if only a pretext could be found. In the meantime, unions representing hotel workers, boilermakers, electrical workers, labourers and dairy workers joined the watersiders, seamen and freezing workers in openly supporting the drivers, promising their own industrial action if Shand went ahead with his deregistration threat.

Negotiations between the Drivers' Union, the FOL, Curtis and the Master Carriers proved fruitless. Following another stopwork meeting on 25 August, the Curtis drivers resumed their strike. Douglas insisted that the conflict be confined to Curtis. Further, and most unusually, he allowed other drivers to pick up Curtis work. It was a clever strategy as the only way that Curtis could be cut off from the rest of the employers was by inducing other carriers to take over its business. An age-old bosses' tactic of divide and rule was turned on its head. In angry response, the Carriers' Association reaffirmed that unless the Curtis drivers returned to work immediately it would regard all members of the union as being on strike. Douglas replied that that was the only tactic now open to the union and, seizing the high ground, claimed that it was the employers and not the union who were turning the matter into an industry-wide conflict.[134]

On 26 August, the *Evening Post* claimed that more than half of Wellington's trucks had been immobilised. No men had been dismissed but many had been kept in the yards on full pay. After a further meeting that day, the Master Carriers determined that no members of the union in their employ would work. The employers clearly hoped that a coalescence of business, newspapers and community antagonism would pressure the government into deregulation. That did not happen, and the Curtis drivers were unfazed. On 27 August they met again and vowed to continue the strike.

Their intransigence began to bear fruit. Other companies began taking some of the Curtis steel-carting work, firstly, with union drivers, before moving on to transport other 'stagnant' cargoes — to and from the Wellington wharf in particular — where there was good money to be made. This was the worst of all scenarios for the Master Carriers; the dispute was now out of their control. The following Monday, at Douglas's insistence, the Curtis drivers approached their employer for more talks. Sensing a need to compromise, the company acquiesced. Thereafter, the drivers all received a weekly above-award payment across the board of 25/- — better, in fact, than their original claim — and the men returned to work that day. The settlement had wider ramifications. The Drivers' Union succeeded in securing an industry-wide agreement, and the new rate became the minimum pay for driving work in the Wellington area.

In this cat-and-mouse game, it was the union that triumphed. Douglas's policy of aggressive confrontation when the union's case was fair and strong paid handsome dividends. One cannot help believing, however, that had not the Master Carriers remained so obdurate and had not Tom Shand inflamed an already tense situation, a consensual outcome would have been reached sooner, causing less industrial dislocation, social strife and lost profits for the company. It was noticeable that when the dispute ended, Shand was nowhere to be heard.

CHAPTER 6

Expanding the stage

By now Ken Douglas was becoming known as a no-nonsense trade union leader — forthright, analytical, thoughtful. But he had also become prominent in the Communist Party, and from 1966 the Socialist Unity Party. This brought him headlines, criticism from within the more conservative wings of the trade union movement, wariness from FOL president Tom Skinner and secretary Ken Baxter, both 'moderates', and savage invective from employers, politicians and a raft of editorial writers. This was no surprise, of course — Douglas foresaw it all. He took sustenance from the way Chip Bailey had handled a similar situation — not only his attitude to the uninformed public criticism, but also the skill with which he had been able to use it to his advantage, highlighting the fact that such criticism meant he was getting up the noses of employers and the state. That meant that he was 'doing a good job for the workers'.[135]

Douglas's office was Room 19 in the Trades Hall in Wellington, premises he shared with three paid Drivers' Union officials and two office workers, as well as a number of other unions. The union also shared a Palmerston North office, with one executive council member representing 300 union members or part thereof. The 19-man council met monthly on a Sunday. Attendance provisions were rigorously maintained — missing three consecutive meetings meant a councillor forfeited their right to belong.[136]

Concerned that too much power and influence was invested in union officials, Douglas took a principal role in making the Wellington Drivers' Union one of the most democratic in the country. The rules the union passed under his watch were explicitly designed to ensure that policy issues were determined by an aggregate vote of as broad a range of the membership as was possible. Meetings were held during the day throughout the Wellington district, which included Horowhenua, Manawatu and the Wairarapa. Notice of motions was always presented at the first meeting, allowing all members the chance to vote on them as the meetings moved on. Members could not 'cherry pick' by introducing different motions at later meetings. In contrast, other unions used devices to restrict members' participation in meetings. In order to hold off potential rank-and-file 'militancy', Tony Neary, for example, once held an Electeral Workers' Union ASM in Pahiatua at 8pm on a Monday evening. Few members could afford the time or expense to make the journey.[137]

Douglas's growing profile within the union and the national Drivers' Federation was owed in part to the lack of able men around him. However, that did not apply to Bill Andersen. The secretary of the Auckland-based Northern Drivers' Union, by far the country's largest, was the exception. Able and articulate, and an outspoken communist who also helped establish the Socialist Unity Party, Andersen became a leading player in the federation. With its president Mick Sullivan, and later with Douglas, he mounted a campaign to establish a national union of drivers that was more activist and powerful than the federation.

The move failed, stymied in the end by the parochialism of the provincial drivers' unions, including Canterbury, which feared their funds, influence and power bases would be swept away in the wash.[138]

Of more consequence at this time was the political damage that was inflicted on workers and their unions. Early in February 1967, the Holyoake government introduced a raft of measures to curb spending in a tightening economy. Some were severe: the government removed subsidies on bread, flour and butter, raised state-house rentals, abandoned the milk-in-schools scheme, raised Post Office charges, cut overseas travel allowances, tightened credit controls and hire purchase restrictions, and imposed constraints on no-remittance vehicle imports.

The Federation of Labour, unions, workers, housewives' groups, and other spokespeople for the unemployed, superannuitants and the poorly paid, were livid. The normally mild-mannered Tom Skinner, who had replaced Fintan Patrick Walsh as FOL president following Walsh's death in May 1963, thundered that workers would not accept this kind of treatment from any government: 'The anger out there is now on a par with the response to Nordmeyer's notorious "Black Budget".' Barry Tucker, secretary of the Combined State Services Organisation, accused the government of 'striking viciously at the New Zealand family'. The secretary of the Auckland-based Campaign Against Rising Prices (CARP), Mrs GJ Schmidt, promised to plan a campaign against the measures. Even the Wellington Housewives' Association, neither a political nor a strident body, sounded a call to arms.[139]

The Wellington Drivers' Union was one of the first out of the blocks, calling for an immediate two- to four-hour transport industry strike. Ken Douglas told the press that his union wanted the government to 'sit up and listen to what the wage-earner feels about these measures'.[140] The idea was sidelined when the FOL promised to coordinate a nationwide protest of all workers, but that took some time. By the time Skinner and his colleagues had organised stopwork meetings, and had them approved by the FOL's national council, the urgency of the protests had been blunted and the changes were well bedded-in.[141]

Skinner's bark was always more strident than his bite. He was conciliatory — too conciliatory for some — promising that if the government stabilised costs and prices in the next few months, the FOL would not apply for a general wage increase in the Court of Arbitration. The government retracted nothing. There was no agitation. Wellington drivers, among others, felt there was no choice but to return to work. Their case was not helped by the Labour opposition, which sat on the fence. Deputy leader Hugh Watt's only comment was that the stopwork meetings 'should have been held outside working hours'.[142]

Holyoake's measures did little to improve the New Zealand economy. Towards the end of 1967 unemployment rose as the terms of trade fell. Among others, drivers were beginning to be laid off. Speaking on behalf of his union's executive, Ken Douglas requested that job delegates notify the union office of any dismissals, and requested of employers that no dismissals should be made while overtime was being worked, and that the principle of last on, first off be applied in all cases where redundancy was proven, with maximum security accorded to job delegates. He also promised that the union would endeavour at all costs to maintain full employment. It was a moderate rejoinder, but sensible. This was not a mainstream union concern; more contentious activity in the future would demand a more assertive union response.[143]

Wage and salary earners did not have long to wait. Early in June 1968, for the first time in its long history, the Arbitration Court handed down a nil wage order. Within hours of its announcement, the Freezing Workers' Union closed works down in protest, and brewery, asbestos, glass and rubber workers all struck immediately. A Wellington Trades Council meeting of 400 union leaders, officials and job delegates unanimously endorsed a resolution supporting a 12-hour stoppage on 26 June, and a march from Trades Hall to a protest rally at the opening of Parliament. The FOL national executive urged all unions to take protest action that 'each saw fit to take'. The Wellington Drivers' Union left it to site delegates and individual workers to take what action they wished. A few refused to drive. Many more looked to the FOL for direction. The federation took a cautious stance. A 4 July meeting of constituent unions decided that immediate strike action would be self-defeating and that a more productive strategy would be to ignore the court ruling and serve immediate claims on their employers for wage increases.

Judge Blair's nil wage order resulted in an unanticipated rapprochement in one industry — the two freezing-worker unions, the New Zealand Freezing Workers' Union and the unregistered North Island Freezing Workers' Union, overcame their previous inability to resolve differences between them by jointly implementing a national load-out ban on exports from all works. The Seamen's Union restricted the operations of the roll-on, roll-off ferries; rubber workers, electrical workers and hotel workers instituted overtime bans, and watersiders threatened to strike if their current wage claim was not quickly resolved 'favourably'. In the end, only a handful of the country's truck drivers took direct action. Drivers at Mulhollands in Dunedin went on a 24-hour stoppage; 15 drivers at New Zealand Breweries' Wellington plant took strike action on 8 July when it became clear that no across-the-board wage increase was forthcoming, and Certified Concrete drivers at the company's Wellington, Porirua and Hutt Valley plants instituted an overtime ban.[144]

Judge Blair had determined that the FOL's case for an across-the-board wage increase of 7.6 per cent had been proved but he had, he said, to take into account the well-being of the country — particularly farmers and manufacturers, who had been suffering considerably under adverse economic conditions. Yet it was a decision that turned around and bit the employers and the government on the backside. There was real anxiety now that the FOL and its unions might reject the Arbitration Court altogether and return to direct bargaining with bosses, with the attendant fear of longer and more militant industrial action. That is exactly what happened. On 4 July hundreds of unionists at an emergency FOL conference unanimously agreed to bypass the Court and negotiate directly with employers for wage rises of between 5 and 7.6 per cent.

Douglas was not surprised at the nil wage order. The system was at fault, he contended, and had been for years. Writing in the union magazine *Wheels*, he commented:

> Because they have been conditioned by successive governments and employers' interests, the vast majority of workers believe that the Court can and does impartially set wage standards. This is not the case now, never has been the case, nor will it ever be. The role of the Arbitration Court is to act as a buffer between the workers and their quest for higher wages to offset the rising cost of living, and the employing interests in their drive for greater exploitation of the working people to achieve greater profit. That the Court has been successful in this has been obvious. If it dispenses wage justice fairly there would be no above award payments — such payments would be written into the award payment. Likewise, the fact that the award payment exists demonstrates firstly that the employers can pay more — and that the unions are capable of forcing the employers to pay more — particularly if there was a labour shortage.[145]

Douglas believed that many spokespeople, including government advocates, endeavoured to present the Court proceedings as some sort of bizarre game. 'The Court finds against the FOL's claims in a "pukka sahib" sporting manner and we are expected to say, well, we played hard and we tried to win. Bad luck old chaps, but you know it's the game that really counts.' He believed it was a 'game' for big business, which was in it to push up profits, but it was certainly not a game for working people for whom the difference between living adequately and struggling to cope was at stake.[146]

As it was, on 16 July, the FOL and the Employers' Association agreed to make a joint application to the Arbitration Court for a general wage order. The government, fearful for the Court's future, also agreed with both organisations that it needed to examine possible changes and amendments to the Arbitration Act as well as the Court's procedures. There was urgency in the case, and the Court responded within a week by agreeing that from 19 August all workers would receive a pay rise of five per cent. Most workers, including the nation's drivers, were appeased. A potentially serious industrial crisis was averted. Within weeks, the whole scenario had made Judge Blair's nil wage order look ridiculous.[147]

Indeed, the judge had done the unions and their members a favour. Workers who had been indifferent to their unions and the FOL for years suddenly sat up in anger at the nil wage order, and put their unions' reactions to it under very close scrutiny. Many became proactive unionists for the first time in their lives. Huge numbers attended the numerous job and site stopwork meetings held in response to the nil order, angry, and determined to respond in kind. This was nowhere more apparent than among Wellington's drivers, called 'militant' by some, who now attended stopwork meetings in numbers not seen for years.

This much-increased enthusiasm for unionism had been a primary factor in the FOL's initially determining on direct negotiation, and when the employers baulked, it speedily marched back to the Court demanding redress. Furthermore, the order encouraged many unions, such as the Wellington Drivers', to turn their backs on the Court and turn to direct bargaining. Such was its success that Douglas wrote in 1972 that the union had achieved more for workers in the past three years than during the previous 30. Through the FOL's, he called for all workers to unite and support any union or group of workers that came into conflict with this 'unrepresentative' government. 'The recent experience of the Seamen's Union [its 1971 deregistration] serves as a valuable lesson as to the dangers of a militant union becoming isolated from the mainstream of the movement.' Solidarity had never been more important. Nobody realised it then, but Blair's nil wage order would be the beginning of the end of the formal arbitration and conciliation system, the backbone of New Zealand's industrial relations since 1894.[148]

On 25 March 1970, to Douglas's delight, oil company drivers, who had been on their own in an 'in-house' grouping since the 1951 lockout, finally became members of the Wellington Drivers' Union. Securing their membership provided the last spoke in the wheel. The union now represented general motor drivers, local body drivers, bus drivers, taxi drivers, tractor drivers, oil company drivers, horse drivers (theoretically at least), earthmoving drivers, ambulance drivers and aerial topdressing loader drivers.

By this time Douglas was observing subtle, slow, but consistent change in the structure and work of the union. He understood that the policy instigated by Chip Bailey, and on which he had expanded — that the rank and file should have genuine decision-making clout in the running of the union — was the right one. While job delegate conferences had been operating since 1958, under Bailey, and particularly Douglas, they were less about rubber-stamping executive decisions than about addressing more meaningful rank-and-file resolutions on a raft of industrial and political issues that were taken on board by the executive, explored and acted upon. As a consequence, Wellington drivers came to feel a closer sense of ownership of, and security within, their union.

There were 146 job delegates in 1972. The significance of their role cannot be understated: they were the conduit between head office and the rank and file in their workplaces, the cornerstone of the organisation. They had regular meetings, seminars and communication training, although their key battle was still to ensure that all drivers in their section were members, having to produce their union cards on demand. There was more pressure on those who worked for smaller companies, where the union presence was weaker.

Delegates were helped considerably by the effect of Judge Blair's 1968 nil wage order in uniting drivers — as it did other trade unionists — into a more cohesive and stronger body with more rank-and-file participation in direct bargaining. Between 1968 and 1972, drivers secured better wages and conditions through direct bargaining on a pro rata basis than they had in 20 years of Arbitration Court decisions. The proof was in the pudding. The Holyoake government in turn reacted by trying to isolate the trade union movement and introducing piecemeal anti-union legislation. This was the thinking in particular behind the Wages Remuneration Act, which was intended to separate sections of the movement and turn one against another. It rebounded on the government as unions, under the aegis of the FOL, grew closer to combat the threat, as they would later under Prime Minister Robert Muldoon who tried to impose more serious threats.

Just as importantly and tellingly in the long term, Douglas monitored the changing nature of the transport industry itself, which was outside his, and his union's, control. Two trends were evident — the change in ownership of trucking firms from family units to nationally and even internationally owned enterprises, and the emergence of the owner-driver, whose membership the union fought hard to retain. These factors, rather than growth in membership, which had slowed, contributed to huge growth in expenditure — from $14,968 in 1960 to $42,366 in 1972 — which for every year between these two exceeded income from subscriptions and entrance fees.

Douglas achieved more prominence than other union leaders simply by dint of the General Drivers' Award being the first to be negotiated and settled every year, and therefore acting as a trend-setter for all other industrial awards. If it was deemed to be too 'generous' he was slated in the press, his most vigorous and uninformed antagonists labelling him a 'greedy Marxist out to destabilise the capitalist system' — his communism, and more specifically his leadership of the Wellington branch of the Socialist Unity Party, a convenient metaphorical stick for these people to hammer him around the head with. But after 10 years as a communist he had become used to such disparagement. Being slated as a political scapegoat for what was wrong in industrial relations washed over him like water off a duck's back. There was an upside to drivers being first off the block. As wage rates were relative, other union leaders rejoiced at any 'generosity', knowing that they and their members, would automatically be able to share in the beneficence, no matter how minor.

Between 1960 and 1972 there were seven drivers' awards, during which the base weekly rates rose from $21.60 in 1960 to $52.60 in 1972. Other improvements won included increased sick pay, more generous allowance for stopwork meetings, a long-service allowance, wet weather equipment or allowance, trailer money, three weeks' annual holiday, additional holiday pay, and 'Hiab' payments — a skill recognition payment for the operation of the 'lifting arm'-type small cranes that were attached to trucks' trays. Since drivers' pay rates were based on the tonnage of a truck, it was important that such specialist payments were in place to acknowledge the skill of the operator.[149]

These upgrades had been negotiated through direct bargaining, although it needs to be noted that the liberal increases in the basic rate were largely offset by increases in inflation, which ranged between 12 and 16 per cent annually. The union achieved a victory in 1973 when, after a long and dogged campaign, all major transport firms agreed to deduct union fees from their men's wages, thus removing from Douglas and other officials the onerous task of chasing up fees and checking the membership books.

Early in 1973, Douglas proposed that in order to re-establish first-hand communication with his members' core business he should take time out from his administrative role and return to driving. The executive was lukewarm on the issue. Understandably, they were concerned about who would be able or willing to do the secretary's job while he was away. Douglas wanted six months; the executive granted him three. He had played rugby for Wellington College Old Boys with Freightways managing director Jack O'Brien, his former nemesis over the negotiating table, and arranged with him to drive one of their trucks.

He enjoyed driving, relishing the freedom that went with it, but one day, after he had been back behind the wheel for six weeks, a wool bale slipped while it was being loaded onto the truck. When Douglas jumped backwards to avoid it his foot became jammed between two bales and he pulled a groin muscle. That meant 'compo' and the end of his employment at O'Brien's. Because Douglas's profile was now high as both union leader and Socialist Unity Party spokesperson, some colleagues suggested that the bale had been deliberately dislodged by 'person or persons unknown'. Douglas laughs this off, confident that it was an accident, as it undoubtedly was.[150]

In July 1974, Douglas was at the forefront of a Drivers' Federation campaign to try to bring together all of the unions involved in the transport industry, representing some 50,000 workers. The proposed Transport Workers' Federation would include unions that covered seamen, waterside workers, harbour workers, railway workers, general labourers and storemen and packers. Such a federation would have real power in wage negotiations, including easier resolution of relativities and the removal of niggling demarcation disputes which sometimes damaged relations among the workers. There was already a precedent in Auckland, where the Northern Drivers' Union and the Storemen and Packers, Engineers, Clerical Workers, Carpenters and Electrical Workers' Unions had set up a joint committee aimed at providing a united front in disputes.[151]

The Federation of Labour gave its assent, but the Transport Workers' Federation did not materialise. Interest among individual unions was lukewarm, and the seamen and watersiders rejected the proposal out of hand. The chance to form a very powerful amalgamated union collective which had the power to affect economic progress — for better or worse — was brushed aside. Parochialism, and a determination to protect their own patch, kept unions small and ineffective on a broader industrial and political scale. It was a blight that would hinder trade union progress for decades.

Later the same year, in September, Douglas faced a nasty in-house crisis. Terry Linton, who drove for an Elsdon street-sweeping firm, filed a writ of mandamus to compel Douglas, as his union's secretary, to call a special general meeting to debate a motion of no confidence in the officers of the union. This followed an earlier refusal by Douglas to call a meeting to listen to the rebel group's grievances as it was not called in accordance with the union's rules. The group's three resolutions were that they had no confidence in the secretary, president, vice-president, council members and organisers of the union; that these officials all be removed from office, and that a secret ballot be held to confirm the resolution. At the court hearing Douglas agreed to call the meeting and the writ was withdrawn.[152]

On the surface, the dispute was over Linton's allegations that Douglas and his officials had transferred union funds from the members to themselves and that Douglas had refused to produce for inspection the union's books, particularly two accounts the union failed to show its auditors, Matthews Clegg and Company. When the law clerk from Buddle, Anderson and Kent had attempted to hand the writ to Douglas at the lift at the Trades Hall he refused to accept it, claiming he was not Kenneth Douglas but Kenneth George Douglas. The clerk then placed the writ at Douglas's feet as he entered the lift.

At a stopwork meeting held on 15 October Douglas admitted he was operating two bank accounts illegally under the terms of the Industrial Conciliation and Arbitration Act. It was an oversight which he quickly corrected, reporting on 19 October that the accounts had become fully authorised under the terms of the new Industrial Relations Act. Douglas denied Linton's claims of skulduggery, claiming that both accounts had been established 'by resolution of the full membership'. At the same time, at a series of stopwork meetings throughout the district, Linton's motions of no-confidence in the executive failed by 1210 votes to 654 — a close to 70 per cent backing for Douglas and his officials.[153]

The deeper reason behind the dispute was that Linton was the frontperson in a campaign to rid the Drivers' Union of its communist leadership — Douglas, Wellington organiser Richie Gillespie, Manawatu organiser Jackson Smith, and John 'Corncob' Andrews, the union's delegate on the Wellington City Council.[154] On a personal level the campaign turned nasty for the Douglas family. Members of a Young National Party ginger group — or their acolytes; they were always anonymous — hounded Douglas by phone every half-hour, day and night. They terrorised his family, issuing death threats against his young children, including threats to lace their milk bottles with LSD and throw Molotov cocktails through the front windows of the family home. Douglas's daughter Jane, a schoolgirl at the time, recalls answering the phone one night to hear a voice say, 'Don't walk down the street, little girl. We'll get ya.' She developed breathing difficulties and had a mini-breakdown, collapsing during a physical education lesson at school.[155]

Douglas's response to the calls was to scream down the phone, while the children screamed and cried and his wife Lesley pleaded with him to have the phone disconnected or at least leave it off the hook. Douglas refused angrily. He believed he had to be available to any union member who needed to contact him at any time, and besides, he averred, 'We're not giving in to these arseholes.'

He now admits his reaction was self-centred, 'It was my stubbornness and pig-headedness that saw the phone left on the hook.' He saw the attacks as a personal challenge to him and reacted in kind, with little acknowledgement of the potential damage to his family. The LSD threat was the nadir. 'I felt totally helpless. What could I do? It frightened the hell out of me. I didn't trust the police. I was afraid to front up to what this was doing to Lesley and the kids. I felt completely isolated.' His resentment and anger over the phone calls made him want to go and deal physically to the perpetrators, if he could find them. 'At all other times when events did not go my way I was able to sublimate personal rage for the common good — but not this time.'[156]

Although nothing was proven, Douglas believed that the National Party was behind the attacks. He challenged Geoffrey Thompson, the MP for Horowhenua and later party president, over the phone calls. Thompson did not deny it. Thompson's law firm had filed all the documents and written letters on behalf of the Linton group. Straight after the vote, Linton was employed as a personal chauffeur by Sir Brian Todd, whose family had close connections in the party. Douglas arranged to be a guest speaker at a Junior National Party conference in Wellington, where he challenged the delegates to work hard for 'proper political leadership' within their party without resulting to underhand practices, and to come and talk to him if they knew anything about the harassment to his family, saying 'We'll get it sorted.' Nobody fronted.

While the Linton crisis was the most worrying for Douglas, it was not the only time his family faced threats from outside. His daughter Helen, who for a time shared a room with her older sister in the front of their Titahi Bay home, recalls bomb threats to which her father paid little heed but which caused her to hop into Jane's bed for comfort.

In 1977, Douglas was voted in as president of the Drivers' Federation. He was in the firing line immediately. Drivers' salaries had now been falling behind others relatively for some years, not keeping up with the high rate of inflation, and held back by Muldoon's wage-freeze policy. A privately employed driver of a 6- to 8-tonne truck was paid $80.75 a week; one driving a 10- to 14-tonne truck received $83.47; and the driver of a big earthmoving machine $86.75. These rates were 24 per cent less than drivers employed by the railways, and 32 per cent less than those employed by Air New Zealand. Many of the country's 20,000 general drivers claimed it was only the overtime rates that kept the job worthwhile. Employers had argued successfully that they could only maintain their competitive edge on rail if they paid their driver employees low wages.

Early in May 1978, the federation claimed a 24 per cent increase in their award talks. There was no consensus, with employers sticking to their offer of a 6.5 per cent increase. Three meetings resulted in deadlock. In response, on 14 May, drivers in most parts of the country struck for 24 hours, promising more if there was no movement. This stimulated Minister of Labour John Gordon to warn drivers to 'cool it', telling them the Labour Department was looking at deregistration of the Northern and Wellington Drivers' Unions as their actions during conciliation appeared to be in breach of the Industrial Relations Act. On behalf of the federation, Douglas then called off all stoppages and work restrictions. On 18 May, the federation gave employers a week to come up with a better offer or face further disruption. Both had moved: the federation was now seeking a 17 per cent rise; the employers were offering 8.5 per cent.[157]

Drivers kept up the pressure with load-out bans, trailer bans, 24-hour stoppages, and in some areas 48-hour stoppages. On 12 June, with no settlement in sight, the FOL weighed in with the drivers. The government then took the threat of deregistration off the table. Tom Skinner was now leading the negotiations for the drivers, with Douglas and federation secretary Stuart McCaffley assisting him. Finally, on 22 June, six weeks after the award talks had begun, both sides settled for an 11.5 per cent wage increase. Employers feared, however, that such a 'generous' settlement would set a 'hot pace' in the forthcoming bargaining season. On 6 July Douglas appeared on Television One in a documentary called *One Pair of Eyes — The Drivers Will Decide*, explaining the case for his members. This publicity angered Prime Minister Robert Muldoon, who repeated a threat that had been made in July 1977, that he would introduce voluntary unionism if the pay round was too 'excessive'. Muldoon later assessed the pay round as 'testing', but did not proceed with his threat.

There was a rerun in 1979 when the federation claimed a 20 per cent increase, still less than the rise in inflation, with the employers offering 7 per cent. There was no agreement. On 12 July, drivers, led by their union advocate Rob Campbell, struck for 24 hours and rejected a subsequent offer of 9.5 per cent. On 19 July the federation dropped its demand to 15 per cent. The employers did not move. Drivers began a series of disruptions — go-slows, load-out bans, 24-hour stoppages — with the federation leaving it to individual groups to decide what course of action to take. The government now threatened a resumption of wage controls. Spot strikes continued into late August, and Minister of Labour Jim Bolger urged both parties to take the dispute to arbitration. The New Zealand Road Transport Association, the New Zealand Contractors' Federation and the New Zealand Employers' Federation paid for large newspaper advertisements blasting the unions and outlining their case. On 5 September, after three months of squabbling, work restrictions and striking, the two sides agreed on an 11 per cent increase, alongside a 4.5 per cent increase already granted in the general wage order. Muldoon raged that it was too high, too inflationary and a threat to the economy. Douglas warned that the government 'would pay the price' if it interfered in the agreement and promised to bring in the FOL, which had the potential to widen the disruptions and lead to industrial conflagration. In implicit support, freezing worker union officials, representing 30,000 men, threatened to walk out of their pay talks if Muldoon interfered with the due process of the law.[158]

On 11 September, a special Cabinet meeting cut the pay rates for drivers by 1.5 per cent. Douglas questioned the legality of this action and brought in the FOL — of which he was now second-in-charge, having been elected as secretary the previous April. New president Jim Knox wasted no time in accusing Muldoon of leading New Zealand towards a 'blatant one-man dictatorship'. On 17 September he called for a snap 24-hour national strike against Muldoon's promise of the cut, which transgressed legal process. This move drastically raised the temperature, one newspaper overstating the case by reporting that it had the potential to be the biggest national stoppage since the general strike of 1913.[159]

The strike was a mixed success. Many workers obeyed the FOL's call. A minority did not. In Auckland the Trades Council organised 250 'temporary delegates' to scan the city's workplaces for staff who were defying the call, and to encourage them to take part in the strike. Union officials threatened 28-day bans on any businesses that were allowing their staff to work, and pickets were placed outside the companies that did not comply. Knox warned employers who tried to intimidate staff into not stopping work that they 'would be in trouble'. Muldoon's 'carless days' restrictions were lifted as bus and train services came to a standstill in all major cities.

There is no doubt that the strike had an impact; it was not 'the sad, lost cause' that Muldoon had predicted. The employers, unions and their umbrella organisations all called for the deadlocked dispute to be sorted urgently in the Arbitration Court. On 25 September, while Muldoon was absent overseas, Deputy Prime Minister Brian Talboys agreed to let it go to arbitration. But then Jim Bolger, the Minister of Labour, exacerbated the tension by claiming the government would not allow the Court to go above its 9.5 per cent guideline, which led Bill Rowling, the Leader of the Opposition, to condemn the government's 'blatant interference in due process and blatant breach of faith with the workers and employers of the country'.

Talboys again backtracked, stating that the government would not interfere. On 1 October, the Drivers' Federation took a 13 per cent claim to the Court, 2 per cent higher than the original agreement of the previous month. The employers replied with an offer of 9.5 per cent, the maximum amount that would have satisfied Muldoon. Chief Judge

JPR Horn split the difference, awarding the drivers a 10.5 per cent wage rise on 5 October, alongside the 4.5 per cent general wage order. The government accepted it, and everyone went home.

This was the last Drivers' Union or Drivers' Federation industrial campaign with which Douglas was involved. Early in 1981 he resigned from the presidency of the federation, thus officially disconnecting himself formally from drivers' union activism, to which he had been wedded for the previous 25 years.[160]

It is difficult to overstate his success in these roles. Being the leader of a union was difficult, and the work was far from glamorous. Douglas worked long hours, forsaking healthy food for the quick takeaway and skimping on rest and exercise, all of which had a negative impact on his health — his weight in particular. He was always on call and his work sometimes required him to be away from home.

He also organised pickets, attended protracted wage negotiations and assisted workers and their families who were in need. His phone never stopped ringing, day or night. He worked hard at being a patient listener and became a very careful checker of facts. On top of this, his remuneration was far inferior to that of company managers and directors. Neither did unions have the resources to employ the expensive public relations firms favoured by big business.

At times, Douglas was voted into office by a small minority of the membership, but he was accountable to all members — unlike employers or managers who were selected or appointed. He understood that he had to perform, or risk being voted out. He often faced criticism from union members at meetings — as well as more from employers, the government and the press. He had to learn to be patient and at ease with individuals and organisations across all these sectors. He became skilled in understanding the parameters and the nuances of how he should behave in every given circumstance. Nonetheless, the thick skin he developed was critical, as it would be in his future leadership roles within the Federation of Labour and the Council of Trade Unions.

By this time, Douglas and his family were living in Titahi Bay. Ken and Lesley had spent 10 months in cramped conditions in the itinerant Hobson Street boarding house after they were married, before shifting into 131 Apu Street, Lyall Bay, the cottage Ken's mother Madge had bought after her parents died. Madge had not had the money to pay off the mortgage so while Ken and Lesley lived in the house and took care of the mortgage, Madge lived in the bach at the back of the property that Attie had built for her. Ken and Lesley's first child, Jane, was born during this period on 2 February 1961. After a year in Lyall Bay, Ken sold the section he owned in Newlands to finance the purchase of a basic three-bedroom house at 20 Opapa Street, Titahi Bay, where the family would live for the following 25 years. This had been a state house, 'pepper-potted' within a range of state and private houses in a suburb that was growing fast. It was a pre-cut Swedish-pine residence built by Austrians brought to New Zealand to transform the Porirua basin into new expansive areas for Wellington's working class, hitherto squeezed into cramped rental accommodation near the central city. Douglas paid £4220 for the house, with a fixed annual mortgage of 3 per cent arranged through the Norwich Union. At close to £6, the mortgage was more than half his weekly salary of £11/10 as a drivers' union organiser.[161]

There were advantages in moving to Titahi Bay. Ken's uncle Terry Farrow, to whom he was close, lived in nearby Dimock Street. The house in Opapa Street was adjacent to a dairy, close to bus transport and next door to the entrance to Titahi Bay Primary School. Jane and her siblings attended the school, and Lesley subsequently taught there for the rest of her career. The bay was a dormitory suburb, with many workers catching buses and trains to the central city. It was a 'mixed' hamlet, with blue-collar freezing workers, watersiders, truck drivers, factory workers and carpenters living close to white-collar civil servants, teachers, nurses and a scattering of other professionals higher on the hill. Among the state houses some belonged to the Ministry of Defence. One of these was next door to the Douglas residence and inhabited by Ron Burton, a navy officer who worked for naval intelligence. The Burtons had no telephone so the Douglases let Ron and his wife Maisie use theirs, until Burton's employers realised with a jolt that their neighbour was a high-profile communist. The practice ceased immediately and the Burtons had a telephone installed. Moreover, an SIS man named Costello lived down the street. 'He would be watching our kids play sport on Saturday and writing a report on me on Monday,' was Douglas's sardonic memory. More irrationally, Costello refused to let his children play with the Douglas kids.[162]

There was also a close relationship between the Wellington College Old Boys Rugby Football Club — for which Douglas played — and its equivalent in Titahi Bay, the former helping to sponsor Titahi Bay's affiliation to the Wellington Rugby Football Union. Roman Catholicism was a primary early influence in the area. Catholics built the first church, and Viard College, the suburb's first secondary school. Despite a lack of facilities there was a real community spirit. Neighbours quickly became friends. Sports clubs were melting pots of race and class. Jane's first memories of Opapa Street were of playing with the many neighbouring kids in the street outside their homes and in local parks.

It was in this house that the Douglases' three other children were born and raised. Jane, Peter, Helen and John all went from Titahi Primary to Titahi Intermediate School, and all except John went to Mana College. Jane, who began school in 1966, was selected for the top class at college, winning university accreditation after two years in the sixth form. After leaving school she took a secretarial course, and later worked as an industrial officer for the Public Service Association. She then worked for Fonterra in Hamilton, before joining the State Services Commission where today she is principal advisor in the Employment Relations section. Earlier she was an active youth member of the Socialist Unity Party, and 'sporty' — playing softball, netball, badminton and tennis through school and into adulthood. While Jane was quieter and more shy than her siblings, the Douglas children never took a backward step and were regarded in the area as 'tough kids'.

None were 'tougher' than Peter, born on 2 November 1962, who went from primary and intermediate to an undistinguished career at Mana College. He was a reluctant student, and one of his earliest memories is his father chasing him with a one-and-a-half-inch-wide strap, which

Ken called the 'tickler', to encourage him to stay at primary school. Expelled from college twice — Ken ensured that he was readmitted — Peter left school at the end of the fourth form, aged 14. He spent as much time wagging as attending class. His memory of his school days is blunt: 'I didn't learn anything at school. I didn't like authority. Mum was my most important teacher.' On leaving school he became a workshop dogsbody at Cameron Contracting Company in Lower Hutt. An uncle, Frank Robins, secured him a maintenance job at the Williams Building in the CBD before he trained as a mechanic at Cable Price, where he worked for 11 years. After a subsequent 10-year stint as a mechanic, Peter is currently studying information technology at Whitireia Community Polytechnic in Porirua.[163]

Helen, born on 14 November 1963, followed the same path as Peter, inheriting some of the same anti-authoritarian traits. 'My big mouth was always getting me into trouble. I was always telling the teacher off, particularly at intermediate school,' she recalled. Her saviour at Mana College was art teacher Robyn Kahukiwa, who recognised her hitherto hidden potential and had her moved from a bottom to a top form. Leaving school after four years, and interested in unionism, Helen first worked as a check-out operator at a New World supermarket and became a union delegate. She then joined the Department of Statistics as a 'lowly clerk', was sacked after falsifying time-sheets, and joined the Public Service Association as an organiser. Leaving the PSA in 2004, she ran a catering business at Titahi Golf Club before leaving for Brisbane and working for Mainfreight. For some years she was the partner of Boycie Paora, with whom she had three children.

John, the youngest, was born on 12 July 1967. Ken and Lesley separated when he was 12, and after his early schooling at Titahi Bay he lived with his father in Wadestown and attended Wellington College. He was also a competent sportsman, playing cricket and football to a high level. He left school after four years to become a trainee multi-lithographer in the Post Office. After marrying young, he shifted to Brisbane at 20, working initially as a builder's labourer and then for a franchise holder at Snap Printing before purchasing his own franchise with the company in

2000. He is the father of four children, two from a previous relationship and two with his present wife.

After Jane was born, Lesley became a Playcentre supervisor, and all her children attended. Conscious that she had not had an ideal start in life, with her childhood years spent in an orphanage, she wanted the very best for her children. Ken described her as 'the most fanatical of mothers — especially to her sons'. As well as her nurturing role she was the fulcrum around which the family operated. She did everything in the home. In public she was shy, and deferential to Ken, but to her children she was their 'best friend'. For them Lesley provided the stability, consistency, constancy, and was the interpreter and reinforcer of the humanitarian values, couched in communist dogma, that their father articulated. She was often on her own with them. Ken left home very early in the morning to meet drivers before working hours and was often home late in the evening — long after the children had gone to bed. Lesley's mother Gwen Winter helped her with the child-raising, and the housework while Lesley was at school. Helen and Jane recall their grandmother Gwen as a gentle, loving, calm, non-judgemental and well-read person who taught them card games. During the school holidays the children also stayed at Madge's house in Apu Crescent, where they developed a close, warm relationship with their other grandmother, now cured of the alcoholism that had so damaged her relationship with Ken when he was young. The Farrows in Dimock Street were another focus for family gatherings, often around a keg of beer.[164]

Lesley returned to teaching in 1972 — next door at Titahi Primary — when Jane was 11 and John was four. She rose through the ranks to take up senior positions, mentoring new and student teachers. Lesley was innovative and hard-working in the classroom, and respected by her colleagues. Somewhat of an 'earth mother', she also took strays into her home — mostly Peter's friends, 'tough' kids, some of whom had dysfunctional relationships with their own parents. She taught one of these boys to read so he could sit his driver's licence. In later years she also helped both Jane and Helen with their children when they were bringing them up on their own.[165]

Lesley both played and coached sport, at school and as player/coach in Titahi Bay's junior women's softball team for a number of years. She was also political, being active in the primary teachers' union — the New Zealand Educational Institute — and the Socialist Unity Party, which she joined independently from her husband, and where she was secretary of the Porirua branch for a period. Through it all she was a loyal and ever-present support and sounding board for Ken in union and political discussion — when he was not too tired from his daily grind.

Ken was often absent from the kids' lives. Not seeing him in the morning, Jane recalls her great excitement when she heard the union car coming up the drive in the evenings. The family also suffered through their father's loose concept of time. On one occasion Jane sat in the gutter in the street outside her home for hours, sharpening ice-block sticks on the concrete, waiting for her father to come and pick her up to take her to an aunt's house. She does not recall feeling angry or sad, and says now she has inherited his habit of keeping people waiting. Her father was always running late. When people he was supposed to be meeting rang the house, the children were instructed to answer the phone and tell them that 'he left 10 minutes ago'.

Today Ken's regret at not spending more time with his children when they were young is manifest. 'I missed out on so much richness of their young lives; being involved in understanding their needs and helping to develop their aspirations,' he says. What he missed out on has become even more apparent to him in in recent years, when he has been able to spend time with his grandchildren — Anthony, Jane's son, and Tama, Henare and Lesley-Ann, Helen's children.

It was not easy being Ken Douglas's child in Titahi Bay. He was well known as much through his leadership in local sporting clubs as for his role as a high-profile trade unionist, a profile raised even higher after he became secretary of the Federation of Labour in 1979. Jane recalled that, such was his profile, 'We couldn't get away with anything.' Ken's other public face was his local leadership of the Socialist Unity Party, which had meetings in the Douglas house. His communism led the older children in particular to become the butt of ill-informed criticism.

Peter, who received much of the flak, recalled being castigated as a 'dirty little Commo' by kids, parents and the occasional teacher even before he understood what the term meant. At intermediate and high school he had scraps with others as he defended his father's honour, and at Mana College he was caned by one of the science teachers after he swore in class. 'Ah, you swear just like your communist father,' the teacher told him. Peter walked out of the class. Unlike Lesley, Jane and Helen who joined the party, neither Peter nor John were 'political', refusing to have any contact with the SUP.

Helen got her first notion of politics when she was nine, when a classmate told her, 'Mum says it's your fault that we've got no bread.' She did not understand that put-down until she learned that the Tip Top bread factory was on strike. On the other hand, at the age of 14, as a young communist, she enjoyed attending a children's camp on the Black Sea in Russia along with 10,000 other teenagers — 4000 Russians and 6000 from other countries, many of whom she recalled as having very sophisticated anti-capitalist beliefs. She learned about the 'revolution', as well as spending hours swimming, hiking and sailing. A highlight was a visit from premier Leonid Brezhnev, who addressed the young people. There was also hypocrisy. Some of the American kids tried to sell souvenirs — 'The American dream, I suppose,' Helen mused. She also learned that many of the Russians were not working class but the sons and daughters of party apparatchiks. Unlike the others, they received food parcels from home.[166]

None of the children had an issue with their father's career. He took them to stopwork meetings from an early age, and as a young boy John would sit under the table at the front of the meeting. Ken recalls taking Peter, when he was four, to a testy Drivers' Union meeting in Levin; when one of the drivers expressed displeasure towards the union — and Douglas — Peter put his arms through his father's legs and held on tight 'in protection'. The Maori drivers in particular loved the sense of solidarity being demonstrated by 'the young fella'.

Today Douglas is close to all of his children, and they all speak of their pride in his achievements. Jane's analysis is that he is an honest and passionate man — with love, hate, anger and joy in equal measure — who wore his heart on his sleeve. He respected others' points of view, believing that the truth was always 'expandable'.

John's earliest memory is acting as his father's caddy on the Titahi Golf Course around the age of seven and being paid the princely sum of one dollar for his labours. He says he always felt close to his father. For a time the two of them lived together in Wadestown, and, John says, his father took him to 'all the best restaurants, almost every night'. 'He has always confided in me. He trusts me more than anybody else; possibly because I live out of the country. He taught me to be positive, optimistic and to always be true to myself.'

However, Douglas was also a man of his time. Helen recalls that she never saw him go shopping with Lesley, make a bed, iron a shirt or cook a meal.

By the late 1970s there was increasing strain in the couple's relationship. Ken was away a lot and inattentive at times when he was at home, where union business continued on the telephone. Married young, they were growing apart. There was less and less mutual satisfaction and fulfilment in their relationship.

'I was arrogant,' Douglas later admitted. 'Lesley was the typical suburban widow. I'd get home from a union meeting tired, and all I'd want was to get in, have a feed and a shower, go to bed and get some sleep.' Lesley would want to talk about her day, and what the kids had been up to. I'd always say we'll talk about it tomorrow but, of course, tomorrow never came. She was a victim both of the times and of my insensitivity.'

Douglas was also having affairs. Women were attracted to him because of his power, energy, broad intellect, seemingly endless confidence and rough charm. Lesley had put up with his philandering for years. Douglas had been totally honest with her, and everybody else seemed to know about it as well. Titahi Bay was a small and, in some respects, an introverted community. 'A lot of people seemed to get a buzz out of telling us about it,' was Jane's memory. She wished she had not known.

When the break-up came in 1979, it seemed to Jane, who was 17, 'close to the end of the world'. The internal tensions and the stresses of torn loyalties were overpowering. Close to both parents, in different ways, she felt as if she was walking a tightrope. 'Mum was a proud woman and continued to hold her head up high, but she never got over it.' Peter's youthful mind reasoned that their separation was his fault, because he had been 'a naughty boy'. The truth dawned much later.

On the surface the parting was amiable — there were no histrionics — but Lesley was deeply hurt. She would have preferred to have continued to live with the pretences. But mere co-existence was not an option for Ken. Jane believed that her father was full of regret, although relations between the two of them remained strained after the divorce, and communication was largely conducted through the Socialist Unity Party.

Ken bought an apartment in Oban Street, Wadestown, where he lived, initially, with Elaine Dean after persuading her to leave her husband. He had got to know Elaine through the golf club, where they were both on the committee. But the relationship did not last. Ken spent six years in Oban Street, shifting out in 1986 and selling the apartment to Jane. By this time he was romantically involved with Marilyn Tucker, an Auckland-based pharmacist and SUP activist.

Tucker, who is 13 years younger than Douglas, was raised in Ponsonby, Auckland, and attended Richmond Road School and later Auckland Girls' Grammar School. She went on to train as a pharmacist in Petone, and has spent her professional life as a research pharmacist in hospitals and later as a clinical pharmacist working in mental health. Her political education began with the protests against the Vietnam War (and against the Soviet invasion of Czechoslovakia in 1968), although she did not join the SUP until 1972 after she had met and married Ian Tucker, a law student and party member. She describes her primary influences as study groups led by party member Peter Cross, and long discussions with Ken Perrott, a Hamilton-based scientist, and Douglas, who both stayed at the Tuckers' home during visits to Auckland. She separated from Ian Tucker in 1984 and later began a relationship with Douglas, moving to Wellington to join him in 1988. The two of them shared a two-storeyed house in Main Street, Titahi Bay, for 10 years before buying the house where they live today, overlooking the Titahi Bay beach at 8 View Road.

Lesley continued to live in the Opapa Street house until the children had all left home, later selling it to Helen. She purchased a small property near the grounds of Takapuwahia Marae in Te Arataura Street, Titahi Bay, where she lived until her death from cancer on 28 September 2006.[167]

Sport was Douglas's main passion outside work and family. For decades he played, coached and took various administrative roles. Rugby dominated in winter. He played for the Wellington College Old Boys Rugby Club (WCOB) for eight years, in teams that moved between the senior fourth and senior second divisions. Playing at prop, he was never quite big or 'mean' enough for promotion to the senior first team, although he was on its fringes as a reserve on many occasions. To 'bulk up' he spent hours weight-training at Koolman's Gym in Cuba Street, which he supplemented with a steady diet of glucose drinks and protein-rich foods. At the same time he coached lesser grade teams at Wellington College for a number of years, as well as primary school teams from Karori in Saturday morning competitions. Though he found it invigorating, behaviour of some of the parents who abused their own children and those from the opposing team angered him.

In 1959, Douglas helped lead the fundraising for a WCOB club gymnasium. At the end of the season he and Bill Wathey were each accorded a special vote of thanks for their efforts collecting 'contributions' from players on Saturday nights — 'strong-arming' donations has become a characteristic of Ken Douglas's modus operandi in all the sports clubs to which he has belonged. In 1961, in his second to last year at the club, he both played in and coached the WCOB's senior second team, taking it to the final of the National Mutual Cup. The club's historian recorded that Douglas displayed his usual enthusiasm, and 'nobody could have tried harder'.[168]

He had been elected to the WCOB club's committee in his second year out of school, and served on it for a number of years. He was also one of its delegates to the Wellington Rugby Union, and took a leading role both within and outside the club in opposing the non-selection of Maori for the All Black tour of South Africa in 1960. Within the club, he was instrumental in persuading members to vote by a majority to oppose the tour because of the South African government's insistence that no Maori be selected. The resolution was taken to the rugby union and seconded by the University Club, but it was not supported by other clubs and the proposal was lost.

In 1963, two years after he shifted to Titahi Bay, Douglas transferred his allegiance to the local club, playing for Titahi Bay in senior and junior teams every year for the next 16 years — many of them as captain. He retired at 44, though he says he would have liked to have played longer — he loved the physicality of the game and the after-match camaraderie. By then, however, he was secretary of the Federation of Labour and Jim Knox among others 'did not think it was a good look to be turning up to work on Monday mornings with black eyes and bruised knuckles'. He had not been at Titahi Bay long before he was elected onto the club's committee and became its delegate to the Rugby Union; after a couple of years he became chairman, retaining that role for 15 years between 1964 and 1979. The biggest campaign he led was trying to persuade the Wellington Rugby Union to amalgamate clubs in the northern region — Titahi Bay, Porirua and Paremata-Plimmerton — as each on its own was never strong enough to be competitive in Wellington's premier club competition. Today he recalls:

> People like Bob Scott and Murray Mexted would come down the motorway in their All Black blazers and cream off many of our top young players for their clubs, Petone and Tawa. We wanted the rugby union to introduce zoning to stop this snaffling of our young talent but the union wouldn't hear of it. So we led a revolt and established our own Western Bays representative team which played and beat both a Wellington Samoan and Wellington B team. We had discussions with the Horowhenua Union to accept this team in their competition. That did not materialise but it put the pressure on the Wellington Union to merge the northern clubs ...

Paremata-Plimmerton pulled out, but in 1989 Titahi Bay and Porirua amalgamated to become Northern United and Douglas soon became deputy president of the club. The local rugby youth have stayed with the team, and Northern United's success in Wellington's premier competition in recent years has been second to none. While Douglas has long retired from playing and more recently administering the game locally, he has kept close links with the club and others further afield, and today he sits on the board of the New Zealand Rugby Union.

Although Douglas played cricket as a schoolboy, and later with Wellington College Old Boys, where he played in the president's grade, the sport did not feature in his sights at Titahi Bay, where softball was stronger. He brought his usual commitment to this game, playing in the local club's senior team for seven years, being on its committee for most of that time, and acting as club captain for three years. For some years he coached the Titahi Bay women's premier team, and for two years he coached or co-coached the Wellington women's representative team. He also played other sports to a 'lesser standard', including wrestling — which he used as fitness training for rugby — and lawn bowls, from which he retired because of its 'mental strain', and for a short period was secretary of the local surf lifesaving club even though he could barely swim.

But his biggest commitment post-rugby has been to golf. After the Titahi Bay softball team had a winning season in 1967, coach Ken Lander organised a party and a nine-hole competition at the local golf club for the players. Douglas, who had never played golf, was quickly hooked, joining the club, as did 12 of the 13 other softballers, many of whom performed highly for the club in subsequent interclub competitions. Since then he has given 43 unbroken years of service to the nine-hole Titahi Golf Club — as an interclub player, as a mentor and coach to young players, most notably Michael Campbell, and as an administrator on numerous committees and sub-committees. He was first elected to the club's presidency in 1980, serving until 1984, and again from 1993 until the present, a record 18 years of unbroken leadership. In recent years he has guided the club to a more professional management footing with a new board structure and revamped constitution. He has led the club's long-term negotiations with the Whitireia Trust Board, the Department of Conservation, which manages the land, and Radio New Zealand, which owns masts on the course, with the aim of both ensuring the club's lease is safe for the future and enabling the development of an 18-hole course on the site and surrounding land.[169]

The Titahi Golf clubhouse has become Douglas's second home, particularly after his retirement from the Council of Trade Unions. Social occasions in his honour, such as birthday celebrations, are held there, and as well as his presidential duties he participates in working bees, fundraising and helping to organise club tournaments. Don McIvor, who joined the club in 1962 and is its longest-serving member, has worked, played and socialised with Douglas for decades. He describes Douglas's contribution to the club as unsurpassed: 'He has an ability to cut through the waffle and get to the point. He's been the principal mover and shaker in the club over the past 20 years. Of that there is no doubt.'[170]

CHAPTER 7

Red Ken

With union and Labour Party local body politics swirling round him in the family, Ken Douglas was politically aware from an early age. His grandfather George (Pop) Farrow's long involvement as Peter Fraser's electorate secretary in Wellington Central has already been noted. Closer to home, his uncle Bryce was for many years secretary of the Northland/Kelburn branch of the Labour Party, focusing principally on raising funds for the party at a local level, choosing and promoting party candidates for local councils — and the Wellington City Council — and supporting electorate candidates in national elections. All the other members of his family, apart from his paternal grandfather George Douglas, were members of the Labour Party. Both as a child, and later as a teenager, Ken Douglas spent considerable time selling raffle tickets for the party.

But Douglas was influenced by other events too. The first stirrings of his interest in communism date from the second world war when the family used to tune into the BBC and listen to how 'Uncle' Joe's brave soldiers were faring against the invading Nazis. Russian troops holding up the might of the German army during its siege of Stalingrad left on his young mind an indelible imprint of Stalin as a brave and fearless warrior, very appealing to a lad of nine or ten. Later he observed that the 'Red Square' waterside workers, who included his uncle Terry Farrow, were the men who provided the intellectual stimulation on the wharf, men who drove the political and industrial debate with clarity, intelligence and strength of purpose. As a very young man he was impressed by their 'seductive and simple' socialist analysis, and their concept of solidarity dovetailed neatly into ideas of the dignity and worth of labour, which in turn translated easily into an understanding of workers' rights.

Douglas stuck with this creed, and as he grew into adulthood Labour was never a serious option. By the early 1950s the party had long abandoned philosophy for pragmatism. It was hard, at this time, to discern a clear ideological distinction between the two main political parties, particularly in foreign policy. Disaffected left-wingers pointed to Labour's aggressive support for compulsory military training in 1949 as the clearest sign, among others, that it wanted to embrace without question the uncompromising anti-communist rhetoric of its new ally, the United States, in the burgeoning cold war. For both National and Labour, the spread of communism was a cancer to be exterminated in mid-stream. Both parties were preoccupied by its threat, real or imagined. Cabinet Minister Bob Semple's hard-hitting 1948 polemic *Why I Fight Communism* set a prejudicial standard for politicians on both sides of the House. Under Sidney Holland, who succeeded Peter Fraser in 1949 and became the first National Party prime minister, the Cold War took on an even more histrionic tone, quickly underscored by events in Korea as the 'red hordes' swept south over the 38th parallel.

For socialists looking for light in a world that seemed to be closing in around them, there was little genuine ideological delineation between

National and Labour. For the young Douglas, there were also 'closer to home' reasons for feelings of distaste towards Labour. The Wellington Drivers' Union had walked out of the Federation of Labour, and the Labour Party, in 1950 following the government's deregistration of the carpenters' union the previous year. The deregistration even upset Labour activists, including Douglas's uncle Bryce, who along with his grandfather Pop Farrow had been his most formative political influence through his adolescence. With his father and uncles active in the deregistered Wellington Drivers' Union before, during and after the 1951 lockout, Labour's equivocation — encapsulated in Walter Nash's infamous statement 'We are neither for them, nor against them' — left a very sour taste in Douglas's mouth.[171]

His political education was a personal journey, independent of family and, at least initially, of party. Based primarily on his own work/life experiences, his early class-based union politics were stimulated by humanitarian ideals rather than ideological dogma. Indeed, as has been seen, very early on he was as vigorously anti-communist as he was anti-Tory, believing communism was more about mind control than class liberation. For Ken Douglas, political 'education' was not a quick transition. Through his early twenties he was more interested in sport, setting up home with Lesley, and their growing family. In February 1959, when he became president of the Wellington Drivers' Union, he was firmly ensconced in the anti-communist camp, in implicit conflict with communist activists in the union and adhering to the notion, common among some unionists, that their paid officials were 'leeches on the backs of workers'. 'If anyone had asked me then who Karl Marx was I would have replied that he was probably Groucho's brother,' he told a journalist in 1983.[172]

But events in 1959 would change everything. His conversion had nothing to do with party politics or trade unionism. It was his love of playing rugby that was the stimulus for a more focused and proactive political stance, when he viewed with anger South Africa's refusal to allow the inclusion of Maori players in the All Black team to tour the republic in 1960, and the New Zealand Rugby Football Union's acquiescence in that refusal. 'I'd been to school with excellent people such as Paul Henare, Kingi Grace and Frank Waiapu. It was shocking to learn that suddenly they did not have the same rights as I had,' Douglas recalls.

Communism's initial appeal was emotional, not intellectual. He joined the New Zealand Communist Party (NZCP) in 1960 not because of a deep philosophical understanding of what Marx was talking about. Rather it 'was the emotive appeal; the search for a sharing, caring society, a valuation of people for what they contributed rather than what they took out of society. It really centred around this question of our relationship with colour — the rights of blacks and Maori. It seemed quite obscene for the world to have gone through the process of defeating fascism in the Second World War, to see those very same ingredients that fascism represented still existing and being supported by the capitalist system.' He could see that the New Zealand Communist Party was the only party taking a proactive stand against the tour — true to form, Walter Nash, now Prime Minister, equivocated at first, then sanctioned it.[173]

On Friday nights, when both Ken and Lesley promoted the Citizens' All Blacks Tour Association's (CABTA) anti-tour petition in Chews Lane, he was often challenged by senior rugby players who were pro-tour. Knowing him well as a prop for Wellington College Old Boys, and often the worse for wear as they staggered out of pubs at six o'clock, they would challenge him to defend his views, sometimes physically. Douglas fought fire with fire, promising to retaliate 'with interest' if any off- or on-field hostility came his way. 'When we met again on the paddock some of them got their comeuppance,' he recalls ruefully. Sometimes the arguments could be heard from one end of Chews Lane to the other. These debates had the advantage of drawing more people to the noise and therefore closer to the table, perhaps to sign the petition. It was most unusual for a senior club rugby player to take such an assertive anti-tour stance in 1960, as it was for the capital's truck drivers, who 'loved their footy'.

Douglas's activism represented a remarkable willingness from an early age to swim against the tide (he was 24 at this time) and risk losing friends among both his driving and his rugby-playing mates, although the Wellington Drivers' Union itself (of which Douglas was then president) was a solid supporter of the 'No Maoris — No Tour' campaign. Many doubters came to respect his stand, but how many changed their minds is hard to ascertain. As far as Douglas was concerned the issue was hugely important, and he was later appointed to the CABTA executive as the FOL representative.[174]

Philosophical understanding came later. Subsequent reading of Marxist philosophy provided him with an intellectual context within which he was able to gain a clearer understanding of racism both within South Africa and in New Zealand. Marxism, as he continued to study it, gave him a framework within which he could see a society being fairly built for the benefit of all rather than torn down for the benefit of the exploiters. He believed that it gave the best chance for workers to be empowered and for class divisions to melt away in silent revolution. The more Douglas read and listened, the more he determined that communism must not be just an armchair philosophy. He needed to live and breathe it. His biggest early influence was Chip Bailey, who took him to his first party meetings. There, he participated in study groups where George Jackson, Jack Manson, George Goddard and Hughie McLeod were formative influences. They encouraged him to read Marxist-Leninist tracts, absorb as much as he could, ask questions, and prepare papers for discussion, particularly on communism's philosophical relationship and application to New Zealand industry and workers' rights.

When Douglas joined the Communist Party he was asked whether in the current political climate and Cold War atmosphere he wished to have his membership publicly identified. In his eyes, the question was meaningless. It was morally important for him to be recognised as a communist. He was proud of it; he would not have joined the party otherwise. Belonging to the party gave substance and structure to political thoughts that up until then had been disparate and uncoordinated. He wanted to learn a lot more, and becoming a 'reading' Marxist enabled him to fill the intellectual gap that was the outcome of his laziness at school and lack of formal education.

The New Zealand Communist Party that Ken Douglas joined in 1960 had been in existence for 39 years, having evolved from a Marxian Association into a fully fledged if small political party by 1921. It did not emerge in a vacuum. Political and industrial radicalism had percolated the New Zealand psyche over the previous two decades in many contrasting, although often interrelated, forms. At its formation, the party promised a purposeful ideological organisation bent on workers' revolution and the overthrow of the capitalist state, to be replaced by a socialist nirvana within which workers would control their own destinies. But the party would never be a large or influential group, being hindered as it grew by factionalism, ego-driven power struggles, ideological differences and splits. It demanded an exacting price for membership — total obedience to its tenets and the ability to work hard, and be seen to work hard, for the party. In 1928 there were just 61 members, 28 of whom were miners — the party's headquarters for a brief period were at Blackball on the West Coast.[175]

By the 1930s the party's organisation was more unified, cohesive and structured, stimulated by the unemployment, poverty and social dysfunction prevalent among working people during the Great Depression. In its early days it had founded the Unemployed Workers' Movement, which became influential, attracting many of the country's dispossessed and poor to its ranks as activists. As the numbers of unemployed soared, recruitment to the party escalated. Nationally and internationally communism flourished among the disaffected, often led by Marxian-inspired middle-class intellectuals. In New Zealand, the state blamed communists for the rioting and looting that erupted in 1932; this led to repressive legislation, followed by police persecution, harsh prison sentences and job dismissals. At the end of the Depression the membership of the party was 300, but it could claim 36 Trades Council delegates among its members as well as six full-time union officials. But the success of Labour at the 1935 elections and the atmosphere of renewed hope that engendered led many in the working class to abandon communism. The party lost support and influence. A portent of things to come was the Communist Party's call for voters to invalidate their votes rather than vote for Labour.

The impact of Russia's heroic resistance to the German onslaught in World War II, alongside New Zealand communists' overt support for the patriotic effort from 1941, stimulated growth in the party and increased its influence in the trade union movement. In 1945/46 the party had a membership of 2000 and a journal circulation of 14,000. It won 3 per cent of the vote in the general election of 1946, the most ever, before or since. In the 1947 local body elections, George Jackson, Arthur Jackson-Thomas and Vic Wilcox won 9666 votes among them for the Auckland City Council, and Connie Birchfield won 6618 for the Wellington City Council. Although none was elected, these results represent the party's highest point in terms of acceptability. Between that time and the 1951 lockout, communists dominated the Auckland Trades Council leadership, and they became more prominent in other unions, notably the Tramways, Drivers', Carpenters' and Railways unions.

The Cold War brought a change. Massive anti-communist propaganda, along with the defeat of the carpenters' strike in 1949 and more particularly the smashing of the waterfront union in 1951, divided and weakened trade unionism. The right was in the ascendant in the Federation of Labour under trenchant anti-communist Fintan Patrick Walsh's autocratic leadership. Already entrenched ideological differences were exacerbated in the 1950s. Both the National government and the Labour opposition treated the party with derision and fear, and it turned its simmering ideological tensions in on itself as a damaging power struggle over the party's direction emerged between general secretary Vic Wilcox and his predecessor Sid Scott.

The fuse burst into flame after the Soviet invasion of Hungary in 1956. Stalinism in practice was exposed to the world as light-years distant from Marxist theory. Many who condemned the Soviet action as Russian imperialism defected, including the bulk of the intelligentsia. Scott was expelled from the party. Others like Wilcox viewed the Russian invasion as necessary to protect Hungary from the 'dark forces of capitalism', exemplified by Senator Joseph McCarthy's anti-communist witch-hunts in the United States. The following years would see a continuation of the factionalism, and the manipulative politicking, as party members continued to resign or were fired for questioning the rigid party line laid down from the top. Russian leader Nikita Khrushchev's dramatic exposure of Stalin's 'crimes' in 1957 and Mao Tse Tung's address to the Communist International the same year revealed for the first time the ideological differences between the Chinese and Russian delegates and their acolytes. In 1960, Fintan Walsh asked Ken Douglas — whom he had grown to respect — why he 'wanted to throw his lot in with the Commies' and told him he would arrange for Douglas to be given an American Field Scholarship if he changed his mind. Douglas refused, telling him that his family would disown him if he did.[176]

In 1963, as the 'pro-Sino' faction assumed ascendancy in the New Zealand Communist Party, men who would later become leaders in the Socialist Unity Party lost their positions. George Jackson was dumped as the party's chairman and Bruce Skilton lost his place on the national committee. These men, and others who favoured Soviet communism, were denigrated as revisionists. Members of branches in Auckland, Christchurch and Lyttelton, and the whole breakaway Dunedin branch, were expelled or walked away from the party, many claiming the leadership was too manipulative.

By this time Douglas had been in the party for three years. For him, too, there were portents of change. The intellectual base which had provided him with the impetus to join the party — with its 'command' culture and preoccupation with discipline — began to fade as the reality of Chinese politics became evident. He believed it was becoming a party of cant and rhetoric, where thousands of people sang slogan-filled songs in praise of Mao, songs which, however, had no relevance to Chinese workers. He recalls standing early in 1964, at the door of a plane which had just landed at Shanghai Airport with a party delegation fresh from a peace conference in Japan, and watching hundreds of seven- to eight-year-old children waving flags in unison and singing patriotic songs. With the delegation was Lu Ning Ye, vice-president of the all-China Unions. Douglas turned to Lu and asked him what was going on. He was told that the children were here to honour him, as the New Zealand Communist Party was the only one in the Western world to continue to support China after its ideological split with Russia.

Douglas was aggrieved by this display. There was a knot in his stomach. These kids, he told his host, would not even know where New Zealand was, let alone understand any of the issues. They were fodder for a political force of which they had no understanding. By this time, the New Zealand Communist Party had divided over the growing philosophical gulf between the two superpowers. As party leaders like Victor Wilcox remained loyal to China, Douglas joined the majority of local members who split away to form the Socialist Unity Party, which pledged its allegiance to Russia, now estranged from its former ally.

The New Zealand Socialist Unity Party (SUP) was formed in Auckland on 1–2 October 1966, with Alex Drennan, an Auckland waterside and Communist Party member since 1929, elected as its first national president and George Jackson as secretary. The party was formed because, as Jackson said at the time, 'the NZCP was following a non-Marxist idcology which was based on nationalism, petit bourgeois adventurism and anti-Sovietism. The leadership of the Communist Party of China had shifted from a Marxist position to one of national petit bourgeois capitalism.'[177]

Some months earlier, on 24 January, Jackson, Drennan, Bill Andersen, Ella Ayo, Peter Cross and Ernie Miller, Auckland party members, had issued a press statement announcing their resignations from the Communist Party. In a foretaste of the deep antipathy that would emerge between the rival groups, the *People's Voice* commented, 'Far from deploring the loss of members [of the CPNZ] we will be pleased that at last the Party is rid of an internal abscess fed with the infection of imperialist and revisionist ideas. The body of the Party will be healthier as a result . . . In fact it is good riddance . . .'[178].

Douglas, by then a key figure in the Wellington branch of the

Communist Party, resigned from the party following the publication of the January statement and was later instrumental in setting up the Wellington branch of the SUP. The party soon became known colloquially as 'the Church', a reference to the fact that of the 17 members of the Wellington District Council of the Communist Party who joined the SUP, 16 were ex-Catholics. The behaviour of this group and the SUP as a whole was often likened to the structure and, tongue-in-cheek, the manners of a church. The name stuck. Douglas liked it; other members proudly identified with it. It was a point of difference.

In June 1983, Douglas explained why he had joined the Socialist Unity Party:

> The Communist Party had believed in the early 1930s, and even later, that the main blow should be against social democracy. It saw the Labour Party as the enemy, not capital or monopolies. This concept led to all sorts of sectarian actions by communist parties all over the world — driven by the Comintern — that damaged the unity of the working class and in particular, of the trade union movement. But the day to day things that related to the New Zealand lifestyle were incompatible with my experience as a worker and union official. It seemed that they spoke about unity yet acted to create disunity.[179]

The other major driver, he believed, was an understanding of the Marxist process of analysis, known as dialectical materialism, where adherents studied everything in terms of its material development, attempting to understand its contradictions — because in every sphere there was a positive and a negative. 'It's not just thought. You have to distinguish what is real and what is not.'[180]

Part of the distinction between the SUP and its predecessor was its members' wish that it remain as relevant within the New Zealand context as possible. It refused to carry over many of international communism's 'commandist' symbols. Thus, it established a national executive, not a politburo; it established a national committee in lieu of a central committee, and it organised and ran national conferences rather than congresses. Having said that, members formally addressed each other as comrades, and 'cadres' were appointed sporadically for specific tasks. Throughout much of the 1970s Douglas was the party's fundraising cadre, and addressed as such.

The SUP had an initial membership of 60, including nearly all of the country's communist trade unionists. The party used its members' organising experience to recruit members, principally from groups with which it had links — overt or covert — such as the NZ-USSR Friendship Society, the Chile Solidarity Community and the Young Workers' Alliance. Members were also recruited through party involvement in anti-nuclear, peace and anti-apartheid protests and unions themselves. As a group, the new party took a stance on many of the issues of the day — protesting against the May 1968 nil wage order, opposing the Vietnam War, becoming involved with the Campaign Against Rising Prices, protesting against French nuclear testing in the South Pacific, renewing May Day celebrations, and supporting Maori issues, which culminated in the land march of 1975 and the Bastion Point occupation two years later. (Some time later, SUP unionists led the debate within the FOL to establish a Maori Committee and Pacific Island fono to encourage greater Polynesian involvement and stimulate awareness of historic land grievances.)

These issues were clear-cut and SUP members marched in sync, both physically and politically, with thousands of other New Zealanders who felt strongly about them. Reflecting the principles of fairness, equity and humanitarianism, these same New Zealanders supported a more tolerant Czechoslovak political order during the 1968 'Prague Spring' under which leader Alexander Dubček loosened the strings of that country's totalitarian regime to allow greater freedom of expression in public and the toleration of political and social organisations not under communist control. Such liberality was too much for Czechoslovakia's Soviet overlords, however, and in August that year Russian tanks rolled into Prague, shut down the city's 'revisionist' radio, television and newspapers, rounded up and incarcerated dissidents, removed Dubček from office and had him locked up in a Russian prison. In protest at Dubček's treatment, a small number of the 80 or so then in the SUP left the party in disgust. The party's leadership described their departure thus: 'Later that year [1968] when the Warsaw Pact countries moved to the support of the Czech communists some, especially new members, lacked the class understanding to grasp the significance of events in Czechoslovakia and fell away, but the newly formed organisation was not deflected . . .'[181]

Even though Ken Douglas was always careful to separate his political beliefs from his trade union practice, sometimes this nexus, which was not watertight at the best of times, rebounded on him. He faced the Czechoslovak crisis head on at the FOL's national conference in April 1969 where, from the floor, Tony Neary, secretary of the Northern Electrical and Electronic Workers' Union, proposed a motion that the 'free' trade union movement throughout the world condemn the August 1968 invasion of Czechoslovakia by the Soviet Union. This was a reaffirmation of an earlier Wellington Trades Council motion which, in turn, reaffirmed a long-standing FOL policy regarding the rights of self-determination of all people. The Trades Council resolved to support the right of the Czechoslovakian people to determine their own economic, social and political form of society and their efforts to develop and protect the Czechoslovak Socialist Republic. It viewed Russia's 'act of aggression' as a threat to peace and security everywhere as well as a denial of the principles of democratic socialism, and called upon the invading nation to withdraw its troops immediately. President Tom Skinner agreed, stating that the FOL had a responsibility to endorse a motion long passed at its conference that there be 'no interference by any nation in the right of any country to determine its own way of life without any interference from outside'.[182]

Douglas wanted to downplay the event. He proposed a motion that the New Zealand FOL delegates to the forthcoming International Labour Organisation conference in Geneva (Skinner and Jim Knox) 'be called upon to refer the whole question of the Warsaw Pact countries' invasion of Czechoslovakia to the trade union centres of Czechoslovakia and the

Soviet Union and report to the National Council of the FOL and request the Council to make an appropriate statement on their findings'. The conference disagreed. Douglas's motion was defeated, and Neary's succeeded.[183]

In 1972, to publicise its beliefs, the party stood candidates for the general election in four electorates. Douglas, standing in Porirua, received just 68 votes. In a mood for change, working people overwhelmingly supported Labour, which was returned to power for the first time since 1957. 'National politics was not for me,' Douglas reflected. 'Mickey Mouse, leader of the Mad Hatters Tea Party, got more than I did in Feilding!'[184]

Yet Douglas stood again in 1975. The party's stated objectives this time were to return the Labour government, keep the National Party out, and advance its own policy and seek members' and supporters' votes in safe seats. Members were chosen to stand in 15 seats where Labour was either not expected to lose or not expected to win. The public's response was disappointing. Douglas collected 46 votes, 22 fewer than in 1972. Yet his vote was the highest, the other 14 SUP candidates each securing between 14 and 39 votes. That the SUP was a 'specialist' organisation in the public mind was the most optimistic conclusion. Even that was euphemistic.[185]

Douglas tried a third time in 1978. This time he was more widely known as president of the Drivers' Federation, secretary of the Wellington Drivers' Union, secretary of the Wellington Trades Council, an executive member of the FOL, chairman of the Wellington Branch of the SUP, and member of its national committee. He only garnered 70 votes. He did not stand in 1981, just five party members did. Andersen won 188 in Tamaki at his fourth try, the highest of any SUP candidate in any election. In Douglas's place, John van der Ven won 52 in Porirua.[186]

Through the 1970s the national executive met four times a year. Regional committees met much more often; in Auckland the committee met once a month. The party's main income, details of which were closely guarded, came from sales of the fortnightly publication *The Tribune* (which, at its peak, had a print run of 2500), subscriptions and donations from members. Members also ran raffles and socials. Every member played an active role in the organisation. All were required to read books and articles espousing Marxist/Leninist philosophy, make vocal or written contributions from their reading at meetings, in newsletters or in *The Tribune*, prepare and participate in group discussions, as well as making financial contributions to the party on top of their subscriptions. 'Laziness' was not an option.[187]

True to their central tenet of 'democratic centralism', debate inside the meetings was open and vigorous. Consensus was important, however, and to the outside world the SUP always presented a united face, at least until 1990 when Bill Andersen resigned.

Robert Muldoon's election as Prime Minister in November 1975 brought the Socialist Unity Party a new level of notoriety — or fame — in the public's eyes. Muldoon was fixated with the SUP in general, and Bill Andersen in particular. In 1976, he told the press that a campaign to 'destroy' the government's stabilisation policy had been orchestrated 'to a considerable degree' by the SUP. In July 1977, Muldoon, without evidence, accused Andersen of being 'the sinister figure' behind the Bastion Point Maori land protests. In October that year, he considered banning the party because of its 'undue influence' in industrial unrest. Early in 1978, he again accused Andersen of using the trade union movement for his own 'nefarious' political ends.

Not many people had the audacity to 'rark up' Muldoon, but Andersen did. Sometimes on Monday mornings they shared the same flight from Auckland to Wellington, and a smiling Andersen would pass a seated Muldoon and proffer a friendly 'Good morning comrade' to his nemesis. Muldoon clenched his fists but said nothing. One time, in 1977, after Andersen had got the better of the Prime Minister in a televised debate, he leaned across to Muldoon in the plane and asked him when he was going to meet him again in the studio. Muldoon growled that Andersen and the SUP already had enough publicity. That was true, but what Muldoon failed to acknowledge was that he was the cause. His attacks on the tiny party gave it publicity beyond its wild imaginings, and membership grew exponentially through this period.[188]

The SUP gave Muldoon the excuse in 1977 to introduce a Bill which gave the Security Intelligence Service (SIS) extraordinary powers to 'hear, listen to, record or acquire' any information that it was authorised to secure under a warrant issued by any Minister of the Crown. Not only did the Security Intelligence Service Amendment Bill permit telephone tapping and the opening of mail, but it also allowed the SIS to do 'any reasonable act' — which could include burglary, intimidation or even the use of physical violence. The ability for agents to break into a desk in a house, and rifle through and photograph papers and diaries, were among specific clauses in the Bill. It also stopped anyone apart from the warrant-issuing Minister speaking out about what these agents were doing. All organisations and individuals, including the press and trade unions, were subject to fines of up to $2000 or imprisonment for two years for disclosing any information about SIS activities. The Bill also contained a clause whereby state servants could be ordered to help the SIS if they were directed by a warrant signed by the Minister. This caused ructions within the Post Office Association, which at its 1977 conference passed a resolution 'totally opposing telephone tapping and mail interception'. It resolved henceforth that its members would refuse to undertake such proposals. Post Office managers themselves believed that employees could not refuse to do the bugging — if they did they faced suspension.[189]

The Bill caused widespread protests. The Labour Party fought it clause by clause in the House — Mangere MP David Lange the most outspoken — but it was not taken to a select committee which meant that the public could not make submissions. This led a number of lawyers and at least one Supreme Court judge to call it a 'very sorry example of subservience to the executive'. Maverick National MP Mike Minogue criticised some of its provisions, including the power of the Minister to issue interception warrants, causing Muldoon's wrath to come down upon his head.[190]

Muldoon erroneously accused the SUP of leading the campaign against the Bill — President George Jackson was flattered, but the accusation was far off the mark. The SUP was just one of 66 organisations, representing civil liberty groups, trade unions, the FOL, church groups, law societies, journalists, city councils, opposition politicians, peace groups, the Workers' Educational Association, and university and high school students and their associations, to actively opposed the measure. In September 1977 many of these groups formed an umbrella pressure group called Oasis (Organisation Against the Security Intelligence Service Amendment Bill), and it organised rallies, protest marches, community meetings, sit-ins, pickets, street theatre performances and newsletter drops all over the country. On 14 October, 15,000 protesters marched in a rally against the Bill to the SIS's Wellington headquarters. It was all to no avail. The government had the numbers in Parliament and the measure passed into law.[191]

There was a close relationship between the SUP and the Soviet Embassy in Wellington. Douglas was on first-name terms with Soviet diplomats and often attended their functions, overindulging in vodka at times. In its first 11 years the SUP sent more than 60 members to the USSR, usually in five-strong 'party to party' delegations. The Soviet Embassy funded these visits. But their purpose was not to enable the participants to learn subversion techniques or industrial sabotage, as Muldoon and other National Party members claimed. Most trips consisted of endless rounds of party congresses, visits to factories and collective farms, dinners with local party apparatchiks and trade union leaders, and free medical checks in sanatoria and treatment in hospitals if required. Douglas made the first of his many trips to Russia in 1970. In 1975, his uncle Terry Farrow, along with Ron Black, an Auckland seaman, and Vic Beganovic, an Auckland taxi driver, participated in an SUP veterans' delegation to Russia for three months' travel, rest and health treatment paid for by the Central Committee of the Communist Party, the Soviet Union's ruling body. Farrow expressed surprise at the hospitality, recorded with delight the funding he received, and took pleasure in the free doctors' visits.[192]

Such visits occasioned a dramatic and ridiculous resonance in January 1980 when Muldoon expelled Soviet ambassador Vsevolod

Sofinsky from New Zealand for allegedly handing over money to the SUP — just days after a Russian journalist, Sergei Zimin, was told to leave the country after being accused of spying. 'I have not the slightest doubt that the Soviet Embassy has been financing the SUP for a very long time and it is subject to direction from Moscow — the personal involvement of the ambassador shows that this was official Soviet policy,' Muldoon told the press.[193]

It was more than just air tickets to the Soviet Union, Muldoon claimed, but rather a sum estimated to be around $10,000. He maintained the grant had been revealed through electronic bugging of an Auckland meeting between Sofinsky and 'a leading SUP official' — later revealed to be George Jackson. This money, it was alleged, had been supplied by Sofinsky so that the SUP 'could meet its Christmas expenses'. Sofinsky flatly denied ever giving money to the SUP, calling the allegations scandalous and absolutely false, contending they were more akin to something emanating from a 'satirical or science fiction magazine'.

Sofinsky believed Muldoon had been deceived by dishonest people pursuing their own ends — those who expressed dissatisfaction about improving relationships between New Zealand and the Soviet Union. He had met Ken Douglas two or three times, and Bill Andersen just once during his 10 months in New Zealand. It was no secret that the Soviet Embassy provided airfares or money for members to attend party conferences, cultural events or medical appointments, or to stay at holiday resorts, but this was a long way from spying. Jackson also denied receiving any money, stating that all he had received from the ambassador was a bottle of vodka for Christmas. So had Muldoon, it was later revealed.[194]

Sofinsky left New Zealand on 27 January, but the debate did not end there. Commentators predicted that New Zealand could face severe retaliation for the action as Sofinsky's twin brother was a member of the Central Committee. This proved to be the case, and within days the Soviet government had expelled Jim Weir, New Zealand's ambassador in Moscow.

By the late 1970s there were significant numbers of SUP members in union leadership positions, although they never became a dominant force. Aside from Douglas, Bill Andersen was secretary of the Northern Drivers' and the Auckland Engine Drivers', Firemen's and Greasers' Unions, and president of the Auckland Trades Council. Tom Downey and John Willis were Northern Drivers' Union organisers. Party co-founder Bruce Skilton retained the presidency of the nightwatchmen's section of the Seamen's Union, while Mike Jackson was secretary of the Auckland Storemen and Packers' Union. Until he was deposed in April 1977, Tom Spiller was president of both the Auckland and the National Tramways Unions. Bob Masefield was vice-president of the Auckland Tramways Union, and before his retirement in February 1978 Frank McNulty was secretary of the New Zealand Meatworkers' Union. Others such as Richie Gillespie, the closest of Douglas's longtime colleagues in the Wellington Drivers' Union, Joe Tonner, Joe Te Pania and Simon Wallace all held senior positions in different unions at various times.

Appointees to senior roles in the Federation of Labour/Council of Trade Unions and associated bodies were chosen democratically. There was a perception among some non-communist unionists that Douglas used his influence to have SUP operatives put in senior positions, such as Te Pania's appointment to a leadership role at the Trade Union Education Authority (TUEA) whose board Douglas chaired. Douglas was accused of nepotism, but it was an unenlightened allegation. All appointees to the TUEA, and other union organisations associated with the CTU, were chosen by its board after a recommendation from its director following advertisements and interviews.

The claims of partiality were probably related to the SUP's secrecy in certain areas. For example, membership figures were hard to verify as the SUP never released names or numbers for fear of retribution from the SIS, but it was unlikely that there were any more than 70 rank-and-file communists out of the thousands of members in the 60 or more trade unions. The party asked two things of its union members: that they accepted its creed, and were active in putting it into practice. For most this meant being active at the delegate and trades council level.

With these numbers they could never dominate a union, and in many other key and/or 'militant' blue-collar unions, such as carpenters, boilermakers, watersiders, freezing workers, seafarers and timber workers, communists were noticeable by their absence.

The challenges Douglas faced as an SUP leader were more pertinent within the union movement than outside it. There was conflict and nearly blood on the floor at the 1978 FOL conference when Douglas and Andersen challenged a report by secretary Jim Knox — based on reports by officials of the International Labour Organisation (ILO) and the International Confederation of Free Trade Unions (ICFTU) — that condemned the communist-led Ethiopian government for assassinating trade union leaders and oppressing unions and their members. Andersen argued that the report was erroneous, being based on false information supplied by the CIA. In addition, he said, information published by Amnesty International — also included in the Knox report — was based on reports from Reuters, 'that well-known capitalist press agency'. Knox's report urged the conference to sanction a delegation to undertake an on-the-spot study in Ethiopia.[195]

Douglas's position was that while it was proper for the FOL to take a stand against worker oppression, this should only be done after a close assessment of the facts. Such oppression was not evident in Ethiopia, as the political situation was the consequence of a widespread people's revolution. 'The working people are now in control in the country,' he claimed. But after a tense, sometimes hostile debate on the floor, Douglas's and Andersen's attempts to persuade the conference to overturn acceptance of the Knox report failed in a hand vote, assessed at being around 70 per cent of the delegates. The debate had erupted after FOL president Tom Skinner attacked the attitudes of the two men. Criticising delegates for allowing ideology to endanger trade union solidarity, Skinner said he was 'amazed' that Knox's integrity should be questioned. 'Whether the delegates like it or not Mr Knox has come to us with a truthful and honest report of what is happening in Ethiopia. If we take action against it we will also be voting against the integrity of the ILO and ICFTU.'

Press reports gloated in the defeat. 'Socialist Unity Party supporters left licking their wounds after being resoundingly defeated,' crowed the *New Zealand Herald*'s industrial reporter. 'Reds beaten in terror vote . . . Atrocities are okay with some FOL members — but only when they're committed by Moscow-aligned countries and abetted by the KGB!' raged *Truth*. At the same time, it was noteworthy that the FOL reaffirmed its long-standing trade ban with Chile, imposed after a junta of army officers led by General Augustin Pinochet overthrew the democratically elected left-leaning government of Salvador Allende in 1973 — and executed him — with CIA help, even though it had meant the loss of work for members.[196]

In the wash, Douglas's personal integrity was not challenged. For many years denied a place on the national executive because of his own politics, in 1977 he had been elected by just one vote. This year, however, he romped home with 523 votes, just 10 behind the leading vote-scorer, the respected Ted Thompson. By now Douglas was secretary of the Wellington Drivers' Union, president of the New Zealand Drivers' Federation and secretary of the Wellington Trades Council. He had intruded into trade union politics more than any other SUP leader. But he always argued that the policies — and the politics — he pursued in the unions, the federation, the trades council and the FOL were in accord with the policies of those organisations. It was remarkable how closely aligned SUP policies were — particularly after Douglas ascended to the leadership of the FOL and CTU — with the policies of those organisations. There was mostly unanimity. Both the FOL and the SUP were active in a range of political causes, and Douglas could choose which hat to wear.[197]

His most scathing antagonist within the FOL was the uncompromising anti-communist Tony Neary. In January 1980 he attacked Douglas, now secretary of the FOL, for justifying the Russian invasion of Afghanistan, which Neary called 'blatant aggression'. Douglas, in Napier to negotiate a drivers' award, refused to engage in a slanging match with Neary — instead inviting observers to wonder at the hypocrisy of condemning Russia for this action and not Turkey, which now occupied about 40 per cent of Cyprus after an invasion. 'In spite of Commonwealth and United Nations calls the New Zealand government did not impose sanctions against Turkey,' he said. For his part, Jim Knox believed that Russia should withdraw its troops immediately.[198]

The Afghanistan issue did have the potential to cause a nasty split within the FOL and its affiliate unions; Bill Andersen was also outspoken in support of the Russian invasion. On 29 January 1980, its executive met to discuss it. Following this meeting, Knox produced a press statement to the effect that the FOL was critical of the Soviet military presence in Afghanistan as it was a serious threat to world peace and a violation of the territorial sovereignty of a small nation. Possibly to deflect internal conflict, the FOL executive resolved to send a representative to assess the situation in Afghanistan for itself. This was pie-in-the-sky, however, and did not eventuate.[199]

Douglas and Knox were at loggerheads on this issue. Wearing his SUP hat, Douglas publicly supported the Russian military presence in Afghanistan because 'its forces were invited to be there . . . a friendship treaty did exist between the two countries which promised that the Soviet Union would give military support to protect Afghanistan's territorial and national sovereignty if requested. It had been requested three times in the past but only on the last time did Russia act,' he claimed.[200]

But led by Knox, the FOL executive condemned the invasion and called for the withdrawal of Soviet armed forces from the country. The invasion, it said in a statement to the press, was a serious threat to world peace and a violation of the territorial sovereignty of a small nation. The executive was reaffirming its long-standing policy of the right to self-determination and non-interference in the internal affairs of all countries and peoples. The FOL had consistently upheld the right of the people of any nation to work out their political future without outside interference, the most recent examples being Vietnam and Chile. It called for diplomatic initiatives to ease the tension and possible military escalation in Afghanistan. Andersen abstained from voting on this issue in the FOL's policy committee, as he did again when the measure was brought before the 1980 national conference. Douglas was silent on the matter.[201]

Within months there was more friction between Douglas and Knox. In August 1980, 50,000 Polish workers went on strike for 10 days in the port city of Gdansk. Principal among their grievances was a demand for the country's trade unions to be free of political control by Poland's communist government. Knox and the FOL executive came out in support of these workers but, as he had learned to be in these situations, Douglas was diplomatically circumspect. Refusing an earlier request from a delegation representing the Polish Association of New Zealand for FOL solidarity with the Polish workers he said, disingenuously, that these workers did not live under the same kind of repressive regime that existed in Muldoon's New Zealand. 'It's just a matter of political opinion,' he said. Tony Neary called for Douglas's resignation. Fellow unionists requested a 'please explain' from him. Others brushed it off, commenting that Douglas was speaking as a member of the SUP, not the FOL.

In an implicit rebuff to Douglas, the FOL executive warned affiliates not to make statements on Poland that were outside FOL policy and could be used by the media to 'split and divide' the organisation and take it away from the mainstream business of furthering the interests of New Zealand workers. Having said this, on 25 August, Douglas and Knox put their joint signatures to a cable sent to the secretary of the Central Council of the Polish Trade Unions which said 'The NZFOL wishes to advise support and solidarity with Polish workers in their struggle for improved living standards and strengthened role of trade unions. We urge early resolvement in interests of Polish people and working class.'[202]

In stark contrast, in a report for its sixth triennial conference in 1982, the SUP made it very clear where it stood on Poland, asserting:

> Imperialism felt sure that its many years of subversive activities in socialist Poland were going to bear fruit . . . so when the

> patriotic forces of Poland took strong decisive action to prevent the planned counter-revolutionary takeover, imperialism's wrath knew no bounds. Once more the Soviet Union was singled out for boycott action by the US administration which demanded that its allies follow suit . . . All of this meant that the class enemy was able to seize on a combination of factors such as a strong sense of nationalism, the entrenched ideological position of the church, and the economic difficulties which arose from the disparity of building a modern industrial base and retention of the backward system of agriculture.

But there was hope. The report continued:

> We side with the Polish people in overcoming the mistakes of the past. We are on their side in defending the socialist system which has brought them out of the backward past more than any other period in Poland's history. We oppose the enemies of Poland because they are the enemies of progressive humanity. We do not expect to win to our position their enemies in New Zealand. We do believe that New Zealand people when they can hear the true position will respond to the side of the Polish people . . .[203]

As discussed more fully in the following chapter, Douglas's primary responsibility, often expressed in debates such as these, was to his professional role as a union leader, not to his politics. But he was always curious. Earlier that year, in February, Douglas had travelled to Cuba with three other trade unionists to attend a World Federation of Trade Unions (WFTU) conference which was also attended by a delegation from Poland, so he could 'find out what was happening there'. Travelling with him were Paul Piesse, secretary of the Canterbury Storemen and Packers' Union, Gus Ricketts, secretary of the Kaimai Trades Committee, and Larry Sutherland, executive member of the Nelson Trades Council (and later, a Labour MP), none of whom were communists. Later Douglas would represent the Oceania Region on the ICFTU executive, sometimes sitting next to Lech Walesa, the leader of Poland's 'Solidarity' movement, and from 1990 the country's president. The two men chatted amicably.[204]

Despite the visit being sanctioned by both the FOL's executive and the National Council, Douglas immediately ran into flak from Neary who stated, correctly, that the WFTU was a communist-dominated body and Douglas's attendance a 'breach of FOL policy because we dissociated ourselves from them in 1949 when it came under the control of the Russian bloc countries'. '[Douglas] was attempting to hoodwink trade unionists and the public,' Neary believed. The controversy was exacerbated by reports that Poland's communist government was still cracking down hard on the Solidarity workers' movement. Individual union leaders had already expressed outrage at the state's treatment of these workers, and the International Transport Workers' Federation had told its affiliated New Zealand unions (seamen, waterside workers, harbour board workers, cooks and stewards, the merchant officers' guild and the marine engineers' institute) to be ready to act against Polish shipping and aircraft. Predictably, Muldoon criticised the visit but Knox defended it. Two remits at FOL conferences in 1974 and 1975 supported continued FOL contact with the WFTU.[205]

In October 1982, the New Zealand Polish Association invited the FOL to participate in its protest action to mark the first anniversary of the introduction of martial law in Poland on 13 December 1981. The FOL executive declined to take part, but Douglas wrote to all affiliates, trade union councils and committees allowing them to support and participate in such activities as long as it was in line with FOL policy. He reiterated that FOL conference decisions had 'consistently endorsed the principles of opposition to martial law, release of all detained trade unionists including Walesa and the right of Polish workers to have the form of trade union of their own democratic decision'.[206]

Earlier, on 17 March 1980, stating that the public needed to be aware of their identity, and calling the SUP a 'disruptive, dangerous and

LEFT Ken Douglas and Lesley Winter, both 21, on their wedding day, 18 August 1956. (*Douglas family*)

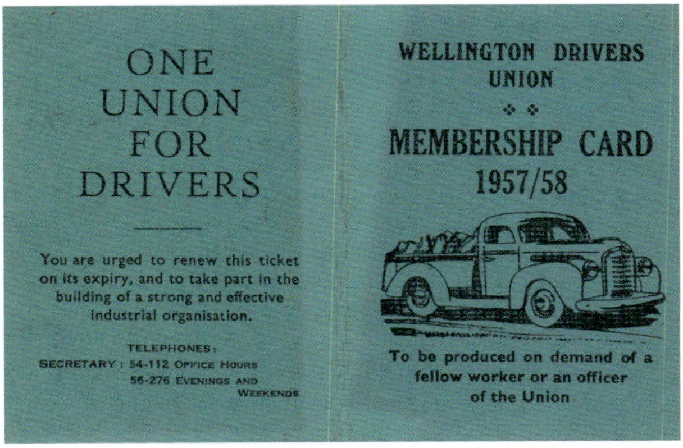

CENTRE Douglas's Wellington Drivers' Union card 1957-58. (*Douglas family*)

BELOW The Wellington College Old Boys rugby team which won the junior first grade championship in 1958. Douglas is second from right in the back row. (*Douglas family*)

ABOVE Munt Cottrell trucks line up on Aotea Quay, Wellington, in 1949. At the time they were the biggest carrying firm in Wellington and one of the biggest in New Zealand. (*Douglas family*)

CENTRE Attie Douglas carting wool in a HW Thomas truck up the dangerous access road at Terawhiti Station, mid-1950s. (*Douglas family*)

RIGHT Douglas (centre) participates in the Wellington Drivers' Union tug-of-war team at the Wellington Transport Unions' picnic in 1958. Tom Poata (partly obscured) is in front of him and Ayson Welsh is behind him. (*Douglas family*)

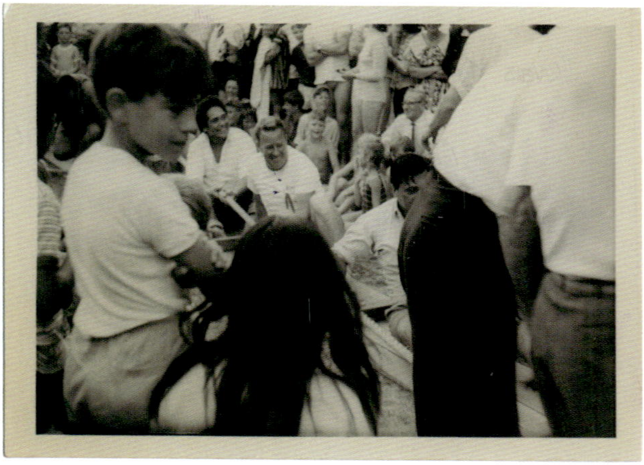

LEFT Three trade union leaders who would play important roles in Douglas's career pictured at the Drivers' Federation conference in October 1960. *From left*: Chip Bailey (secretary of the Wellington Drivers' Union), Jim Knox (organiser for the Northern Drivers' Union) and Bill Andersen (secretary of the Northern Drivers' Union). (*Douglas family*)

CENTRE Acclaimed American singer and socialist Paul Robeson addresses workers in a Wellington wharf shed in 1960. Douglas recalls that the crowd hung on Robeson's every word. 'You could feel the electricity.' (*Douglas family*)

BELOW Attie, Terree, Madge and Ken Douglas at Terree's 21st birthday party at Apu Crescent, Lyall Bay, October 1960. (*Douglas family*)

ABOVE The Wellington Drivers' Union Executive 1961. *From left in the front row:* Ken Douglas (city organiser), Chip Bailey (secretary), Andy Thomsen (president), Jimmy Smith (vice-president), Maxi Harris (assistant secretary and office manager) and Felix Harvey (country organiser). (*Douglas family*)

CENTRE Douglas (holding ball), captained the Titahi Bay Rugby Football Club Senior Third Division team in 1966. (*Douglas family*)

RIGHT Douglas as coach of the successful Titahi Bay United Senior Women's softball team. This team was runner-up in the Wellington competition in 1970-71. (*Douglas family*)

ABOVE LEFT Ken Douglas in June 1970, after he had been elected as president of the New Zealand Drivers' Federation. He was photographed on his way from Trades Hall in Wellington to meet with tanker drivers over their award. (*Alexander Turnbull Library, Wellington*)

ABOVE RIGHT Socialist Unity Party founder George Jackson. (*Douglas family*)

BELOW Douglas addresses the NZ Drivers' Federation Conference, New Plymouth, 1973. *From left:* Stuart McCaffley, Douglas, Minister of Labour, Sir Basil Arthur, and Dougal Soper. (*Douglas family*)

RIGHT Douglas addresses a May 1975 stop work meeting of Wellington drivers in the Wellington showground buildings. (*Evening Post*)

CENTRE Douglas at the forefront of this May 1974 Wellington Drivers' Union march in Lambton Quay in support of the Northern Drivers' Union and its secretary Bill Andersen, who had been imprisoned after refusing to surrender the assets of his union after they were sequestered by ship owner Leo Dromgoole. (*John Miller*)

RIGHT Douglas addresses a January 1976 stopwork meeting of the Wellington City Corporation employees in conflict with their employers over the latter's refusal to recognise a new award. Seated beside Douglas is Russell Jarvis, a Labourers' Union official. (*Alexander Turnbull Library, Wellington*)

LEFT FOL president Tom Skinner leads delegates into the opening session of a special conference on wage regulations in the Wellington Town Hall on 8 June 1976. Behind Skinner are other prominent unionists, Tony Neary (far left), Pat Kelly (2rd from left), Frank Thorn (3rd from left) and Sonja Davies in the background right. (*John Miller*)

CENTRE Drivers' Federation president Ken Douglas looks grim as he discusses problems with the drivers award under Muldoon's wage freeze regulations May 1976, with federation secretary Stuart McCaffley (left) and union assessors. (*Douglas family*)

LEFT Ken Douglas addressing a Drivers' Federation stop work meeting at Newtown Park, Wellington, 1976. Tom Skinner and Jim Knox sit at the table. (*John Miller*)

RIGHT New Zealand, Australian and Indian communist trade union delegates as guests at an All Unions Central Council of Trade Unions (USSR) conference in Moscow in March 1977. Douglas is back left. Second from the right in the front row is Eliot V Elliott, the New Zealand-born leader of the Seafarers Union of Australia between 1941 until 1978. (*Douglas family*)

CENTRE Douglas with fellow FOL executive members leaving Parliament in May 1978, after discussions with Prime Minister Robert Muldoon. *From left:* Douglas, Jim Boomer, Jim Knox, Wes Cameron, Tom Skinner, Ashley Russ and Sid Wheatley. Absent was Ted Thompson. (*Douglas family*)

RIGHT Jim Boomer (vice-president), Jim Knox (president) and Ken Douglas (secretary) on their way to a FOL council meeting 25 September 1979. (*Alexander Turnbull Library, Wellington*)

subversive' organisation, Muldoon had sent the news media a list of 32 names of alleged SUP members who were prominent in the trade union movement. Douglas was included on the list. Muldoon's intention was to stimulate widespread feelings of outrage among the population at large over the allegedly inordinate influence of communists in trade unions, and to cause embarrassment to the SUP members themselves, but he sadly misjudged the situation. Many commentators, including Opposition leader Bill Rowling, Labour Party president Jim Anderton and a number of newspaper editors, contended that the SUP could not have wished for better publicity. Rowling believed the list's publication gave the party a glamour that could only strengthen its overall impact in New Zealand. Social Credit leader Bruce Beetham called the release of the list 'a political stunt designed to outmanoeuvre and embarrass the Labour Party'. Even Neary lambasted Muldoon for 'making a serious mistake in giving SUP members a place in the political arena which they did not deserve'. Eighteen of the 32 later contacted by the *New Zealand Herald* commented publicly that they proudly carried the SUP flag, and that Muldoon was using them as scapegoats to cover up ongoing industrial conflict at the Kinleith pulp and paper mill in Tokoroa (the detail of which is set out in the next chapter) and other government-inspired 'industrial messes' around the country.[207]

Most newspapers carried the story on their front pages, complete with the names of the 32, but two — the *Auckland Star* and *Nelson Evening Mail* — refused to publish the names, asserting there were doubts over the list's accuracy and its morality. The *Star* editorialised that it was not in the business of publishing lists, commenting, 'Senator McCarthy made a name and an infamous place in history out of this system. We don't go along with it.' Even those papers which did publish the list, and were generally condemnatory of the SUP, were critical of Muldoon's use of the names — gleaned from the SIS — as part of a campaign against a legal political party. 'The SIS cannot be allowed to be seen as a tool of the National Party in office,' exclaimed the *Press*. Doubts about the accuracy of SIS information and fears it would be used for political purposes had been expressed during the 1977 debate on the Security Intelligence

Service Amendment Bill. 'This present performance is not reassuring,' the paper concluded.[208]

Indeed, there were inaccuracies in Muldoon's list. 'Joseph' Roberts, an organiser for the Northern Drivers' Union, was in fact Graham Roberts, and not a party member; neither was Ian Brown, an organiser for the Storemen and Packers' Union. Brown believed he was put on the list erroneously because he had spent some weeks in Russia in 1979 along with four other New Zealand and 20 Australian unionists as guests of Soviet trade unions. 'I will be voting Labour in 1981 as I have all my life,' he said. Neither was Jan Farr a member, although she was a supporter and would join the party later. Alongside these inaccuracies, four others complained that their titles were wrong. Norman Evans, an FOL national councillor and secretary of the Buller Trades Council, was not a member of the SUP but was a very keen supporter — he was annoyed that he had been left off the list, and considered putting through a personal call to 'my mate Mr Muldoon to put the matter right'.[209]

These errors brought the accuracy of the relevant SIS files into serious question. Muldoon felt the pressure, and soon he was accusing the Labour Party of harbouring SUP members within its ranks. That was a nonsense. Since the late 1920s the Labour Party had banned people who belonged to other political parties from joining. On 26 March, just over a week after he had released the names, Muldoon — hoping to capitalise on his belief that the country at large hated communists — took his antagonism towards the SUP a step further by threatening, in a speech to the Employers' Federation, to pass legislation to outlaw these 'paid servants of Moscow' altogether. He did not follow through with this threat, however. An *Auckland Star* poll taken at the time showed only 19.1 per cent of the respondents thought the SUP should be banned, a view also expressed by opposing political parties, civil libertarians, newspaper editors and even the Police Association.[210]

Rather than leading to condemnation and disgust, this extra publicity of Douglas's SUP connections, as well as his status as FOL secretary, led to his receiving more and more invitations to talk to Rotarians, Lions, Jaycees and business groups about his take on a variety of issues, including the class struggle. It was a demonstration of the truth of Jim Anderton's assertions that the SUP was only effective when it was under 'senseless persecution'. 'They get this tame Commo over to amuse them over lunch,' was Douglas's sarcastic take on it.[211]

The SUP stood just five candidates in the 1981 election but also supported Labour, seeing its success as the only possible electoral outcome that was in the interests of working people. While Labour's policies of 'class collaboration' continued, it retained the support of most of the working class and pursued some progressive policies such as the campaign against nuclear ships and withdrawal from ANZUS, alongside its support for the workers in industrial struggles such as that at Kinleith and for worker rallies in 1979–80 protesting against Muldoon's succession of anti-union laws. In most cases the SUP's voting figures increased over previous elections, 'but were still very low'. This was the last election in which the party stood candidates.[212]

It remained a tiny organisation. Just 30 delegates attended the party's sixth conference in Wellington in October 1982 — 23 from the North Island, seven from the South. Twenty-five held positions within the party at some level, and all but two were carrying out private study of some sort. There were around 120 members altogether, in four Auckland branches (Auckland City, Mt Albert, South Auckland, West Auckland) and others in Hamilton, New Plymouth, Palmerston North (all of which were struggling), Porirua, Hutt Valley, Christchurch and Dunedin. In the late 1980s there was a small branch in Invercargill.[213]

Douglas inadvertently caused controversy in 1983 when the Carterton town clerk, John Anderson, acting on behalf of the borough and the South Wairarapa County Council, invited him to be guest speaker at the town's Anzac Day parade. Anderson's choice was met with hostility from members of the Carterton RSA, who were unhappy that a man who, they claimed, as a communist had refused to swear allegiance to Queen and country, would parade with them. 'There is no way I am going to put up with the abuse that I have received for not having done anything about the choice of Mr Douglas,' RSA president Jim Yuille commented. 'I have heard him speak twice and I don't adhere to his language.' The service would be attended by representatives of many organisations, he said — Cubs, Scouts, Guides, 'you name it' — and he could not guarantee they would come if Douglas was guest speaker. Yuille contacted Sir Williams Leuchars, the RSA's Dominion president, who confirmed Douglas's unacceptability. Douglas knew Leuchars well. Not only was he president of the Wellington Employers' Association, but he had also been Douglas's commanding officer during his time as a territorial in the Armoured Corps in the 1950s.[214]

The issue reeked of prejudicial nonsense, but faced with the antipathy of the RSA Carterton's mayor Barry Keys withdrew Douglas's invitation in favour of local Anglican vicar Douglas Weavers. In fact, Yuille and Leuchars were wrong about Douglas's 'patriotism' — he had been required to swear allegiance when he joined the 11th military training intake in 1955. 'That wasn't a problem,' he said. 'In the party we continued this loyalty. The only change was that we did it by affirming rather than swearing the oath, therefore removing its religious aspect.' He criticised the RSA's comments as a slight on the trade union movement, describing them as an indication of the reaction and bigotry that were themselves fundamental to the rise of fascism.[215]

As always, Douglas was putting in very long hours at work and sleeping little, an average of five hours a night. His health was suffering. He had had problems with his weight since he stopped playing rugby, stimulated in part by an unhealthy diet and lack of exercise. His usual sustenance was a rushed cup of tea and toast for breakfast, a sandwich or biscuits for morning tea, two pies or fish and chips for lunch, and more fast food or a sandwich in the late afternoon. By 1984 his weight had ballooned to more than 130 kg and he began to suffer problems associated with obesity. He undertook some remedial treatment in Russia, one of the benefits of his close reciprocal links with Russian trade unions and his communism.

In 1984, a Soviet delegation visiting New Zealand to attend an FOL conference offered Douglas treatment to remove his failing gall bladder after the local health system could not accommodate him at a time when he was not busy. At Christmas that year he travelled to Moscow, where he spent three weeks in hospital undergoing both herbal and medicinal treatment before surgeons found his stomach lining was damaged and probably not strong enough for the operation. In November 1985, lighter and healthier, he went back, undergoing tests at a workers' sanatorium on the Black Sea coast before returning to the same Moscow hospital where his gall bladder was successfully removed by a Glasgow-trained surgeon. The treatment was free, and Douglas was enthusiastic about the post-operative treatment which included drugs, herbs, massage, acupuncture and muscle manipulation.

(This was Douglas's fourth journey to Russia. His first visit in 1970 has been noted. His second trip, late in 1972, was as a guest of the All-Unions Central Council of Trade Unions, the central Soviet trade union organisation. In June 1976, after attending a French Communist Party Congress, he went to Moscow to have discussions with the Soviet Communist Party's Central Committee. His fifth stopover came after an international trade union conference in New Delhi in December 1985, which tried, unsuccessfully, to find an accord between the International Congress of Free Trade Unions and the left-leaning World Federation of Trade Unions.)[216]

Ken and Marilyn Tucker (now the SUP's full-time secretary) visited Moscow again in December 1988–January 1989. Their objectives were wide-ranging — to increase understanding of the 'renovation' progress within the Communist Party of the Soviet Union (CPSU) and the international working-class movement, to experience the consequences of perestroika and glasnost, to learn more about the nationalist developments in the Baltic republics and their causes, to meet with the new leadership of the International Department of the CPSU, and to have medical check-ups. Later, in May 1989, Douglas returned to attend a Moscow symposium on 'The Future of the Working Class, the May Day Tradition and the 2nd International' and to celebrate May Day. He had been invited as both president of the CTU and chairperson of the SUP. The symposium was attended by representatives of the Soviet trade unions, the Lenin Institute, the Institute of the International Working

Class, and 40 representatives from 26 countries as well as the Socialist International (a worldwide organisation of social democratic, socialist and labour parties) and several socialist parties in Europe, eight European communist parties and five trade union centres. This was the first time in 75 years that such an expansive dialogue among so many international parties of the left had taken place.[217]

In 1990, Douglas led a small SUP delegation to a World Marxist Review Congress in Prague, after which they visited Moscow to talk with Communist Party leaders then reeling from Mikhail Gorbachev's reforms. His final official trip, this time representing the CTU, was to participate in a Federation of Independent Trade Unions of Russia Congress in 1996. Some unionists expressed annoyance that Douglas was away during wage-round negotiations, but more than half of his trips were on FOL business and he always obtained permission for those sanctioned by the SUP. Like many members of official delegations, Douglas always visited sanatoriums for a health check, visits which sometimes lasted for a week.

Through the 1980s, there were increasing differences between SUP heavyweights Douglas and Bill Andersen over the party's direction and leadership. Andersen had been general secretary since 1982. In August 1985, Douglas wrote:

> I have growing concerns at the methods of work of Comrade Andersen and suspect that there has been little improvement in the region [Auckland] because in part those methods are much about bad decisions. His great experience is offset by his 'serious' theoretical weaknesses; for example his method of work and approach often neglects the recognition of learning from the experience of the activity. There has been and remains much of the approach of 'put off and hope' . . . Comrade Andersen has wanted to experiment on leadership by identifying a newer comrade and taking a 'punt' on such an 'emerging star'. I am opposed, and will continue to be

opposed to such an approach. The whole world experience of Marxist/Leninist parties shows the need to understand and be aware of the dialectics of change and its influence on the process of leadership. Emerging leaders have to win the right to be considered for leadership responsibilities, not to have experiments made on a let's try it basis.

At the same time Douglas, who had long been on the national committee and chaired the Porirua branch, disqualified himself from putting his name forward for the national leadership of the party because of his increasing commitments as secretary of the FOL.[218]

Andersen resigned as secretary in July 1986, citing a desire to focus on his union career, despite having resigned from the FOL executive the previous year to enable him to devote more time to the SUP. He went further, trying to resign from the SUP altogether early in February 1987, citing 'severe differences of opinion on key aspects of the party's political philosophy and other serious difficulties about central office functioning and allocation of responsibilities'. He threatened to form a new 'socialist' party, but Auckland members persuaded him to continue.[219]

This change of mind, and Andersen's subsequent decision to nominate himself to the FOL executive from which he had resigned only two years prior, was in abrogation of traditional consensual party practice, and annoyed Douglas. Earlier, when Andersen had decided to pull back from national trade unionism, he had promoted Mike Jackson for the FOL executive, but now he engineered Jackson's non-renomination for the FOL position that he coveted. 'I had a real problem with this,' Douglas remembers. 'It was Bill imposing a kind of dependence of personality on both the SUP and the FOL — the type we had through the undemocratic practices of Walsh and Skinner in years gone past. Our structures had always been democratic. Bill had not moved on. He was a good headmaster — always telling people what to do.'[220]

The tensions remained. The spark which finally split the SUP asunder was disagreement between Andersen and Douglas, and the party's national committee, now based in Wellington, over the strategy for the 1990 general election. Douglas and the committee wanted to support Labour, while Andersen wanted the SUP to support candidates from third-party alternatives such as the newly formed New Labour Party. In a March 1990 paper, Andersen warned that unless the approach to this election was made clear, and it was handled very carefully, the party ran the risk of a very serious split. 'If we put forward a "return Labour" call as one of our approaches we will engender very serious problems. It has come to our notice that some of our colleagues did not vote Labour in 1987. There is much less desire to vote Labour in 1990 as far as these comrades are concerned.' The party, he contended, should be concerned with 'general politics' as well as 'electoral politics'. 'It is reasonable to estimate that our Party's past electoral approaches have been based on short term considerations and not on long term development of a mass movement for democratic change.'[221] Andersen continued:

> Historically we were correct in advocating a 'vote Labour and build the mass movement' in 1984. Such an approach was appropriate in 1987 but 1990 is a very new situation. The Labour Party is 'two-class'; the employing class has increased dramatically and the working class has dwindled proportionately. There is wide hunger for another electoral alternative. We must assist to develop some. The alternative could be the development of a democratic alliance firstly as a voting mechanism in the election but also developing into a longer term political force. There are a number of these forces in the Labour Party, New Labour Party and Mana Motuhake, and in other left groups and such a democratic alliance would preclude us standing candidates. Through them we could look at issues such as socially responsible State spending, ecology and its defence, Treaty implementation and anti-monopoly orientations . . .[222]

Andersen attempted to circulate his document to an SUP gathering over Labour Weekend but this was thwarted by the party leadership — Douglas and secretary Tucker acting on behalf of the national committee (Douglas, Tucker, George Jackson, Alan Ware and Joe Tonner). They argued that the document acted against the overall SUP strategy, which was to promote democracy; to oppose the anti-worker policies promoted by the Business Roundtable, implemented by the Labour Party and promoted by the National Party; to put forward an alternative economic and political programme, which meant rebuilding the strength of the labour and progressive movements — and to campaign for a proportional representation political system. This included not standing candidates in the election (because the SUP was in a 'reorganisation' phase) but instead working hard to support the election of progressive Labour candidates. Andersen refused to concede, and on 28 June 1990 he quit the SUP.[223]

Tucker believed that the SUP shared many of the criticisms of the Labour government, but felt that the political priority was to unite to change it, not let the right-wing win by default. It was significant that there were some close relationships among activists in both the SUP and the Labour Party, with whom the CTU had just signed a compact which the SUP supported, drawing the ire of the Communist Party. Douglas was close to Mike Moore, the compact's architect; Tucker was close to Labour Party president Ruth Dyson; and Don Farr, a Labourite CTU official, was married to Jan Farr, a member of the SUP's central committee and long-term editor of the *Tribune*.[224]

Douglas, by then the party's national chairman, was unimpressed with his former comrade's defection. 'It's really tragic he is now so obviously confused about so many of the principles he has stood for,' he told the press, more in sorrow than in anger. 'His criticism that the SUP had not come to grips with moves toward democracy was a bit pathetic, frankly.' A new Auckland branch of the SUP was formed soon after, on 22 July 1990, but with far fewer members. In turn, Andersen formed a new party, the Socialist Party of Aotearoa. Around half of the SUP's Auckland members went with him, including activists Doug McCallum,

Peter Cross, Pat Shepherd and Stan and Gloria Stanford; the rest stayed 'loyal'. It was an unhappy time, with pro- and anti-Andersen factions verbally harassing each other. Friends became antagonists overnight. Douglas and Andersen, who had been close friends and confidants in both politics and trade unionism, were now permanently estranged.[225]

At this time events in Russia were lessening the party's continued relevance. From 1988 on, Gorbachev's radical 'glasnost' reforms — the first rejection of established communist practice as interpreted by Stalin and his successors — caused a frantic and panicked response from the members of communist parties around the world, and more than a little disillusionment on the part of the traditionalists, many of whom resigned. It was the same in New Zealand, where the Communist Party tried to stick to the hard line, unbowed by the new order — and became even more irrelevant. In contrast, the SUP began to swim in the new ideological current with a new-found willingness to collaborate with right-wing (in the Communist Party's eyes) social democratic parties in a restructuring of capitalism — exemplified by the SUP's strong support for the trade union's compact with the Labour government. It was no coincidence that Ken Douglas was a key player in both the trade union leadership's and the SUP's espousal of the compact.

This did not help an organisation whose membership was declining even before Andersen's defection. In 1989 it was decided to close down the *Tribune*; according to the feedback that editor Jan Farr had been getting, it was no longer 'relevant'. It was revamped as a cyclostyled production. Just 26 members attended the SUP's ninth national conference in Wellington in October 1991. The following year the number had halved. By this time, the national committee, the fulcrum around which the party had operated for decades, had been abolished.[226]

The fall of communism in Russia and its satellite states affected Douglas deeply. Rob Campbell maintained the SUP was always the bedrock that kept Douglas on track intellectually — his 'personal motivator'. Peter Harris, who worked closely with him at the CTU as its economist, identified two Ken Douglases. The first was the man from the communist-Russia era, very much under the influence of the Soviet world view, although tempered by a more pragmatic realpolitik. The other was the man from the period after the collapse of communism, who 'almost lost his anchor' and, partly in response, became more involved with international trade unionism. Unionist Robert Reid, who had worked closely with him, believed that the the introduction of Gorbachev's reforms — which began the transition from a command economy to one that was determined by market forces — meant that Douglas had lost his 'spiritual home'.[227]

Yet the collapse of communism in eastern Europe, the defeat for Albania's Stalinists, and the devastation of socialist parties in the French general elections through the early months of 1992 had less of an impact on Douglas than might have been imagined. Long calling himself a Marxist/Leninist, and his SUP the only true Marxist/Leninist party, he had also long despaired of the Soviet and Chinese models which were now, in his view, distortions of the principles identified by the early Labour leaders and philosophers such as Karl Marx.

Remarkably, he believed that the key reason Marxists were not thrown into despair by the Soviet debacle lay in Japan, that bastion of capitalism, which had managed to get closest to the communist ideal of socially responsible, collaborative partnership between big business and labour where the latter had genuine input. This was Marxian, he contended: 'Marx believed quite specifically that socialism would come into being in a highly industrialised society where there was a huge increase in the cultural and educational levels of the population.'[228]

The following December Douglas was back in Moscow, staying in the Sputnik Hotel on Lenin Prospect. He felt disgusted as he peered out the window at the snow-covered scene. 'The city used to be so clean, pristine. Now it is dirty with ugly advertising and hoardings along the roadside. It was even worse with litter everywhere and beggars in rags.' He recalled a quote from a visitor to the Soviet Union soon after the 1917 revolution who said he had seen the future — and it works! Retreating from the window he wrote in his diary, 'Now this? What is it? A trick of life?' The message was clear. Since the country had abandoned communism — or successive leaders' interpretation of it — clearly Soviet society was in some kind of morbid decline, and with no paradigm to provide a moral compass, it was suffering from the worst excesses of capitalism.[229]

While Gorbachev's attempts at reforms were inevitable and overdue, he felt, there was little follow-through. 'What he did not do was invest a sense of ownership in the people. His restructurings were intended to democratise the country and disempower the party apparatus. That failed because he could not manage the twin processes of the rise in authority of the community and a decline in the authority influence of the party approach . . .' In 1993 Douglas called Gorbachev's successor Boris Yeltsin's corrupt administration 'a farce' as it lurched from one economic and political crisis to another, wallowing in rampant corruption. By this time his visits to Russia were mainly matters of nostalgia — meeting old friends, reliving old glories, and bemoaning the shocking increases in the cost of living. Johnny Walker Black Label was now a 'ludicrous' $US60 a bottle.

Douglas cares little for people's opinions of him, but he does concede that his SUP membership has put great pressure on his ability to retain a good humour. In 1983 he commented:

> I've had some quite unpleasant situations face to face; physical threats; death threats. But I go out of my way not to be provoked. I've always believed that those who lose their temper lose the fight. Mind you it can be tough in pubs. I've had to tell a few drunken characters that I'll put their big, flat feet down their bloody throats. And I've done exactly that on one or two occasions.[230]

Much of the enmity towards him came not from the 'right' but from the remnant of the New Zealand Communist Party and its offshoot, the Workers' Communist League. Through the pages of their journals, and at protests, both groups attacked the SUP continuously, even more vigorously than they berated the CTU which Douglas led. Their accusations, which grew more virulent over time, were based around the view that the SUP had 'sold out' — it was no longer a pure Marxist organisation but rather a pseudo-capitalist party of 'collaborationist revisionists'. For the most part the SUP refused to be dragged into the argument. Instead, it focused its resources on fighting for workers' demands, and struggling to unite working people and non-monopoly forces against the monopolies and against state-monopoly capitalism.

By 1995, the SUP was fighting for its life. The Soviet Union had collapsed, as had other Soviet bloc countries; new-right economic policies were in the ascendancy both in New Zealand and internationally as social democratic parties moved to the right. In contrast, the left was suffering a theoretical and ideological malaise. An SUP report bemoaned the inability of the world communist parties — now either gone altogether or marginalised from the mainstream of power — to redevelop their ideological and theoretical base. The pragmatic effect on the SUP was that resignations increased, a process which had begun with Andersen's departure and the establishment of the Socialist Party of Aotearoa, which was fighting for recognition within the same constituency. The SUP was still alive, just, in 1997. Joe Tonner represented it at a Russian Communist Party Congress in April of that year — that party, of course, was no longer in power.[231]

Douglas believed that Gorbachev's 'misjudgements' and Yeltsin's subsequent capitalist decadence had damaged the integrity and moral authority of political leadership in Russia. He was also influenced by the democratisation of the Mongolian Communist Party, which had forgone some of its central control and given more 'back to the people'. But, ever the pragmatist, he understood that there was no going back and that the political future lay with social democracy, the only means of counteracting the threat of globalisation. The SUP's last act was to disburse funds to the New Zealand Labour Party from the $40,000 that remained in its bank account.

While the SUP is not deceased, it is 'on ice' and unlikely to be revived. In 2002, Douglas made his break permanent with it when he joined the Labour Party to contest, and win, a position on the Capital Coast Health

Board on a Labour ticket. To do so he signed an oath of allegiance to the party, which accepted his proviso that it acknowledge he was a trustee of the inactive SUP's assets.

CHAPTER 8

The Big Cheese — the Federation of Labour

By the early 1970s, Douglas was making his mark within the Federation of Labour. President Tom Skinner always wanted FOL conferences to run smoothly — like his predecessor Fintan Patrick Walsh, he abhorred dissent. Mostly he got his way, unlike Walsh, without the use of behind-the-scenes bully-boy sycophants who beat up malcontents.

In general, union leaders in the 1960s and 1970s were compliant and conservative. Douglas was different. When the occasion warranted it, he was critical of the leadership. In October 1973, he put his name to a document that indicated his union's belief that the FOL was failing to take a lead — for example in its continual failure to successfully negotiate demarcation disputes, which were happening more frequently as new technology replaced manual labour and unions were downsizing and merging.[232]

In May 1974, Douglas took a lead on the FOL conference floor, protesting over the use of injunctions to try to solve industrial disputes and calling for concerted opposition from unions to 'this latest union-smashing device'. This was a reference to Les Dromgoole, the owner of the North Shore Ferry Company. In April Dromgoole had won an injunction to force Auckland drivers to supply fuel to his vessels, whose crews he had banned from joining the Seamen's Union in favour of his own in-house 'union'. Dromgoole used a writ of sequestration to have the government seize the assets of both the Seamen's and the Northern Drivers' unions. When Drivers' Union secretary Bill Andersen resisted, Justice Peter Mahon had him arrested and incarcerated in Mt Eden Prison, an action which incensed workers around the country, with 20,000 walking off the job in Auckland alone. They saw the injunctions as a back-door means of denying them the legal right to withhold their labour but despite union and subsequent FOL protests, the use of injunctions stayed.[233]

When Douglas was in full flight on the FOL floor during this and other disputes, fellow delegates sat up and took notice. He was expressive, waving his hands in the air when agitated, although he tended to slur or mispronounce words as his tone rose and dialogue sped up. At other times he was quieter, calm and more articulate. In major speeches he moved effortlessly from one mode to the other. Yet being noticed did not translate into support. For nearly a decade from 1969, Douglas was nominated but failed to win a seat on the FOL executive. He secured 141 votes at his first attempt, far behind Frank Thorn (of the Clothing Workers' Union, who won 386), Wally Molineaux (Carpenters' Union, 286), Len Hadley (Motion Pictures Projectionists' Union, 257) and Bill Martin (Seamen's Union, 235) who were elected, and Norris Collins (National Union of Railwaymen, 171) who was not. In 1970, he received just 100 votes, far in arrears of Martin (360), Hadley (356), Thorn (317) and first-timer Jim Boomer (Engineers' Union, 273) who were elected, and Collins who again missed out.[234]

This set a pattern for the next six years. Between 1971 and 1976 Douglas received 129, 155, 178, 217, 205 and 252 votes respectively, none of which were high enough to win selection. He watched others — Boomer, Ashley Russ, who succeeded Molineaux after his retirement, Wally Clement (Plumbers' Union), Ted Thompson (Waterside Workers' Federation) and Sid Wheatley (Dairy Workers' Union) stand for office after him and win selection ahead of him. Finally in 1977, in a small field, he succeeded with 402 votes, defeating Clement for a seat on the executive by just one vote. Ahead of both of them were Thompson (536), Wheatley (531), Russ (526), Thorn (451) and Wes Cameron (Freezing Workers' Union, 411).[235]

Douglas was the first known communist to be elected to the FOL executive. That had been his problem. While he commanded respect as an able leader of the Wellington Drivers' Union, the New Zealand Drivers' Federation and the Wellington Trades Council, as well as on the floor at FOL conferences, his political affiliations held him back. The bulk of the moderate unionists, many of whom represented 'craft' unions, shared most New Zealanders' distaste for ultra left-wing activism, with attitudes that ranged from distrust to anger and fear. They consistently voted for 'caution' and returned long-term executive members, some of whom had not shown the degree of leadership exhibited by Douglas, who was always prominent at FOL conferences speaking on a wide range of industrial and political issues. But slowly, as his profile rose so did the respect, despite his politics.[236]

Douglas did not canvass personally within any union for election to higher office. In 1969 he had contested the FOL executive at the behest of the Socialist Unity Party. George Jackson, Ernie Hunter, Bruce Skilton and Frank McNulty, all trade unionists, had believed, like Douglas, that the FOL was stultifying under the 'steady as she goes' leadership of Tom Skinner. This group spoke to the SUP's national council, which voted unanimously that Douglas should stand for office in the FOL.[237]

There was much truth in the party's assertions. Through the 1970s increasing calls for change were coming not from the executive but from the FOL's national council (on which Douglas sat), which represented a wider cross-section of unionists across the country. From them, and from district trade councils, came initiatives such as recognising the importance of celebrating May Day, introducing or reintroducing social occasions such as picnics and sports competitions among workers and their unions, and taking stands on issues such as the 'No Maoris — No Tour' campaign, political recognition of communist China and opposition to French nuclear testing in the South Pacific.

Once elected in 1977, however, Douglas's ascension was rapid. In the following year he proved his worth and became the FOL executive's third highest polling candidate with 523 votes, just behind Thompson (with 533) and Cameron (526). This proved the 1977 result had been no fluke, and demonstrated that the 'threat' of his politics was more about perception than reality. In June 1979, after Skinner's retirement and Jim Knox's elevation to the top job, Douglas was elected secretary of the FOL. It was a tight battle. Douglas defeated Ashley Russ, secretary of the New Zealand Carpenters' Union, by 273 votes to 247. In order to win, however, he would have needed at least one of the big three large 'conservative' unions to have been on his side — the Hotel Workers', Engineers', or Clerical Workers' — all of which were entitled to a high number of votes on the ballot based on their size. It is not known which unions voted for Douglas, although he believed the first two were in his corner. He succeeded partly because Knox wanted Russ as his running mate; the two were close friends. The vote rebounded against Russ because there was no guarantee that such a pairing would change much. Further if Russ had been elected the FOL's power-base would have remained in Auckland, to the detriment of the rest of the country. Russ neither enjoyed the same prestige nor possessed the same abilities as his predecessor, Wally Molineaux. Douglas was a Wellingtonian and he promised change.[238]

Yet it seemed his hands were tied to a degree. Knox, wary of Douglas's communism, had managed to win from the organisation 'special powers' that related only to him, and to which Douglas was not privy. Essentially, Knox promised to 'keep an eye' on Douglas's performance to see that he acted solely in the interests of the trade union movement. It was a less than oblique message that Douglas's political affiliation needed to be subservient, indeed irrelevant, to his new role as second-in-charge of the country's trade unions.[239]

Historically, communists 'mounted the barricades' in industrial disputes, compromise being at odds with the tearing down of capitalist ideology. But sound union leadership rested on an ability to be much more far-sighted than this. There was a time and place for uncompromising direct action. At the other end of the scale, there was a time for nuance in negotiation. The skill was in knowing when to use what, against whom and for how long — and an ability to read changing tides and adapt accordingly. Where possible, Douglas always championed negotiation over direct action. This was the pragmatic Douglas in action; personal politics had no place. He was careful to try to ensure that the two roles were not in conflict. In fact, he took a leading role in drawing up a Socialist Unity Party document which stated that it was the responsibility of party members to abide by the majority decisions of all the organisations they belonged to.

His job as a union leader was always to advocate for and promote either the union's or the FOL's position. There were a significant number of events, mostly international, as we have seen, where his political views conflicted with his professional responsibilities — and where antagonists, such as anti-communist unionists (although there were just a handful of them who bothered; in the FOL Tony Neary was his only persistent adversary), the media and conservative politicians would try to distort or misrepresent his position with accusations of 'disloyalty'. Douglas raged against this 'personalisation' of the issues, which demeaned the union movement as a whole and gave a perception of splits within it.

When it came to the crunch he was a team man. There was no debate on political issues when he was representing his union or the FOL. His personal politics were reserved for statements that he identified strictly as coming under the aegis of the SUP, and nearly all of these were for private consumption. Conversely, collective responsibility was paramount when he put his signature to FOL executive remits condemning communist 'imperialism' or 'autocracy' in Ethiopia, Afghanistan and Poland.

Douglas won the race to become secretary, eventually, because of his highly regarded administrative skills and political and analytical judgement — skills and judgements honed after long experience as leader of the Drivers' Union, the Drivers' Federation and the Wellington Trades Council. For his part he promised that his leadership would be participative, not paternalistic, and he rarely wavered from this principle throughout his trade union life.

At the landmark 1978 FOL conference, decisions were taken to decentralise structures so that more decision-making power was placed in the hands of union affiliates and trades councils — and the FOL's national council, which had representatives drawn from all centres. The aim was to create a stronger, more flexible and accountable organisation and to move on from past criticisms that members merely rubber-stamped decisions taken by the executive. Once Douglas became secretary he assumed much more influence within the FOL. He exercised this in part through his authorship of the organisation's annual report — in which he not only reported but also took positions and argued for those positions — as well as encouraging unions through their delegates to be proactive rather than reactive. Long-standing convention required the annual report to be considered and endorsed by the FOL's national council — and it always was.

Douglas's elevation to the position of secretary came at a time of increasing tension between unions, the FOL and the Muldoon government — with the latter's increasingly hostile attitude towards unionists exemplified by the increasing number of anti-labour laws being passed. On 17 May 1979, close to 6000 workers and supporters marched through the streets and gathered at the grounds of Parliament to listen to Knox, Douglas and Labour Party president Jim Anderton berate the government's dismal economic performance, anti-union legislation and high inflation. Muldoon responded by calling the protest a shameful affair led by 'one Douglas of the Socialist Unity Party'. Four days later the Auckland Trades Council staged a solidarity week to protest against falling real wages and growing unemployment.

On 1 June, Knox persuaded a rally of thousands in Christchurch to call on the government to resign, and Douglas was a key speaker at a rally of 2000 unionist marchers to Hamilton's Garden Place condemning the government and calling on it to act over the rising cost of living and burgeoning unemployment.[240]

In August 1979, with industrial conflicts swirling with ever more intensity around him, Muldoon set about repealing the General Wage Orders Act — which was just two years old, and essentially entrenched the award and arbitration systems — restoring the right of the Arbitration Court to make general wage orders. He replaced the Act with a Remuneration Bill which allowed for any pay agreements handed down by the Arbitration Court to be binding — but pay rates agreed to in conciliation and ratified by the Court were subject to non-negotiable alteration by the government. This gave the state unparalleled power to nullify or amend any industrial award not determined by the Court. Free wage bargaining was out. If the settlement was too high, the country could not afford it, was Muldoon's argument. He had already identified a potential ready-made antagonist, vowing to step in to stop any direct action by SUP-led unions. 'Direct action by the drivers, storemen and packers and now I understand the dairy workers will not be tolerated. We have a duty to interfere. We will interfere . . .'[241]

Outside the government, the measure found little support. Employers called the proposed legislation 'unpalatable' and implored the government to consult them before it amended or nullified any wage agreement. The New Zealand Law Society expressed concern, noting that such changes to repeal the existing law should be made by Parliament after consultation, not by the government. The new law gave the government the power to unilaterally usurp the role of the Court and Parliament, it argued. But it was all to no avail. On 9 August 1979, the Remuneration Bill became law.[242]

Union reaction was not long in coming, and Douglas was in the thick of it. On 18 September the FOL called for the first 24-hour nationwide stoppage since the general strike of 1913 in protest at the government's decision to pare 1.5 per cent off the already agreed drivers' award — after

Knox and Douglas had pleaded in vain with Minister of Labour Jim Bolger to reverse the decision. Muldoon derided the proposed stoppage as a 'lost cause' and indicated that if that was the way the FOL wanted to play, his government would return to wage regulation 'quick and lively'. Bolger, more temperate and sensible, renewed his offer for an all-party conference on wage fixing. It didn't take place, and the strike went ahead.[243]

On the day, factories, including freezing works and dairy factories, closed as did some schools; hospital and hotel services were greatly reduced; buses, trains, ferries and trucks did not run; planes did not fly; mail and milk were not delivered, and no newspapers appeared. It was estimated that those who did strike lost close to $16 million in pay. But many white collar workers did work. Shops and supermarkets stayed open, as did banks. The Auckland Trades Council employed 250 'temporary delegates' to scour the city to find staff not obeying the strike call and encourage them to do so. These were similar to the 'flying pickets' British trade unions used for similar purposes during strikes.

A number of rallies were held. In Auckland an estimated 2000 protesters marched down Queen Street before listening to Bill Andersen and other speakers from the local trades council blasting the new legislation. On the same dais Labour Party junior whip Richard Prebble expressed 'full support' for the strike. Muldoon was unimpressed, calling the strike 'an absolute fizzer', and soon afterwards passed a Commerce Amendment Act which enabled the government to selectively control the charges and profits of every firm in the country. No government, before or since, has exercised such hegemony over the working lives of New Zealanders and the businesses in which they work.[244]

The 24-hour stoppage was merely the beginning. The biggest street campaign against the Act and associated issues — such as the right to direct bargaining, the right to a minimum living wage for workers, concern about declining living standards in the wake of growing inflation, rapidly increasing prices and increasing unemployment — was remarkable for its strength and militancy. On 29 August 1980, 30,000 unionists and others gathered in Post Office Square at the bottom of Queen Street to march up to Aotea Square, where another 10,000 awaited them. Knox recalled: 'As we marched I was somewhat surprised and taken aback because people were coming off the footpath and shaking hands with me — young women with children, old people . . . I was so very proud to be a trade unionist that day.'[245]

The FOL's next fight was with New Zealand Forest Products at their Kinleith timber mill near Tokoroa, the largest mill in the country. Forest Products had had a good year in 1979, making a profit in the first half-year of about $18 million. But trouble began in December when annual wage talks between management and unions broke down after a long series of meetings, and the latter sought help from the FOL. It took over the dispute in January 1980. The important issue was that workers at Kinleith wanted parity with their mates at Tasman Pulp and Paper at Kawerau, where a $4.80 per week pay rise had been agreed. Forest Products did not budge. Five hundred and sixty tradesmen went out on strike. Production ceased in January and the company laid off 1200 men and women for whom there was no work. Forest Products — which had probably hoped for government intervention that was not forthcoming — then acquiesced and, on 24 February, agreed to the $4.80 figure. On 5 March, Muldoon invoked the Remuneration Act and cut back the rise, for both companies, from $4.80 to $4.69. It was a remarkable act of insensitivity, and overnight the whole of the New Zealand trade union movement, and many others, including newspaper leader-writers, came in behind the Kinleith workers, giving heart to the FOL to push the conflict to the very end.

Tokoroa became a town under siege. Mortgage and hire purchase payments were under threat of default with no money coming to workers' families. A welfare centre was set up and run by workers' wives in the old Jaycee Hall. The 560 strikers and their families received donated money and food. There was also a drop-in centre, a food exchange and school clothing swap. Women developed a roster and produced meals every day, countless cups of tea, and counselling for families under stress. There were social activities including children's parties, where Woolworths provided chips and jellies. The union organised film showings and even a concert with island, folk and country-and-western items. Knox and Douglas spent considerable time in the town, addressing mass gatherings and holding meetings with union delegates and local officials. Knox indicated that it was not just Kinleith that was at stake. If the FOL did not win here, where would the government use the iniquitous act next, he asked. The FOL refused to agree to any limit for wage negotiation.[246]

Muldoon again directed attention to the SUP, taking potshots at Douglas in particular. But his outbursts were a sideshow, a deflection from the main cause, and they failed. Douglas and Knox remained calm. After four weeks of stalemate, costing the company hundreds of thousands of dollars in lost production, and with the workers continuing to hold firm, Muldoon yielded. He offered a new proposal — if the FOL agreed to enter wage talks with the government it would discuss a composite agreement for the whole industry. Knox insisted that there would be no return to work unless the regulations were lifted and the $4.80 rise restored. In May, after several more weeks of fruitless negotiation, and realising that neither the Kinleith workers, their union, nor the FOL were going to buckle, the government finally agreed. It was a complete surrender. The men returned to work in June. The FOL then explored the possibility of developing a single wage-bargaining structure within the industry.[247]

The settlement at Kinleith became the foundation on which the continuing demand for the revocation of the Remuneration Act was based. Douglas concluded in the FOL's 1981 conference report that if in every industrial dispute the militant actions of the workers were supported by the wider trade union movement and the community, then the forces of capital would have an extremely difficult job resisting the united pressure of the working class. 'Employers in the main are only able to resist the expressed needs of workers when they are capable of creating disunity and confusion among the unions' rank and file and division among the unions . . .' It was noteworthy that the sheer volume of donations for the striking Kinleith workers was more than enough to meet all expenses — indeed, the FOL had to decide what to do with the surplus.[248]

The Kinleith dispute was a turning point for the FOL and the wider trade union movement — Muldoon's anti-union prejudices had united the unions as never before. Up to this time the FOL had often acted as a sort of industrial undertaker — called upon to bury disputes rather than to join in the fight. Knox and Douglas went to Kinleith, listened to the workers and backed them with the full weight of the federation. Crucially, and unusually, state unions added further support. Muldoon's attempt to divide and rule failed miserably.

The main target, the Remuneration Act, was left in tatters. After the victory, Knox and Douglas were hailed within and without the FOL as an effective team. It was Knox's first public showing as president, and Douglas, as secretary, had set the platform by organising meetings, coordinating plans of action with locals, distributing literature and keeping the media informed. He remained calm and measured in his dealings with all, a perfect foil for Knox, who was often loud and sometimes flustered in his assertions. There was huge euphoria and back-slapping at the subsequent FOL conference, which began on 9 May 1980, and where Douglas again played the key administrative role. The divisions that the Soviet invasion of Afghanistan had caused at the 1979 conference were a distant memory. Delegates welcomed Isabel Allende, daughter of the murdered former president of Chile, and South African political exile Zola Zembe.

But there were other concerns besides the Remuneration Act. Union leaders and workers were sick of rampant inflation which eroded their purchasing power. They were sick of paying more and more tax while companies were paying less. They were sick of the government meddling with their pay agreements, and they were sick of Muldoon's insults. Keeping up the momentum, Douglas suggested that the FOL seek a general wage order of between 30 and 40 per cent if the government did not repeal the Remuneration Act by 15 July. If it did not come up with alternative wage-fixing procedures then 'it's war', he told the press. The government was silent. On 1 July, the country marched, demanding an end to government-imposed wage restraints and repeal of the Act. Five thousand protested in Lower Hutt alone, marching on Vogel House, the Prime Minister's residence. An equally large number marched to Parliament, where Douglas led a protest delegation inside to see Muldoon.

In the meantime the FOL continued in tense talks with the government over an alternative wage-fixing package. Progress was slow, the Remuneration Act being the main stumbling block. The FOL simply would not accept its continuance. The pressure told. On 6 August, the government promised to repeal the Act. In return the FOL promised that the current round of award negotiations would proceed on a 'reasonable' basis — increases of about 13 per cent being regarded as reasonable. It was a remarkable victory for the FOL and trade unionists generally. Ken Douglas had no doubt that it was the strength of the rallies and the anger of the participants, and the fact that the campaign united the FOL and the state unions, alongside Muldoon's continued attacks on unionists — both personally and through their pay packets — that led to the Act's demise.[249]

It was during this period that Muldoon released his list of alleged SUP members, illustrating the degree to which he blamed the party — this 'dangerous, disruptive and subversive' organisation — for much of the industrial strife. All this did was give the SUP publicity and lead to increased membership. More galling was the anti-union 'Kiwis Care' march down Queen Street early in 1981. Led by a 22-year-old sales representative, Tania Harris, it attracted 30,000 people — and had implicit state support and significant employer sponsorship, with many giving their employees time off to attend and even providing buses to get them there. Among many others, one banner read 'Death to Communist Trade Union Leaders!' The FOL organised a counter-demonstration four days later but it attracted only 3000 supporters, who faced abuse and egg- and tomato-throwing from the sideline. The small number was not surprising. Workers were otherwise occupied, sorting out their own wage claims and marching specifically against Muldoon's raft of anti-union legislation and subsequent regulations which suspended the conciliation and arbitration procedures of the Industrial Relations Act.[250]

Further industrial strife inflamed tempers even more. Disputes involving Air New Zealand engineers, cooks and stewards in Wellington and workers at the Ravensdown fertiliser plant near Dunedin saw Muldoon threatening to sue Knox after the FOL president made derogatory comments about him on television. The FOL refused to allow Muldoon to address their annual conference in 1981 — the first time in decades that an incumbent leader had been denied this privilege. Douglas wrote that the executive 'did not think it was appropriate or desirable for a direct representative of a government that sponsored, promoted and implemented anti-union policies having disastrous effects on living standards and employment levels, to participate in the work of the conference'.[251]

Under Knox and Douglas, the FOL was also taking a more proactive and public stance on political and social issues outside the trade union mainstream. Racism was an ongoing concern. At its 1981 conference the FOL, noting widespread opposition to the forthcoming Springbok rugby tour, passed resolutions expressing strong protest at the failure of the government to honour and implement the Gleneagles Agreement (under which Commonwealth leaders had agreed to 'discourage' sporting contact with South Africa), reaffirmed its policy of support for the South African Congress of Trade Unions in its struggle for recognition, restated its total opposition to racism and the involvement of New Zealand in assisting the perpetration of racist policies in South Africa, and the spreading of that racism to New Zealand by a refusal to act decisively to demonstrate this country's opposition to apartheid. It also supported the call made by the South African working class to demonstrate New Zealand's opposition to apartheid by striving to prevent the proposed rugby tour — but notably fell short on instituting a campaign itself to stop the tour. This conference was addressed by Andrew Molotsani, a representative of the South African Congress of Trade Unions, who was given a standing ovation after outlining the plight of black workers in South Africa.[252]

Through 1980 and much of 1981 the government and the FOL tried to negotiate a wage/tax trade-off but talks were called off in June 1981 after 15 months of negotiations. The government and the FOL blamed each other for the breakdown of these talks, and the relationship between the two reached an all-time low when Muldoon expressed fury at Knox's address to the International Labour Organisation conference in Geneva on 9 June. Knox was critical of the fact that New Zealand workers were becoming 'captives' to multinationals, stating that the social welfare system was being run down, that the state was sanctioning the arrest of peaceful picketers, and that while 100,000 New Zealanders were unemployed, the government continued to import foreign labour. Muldoon believed Knox had broken an 'unwritten law' that New Zealanders abroad did not disparage their country. 'It was a distorted tirade,' he said. He threatened in the future not to pay union delegates' fares to future ILO meetings.[253]

Jim Bolger was president of the ILO at this time, the first New Zealand Minister of Labour to hold that position. He was chairing the conference when Knox was speaking, and interrupted him on the dais when he went over time, telling him that his time was up. Knox, infuriated, ignored Bolger and continued to speak, berating the government. After a few more minutes Bolger turned off the microphone, and to the delight and amusement of the several hundred delegates present, the two men continued to harangue each other as if they were in a silent movie.

Muldoon blamed Douglas. 'I have not the slightest doubt,' he fumed, 'that this speech was ghost-written by Douglas. It would bring great joy to his Communist mates.' Knox fought fire with fire. 'Unwritten law be damned,' he exclaimed; 'There's no such thing. What I said was absolutely correct . . . As far as I'm concerned he can make all the threats he likes about me. If he withdraws fares, he will have to do that for the whole delegation.' He also denied that Douglas had written the speech. 'It was mine. I wrote it in the plane on the way over.' At the conference Knox was re-elected with a bigger majority as the substitute, or 'second in charge', workers' representative on the ILO's governing body.

Muldoon continued to hammer workers with legislation. From

October 1981, a new Industrial Relations Amendment Act gave increased powers to employers to enable them to adopt a more aggressive bargaining stance in disputes. Employers could now suspend workers operating restrictive practices without pay, and had greater powers to lock out workers without being liable for their wages. The FOL was not consulted.[254]

The challenges intensified in 1982. Unemployment continued to rise, and workers were increasingly concerned about the level of tax they were paying. The real issue was not the total level of tax but who was paying it. Labour Department statistics indicated that in 1971 salary and wage earners were paying 49 per cent of the country's tax take. In 1981, this figure had risen to 68 per cent, while the company tax take had fallen from 29 to 11 per cent over the same period. To take workers' minds off this increasingly unfair distribution of tax, Muldoon introduced a wage/tax trade-off. This was supposed to be enacted as a small cut in the award round in exchange for a tax cut, the rationale being that there would be a reduction in the rate of inflation in future years. But the FOL and the unions rejected wage/tax trade-offs because they were unfair: only workers were asked to take cuts in their incomes, in exchange for tax cuts which went to everybody. In addition, they would not stop rising inflation, nor could they be imposed in isolation from other policies. The government, Douglas protested, was 'playing politics' with the trade union movement.

Tax/wage trade-offs had been one cornerstone of the government's industrial relations policy, but after this rejection a frustrated Muldoon imposed a 12-month wage/price freeze beginning on 23 June 1982. Effectively, however, as workers had received their last wage rise between October 1981 and February 1982, they were being asked to have their wages frozen for 18 months. Moreover, people other than wage and salary earners were not subject to the regulations, and there were so many exemptions to the price freeze that you could, as one commentator noted, 'drive a truck through them'. Meat, second-hand goods, goods sold at auction — such as cars, furniture and fresh fruit and vegetables, which were staple items in all homes — were exempt, as were some luxury items such as women's fashion wear. Furthermore, other prices could increase as a consequence of increases in import prices, indirect charges or government charges. Petrol prices, for example, were not frozen. Muldoon also tightened controls on interest rates and restricted the level of redundancy payments that could be negotiated between unions and employers. To offset this, he promised 'substantial' but unspecified income tax reductions in the October budget.[255]

Muldoon's institution of the freeze ran directly counter to the advice he had received from Treasury, the Department of Trade and Industry, the Labour Department and the Reserve Bank. The FOL and the unions denounced the package but, initially, played down thoughts of a major confrontation with the government. Muldoon was a lone ranger. His main motivation, he said, was to bring down the country's rampant inflation, currently running at close to 18 per cent. The government also completely ignored a special FOL conference in November 1982 which called for an immediate $20-a-week wage increase across the board for all union members, a new wage-fixing procedure, and an alternative economic strategy.[256]

Bill Andersen was first out of the blocks, calling for 'more meetings, more marches, more strikes' to combat the freeze. As other unionists promised disruption Muldoon threatened a snap election, initially blaming SUP unionists for stirring up 'unwelcome' agitation. In July, Knox challenged Muldoon to call a snap election to test the public's reaction to the freeze and restrictions on redundancy payments. In response, on 20 August, Muldoon tightened the freeze still further by introducing new regulations forbidding any conciliation council being formed, and banned the Arbitration Court from hearing cases until the freeze was over. Conversely, he eased the clamp on wage rises and broadened the circumstances under which manufacturers and retailers could pass their costs on.

The bad news continued. Muldoon's budget that year gave tax concessions to those at the higher end of the wage scale but little or nothing to those further down, including the great bulk of the country's workers. For part-time workers and married women, tax actually increased. The combination led to a joint FOL/Combined State Unions (CSU) campaign against the freeze, which resulted in rallies in all parts of the country from mid-October.

The size of the crowds attending these rallies was remarkable — 40,000 in Auckland; 3000 in Whangarei; 4000 in Christchurch; 6000 in Wellington, and 2000 in Rotorua. Even Tokoroa attracted a crowd of 2000, mainly Kinleith timber-workers and their families. There were 38 rallies altogether, including many in small rural towns with relatively few workers. Otorohanga, for example, attracted 65 protesters, Te Awamutu 75, Taihape 90, Levin 150 and Westport 150.[257]

Following consultation with the FOL executive, the Drivers' Federation then sought a hearing in the Arbitration Court on the legality of the wage freeze regulations, and when it lost this case it went to the Appeal Court. It lost there too, but on a split decision. Its November 1982 conference reaffirmed its decision to press for an immediate $20 wage claim. In the meantime, unemployment was growing by 1500 a month and inflation was striking 20 per cent. There was even more pressure from poorer wage workers for pay relief because they had been denied increases in their awards as a result of the freeze and received little or no tax relief. In some cases they had ended up paying more in the recent budget. The November conference also proposed the establishment of an independent body, including union and employer representatives, to review wage-fixing procedures to try to make them more flexible.[258]

The government responded with a quick 'no' to the $20-a-week proposal, although Muldoon left the door open for talks with employers and the FOL to review the wage-fixing system. He reaffirmed, however, that the wage freeze would remain until the following June. On 15 April 1983 he tilted the playing field again by proposing two options: either to extend the wage freeze for a further six months with no wage adjustment, or to institute a small wage order — 2 per cent — to apply after 23 June, followed by a continuation of the wage freeze for a further six months from that date.

The FOL and the CSU rejected both (4600 workers had been laid off since the freeze began) and determined that they would not agree to any extension of the wage freeze. Knox and Douglas wanted to enter into meaningful wage adjustment negotiations immediately. Muldoon refused. The stage was set for the stoush to intensify. Douglas even feared that Muldoon's 'less than hidden' agenda was to use the freeze to try to crush the union movement altogether. In May, in response to the FOL's continued 'aggressive' and very public stance against the wage freeze, the government suspended the tripartite wage discussions — for the fourth time. There was no consensus. Muldoon extended the wage freeze to 29 February 1984.[259]

In response, the FOL and many individuals instituted a campaign of go-slows and a series of rolling 12- or 24-hour strikes. One newspaper called it 'a campaign of industrial guerilla warfare'. That was an overstatement, but the anger among workers and their union leaders was palpable. The cornerstone of the FOL's response to Muldoon's extension of the freeze was to defuse direct industrial action and instead to continue to negotiate, with a new demand for a one-off, interim across-the-board $20 wage rise for all wage and salary earners. It was a measured response, but drew nonsensical replies from FOL adversaries. Peter Johnson, president of the Auckland Employers' Association, called the '$20 a week' campaign a 'Socialist Unity Party plot to make New Zealand a communist country'.[260]

Ken Douglas's energies at this time were directed elsewhere. Late in April 1983, 650 Kawerau pulp and paper workers went on strike (and a further 500 were locked out by the company as a consequence of the strikers' action) over the refusal of their employers, Tasman Pulp and Paper, to give them back-pay owed to them during the freeze. The dispute dragged on until 31 May with no resolution until the workers' union, the Northern Federation of Pulp and Paper Workers, called on the FOL for help. Douglas travelled to Kawerau and after an 11-hour meeting with both sides, thrashed out a proposal to settle the strike to everybody's satisfaction. The men received their back-pay.[261]

This brought Douglas unwelcome praise from Muldoon, who commented that he would sooner work with SUP leader Douglas than 'moderate' president Jim Knox, who had recently described him as a 'bully and a ranter'. Muldoon went on to say that there were people on the FOL executive who *could* lead the union movement responsibly, adding, 'I'm not going to give you the names of them because if I did it would be the kiss of death for them.' That was astute, and Douglas — fully aware of the damage any praise from Muldoon could cause him among unionists — breathed a sigh of relief. He rejected claims that he personally had ended the Kawerau conflict or that his mediating role was ironic in light of his reputation as a communist trouble-maker. 'There was nothing magical about it. The same result would have happened had any other FOL executive member been there,' he said. His function as FOL secretary was to give effect to the policy decisions of the organisation.

The Kawerau dispute and Douglas's role in helping to settle it in Knox's absence put him in the media spotlight as never before. He was discomforted, even alarmed, mainly because journalists and television reporters, as was their wont, personalised the situation, describing Douglas as the workers' saviour. It was an inaccurate assessment. The Kawerau settlement was a joint agreement signed by management and labour, among whom Douglas was but one signatory, albeit an important one. He was also uneasy when some commentators called him the 'strong man' of the FOL. The 61-year-old Knox was still in charge, although his intemperate language under pressure was turning people off. Douglas, by contrast, was more considered in his statements to the press. They were fewer in number than Knox's, but more and more widely read. It was hardly a changing of the guard, but Douglas was gaining widespread respect and some correspondents were suggesting that he should now replace Knox as head of the FOL.

It was true that the Kawerau settlement had required no magic on his part. The timing of the talks was not determined by him as a part of any grand strategy. But Douglas was also being self-effacing when he downplayed his role. At a time when trade unions looked to their umbrella organisation for direct intervention in seemingly intractable disputes, Douglas used a combination of persuasive oratory, bluff and personal charisma to persuade 650 'militant' pulp and paper workers that the agreement finally reached — where the employer had moved considerably closer to the unions' positions than the other way round — was the best deal they would win. Speaking to a journalist, he invoked Roman history in an analysis of the Kawerau resolution: 'You know, history is not the recording of brilliant individuals. It's the recording of consequences of the clash of classes, of class struggle. Spartacus might have led the slave revolt but he was thrown up as a consequence of all the social factors which created the conditions of the revolt itself.'[262]

Focus on the FOL's campaign for a $20-a-week rise was overtaken in July 1983, when Minister of Labour Jim Bolger drafted a new bill outlawing compulsory unionism. It was a bold move, bearing in mind that similar proposals had failed in the past partly because unions, employers and their associations had opposed them. This time, some employers nodded their heads in agreement, as long as it was accompanied by a long-term wage-fixing agreement. Conversely, unions threatened to impose closed shops and use 'strong arms' to maintain recruitment. Even Muldoon conceded that closed shops and standover tactics would be 'probable' if voluntary unionism went ahead. There was also likely to be conflict between union and non-union workers on site. This had happened before, in particular during and after the 1951 waterfront lockout, and had led to violence. It was the basis on which a number of employer groups also opposed voluntary unionism. The management of New Zealand Forest Products, for example, believed it would lead to loss of productivity, decreased profits and reduced export income.[263]

But the proposal went ahead. In October, Muldoon introduced the Industrial Law Reform Bill into Parliament — its main aim being to remove unqualified preference and introduce voluntary unionism. It also proposed penalties and remedies for discrimination, undue influence and strikes aimed at 'closed shop' situations, and a toughening up on unionists' right of entry into workplaces, promoting employer collection of union dues and imposing limits on union fees. There were also proposals for increases in the penalties for strikes in essential industries — and the introduction of youth rates. It was the most severe of Muldoon's many 'anti-union' laws since the 1979 Remuneration Act.

The FOL responded with a huge submission to the select committee studying the Bill. It pointed out that in 1977, 89.2 per cent of workers covering 67 per cent of unions and 81 per cent of total union membership supported compulsory unionism. Muldoon wanted voluntary unionism to stem union work stoppages and give individual workers the right to opt out of their union in protest. The first claim was not supported by the facts. Statistics in the 1982 *ILO Year Book on Labour* recorded that between 1971 and 1981 New Zealand had lost 314 working days per thousand workers per year. That stood in stark and favourable comparison with 369 for the United States, 513 for Ireland, 562 for Australia, 536 for the United Kingdom, 850 for Canada and 990 for Italy. Furthermore, there was already provision for conscientious objection for workers who did not wish to belong to a union. Ken Douglas made particular mention of the potential for damage to unions with large memberships of minority racial groups and/or low-paid women workers in small workplaces — the latter view strongly supported by women's groups, led by the National Advisory Council on the Employment of Women.[264]

The Employers' Federation also opposed the measure because it was too negative, emphasising penalties rather than positive industrial relations. Its executive director Jim Rowe saw troubled times ahead, particularly as the Bill seemed to indicate employers would be regarded as culprits in discrimination over union membership. On top of this, there was no public consultation and the select committee hearings were stopped early, meaning a number of people were not heard. Other employer groups were also opposed to the proposed legislation. The Freezing Companies Association and the Association of Waterfront Employers, both umbrella groups for organisations that employed thousands of workers, believed that voluntarism would worsen industrial relations in their spheres.

These objections cut no ice with Muldoon and Bolger. Through November and December the Bill was debated, its main features — voluntary unionism, youth rates and increased penalties against those on strike in essential industries — surviving rigorous opposition in the select committee hearings. But not in the House, where the first vote resulted in a 45 to 42 margin against the Bill as independent MPs (and former Labourites) John Kirk and Brian MacDonell, Social Creditors Bruce Beetham and Garry Knapp, and National mavericks Marilyn Waring and Mike Minogue voted with the Opposition. This was unprecedented; it was the only time any government had suffered a first-division loss since the Second World War. The Bill looked doomed to fail. Muldoon then ditched the clause imposing youth pay rates, which persuaded Kirk, Minogue and Waring to change their minds, and parliamentarians agreed, by 44–43, to allow the measure to go back to further select committee hearings.

The Bill was finally passed on 13 December 1983, 46–45, to become law on 1 February 1984. Waring, Beetham, Knapp and MacDonell still voted against it. It succeeded on the decision of John Kirk, the Sydenham MP and son of former prime minister Norman Kirk, with some in Labour calling him a 'Judas'. David Lange, Leader of the Opposition, promised his party would scrap the legislation if Labour won the 1984 election. At the same time, Muldoon extended the wage freeze indefinitely. Unemployment numbers skyrocketed. In March 1981, there were 47,464 unemployed with another 15,750 on special work. By March 1983, those figures had increased to 72,770 and 22,583 respectively; by December 1983 they had reached 81,062 and 47,478. Together this was more than 10 per cent of the workforce. There seemed no end in sight.[265]

The new law infringed clauses 87 and 98 of the International Labour Organisation's conventions in overriding, by legislation, freely negotiated award clauses. Moreover, it passed in spite of unions being forced to hold an 'officially supervised' ballot among their members which had resulted in an 82 per cent vote to retain the 'unqualified preference' clause. Clearly Muldoon, his parliamentary colleagues and many employers thought the figure would be drastically lower.[266]

The Act neither reformed industrial relations nor promoted the harmony that Muldoon had prophesied. On the contrary, the reverse eventuated. Within three months, between February and May 1984, there were 25 significant stoppages because of the law, the most in such a short time for decades, as unionists refused to work alongside non-union men and women. They included disputes in freezing works; railway workshops; dairy, rubber, concrete, aluminium extrusion, phosphate and paint factories; knitting mills, and on construction sites up and down the country.

Collectively, these disputes represented more than 14,000 work days lost, the Auckland Employers' Association estimating 8700 days were lost in its area alone. In the freezing industries, up to 18 April there were 5916 days lost, leading 2850 workers to forfeit $491,000 in wages. Some freezing works did not recover from this. Reeling from the quickening pace of the introduction of labour-saving technology, they closed altogether. The voluntary unionism legislation did not affect large, more militant unions, the great bulk of whose members stayed. But, in a foretaste of things to come, whereby 'reluctant' unionists saw little value in staying within the fold, by June 1984, four months after the legislation was introduced, the Auckland-based Clerical Workers' Union had lost over 3000 members, 15 per cent of its total membership.[267]

By 1984, leading up to the Industrial Law Reform Act, the government had passed or introduced 19 Bills that were anti-worker or anti-union. Ken Douglas, the FOL, and its constituent unions all looked forward in hope to the election of a Labour government later in the year to repeal much of this legislation, including that relating to voluntary unionism. It was clear Muldoon was relying on prejudice against unions in marginal provincial seats to try to win or hold on to them. Alongside pro-Springbok tour supporters they had been his saviour during National's narrow victory in 1981. In June 1984, the International Confederation of Free Trade Unions (ICFTU) named New Zealand as a 'violator' of human rights, and argued that such rights had been cut back to a bare minimum. Earlier Muldoon had declined to meet an ICFTU delegation when it was in New Zealand.[268]

Muldoon had a remarkable, albeit subliminal, regard for Douglas. Away from the glare of the press, where Muldoon was prone to rant and hyperbole, he acknowledged Douglas's abilities and importance as a union leader. (He barely tolerated Knox, who despised Muldoon.) Douglas and Muldoon sometimes met in one-to-one or tripartite talks and the Prime Minister's office was always open to Douglas (and in fact Knox, with due regard for his role as FOL president). The personal regard in which Muldoon held Douglas was best illustrated by his astonishing attempt to bring him 'alongside' as part of his think tank, in part to combat a political ideology pervasive in Treasury that Muldoon considered too right-wing. In May 1983, Bernie Galvin, head of the Prime Minister's Department, approached Douglas on Muldoon's behalf to sound him out about whether he would be interested in leaving his job as secretary of the FOL for a two-year secondment to the department. Douglas was taken aback. He asked Galvin why. Answering in generalities, Galvin indicated that his expertise could be useful in providing a different political and economic perspective than those emanating 'from other sources'. Douglas was intrigued but non-committal, saying that he would need to have a confidential discussion with Knox first.[269]

When the two of them met, Knox laughed. 'Why would you want to do that?' he asked.

'I don't really know, but of course I'd have to step down as secretary,' Douglas replied, explaining the likely scenario.

'That's probably why they're doing it!' retorted Knox, shaking his head.

Muldoon's approach was not as radical as might be thought. Various business people, some of whom opposed his autocratic tendencies, had been seconded to the Prime Minister's Department for periods, although many of these were 'single issue' appointments. As it was, Douglas turned down the offer. There was probably truth in Knox's assertions that Muldoon was trying to 'buy him off'. Douglas was a trade unionist through and through, and he envisaged a future as president of the Federation of Labour, seeing it as an exciting challenge. He offered Galvin the name of another union principal to take his place but Galvin told him he did not have a mandate for that. Clearly Douglas was the man Muldoon wanted.[270]

On 1 April 1984, the government gave an $8-a-week gross hand-out to wage and salary earners — equating to a 2.9 per cent increase in the average basic wage. It was little enough, coming, as it did, at the end of the two-and-a-half-year wage freeze. It was a 'take it or leave it' offer. The FOL decried it as far too low but took no direct action. Knox urged workers to reject it and request their bosses to engage in direct wage bargaining. He and Douglas preferred to look ahead to the end of the year and work towards a Labour Party victory in the general election.

This approach resonated at the FOL's annual conference the following month, with the 380 delegates cheering Opposition leader David Lange when he promised that a Labour government would immediately dispense with voluntary unionism and the freeze on wage bargaining. This sealed the closest relationship between the industrial and political wings of the labour movement in years. It was also the smoothest, happiest conference for years. One notable absentee was Tony Neary, whose 10,000-member Electrical Workers' Union had pulled out of the FOL because it 'did not like the way the organisation was heading'. Neary believed Knox should go — although he did not identify a preferred replacement. The conference vowed to work hard for a Labour victory at the polls at the end of the year.[271]

In fact, workers did not have to wait that long. On 14 June, Muldoon, visibly drunk, announced a snap election for 14 July after National MP Marilyn Waring told him she would not support the government over its opposition to a Labour-sponsored anti-nuclear bill. He did not have to — Waring had not threatened to block confidence and supply — but Muldoon wanted a mandate for his policies. He miscalculated badly. With the recently formed laissez-faire New Zealand Party, led by property developer Bob Jones, splitting the right-wing vote, Labour romped in with 65 seats to 37, voters rejecting Muldoon's paternalistic and increasingly authoritarian rule. Workers rejoiced, and the

Federation of Labour looked forward to a close working relationship with a new, more sympathetic government which, initially, was promising longer-term wage reforms.

At the same time the FOL could ponder, with some pride, its successes during recent years under difficult conditions. In 1983 it had resisted a government and Employers' Association agenda to destroy the national award system, and it believed that in its place the campaign for a $20-a-week rise had been largely successful. More specifically, it had forced the government to abandon the iniquitous Remuneration Act as a consequence of its 1980 victory at Kinleith. It had successfully resisted a two-and-a-half-year lockout of Mangere Bridge workers in Auckland — the longest in New Zealand's history — and won a major redundancy deal for the workers, also securing the agreement of construction industry employers to include redundancy provisions in all future contracts. The FOL also secured a decent redundancy deal in 1981 for Levin's 67 sacked Rixen factory strikers after the owner had offered nothing (which had resulted in the workers 'sitting in' at the factory for 11 weeks), and enjoyed a successful resolution of the 1983 Kawerau dispute in the workers' favour. It had won site agreements on major construction jobs in the face of employer intransigence, and had controlled the importation of foreign riggers when qualified local men were available to do the work at Marsden Point. With the promise of a more sympathetic industrial environment to come, Ken Douglas looked to the future with optimism.

CHAPTER 9

Douglas and Douglas

Knox, Douglas and other trade unionists greeted Muldoon's demise with huge sighs of relief. Ever fond of flowery language, Jim Knox wrote that the FOL had suffered an eight-year 'political trial' under an 'economic wizard' who turned out to be a 'sorcerer's apprentice'. There was encouragement, too, in that the essence of Labour's election platform had been based around the mantra of 'social and economic consensus'.

The early portents were promising as the new government 'opened its doors' and allowed trade union leaders, among others, to speak frankly at an economic summit conference in September 1984 which brought together capitalists, unionists and politicians. The gathering was a watershed, the first of its type in New Zealand. The FOL and union leaders were keenly anticipating some kind of consensus between the state, capital and labour where they could move forward. They saw 'bread and butter' issues such as wage negotiation being addressed with little angst, and their role expanding so that they had a more direct impact and influence on the future economic direction of the country. Knox called for government policies to be appropriate for the people's needs, for recognition of social and cultural diversity, and for greater public participation in the decision-making process.

Ken Douglas was more circumspect, warning that the summit would not be a cure-all and that a comparison with a recent similar summit in Australia was erroneous. In that country, he noted, there was concentrated union action, whereas there was division among New Zealand trade unionists (with Tony Neary having formed his own predominantly white-collar, 'non-aligned' union grouping outside the FOL). Moreover, unlike New Zealand, there had been direct participation by the Australian Council of Trade Unions in Australian Labor Party policy in that country before their recent election, which meant that neither the media nor capital interests could destroy it — and there had been live television coverage of the event, meaning there was no distortion the reporting.[272]

Twenty-six union leaders (but not Neary, who was left off the list), including the full FOL executive, attended the summit between 11 and 13 September. Seven more came from the Combined State Unions. There was no direct political representation, although Prime Minister David Lange and new Finance Minister Roger Douglas were chairman and deputy chairman respectively. Its broad aim was to search for a consensus on ways to achieve sustained economic recovery. At its end, delegates issued a joint communiqué pledging their support in promoting unity, cooperation, greater understanding of the country's economic standing and a commitment to assist and cooperate in dealing with these issues. Knox's public offering of his hand to the 'high prince' of capitalism, Ron Trotter — chairman of directors and CEO of Fletcher Challenge and soon to be the inaugural chair of the Business Roundtable — remained for many in the years to come the conference's most compelling image.[273]

Union delegates at the summit called for more specific aims — an immediate wage increase accompanied by tax changes, and spending policies that paid particular attention to the plight of low-paid workers, an immediate relaxation of the wage freeze regulations, the protection of workers against price increases, and the urgent renegotiation of the state-pay-fixing legislation so that when full wage bargaining resumed in the private sector negotiations would take place in terms of a fair and equitable legal structure. This was both idealistic and optimistic; the proof of the pudding would be in the eating.[274]

Indeed, the euphoria manifest at the summit's end soon dissipated when the government was tardy in granting an interim wage increase, postponing it for three months. The FOL's call for an immediate $15 a week increase (around 5 per cent of the average weekly wage) to assist the country's workers, who were in a dire way as a consequence of Muldoon's wage freeze, a recent devaluation, a substantial fuel price increase and rises in the cost of living, was ignored. Lange told unions to 'await developments' in the November budget. This reaction tested the FOL and union leaders and threatened very quickly to unravel the goodwill the government and the FOL had forged at the summit, particularly after news emerged that New Zealand's top 10 companies had achieved profits of between $130 and $180 million during the 1983/84 tax year.

On 2 October, Ken Douglas warned that if the wage increase was not forthcoming he would ignore the continuing freeze and tell unions to negotiate directly with the employers. Roger Douglas seemed to be the stumbling block, stating he was against an early move. Contending that the FOL's request for an immediate $15 a week across the board increase would cost the government about $800 million, which he said was not sustainable, and that 'relief' for workers should come through tax cuts and use of the social welfare system, it was clear that he was moving to a different agenda, one where 'reaction' to Muldoonism had no place. When the unions disregarded the 4 per cent guideline that the government proposed, David Lange, to the FOL's fury, raised the spectre of reimposing a system of centralised wage fixing. Within a fortnight the government's accord with the FOL was in danger of collapse, with both parties sticking to entrenched positions on the pay issue.[275]

The FOL held out for increases of close to a minimum of 9.6 per cent. Unions wanted a lot more. The Engineers' and the Electrical Workers' Unions each sought a 20 per cent wage rise, the Waterside Workers' Federation wanted 25 per cent, while the Drivers' Federation looked for a $25 rise in the award round set down for early in 1985. Crisis talks between Lange, his Minister of Labour Stan Rodger, employers, Federated Farmers and the FOL and CSU on 23 November quickly broke down over the impasse. A gap was yawning, with the potential for serious industrial dislocation. The enthusiasm manifest at the summit had lasted a very short time indeed. Any government–union accord was now in tatters. The summit had been window-dressing, not the dawn of a brave new world.[276]

One minister in the Labour Cabinet wrote that the stand-off was Jim Knox's epitaph. Another bewailed the absence of Ken Douglas from the talks, commenting that he would have kept the whole business on track. (At the time Douglas was in Russia, undergoing medical treatment for his damaged gall bladder.) It was noteworthy that Douglas was now receiving as much attention in the media as Knox, if not more, with journalists reacting positively to his more consensual and slogan-free approach.

Lange, concerned, looked for a solution in private discussions with Knox, Ron Burgess (chairman of the Combined State Unions) and, in Douglas's absence, FOL vice-president Sonja Davies. As a result of these discussions, Stan Rodger introduced a Wage Fixing Reform Bill which set in place the government's new wage-fixing procedures. Within days, the government decided on wage rises of between 6.2 and 7.2 per cent for skilled workers, higher than the government guideline of 4 per cent but considerably lower than the unions' initial demands. The government on wage fixing cut across the negotiation and conciliation procedures that employers and unions had been engaging in, to their chagrin. Lange told the unions to settle at that figure or face direct wage controls.[277]

Contemporaneously, the corporate sector began to flourish, freed of many of Muldoon's draconian policies. Over the next 18 months, monopolies made huge profits and their directors and shareholders grew fat. They came to dominate the economy more and more. Many were overseas cartels whose profits left the country. Company directors, fresh from joining in the litany of praise for the new government's message of restraint at the September summit, rewarded themselves with massive rises in directors' fees. Typical was a 40 per cent rise — from $100,000 to $140,000 — awarded to the nine directors of the ANZ Group on 16 January 1985. More followed. Newmans Group awarded its directors a massive 66 per cent rise; Cable Price Downer 60 per cent; R and W Hellaby 40 per cent; Watties 27 per cent, and Dominion Breweries 21 per cent.[278]

Management salaries also kept rising at a much faster rate than those of the workers they employed. In April 1985, an Auckland recruitment company reported that top executive salaries had increased by between 20 and 30 per cent since the end of the wage freeze the previous November. Chief executives of big companies enjoyed salaries and bonuses, plus added extras like company cars, that far exceeded $150,000. This failed to stem an exodus to Australia, where executives could earn more; neither did the 6 to 7 per cent rise for wage and salary workers stop their emigration to Australia, where they, also, could earn a lot more.[279]

Looking back on the first six months of the new Labour government, it is apparent that the economic summit resulted in nothing but a raft of failed ideals and the sacrifice of workers' jobs in the restructuring and corporatisation of state-owned industry that was the hallmark of Roger Douglas's new agenda. Ken Douglas felt angry and cheated. He wanted to believe in this government, but it was betraying that belief: 'I saw the confidence that workers and their families felt about the election of the government, the promise it held out and all the fine things that were said.' What offended Douglas and union members most was having their keen desire to cooperate — after years of being Muldoon's scapegoats — slammed back in their faces by the very party that had promised to deliver them from all of that.[280]

Working people would come to be hurt by the government's policies, enshrined in its radical new economic direction under Roger Douglas — 'Rogernomics' as the laissez-faire monetarist reforms he introduced came to be called. Protections against cheap imports mostly from Asia were removed, allowing them to flood the market, forcing many local manufacturing businesses to close with the loss of thousands of jobs. Clothing and footwear manufacturers were particularly hard hit. Floating the exchange rate led the dollar to rise and export returns to fall, putting pressure not only on farmers but also on the thousands of workers who processed and transported the country's exports — freezing workers, timber workers, drivers, waterside workers and seamen. Many hundreds lost their jobs, the situation exacerbated by increasing scientific and technological advances which led to more and more workers being replaced by computer or machine — particularly among the unskilled or semi-skilled.

Rural towns, in particular, suffered as a consequence, and this was made worse when Richard Prebble — as Minister of Railways and Postmaster-General — closed down railway lines and nearly half the country's Post Offices, leading to even more unemployment. Some communities became little more than ghost towns. For the FOL the one positive note was the introduction of the Union Membership Bill in December 1984, which led to the reintroduction of compulsory unionism on 1 June 1985 under the Industrial Relations Amendment Act. The following month, the government also lifted the long-static minimum adult pay rate from $100 to $170 a week.[281]

These measures aside, within months the labour movement's industrial and political wings had become estranged as the full effects of the Rogernomics reforms took hold. Roger Douglas 'freed' everything except wages, devastating the lives of workers already faced with rapidly increasing unemployment. It was done stealthily, with no union input into the changes. To combat Rogernomics, the FOL and the unions developed policies on a much wider range of issues well outside the traditional union sphere of wages and conditions. The grand plan was that by producing an alternative economic policy the movement would be better placed to fight 'the media war'. Along with his constituency, Ken Douglas had been duped into believing that 'utopia' had arrived with the election of the fourth Labour government, and the enthusiasm of the subsequent summit had confirmed that optimism. But it all turned to custard as Roger Douglas began to deregulate the economy. Unlike Muldoon, Douglas refused at all times to consult with the FOL before introducing reforms that affected workers.

Ken Douglas believed the real game plan was being set by Business Roundtable ideologues. Certainly they had the ear of Roger Douglas, Labour's most powerful politician in its first three years in power. Under Douglas, corporatisation was following international agendas. Hatchet men with no links or empathy with the grass roots, and whose modus operandi was totally focused on profit and loss irrespective of the hurt they might cause along the way, were arriving thick and fast. This course, Ken Douglas believed, was irreversible. Business liked it. Even if Roger Douglas fell under a bus his agenda would continue, and there were already signs that under a National Party administration it would intensify.

Rogernomics became the personification of neoliberalism. Roger Douglas seemed to share Muldoon's belief that a low-wage policy was the only path to economic prosperity. In the wash, companies enjoyed big profits and even bigger dividends, proportionately, for their shareholders. This was a Labour government like none before it. Not only unionists but also left-wingers in the government — shut out from Cabinet — watched helplessly from the sidelines, the latter keeping quiet under the pressure of collective responsibility.

The May 1985 FOL conference should have been celebratory in tone, a welcome to the first Labour government in nine years. It was anything but as speaker after speaker berated the government's economic policies, including the imminent introduction of a Goods and Services Tax which was about to impose a further financial burden on low-income earners. David Lange's address failed to turn the tide. When he called for union restraint he was heckled by a minority yelling 'Rubbish' as he spoke. He was unfazed, but such a reception was unprecedented for a Labour politician — let alone a Prime Minister — at an FOL conference. The feeling on the floor was that workers had been betrayed by 'their' government, although as Jim Knox warned the delegates, the FOL never had any intention of divorcing itself from the administration. 'We want you there and we intend to keep you there,' he said. That was all Lange and his deputy Geoffrey Palmer wanted to hear.[282]

Ignoring the temptation to continually bewail the impact of Rogernomics, Ken Douglas preferred to look ahead. He implored unions to improve their acts to be more competitive, and match the new aggression of the employers: 'What we are saying to the unions is "Cut the rhetoric and word polishing, get out there to your membership, organise delegates, seminars, memberships, work your Maori and women's structures and widen the base of your operations."' This was new — hitherto the union movement had been slow to offer fresh solutions because there had been little need. It was involved just in salary negotiation and (except in 1968) always guaranteed a wage rise after agreement in the Arbitration Court, to compensate for inflation if nothing else. Traditionally unions believed they determined when a strike began and when it ended. For Ken Douglas, it was a reminder of how things had been at the turn of the 20th century, when the labour movement was taking root. Then, the workers' movement needed parliamentary representation to control, restrain and regulate capital. Now, he believed, the heirs of the very people who had created those regulations were tearing them down. Douglas would hold on firmly to these beliefs for the remainder of his union career.[283]

In September 1985, unions began bargaining in the Arbitration Court for increases of between 15 and 45 per cent — a figure both the government and employers looked at askance, although Lange promised the government would not intervene. The FOL also called for a gross minimum wage of $208 a week — supermarket workers at the time were being paid between $130 and $150. At the same time, on 9 September, the Higher Salaries Commission awarded David Lange a 37 per cent pay increase, Cabinet ministers and the Leader of the Opposition 38 per cent, and senior public servants between 35 and 38 per cent, all backdated to 1 April on the excuse that state sector salaries for senior managers had not kept pace with their equivalents in the private sector because of the recent wage freeze. The timing of the Commission's decisions, on the eve of the wage round, left the government with egg on its face. Even Lange called it 'pitiful' — but he did not reject it. In November, the Commission awarded judges rises of between 33.7 and 38.3 per cent.

These increasing disparities raised tensions over the wage round, causing Ken Douglas, in a rare display of public aggression, to tell Cabinet ministers Roger Douglas and Richard Prebble to 'shut up' after the two issued persistent warnings in the press against 'excessive' wage increases for workers.

> They should not be interfering with the wage round and the parties involved need to get on with their negotiations without political interference. What people need to remember is that unions are asking for only two things — a fair increase to help the low paid and that living standards for all workers must fall no further. It's the government's monetary policy that is causing unemployment, not the unions' wage claims.[284]

Later that month, Tony Neary's Electrical Workers' Union set the bar high when it sought a 24 per cent rise on which it initially refused to budge, although it finally settled for 15.5 per cent. Soon afterwards, the government released the latest inflation figure of 16.3 per cent. In terms of the real value of their increase, working people's salaries were just treading water. Nevertheless, Lange was unhappy, describing the electrical workers' settlement as 'pushing the tolerance of the government to the very limit'. Yet other awards agreed to through October and November ranged between 14 and 17 per cent. Only five unions settled for less than 15.5 per cent and some received a lot more, ignoring Stan Rodger's call that they should be between 10 and 13 per cent.

The May 1986 FOL conference represented a significant milestone for the working class and the trade union movement. It was the 70th anniversary of the founding of the New Zealand Labour Party and the 35th anniversary of the 1951 lockout. But many delegates were bewildered and confused. They had a Labour government, but it was one with which they found it hard to identify. There was just token applause for David Lange when he left the podium. His speech had drawn an indifferent response, and less than a third of the delegates had stood for his entrance. This despite Knox telling him that he could be assured of a warm welcome: 'And do not get me wrong. It comes from the heart.'

But he misjudged the mood. Knox, a tried and true Labour man from 'way back', was indulging in nostalgic unreality. As Rogernomics rolled on with no signs of abating, any visions of a 'working class' labour political movement were wistful sentimentality. Delegates looked for comfort elsewhere. In sharp contrast to the response given to Lange, most were on their feet in thunderous ovation as Therese O'Connell of the Clerical Workers' Association celebrated her election to the FOL's Women's Advisory Committee by singing a satirical ditty she called 'A Song for Ruthless Ruth Richardson', referring to the National Party's youth issues spokesperson.[285]

For his part, Ken Douglas was elucidating a broader vision. In a precursor to what would become an integral to his modus operandi, he told delegates that he envisaged change, with labour market flexibility becoming a byword for a deregulated economy irrespective of which political party was in power. Unions, he argued, would need to deal proactively, not reactively, with this new order — as they were already doing in most European countries and the United States. Yet there were massive problems. Unions had to come to terms with the new order. Labour market flexibility maximised profit for corporations while diminishing, or trying to diminish, rights that unions had won by hard graft over decades — national award minimum wages, penal and overtime rates, holiday pay, sick leave and safety standards.

'Attacking these rights has to be confronted,' he told delegates. 'This is where we need to focus our energies . . . Time is short.' Douglas spoke commandingly, reinforcing his already considerable prestige within the organisation. The *New Zealand Herald*'s industrial reporter Ross Barrett called it a virtuoso performance.[286]

It needs to be stressed that beyond the core of Rogernomics, Douglas and the FOL welcomed the Labour government's assertions of nationhood after decades of colonial mentality, praised the new 'Tomorrow's Schools' education reforms, lauded the first-ever Ministry of Women's Affairs, applauded its efforts to preserve the Maori language and, most important of all, congratulated it for its implementation of a 'sane', independent and non-nuclear foreign policy. In industrial issues, aside from the reintroduction of compulsory unionism, the FOL welcomed extra funding for child care, the introduction of a low-pay unit within the framework of the tripartite wage conference, increases in the medical services benefit for children, the introduction of permanent status for part-time public service employees, as well as legislation allowing for a Trade Union Education Authority and paid educational leave.

The only other union leader with Douglas's level of foresight at the time was Rob Campbell, a university law graduate and a committed unionist who, by this time, was on both the Labour Party's national council and the FOL executive representing the Distribution Workers' Federation. Young, energetic and outspoken, Campbell was impatiently promoting the kind of consensual industrial relations that Ken Douglas was working towards, and looked towards an expanded union body (akin to the merger of the private and state unions which was yet to come) to give the movement strength and wider acceptability. He had the support of Douglas, but not Jim Knox nor the majority of the organisation's blue-collar executive, hidebound by the status quo. Specifically, Campbell was angry that the FOL under Knox's stewardship was not ascribing urgency to the formation of the bigger body, as the first prerequisite for any union/government accommodation.

Douglas was in an awkward position. He agreed with Campbell, whom he had promoted as a protégé in the movement through the Wellington Drivers' Union. He saw Campbell as a new breed of trade union leader — brimming with new ideas, not constrained by traditional ideologies. But after some stressful internal debate Douglas sided with Knox. He had worked side by side with Knox since 1979 and had deep respect for his qualities despite deep-rooted concerns over his 'immovability' on new ideas. Traditional loyalties ran deep. The status quo remained.

As it had with other union leaders, the Labour government appointed Campbell to a board, in his case that of the Bank of New Zealand. In July 1986 the BNZ board decided to partly privatise the bank to allow it to raise $150 million through a public share issue. Campbell expressed no issue with this, as it was explained to him that it would then be able to operate competitively abroad with a capital base more in tune with internationally accepted standards. In August, a majority on the FOL national executive gave its official blessing to Campbell's stance on the sale of BNZ shares, even though its annual conference the previous May had unanimously passed a resolution opposing the sale of any part of state-owned enterprises to private shareholders. But a minority of the executive, which included Jim Knox, did not, and the issue went to the federation's national council for resolution. The council voted on 31 July to reject the government's plan to sell part of the BNZ. Campbell's was the only dissenting voice.[287]

Campbell found his position untenable, and on 18 August he resigned from the FOL executive. His promising career as a union leader was nipped in the bud. Initially there was no explanation given for the resignation, but on 24 August he publicly lambasted the FOL as incompetent and its leadership as intolerable. He was particularly critical of its frosty relationship with the state 'because the FOL had failed to adapt to the new economic and political environment created by the government' — the FOL had been incompetent in not seeking an incomes agreement for the wage round, he said, believing it would undermine the prized ideal of free wage bargaining. Notably, within a few days, tripartite pre-wage negotiations broke up in disarray.[288]

There were huge divisions between the articulate, complex, enigmatic, feisty 'new-age' 35-year-old Campbell and the honest, sincere, hard-working but one-dimensional and often inarticulate Knox. The latter was 32 years Campbell's senior, and the fire and thunder that had once characterised his persona in the public arena had long since lost its ferocity. His image now was that of a benign father figure although, it must be stressed, one who still commanded the loyalty and respect of the bulk of the country's workers. Knox had integrity, always having the workers' best interests at heart. He did not do deals like Fintan Walsh or Tom Skinner. His work was always honest and transparent.[289]

Campbell had ambition. Before he resigned, nobody had seemed sure of his commitment to trade unionism, short or long term. Those critics who now lambasted his apparent turnaround — traitorous in some unionists' eyes — forgot that he had been working hard as a unionist for nearly all of his working life, first in the Wellington Drivers' Union (and writing a book on its history), in the Drivers' Federation, and latterly as leader of the Distribution Workers' Union. Reflecting his skill, his rise had been rapid. He was the son of a bank manager, and the more scathing among his detractors believed that with the BNZ share issue controversy he was now 'going full circle and returning to family business'.[290]

Yet the more far-sighted among his colleagues understood that Campbell had the nous and flexibility to take a new union structure into the future, not being hidebound by ideology and the traditional ways of operating to which Knox was wedded. The events of 1986 did not come out of nowhere. In 1983, with Alf Kirk, a former FOL economist, Campbell had written a book called *After the Freeze*, in which they argued that New Zealand's wage-fixing procedures were badly in need of reform as real wages could not go on rising forever and wage fixing had to take into account the overall economic situation. While acknowledging the need for more flexibility in the system, Campbell and Kirk rejected free wage bargaining as being out of step with the underlying philosophy of the trade union movement and ruled out market forces as the main factor in wage fixing. A new form of wage fixing needed to be introduced which was much more centralised, they believed. David Lange, to whom Campbell was close, saw in him a conduit for a more productive relationship between the government and the FOL. Knox's 1986 attack on the government's free-market economic policies was predictable, he believed. Campbell saw himself as a realist promoting an industrial approach closer to political populism. His antagonists castigated him as an unrepentant 'Rogernome'. Whatever the analysis, the actuality was that it was a very different world from the previous Labour government of Norman Kirk — and that of Robert Muldoon and his interventionist obsessions.[291]

Campbell's promise as a 'new age' trade unionist had had a significant impact on Ken Douglas, and his withdrawal from the movement was both a huge hurt and an immense disappointment. Douglas saw Campbell rather than himself as Knox's successor and as the first leader of the future Council of Trade Unions, and he had taken a leading role in mentoring him towards this end. But loyalty was also immutable in his book, and therein lay the conflict. In August 1996 he told a television audience:

> I believed that the CTU needed someone to lead it with a good intellect and academic qualifications to deal with the huge challenges ahead. I read too slowly and it takes me bloody hours to wade through all the stuff that Treasury put out. I had great expectations of Rob Campbell. It seemed to me that he was what was needed to lead the movement — he had that sort of ability. But it was too slow for him. He wanted Knox's job the day before yesterday. He said he'd outlived his usefulness . . . and that the movement should just dump him. I said no. I told him we treat people decently . . . In the end I think leadership is important but it's not the determinant.[292]

Douglas articulated the well-known characteristic of 'small, incestuous' New Zealand, where economic phenomena were personalised: 'Muldoonism, Rogernomics, Ruthenasia — they are all gone now but their policies survived beyond them . . .' With Rob Campbell, the same phenomenon might have occurred.[293]

Although the argument remains hypothetical, had Rob Campbell stayed within the movement he may well have ascended to the top of the CTU hierarchy, either in place of Douglas or succeeding him. He had aspirations to become Labour Party president and later a Member of Parliament. Had all these roles been forthcoming he would have achieved huge public prominence as well as securing for the CTU a high public profile and considerable political clout.

But there was another side to Campbell. He was not as 'democratic' as he should have been, some said, reputedly being inclined to 'make deals' behind closed doors in the Skinner tradition and not tell his fellow unionists any more than they needed to know. This was patently obvious during the 1986 pay round when, in defending his 6 per cent drivers' settlement, Campbell telephoned Steve Marshall of the Employers' Federation and told him a 6.75 per cent wage increase would fix the retail non-foods award. Although these negotiations were part of the Distribution Workers' Federation and he was not directly involved in them, he did not advise the union negotiators of the call until after the event — a lapse which caused resentment. Like Skinner, Campbell was by instinct more of an individualist than an institutionalist. As it was, his sudden departure from trade unionism and subsequent work as a business consultant who would, in 1990, set himself up as a 'bargaining agent' to replace unions in wage negotiations under the iniquitous Employment Contracts Act, reduced him in many unionists' eyes to a 'treacherous turncoat' whose ambitions were totally self-serving.[294]

Douglas now had the inside running for the FOL leadership and the new merged organisation with the state unions that was about to come into being. Jim Knox was presenting a sad figure, increasingly out of touch with political and industrial realities. Denis Welch, the *Listener*'s political commentator, described Knox's performance at the FOL's 1986 conference:

> . . . pride of place is reserved for FOL warhorse Jim Knox who comes slowly on to the stage to deliver what is in effect a

> tragic valedictory for the old movement. Bluntly, badly, almost despairingly he indicts the Labour government for turning away the workers it was originally formed to represent . . .
>
> A portrait in pathos and dignity, he stands like a ruined boxer out of another age. Sixty-seven now, Jim was probably a booming baby once, but he's no baby boomer. They're the ones who fix the fights these days with their talk of 'contestability', 'corporatisation' and 'increasingly competitive environment' . . . Some delegates even heckle him — this man who once commanded the rapt attention of Labour audiences on the strength of his mispronunciations alone. The hecklers include certain MPs and at least two of them decline to stand in the obligatory standing ovation. They remain in their seats, tight-lipped and sulky. Stand up, Judy Keall and John Terris. Have they no respect for their elders?[295]

But Knox was not done yet — he would see one last FOL conference. In the meantime he also had to face barbs from his former leader Tom Skinner, who had not wanted Knox, his 'intellectual inferior', to succeed him as FOL president in the first place. Launching Tony Neary's memoir, *The Price of Principle*, Skinner unleashed undeserved criticism of the FOL as an 'absolute shambles' which had lost its pride and lacked leadership. 'It was a good, strong, recognised movement in my day,' he said. Skinner bewailed the practice of piecemeal industrial agreements instead of fighting for a centralised wage-fixing system. That was reactionary as well. In-house agreements were quick, easy and left management and workers content, whereas there was evidence that the award system was beginning to haemorrhage. Skinner, the dealer, was playing the man. Later, in May 1987, Sir Tom refused to attend the 50th and last annual conference of the FOL despite receiving an invitation to do so as a special guest.[296]

Late in 1986, Minister of Labour Stan Rodger accused the FOL of embarking on a propaganda exercise by using the news media rather than more formal channels of communication. Ken Douglas countered that it was using all available channels to get its message across. The FOL, he said, wanted a commitment from the government to provide more jobs and industry development; maintain workers' living standards and protection of their rights; provide balanced economic development between urban and rural areas, and stand by its anti-nuclear policies and support of worldwide disarmament issues. What Douglas did not want — and he repeated this time and again in different guises throughout his career — was to be drawn, along with the union movement, into provocation and become isolated and defeated, as the watersiders had been in 1951. He never forgot that lesson. The problem with Rodger, he later surmised, was that he was all talk and little action: 'Stan had real problems taking the hard decisions.'

In February 1987, Ken Douglas was despondent. Musing on the dramatic changes to trade unionism over the past two and a half years, he was querulous and concerned about a future in which corporate profit — read greed — seemed to be the new byword for economic prosperity, with workers and their unions flailing in their wake. In 1983 he had told *Listener* journalist Tony Reid that there was no greater power than that of organised labour. Now, he told Reid, 'I would have to say that there is no power greater than that of speculative investment.'[297]

By this time his words meant a good deal, not only to unionists but to a broader audience. He was widely regarded as the person who had brought the most brains and heart into the trade union movement. It hurt him to reflect on this turnaround, yet his clear-headed honesty compelled him to admit the power of big business had so battered the FOL that it could not even cling easily to the traditional rhetoric. The union movement had buckled like a rubber band stretched to breaking point. Yet he remained defiant. 'If the FOL bends to the knee then we are saying that all the traditions, all the investment in the struggles of trade unionism historically will be denied,' he told Reid. 'I can't do that in conscience and I won't do it.'[298]

His grouchiness and bafflement were easy to understand. While trade unions had given birth to the Labour Party, this government had merged the interests of the state with monopoly capitalism. The change had occurred so quickly that unionists could not comprehend it or react to its specifics. Douglas had not seen the tsunami coming. Before the 1984 election both the FOL and the CSU had agreed on a statement of economic principle with Labour — including strengthening the rights of the labour movement, involving it in government decisions and working towards restoring full employment. 'We had a very intense input to get this government elected. The fact that their word has been betrayed in a very savage way is now causing considerable disenchantment with politics in general.' Douglas's anger at this duplicity was palpable, and there were plenty of facts to justify his annoyance. In 1979, Department of Statistics figures showed around about 47 per cent of workers affiliated to the FOL earned less than the average wage. In 1986, this figure had nearly doubled to 85 per cent and unskilled workers, in particular, were being discarded on the scrapheap.[299]

Douglas was also disillusioned that FOL muscle did not have the same impact as it had had under Muldoon, winning fights against the industrial giants in the Kinleith and Kawerau disputes for example. Late in 1986 there had been a 10-week dispute at Tasman Pulp and Paper's Kawerau mill. The scenario had changed since the earlier dispute. Tasman was now part of the Fletcher Challenge conglomerate and Fletcher Challenge, through its wealth and the diversity of investments at home and abroad, was able to hold out, sacrificing profits and locking out the labour force until the striking workers, close to penury, agreed to return to work on the company's terms. Douglas bemoaned the fact that even if the 12 unions on the site had been united (which they weren't) they would not have 'stood a bolter's chance in hell' of winning this battle. 'Oh, the extreme right-wing ideologues are in control all right,' he reflected.

> Ron Trotter [Fletcher Challenge's chairman and chief executive through this dispute] is probably the strongest representative of capital in the land. And Trotter has appointed himself as

> a full-time organiser and propagandist for the government, more powerful than Lange. We should understand that the Prime Minister is not the organ grinder. He is the monkey with the cup and he does what the organ grinder tells him. Now all governments represent class interests, all of them like to dance to the organ grinder's music. Under Labour what's changed is that we have a bigger monkey, a smaller cup and a more strident tune.[300]

It was some small solace that many New Zealanders, including some union leaders, saw the 1986 pay round as a shambles (which it was) and Kawerau as another costly fiasco which ended in capitulation for the workers and their unions.[301]

All this had earlier played out in the United Kingdom. Conservative Prime Minister Margaret Thatcher's vigorous campaign against union 'power', and in particular her long-drawn-out, often brutal but ultimately successful fight against the country's miners, their union and its leader Arthur Scargill, led to the virtual destruction and deunionisation of the workforce, with the closure of all but a handful of the country's pits. But other workers had benefited in the interim during Thatcher's reconstruction of the British economy. It was a country divided between the thousands of casualties, victims of her hard-line approach to the 'militants' and others who benefited from her divide-and-rule policies. It was galling for the former, and hard for them to understand, that 47 per cent of the country's unionists voted for Thatcher in the 1987 general election. Old truisms such as 'solidarity' no longer meant much as the cult of the individual took hold. It was every man, and woman, for him- or herself in the country's workforce. 'Free market unionism' had taken hold; unions were fighting each other for membership, or 'market share'.

It seemed to Ken Douglas in 1987 that New Zealand might go even further along the same road. After all, this country, the most loyal of Empire sons, had adopted the British political and industrial systems holus-bolus. The Labour Relations Act of 1987 specifically allowed unions to compete against each other for coverage. It also encouraged wage bargaining based on an employer's ability to pay, rather than, as had been the practice for generations, on a nationally established rate for the job. This created obvious incentives, and those who were well-organised and in profitable industries would be able to separate themselves from the pack and pursue bigger increases. The only difference was that New Zealand once again had compulsory unionism, but that was under threat from any incoming National administration which was also promising welfare cuts.

That prospect was too terrible to contemplate and Douglas and other union leaders looked instead for inspiration from those European states that had a highly centralised industrial relations model which, from the union perspective, was tightly disciplined. It was predicated upon tripartite cooperation between the central union, employer organisations and the government, and was not aimed at resisting change but rather at controlling it so that individual unions and their members were not too badly disadvantaged in the process. In the meantime, the May 1987 FOL conference was about to witness the most dramatic structural change in New Zealand trade union history.[302]

CHAPTER 10

Transition — the formation of the Council of Trade Unions

For a decade and more, there had been growing cooperation between the Combined State Unions (CSU; formerly the Combined State Services' Organisation) and the Federation of Labour over issues of mutual concern such as unemployment, opposition to the Remuneration Act and other anti-union legislation. A merger between the two groups was first discussed in the early 1970s. This growing compatibility represented a sea change from previous years, when the two organisations — reflecting two very different catchments — were mutually suspicious and kept their distance from each other. The FOL represented traditional blue-collar 'working class' trade unionism whose ethos was based around 'all for one and one for all', a mantra for class solidarity and aggression in industrial disputes. The CSU had evolved out of the Combined State Services Organisation (CSSO) which represented white-collar state servants, many of whom (although not all) were industrially temperate and cautious, contending that withdrawal of their labour, no matter how justified the cause, was contrary to sensible industrial relations. Many of these people did not belong to 'unions' per se, but 'associations', 'guilds' and 'institutes' — more than a few of them felt anxious about being identified as 'unionists' in the traditional sense of the word.

But by the 1980s, the business community had rationalised in the wake of company takeovers and mergers and become more robust. On the back of this, the Employers' Federation became bigger, stronger and better organised and the Business Roundtable, composed of the most powerful capitalists in the land, had the ear of the Lange/Roger Douglas government. Unions on the other hand remained small, despite FOL policy recommending amalgamation. (The only exception up to 1985 was the New Zealand Distribution Workers' Federation, which covered 65,000 workers including drivers, storemen and packers, and shop employees.)

Small unions were under-resourced and lacked industrial effectiveness. Moreover, longstanding inter-union rivalries, demarcation disputes, divisions between skilled and unskilled workers and their unions, personal ambition and lack of job security all blocked progress. But Robert Muldoon's anti-union legislation, wage freezes and the unremitting high inflation and growing unemployment brought a closer cohesion among these groups in resistance. In 1978 the CSSO became the Combined State Unions, representing a more union-focus in its operations. As the numbers of mostly blue-collar workers fell, victims of evolving technology, all unions and 'quasi-unions' looked for more cooperation.

Throughout the 1970s, before representatives of the CSU and the FOL had their first joint consultation on 28 January 1981, the two organisations had been working together on a number of industrial and political issues, such as cost of living campaigns, wage round agitation, and wage adjustment advocacy. Following this meeting, which was the first of six during that year, they organised joint campaigns against the cost of living order, conducted wage policy discussions with the government, including proposals for a wage/tax trade-off, prepared a joint submission to the Task Force on Tax Reform, promoted trade union education and ran a joint defence of living standards operation alongside campaigning against the Springbok rugby tour and French nuclear testing in the Pacific. In August they jointly organised and ran an unemployment conference, the first of its type, which attracted 260 delegates from around the country. By this time, also, Jim Knox was refusing to negotiate on wages with the Muldoon government unless the state unions were involved. The degree of unanimity among delegates surprised even the most enthusiastic of devotees to the cause of closer ties.[303]

The initial stimulus to take the process a step further came from the Public Service Association (PSA) whose 1982 annual conference resolved to approach the FOL with a proposal that a joint working party be established to consider a Confederation of New Zealand Trade Unions combining private and state unions. The FOL executive was supportive, resolving to 'endorse the formation of one trade union organisation representing all trade unions within New Zealand'. It circularised its affiliates, encouraging them to be equally supportive. Most were. By this time the two groups were holding joint campaigns in protest against Muldoon's wage freeze.[304]

The inter-union working party on unification that was established in October 1982 combined heavyweights from both sides — Knox, Thompson and Douglas from the FOL, and Barry Tucker (CSU secretary), Ron Burgess (general secretary of the NZ Post Office Union and CSU chairman), Bruce Webster (general secretary Post Primary Teachers Association and CSU vice-chairman), Don Aimer (general secretary New Zealand Bank Officers' Union) and Bill Anton (secretary Local Body Officers' Union) from the CSU. Colin Clark of the PSA became secretary to the committee; subsequently, both he and Tucker worked tirelessly to bring the Council of Trade Unions to fruition. The main aim of the working party was to provide a framework for an improved and effective trade union organisation that would encourage greater participation in the union movement and represent the aspirations of all wage and salary earners.[305]

Progress was swift. By the end of the third meeting of the working party on 23 February 1983, a draft constitution had been hammered out. This included the stated objects of the new body, conditions of membership, the arranging of biennial conferences and voting thereat, levels of representation at the conferences, the composition of a national council and a national executive, possible groupings of unions for nomination to the national executive, election of national officers, a proposed regional structure and funding issues. It also had the implicit support of the government; Minister of Labour Stan Rodger would be a keynote speaker at the FOL/CSU's preliminary constitutional conference in February 1985.[306]

The draft constitution included four basic principles: that the great majority of unions needed to agree and participate in the process; that the autonomy and independence of each union be protected; that the council would not have authority to direct individual affiliates to take industrial or any other action, and that provision be made for separate group identities to be maintained. Seminars followed in Auckland, Hamilton, Wellington, Christchurch and Dunedin. These were well attended and the proposals were received positively, although some blue-collar union delegates questioned whether the new body would diminish the traditional working-class strength and nature of the union groups, diluting them by bringing in white-collar workers who had a different heritage and culture.[307]

Ken Douglas's plan for the expanded body was that it should be an extension of the present structures of the two unions, but better organised and funded, and more efficient. It would grow and develop organically. Of prime importance, he believed, was addressing the weaknesses apparent in the FOL's sub-structures, particularly in the regions where on-the-ground liaison between unions and their members was often poor. The other aspect of the development of the expanded body was the hope that it would put an end to the internal wrangling that infested the FOL from time to time and had led to some unions leaving the fold. Some unionists made no secret of their wish to see an end to Jim Knox's perceived 'fire and brimstone', confrontational style of union leadership, which had become less and less effective. The creation of the CTU was the perfect opportunity for such a transition to occur. While no participant was prepared to pick a new leader, Ken Douglas's more pragmatic approach had wide appeal.[308]

In July 1985, speaking at the Post Office Union conference, Douglas warned that unions had to unite and adapt or they would become irrelevant — ending up as relics if a National government ever returned to power. While welcoming the very recent return of compulsory unionism, he noted it was not as important as a 'concept of conviction'. Unions both private and public had to change — not putting their heads in the sand, screaming blue murder and looking back to the old days when wage rises were guaranteed under an arbitration system that was now under threat. 'We have got to stop running away from the ghosts of the past. We cannot remain as we are now,' he warned.[309]

There were opponents of the proposed merger. In addition to the blue-collar workers who feared dilution of their message, some state employees feared dictation from the FOL which was, they believed, in the grip of the Socialist Unity Party. Both arguments were nonsense, but they took a lot of knocking down. In the end, however, rational argument won the day, and it was agreed that one strong, unified union movement was the best way to confront the demands for change head-on. Clearly the problems unions had had under Muldoon were not going away under Lange. Privatisation, contracting out, and increased 'casualisation' of labour were here to stay. The union movement had to deal with it. There was also a common feeling, which Ken Douglas had long articulated, that the new body had to be up and running before the 1987 general election, following which a new government might implement legislation to stop the merger.

Over the following year more private and state unions came on board. Opposition from the minority coalesced into what became known colloquially as the 'Third Force'. Some of these unions were reacting to majority plebiscites among their own members who opposed the merger. The 5000-strong Waterside Workers' Federation was one of these. Its secretary Sam Jennings articulated a common complaint when he contended that 'these new young people from academic backgrounds know nothing about trade unions'. The 'Third Force' made its play at the 1986 FOL conference. At the end of a marathon debate on the CTU's formation — which was endorsed by 318 votes to 99 with 63 abstentions — Dave Morgan, president of the New Zealand Seafarers Union, Jennings, Dave Graham of the Cooks and Stewards' Union and Don Goodfellow of the National Union of Railwaymen walked out and boycotted the rest of the conference.[310]

Morgan was annoyed. 'Bluntly,' he intoned before the vote, 'it means the demise of the FOL — think about that. All the fine words and gilt-edged theory notwithstanding, that's the bottom line. There will be no loyalty once the FOL shuts down to any other organisation other than the working-class movement. A vote for the monolithic structure like the CTU will rip the heart and guts out of this conference.' Morgan wanted the FOL to extend and invite others to join it, rather than disappearing altogether. In the context, that was naive. After the conference, the Waterside Workers' Federation, Seamen's Union and National Union of Railwaymen established their own conglomerate, the New Zealand Maritime, Transport and General Workers' Federation.[311]

For his part Jennings believed that his union did not leave the FOL. 'The FOL left us. For our efforts we have been subject to snide remarks from the CTU hierarchy and accusations have been made against us. But history will show whether we were right or wrong.' History showed that he was wrong. Within three years, after waterfront reforms under which thousands of workers lost their jobs, the Watersiders' Federation joined the CTU and the Maritime, Transport and General Workers' Federation was no more.

To the minority of workers who were unhappy with merging with white collar workers in case their unique voice and perceived 'militancy of long standing' was lost in the larger body, Douglas was unsympathetic. It was true that a number of those who opposed the merger had earlier opposed both the FOL and the CSU on other matters, including their refusal to accept policy positions in respect of unions' economic needs and their approaches to the 1984 election. Douglas was at pains to repeat the working party's view that all workers depended on a job or salary for their livelihood. Unionism was about unity, not separation.[312]

There were differences, of course, among workers — female, male, manual, clerical, private sector, public sector. But in terms of economic dependence all were the same. It was also a myth that at least some white-collar workers were less militant than their blue-collar counterparts. A perusal of the record of industrial action showed that. The secondary school teachers' union, the Post Primary Teachers' Association, for example, had a recent history of industrial militancy that rivalled any of the blue-collar worker unions. Douglas believed all those joining the expanded body would accept its agreed objectives: 'To promote the economic, social, industrial and educational interests and civil rights of the working people of New Zealand including the right to useful and more secure employment' and 'to achieve and maintain a united organisation for all workers and employee organizations in New Zealand'.[313]

More astute than some of the older union leaders who were uncomfortable with change, and in words that would also ring out loudly in the subsequent debate over the contentious Employment Contracts Bill of the early 1990s, Douglas reiterated that New Zealanders lived in a rapidly changing world and workers and unions had to adapt to those changes, not only to survive but also to thrive. He had watched the long-running British Miners' Union strike fold in the face of Margaret Thatcher's intransigence and police brutality despite their charismatic leader Arthur Scargill urging delegates at the 1984 British Trade Union Congress to support the miners' cause — just days after, in fact, the union had capitulated. Other governments, both conservative and socialist — in France, the Netherlands, Italy, Germany and the United States — had also forced crippling defeats on trade unions and their members over strikes, in blithe disregard for the social cost. Furthermore, it was recession time, and increased unemployment and the introduction of new technologies had seen union membership decline in these countries by up to 20 per cent in less than two years.

Internationally, unions were losing the political and economic clout that had made them such a dominant force a decade earlier.

Douglas foresaw similar problems in New Zealand — also suffering from a recession and the ever-increasing introduction of new technologies, in manufacturing and transport industries in particular. Already some unions — notably those representing shop employees, clerical workers, cleaners and caretakers, carpenters, drivers and bank officers — had lost up to 20 per cent of their members through downsizing, retrenchment and, in the drivers' case, more satisfaction and better pay as non-union owner-operators. They were business people now.

History told him that merger meant strength, as well as opportunities for unions to tap into a broader range of expertise, improved research, training and facilities, and economies of scale in its offices. The past few years had not been kind to working people. In 1985 the FOL was keeping pace, just, with the Lange government, with the removal of subsidies yet to hit low-paid factory workers. But under Muldoon, from 1976, unions had suffered a three-year wage freeze, voluntary unionism and a raft of anti-union laws. In the view of some New Zealanders the FOL had not helped itself with its $20-a-week campaign, which they maintained was greedy, and by its unapologetic stand on issues beyond 'core business' such as the Russian invasion of Afghanistan, the Chile trade ban and the union clampdown in Poland. Moreover, there was a feeling that the FOL was supporting the interests of the unskilled at the expense of the skilled. And there were still lingering suspicions of communist influence.

The charges of communist influence were wrongly ascribed. Douglas made a point of keeping his politics out of union affairs, although sometimes, as we have seen, this came back to bite him. His growing reputation was one of pragmatism, eschewing direct action where possible in favour of conciliation around a table. He was primarily responsible for the FOL not tackling the Muldoon government head-on over the wage freeze because he knew it was a battle the organisation could only lose. He won this argument around the FOL executive table.

He was also at the forefront of the FOL move to adopt a 'political thrust' as opposed to an 'industrial thrust', whereby unions could best survive and progress by better education on the shop floor and more political influence at the national level.

He was also championing a newer, younger reformist brand of university-trained union leaders such as Rob Campbell, Peter Harris of the Public Service Association (both trained economists) and 33-year-old Rex Jones, who in August 1983 had taken over as secretary of the 51,000-strong Engineers' Union and would, two years later, be elected onto the FOL executive. (This did not sit well with the more conservative cloth-cap brigade, suspicious of union leaders who were not 'working class' — their own politics hewn from the dignity of their manual labour on the factory floor, but by this time in danger of becoming sentimentalised.) The marriage between the private and public sector unions at a national level would further consummate a 'new look' transformation of New Zealand trade unionism that was overdue.[314]

The working party's final report, presented to the 1986 FOL conference, called for an inaugural conference of all CTU delegates to be held in October/November 1987 to formally adopt a constitution, adopt a codified policy, elect officers, set up structural and administrative machinery and consider any new proposals arising from a constitutional conference planned for later that year. Only a few unions had objected to the working party's plan to group them in 'electoral colleges' for the election of its national executive. This was because the grouping system ensured that a new executive was broadly representative of all industries and groups of workers, and prevented large unions winning additional places on the executive at the expense of smaller unions. These groupings also enabled small unions to have their views represented by their group of nominees, and allowed groups of unions to get together to sort out their representation amicably.[315]

In September 1987 the new Council of Trade Unions appointed its first staff member. Kate Clark, assistant secretary of the CSU, became assistant to the secretary when the council was formally established after the conference. Another key first-day employee was the PSA's Peter Harris, who became the CTU's first research officer. He had been assistant secretary of the Combined State Unions. His astute grasp of politics, alongside his ability to analyse national and international economic trends and government decision-making in this area, would serve the organisation well.

The Wellington Drivers' Union put forward Ken Douglas's name for the CTU's presidency, and the Post Office Union endorsed its retiring secretary Ron Burgess for the post of CTU secretary. They were elected unopposed at the CTU's first conference, and honoured with a standing ovation. Both were popular and enjoyed almost unanimous support within their own constituencies. Only one 'top table' position was up for grabs; Therese O'Connell — the FOL women's advisory committee convenor, Wellington Trades Council vice-president and Central Clerical Workers' Union education and women's rights officer — challenged Angela Foulkes, a bank accountant and Bank Officers' Union president, for the vice-presidency.

Theirs was a close tussle. O'Connell had strong feminist credentials and was personable, gregarious and popular with many delegates, but was questioned by some who doubted her track record in organising successful industrial campaigns. The more serious but strong-willed Foulkes had led bank officers from obscurity to coherency in an effective union, winning a number of successful confrontations with the nation's bankers. And whereas Douglas and Burgess represented the private and state sectors, Foulkes represented a non-aligned union that the CTU was trying to woo, which many delegates felt would make an appropriate balance. O'Connell, a strong advocate for the autonomy of women and Maori unionists within the CTU, supported separate structures so that they could elect their own representatives on the executive. Foulkes opposed this, believing it would marginalise these groups by shunting them out of the mainstream of CTU activity. She recalled the election campaign as being 'quite nasty, personalised and divisive . . . traditionalists saw me as a bureaucrat or a corporatist . . .'[316]

In the end the desire of many delegates for a representative of a non-aligned union won out —Foulkes, the banker, was that representative. Thirty-nine years old, and a university-trained accountant with the ANZ in Petone, Foulkes had been born in Manchester, England, emigrating to New Zealand when she was 25. Before coming to this country she had had no previous experience with trade unions. Locally, however, she became active on her branch committee, then worked as a job delegate, district and national councillor before becoming president of the Bank Officers' Union in 1982, winning plaudits for her outspokenness and dogged determination.

A feature of the 13-strong executive was that there were just five survivors from the FOL's executive — in part because of the electoral college/ward system of voting. These were Bill Andersen (Northern Drivers' Union and Auckland Trades Council president), Rex Jones (Engineers' Union), Len Smith (Northern Labourers' Union), John Slater (Clerical Workers' Union) and Rick Barker (Service Workers' Federation). Others elected were Peter Kovacevich (North Local Government Officers), Don Farr (New Zealand Photo Lithographers), Roger Middlemass (New Zealand Meatworkers), Steve Grant (Railway Tradesmen), Des Long (Post Office Union), Colin Clark (PSA), Kevin Bunker (PPTA) and Gay Williams (Nurses' Association).

When, on 19 October 1987, the Council of Trade Unions came into being, it was a red letter day for New Zealand trade unionism. It had been a smooth ride. The creation of the CTU had been ratified just seven years after the possibility of such a merger was first discussed, the speed driven by the fourth Labour government's hasty and aggressive attacks on hard-won trade union freedoms. Representing 76 unions and more than 560,000 unionists, the CTU was not only, by far, the largest conglomerate of unionists in New Zealand's history, but was also, on a proportional basis, one of the largest in the western world. It was also the largest organisation of any type in New Zealand.

The CTU's emergence was not before time. The FOL's focus on manual labour was becoming anachronistic in an increasingly technological age. For its part, the Combined State Unions needed a buffer to prevent its relations with the government becoming overheated. But while the CTU was a necessary merger, it was far from perfect. There were differences of social class and some middle-class white-collar unionists, preferring to call themselves 'professionals', found working-class blue-collar unionists uncomfortable bedfellows, and vice versa.

Language and cultures were different. There was distrust between some union leaders, who had worked their way up to leadership positions from the rank and file, and often had only a primary school education, and the new breed of university-educated unionists, whose abilities helped them quite quickly gain prominent positions. Unskilled and semi-skilled workers and their unions who remained in strength — freezing workers, engine drivers, timber workers, labourers, drivers — were similar in culture to the collective which had refused to join, seamen, watersiders, cooks and stewards chief among them. While the latter's non-appearance within the CTU signalled their end as any kind of force within trade unionism — becoming an ineffective ginger group estranged from the mainstream — it also meant the CTU lacked some sense of blue-collar solidarity, community, colour and historical militancy.

But in many ways the new body reflected a changing New Zealand society. Most New Zealanders, including the sons and daughters of working-class people of yesterday, aided by better access to advanced levels of education along with a dramatically changing world of work, had aspired to and reached the 'middle class'. The white-collar unions which represented this new constituency were also becoming more militant, but for them the 'class struggle' was never part of their consciousness. The Labour Party reflected changes akin to those evident in the CTU — once the workers' party, it had for decades been attracting more and more middle-class, educated liberals into leadership positions.

There were practical differences, too, between the FOL and its successor. The FOL tended to cover workers employed on a wide range of sites across a range of industries spread throughout the country. Many FOL unions were regional in nature. The watersiders' unions, for example, were based in ports where the men worked with their own officials and budgets. In contrast, most white-collar unions were centralised and monolithic, with power invested in a Wellington head office. This meant they tended to have fewer rank-and-file meetings, and decisions were oligarchic rather than democratic, as they were in well-run blue-collar unions among which plebiscites were frequent. The CTU therefore had to try to cater for members from widely differing cultural, class and organisational backgrounds — and do so on an inadequate budget. Its fees did not keep pace with inflation and the organisation would continue to leak numbers through restructuring, lay-offs and later, under National, the removal of compulsory unionism.

The CTU's most basic responsibility was to exercise influence wherever it could and by whatever means. For its members and affiliates that is what it was there for. The leadership was a formidable team. The political avenue was now more critical because Ken Douglas, Angela Foulkes and Ron Burgess were all pragmatists not given to direct forms of protest. Affiliates and their members all saw the need for a strong central power base. Burgess's long commitment to state unionism had given him knowledge, lucidity, wisdom and acuity. He also proved a steady, calming influence over Foulkes, who was sometimes sharp with her affiliates and co-workers, but was very able. Like Douglas, Foulkes was a strong character and often blunt, and the two came from very different backgrounds. They sometimes clashed, and Burgess would at times be the bridge between them. Nonetheless, collectively the three would manage the transition from the FOL to the CTU, a very different beast, with considerable skill.

CHAPTER 11

A new dawn

The FOL had wound down with a whimper. Retiring president Jim Knox told its last conference in May 1987 that he was a 'little bit emotional'. That was understandable — now 68, he had been in and around the FOL since he was 15. But what tears there were, were sublimated. The FOL had had its day. There was no singing of the 'Red Flag' as there had been in 1937 — or any other song for that matter. There were no cries of angst — just a mandatory shaking of hands when veterans were acknowledged. Most emotion was displayed at the farewell to the movement's esteemed vice-president, Sonja Davies, soon to become MP for Pencarrow. Her influence would not be nearly as strongly felt in Parliament, where her left-wing and feminist views became marginalised under the weight of the neoliberal agenda of the fourth Labour government.[317]

Knox's usual rhetoric was missing. He was tired, worn out by the struggle. His retirement signalled the end of an era. Old school, and with working-class blood pumping through his veins, he was educated in and only understood the politics of confrontation. He had been ambivalent about the concept of the CTU and could not contain his anger that Labour, 'his' party, after promising much, had betrayed the working people by pursuing an agenda that was foreign to him — an anger deepened by years of fighting Muldoon's excesses. He felt betrayed and had become immobilised. Knox had been widely regarded for his integrity, diligence and honesty — and his undying, aggressive support for the unions and belief in an assertive working class. But the world of work had moved beyond him. He did not have the flexibility or foresight to understand or deal with the revolutions that were swirling around him during his last years in charge of the FOL.

Despite his superior intellect and bouts of frustration at Knox's heavy-footed sophisms, Douglas remained loyal to the older man. He shared a similar heritage and understood clearly where Knox was coming from — and he empathised with his strengths and weaknesses. But in the new politics, the Council of Trade Unions had little influence in the growth areas of the economy where microchips and 'push-buttons' were beginning to supersede the hairy arm and the mallet as the most relevant symbols of primary and secondary production. Manual workers, for decades the life-blood of the country's economy — on its farms, construction sites, roads, railways, wharves and ships, and in its factories, forests, timber mills and freezing works — were disappearing in the wake of new, more sophisticated machines, more open international competition, retreating overseas markets, depressed prices and the government's deregulatory obsessions. By August 1988, the unemployment rate was 8.5 per cent and rising. Former delegate Wayne Ewart articulated the pain during a Meat Workers' Union conference, when he commented on the closure of the Whakatu Freezing Works near Hastings: 'I walked along the top chain and I bloody well cried. I cried for the people who lost their jobs. I cried for their families. I cried for the whole meat industry. Where the hell do we go now?'[318]

Neither was the state, dominated by neoliberals Douglas, Prebble and Michael Bassett — supported by Prime Minister Lange — about to engage with trade unionists any time soon. Capitalism held sway. Local strength was enhanced by ever-increasing inflows and outflows (for directors and shareholders) of huge amounts of money as multinationals, relishing the deregulatory freedoms, made their presence more and more strongly felt. Internally, the bigger the enterprise and the fewer the bureaucratic restrictions imposed on its operation, the more politically powerful it was. The huge Fletcher Challenge conglomerate was the most powerful of them all. Its principal Sir Ron Trotter also chaired the Business Roundtable. Trotter, who had the ear of Roger Douglas — and, from 1990, his National Party successors — displayed an enmity towards 'that communist' Ken Douglas that was deep-seated and long-lasting.[319]

For his part, Douglas was keen on a new way for the CTU and its constituent trade unions to operate. He was tired of 'playing second fiddle' — being reactive and confrontational — a role that often ended in strikes where workers, more often than not, lost the battle, their families having to forsake the weekly pay packet and their unions wallowing in the despair of another lost public relations campaign. From his earliest days as a trade unionist Douglas had addressed wages, conditions, relativities, wage and price freezes and other industrial issues by marching in the streets, placarding on street corners and listening to other union leaders on loud hailers, as they criticised the forces of capitalism and the state in a vain attempt to influence events. When he led the Drivers' Union and the Drivers' Federation, and when secretary of the FOL, he was often at the forefront of these marches, pleading through the loud hailer for justice from an absent 'enemy'.

When he ascended to the CTU leadership, much was expected of him both within and without the union movement. No longer perceived as a communist ogre dedicated to the destruction of Western-style democracy, he had won respect from a broad spectrum of employers, unionists and politicians as a skilful, unruffled but unrelenting negotiator. He had smartened his sartorial act, and on television he exuded a calm and knowledgeable confidence — a pressed suit, smart tie and ironed shirt replaced the crumpled cardigan, baggy pants and unkempt hair of yesteryear. Douglas understood the power of television, contending that a reasoned and intelligent presence on the medium could go a long way towards winning the public relations debate. The serenity of his television persona — interspersed with occasional flashes of wit — hid, superficially at least, a sharp mind and a broad and determined understanding of how the CTU and its constituency should operate proactively in a new industrial world. Extensive reading, mostly of political tracts, had increased his vocabulary and he had become more lucid. He was connecting more easily and accurately with audiences.

As he grew in confidence and self-belief on the public stage, journalists found him readily accessible, not defensive or aggressive — yet also not a person who would be diverted from a vision of where the union movement could go. After an interview with Douglas for the *Dominion Sunday Times* of 21 August 1988, Sharon Crosbie described him as 'totally disarming, able to express the ideals of pure socialism in a way that's almost evangelical and would do Marx and Lenin proud. It's no wonder others describe him as a father figure, the man who keeps unions together, a conciliator in a class of his own, a man who is liked, respected and feared; a man who is very, very clever.'

Douglas always saw himself as part of a movement — a true democrat, neither oligarchic nor autocratic in his thinking. 'I never see myself as carrying the world on my shoulders. I'm a conduit for the accumulated experience of what's gone on before and who we have with us now,' he told a journalist in 1989.[320] That was disingenuous. There was no doubt that as the leader of the country's unions his words and actions would be keenly viewed, followed, analysed and assessed by everyone involved in industrial relations. Douglas understood that criticism, often loudly expressed, was concomitant to the role, particularly given his personal politics. It was life in a goldfish bowl.

Along with some of his key allies in the CTU hierarchy — Foulkes, Burgess, Rex Jones and Chris Eichbaum of the Engineers' Union, Owen Harvey of the Distribution Workers' Federation and Mike Jackson of the Northern Stores Union — Douglas tried to push for a more inclusive tripartite operation whereby the CTU, unions, employers and their organisations and the state would negotiate issues of common concern in an atmosphere of positivity. Such a model was focused around controlling or managing change for the common good of all concerned. Douglas wanted a New Zealand trade union akin to the Swedish model, which meant a high degree of centralisation and tight discipline from the constituent unions and an acceptance that full employment and productive efficiency were prime targets. But it also demanded that when times were tougher, union leaders needed to be prepared to moderate wage demands on the understanding that economic viability was vital to living standards — and jobs for workers in the long term. In return for this restraint, they demanded real input into government decision-making, and particularly economic direction. There would be a similar scenario in the workplace, where unions would promise quality assurance and productivity improvements in return for the right to be consulted on and involved in management issues.

But he understood that to shift employers and many unionists to this new proactive approach would be a massive uphill battle. Blue-collar union leaders, and in 1988 that was most of them, were steeped in a tradition of confrontation and regarded any kind of cooperation and consensus with employers, rapacious or otherwise, as 'supping with the devil'. That a shift to a more cooperative mode would be difficult, if not impossible, at least in the short term, was well illustrated in the ideological debate that raged over the so-called 'Nissan Deal' in February 1988. The Engineers' Union — representing the biggest group of workers in the plant — signed an agreement with the company which introduced a version of Japanese work practices in Nissan New Zealand's Wiri plant. It was based on the Kaizen principles of teamwork and devolution of responsibility to the shop floor, with workers being awarded pay rises on merit. The measure promoted industrial democracy and its implementation resulted in improved productivity. But most of the other site unions slated it as a sell-out; in the words of one opponent, it was an attempt 'to encourage a dangerous worker identification with the company'. Unions representing store workers, clerical workers and cleaners went on strike, unsuccessfully.[321]

The inaugural council of the CTU held its first meeting on 18 July 1988. The formation of this body represented a massive cultural change, from an exclusively blue-collar grouping to one which, in large measure, was taken up by a new breed — mostly middle-class workers for whom 'solidarity' was not a byword for class understanding. Numerically they were ascendant in the CTU, with public servants, teachers, nurses and bank officers showing the way. Though she would deny it, Angela Foulkes, Douglas's deputy, was their most natural representative. Apart from bank clerks these employees belonged to state unions and they probably needed confederation more than the blue-collar workers. They had been traumatised by the speed and scope of the government's reform of the public service and needed a buffer to prevent their relations with it becoming overheated to the stage where they became completely unworkable.

There were other portents of change. The Federation of Labour had operated from cramped premises in central Wellington's Lukes Lane but the CTU purchased, at significant cost and huge overdraft, the Tasman Hotel on the corner of Willis and Dixon Streets, where it established itself in sumptuous new offices. These came with smoked-glass partitions, newly laid grey carpet and mushroom-coloured walls, all of which evoked an almost corporate image which was not lost on wags who dubbed it a 'not-such-a-down-at-heel version of Judgecorp'. Douglas took time to get used to the new quarters but understood that the symbolism was important — the CTU meant business and would be making a serious, determined bid for political influence. Yet the organisation was in serious debt after the purchase of the new and sale of the old building, having been caught in the financial downturn associated with the October 1987 sharemarket crash. There were crippling interest bills on emergency loans to be paid, estimated to be as high as $35,000 a month. As journalist Patricia Herbert recorded, beneath the CTU's exterior gloss, the structure was shaky, as apt a metaphor as any for the predicament that New Zealand unionism was in.[322]

In his opening address to delegates at the first council meeting Douglas found it hard to be positive. It was a time, he said, of social confusion, disillusionment and despair. Travelling around the country he had found that workers felt a trust had been betrayed and they feared for the future — wondering if they would still have a job in six months, scared that they would not find another, worried that they would not be able to pay their bills. He believed that workers felt used by politicians and as a result were disillusioned by the political process.

There was a feeling among unionists of being overwhelmed by the task ahead, but Douglas saw it as a challenge from which he was not about to walk away:

> We recognise the need for change and stand ready to participate in its process. However, we are not and can never be indifferent to that form of change. Change that destroys jobs without creating alternative work will be resisted; change that takes no account of the future of small communities cannot be accommodated. Change that does not recognise the values, traditions and vision of society has nothing to offer us . . . Any economic reform must have underlying objectives of jobs, social equity and stability. The free market has no heart and soul. Our central policies are to identify the constraints on the free market which are necessary to achieve full employment and society equity needed for a decent society . . .[323]

It was a dogged call to arms.

On 1 August 1987 the government passed the Labour Relations Act, its most important piece of labour legislation. The Act's most radical demand required all unions to find 1000 members within 18 months or be disbanded — half the number the Labour Department had suggested some months earlier. In the end it was a demand that would strengthen the hand of unionism as fewer, bigger unions led to the emergence of more capable leaders, a higher profile and more political strength. On the other hand, mergers left some union leaders surplus to requirements, resulting in a loss of institutional knowledge, and often — particularly in small enterprises, or in rural towns — a loss of personal contact between workers and their union delegates. On 31 December 1986 there had been 227 unions; by 12 December 1987, there were 176.

The Act also brought 'modernisation', a positive step. It preserved the union registration system, which gave unions bargaining rights and enabled them to choose whether to bargain with employers as a group or on a one-to-one basis in award negotiations. While retaining compulsory unionism it dispensed with the Arbitration Court in favour of more formal Labour Courts. It also removed wage controls, introduced voluntary arbitration — which also meant dispensing with the contentious relativities — moved back from interference in wage bargaining, reformed state wage-fixing, and limited some monopoly coverage by unions.[324]

Other changes under the Act created a climate that made it easier for New Zealand to follow Britain's Thatcherite reforms. Not only did it allow unions to compete against each other for coverage, but it also encouraged wage bargaining based on an employer's ability to pay rather than the former practice of a nationally established rate for the job. This created an obvious incentive for those workers and their unions who were well organised and in profitable industries to separate themselves from the pack and pursue bigger increases.

It also narrowed the legal right to strike. Workers and unions who withdrew their labour risked damage suits in the Labour Court — and employers were quick to take advantage. The Labour Court changed the whole business of industrial negotiation. It was now bound up tightly in a legal framework, with lawyers the main financial beneficiaries as it faced an ever-growing workload. The legislation, as well as the economic recession, had resulted in far fewer strikes over traditional sore points such as demarcation, second-tier bargaining, dismissals and interpretation of award provisions — because these were now all illegal and unions faced massive fines if they transgressed.

By 1988, increasing numbers of employers were avoiding the Labour Courts, contracting out jobs and thus avoiding unionised labour altogether. This was manifest initially when state-owned enterprises placed some public servants on short-term contracts. The Forestry Corporation and the Tasman Pulp and Paper management in Kawerau rid themselves of thousands of workers through voluntary severance and began employing contractors to do much of the work. Since the late 1970s, freight-forwarding and haulage companies had employed fewer of their own drivers and had contracted work instead to independent, non-unionised owner-drivers. Building firms were divesting themselves of carpenters, plumbers and electricians, and contracting freelance non-union men instead. Their wages were not guaranteed and they could be paid less than the minimum under the various awards. Workplace structures were undergoing a revolution.

In the meantime, more jobs were being lost. Business was volatile. Apart from a short period in 1985, reflecting Labour's early 'honeymoon' with workers and their unions, when pay rates increased to cover Robert Muldoon's long-standing wage freeze, workers' real pay decreased in value between 1982 and 1988. In 1987, the corporatisation of State Coal to become Coal Corporation led to 836 of 1728 miners being made redundant. There were also job losses at Telecom Corporation (3146); Ministry of Transport (347); Panelcorp (650); UEB Carpet (114); Kiwi Bacon (70); Lane Walker Rudkin in Westport and Temuka (83); Golden Bay Cement at Tarakohe (150); Leespower, Papakura (160); Tatra Leather, Wainuiomata (17); Amalgamated Batteries, Woolston (78); Tendabird Poultry (20); DIC at Lower Hutt and Palmerston North (48) and Coachwork International (70) among others. In July 1988, 250 jobs were lost when the *Auckland Sun* newspaper shut up shop, and another 150 when Golden Bay Cement closed its Nelson plant because it was cheaper to import the product.

These jobs all disappeared for a variety of reasons, but wages being too high was not one of them. They included relocation of business — usually to Asia, where labour costs were so much lower — cheaper imports, lack of work exacerbated by employers contracting work to outside companies, company restructuring after takeovers, the impact of the high New Zealand dollar, labour displacing technology, budget cuts, a depressed retail market both locally and overseas, the removal of development assistance funds, and deregulation. Concurrently, industry slashed apprenticeship numbers by 40 per cent between 1985 and 1989. Just 5 per cent of the workforce was trained to apprentice levels, one of the lowest among OCED countries. Employers were reluctant to take on apprentices in tough economic times.[325]

The worst off was the freezing industry. In July 1988, the Westfield Freezing Works in Auckland cut its workforce by 650. Later that year, Westfield in Whakatu (Hastings), Islington (Christchurch) and Burnside (Dunedin) closed with the loss of 3220 jobs. Others were just hanging on or spending millions of dollars upgrading plant to meet new EEC hygiene requirements, dispensing with employees in the process. The state of the industry was dire. There were falling prices for sheep meat overseas, a high New Zealand dollar, rising transport costs, the introduction of tariffs in key markets, competition from other foods as eating habits changed, the effects of high interest rates on farmers causing them to cut back on farm inputs and reduce stock numbers, the removal of subsidies, poor market development by companies, uncoordinated selling, and the expansion of killing capacity after delicensing. Other 'economic mainstream' workers were suffering as well. In October 1989, 1500 watersiders — mostly in Auckland — lost their jobs after drastic albeit overdue waterfront reform. By now there were 151,011 registered unemployed in New Zealand compared with 63,417 in October 1984 and 7213 in August of 1977.[326]

In a portent of the future, in November 1988 the widely dispersed but numerically strong 27,000-member Clerical Workers' Union, which had only small numbers of members in each workplace, failed to gain a renewal of their award. Employers, seeking flexibility, wanted to change the part-time clause which defined 30 or more hours as full-time work. The union did not agree. It contended that the removal of the clause meant opening the door to casualisation of the workforce. They were right. It was this union, with a high number of women and part-time workers, that suffered most losses when voluntary unionism was brought in under Muldoon, and would do so to an even greater degree under the coming National government reforms of Jim Bolger and Bill Birch.

On 21 November 1988, more than 12,000 unionists attended a CTU-organised mass stopwork meeting at Auckland's Mt Smart Stadium, concerned about a raft of stalled award negotiations but also the government's intensification of its deregulatory agenda. Ken Douglas accused the Business Roundtable of using the Labour Relations Act, its wealth and its political influence to direct economic policy in its favour. The Labour government, he believed, was not a passive actor but a willing tool of the Business Roundtable. He called for a campaign of industry-specific stoppages as the most effective way to combat the government's economic policy and employers' refusal to negotiate award agreements. Less than a month later the Higher Salaries Commission announced another 4.5 per cent rise in MP's salaries, bringing their total rise to 14 per cent since the previous May. This compared with the average wage round of between 3 and 5 per cent for those that had settled.[327]

Remarkably, Douglas and Ron Trotter were both rumoured to have been shortlisted to become directors of the Reserve Bank — Douglas to replace businessman Sir Lawrence Stevens, whose three-year term was about to expire. This caused animation in the media, particularly after the National Party opposition received news of the story and leader Jim Bolger angrily condemned the consideration of country's 'top communist' for such a position, a comment which resulted in his expulsion from Parliament by the speaker, Gerry Wall. As he left Bolger tried to have the last word: 'Well that's all right. If he [Wall] keeps sending us out [Muldoon, Birch and Venn Young were also evicted] then there'll be more room for the Commos inside . . . when are the Comms going to march?'

After the government would neither confirm nor deny Douglas's possible appointment, National Party MP George Gair ostentatiously described the idea as 'one further example of the Labour government trying to buy the ongoing support of the SUP and the industrial labour movement'. After all, there had been precedent. Less than a year earlier Douglas's erstwhile friend, Rob Campbell had become a director of the Bank of New Zealand. But it was all a damp squib — the whole issue was a media and opposition beat-up. Former FOL executive member Sir Len Hadley had been on the Reserve Bank board and on his retirement Douglas was asked if he would like to replace him. Douglas said that he would but heard nothing further.[328]

In September 1989, the CTU held its first biennial conference. While union numbers had been dropping, it was still an impressive organisation with 61 affiliated unions representing 505,773 members. There were 24 district CTU councils up and down the country, each with its own president and secretary. Head office held three officers (Douglas, Foulkes and Burgess), and 17 other staff in technical services, accounts, administration and secretarial/clerical positions. There were 20 members of a national executive representing private and public sector unions, and six regional coordinators in the Northern, Auckland, Central, Wellington, Canterbury and Dunedin regions, all with administrative assistants.[329]

The principal aim of this conference was for the CTU to assert itself as a dynamic and purposeful leader for the country's workers and more generally as a relevant force in the market-driven economy of the 1990s. The challenges facing the organisation were on a scale never experienced before by the country's unions and their national body — deregulation of the economy, privatisation of state-owned or -managed businesses, a technological change in the workplace that was startling in its breadth, new labour laws and industry restructuring. Thousands of workers had lost their jobs — more than 2000 members of the Auckland Engineers' Union alone in the past two years — most with no redundancy. Many others watched helplessly as their real wages and working conditions were eroded.

But there were successes. Demarcation disputes had become a thing of the past as unions merged. Ken Douglas presented a voice of reason, and his long-established prestige not only helped keep the organisation relevant but also remained a key behind-the-scenes influence on the resolution of industrial disputes. Ron Burgess and Angela Foulkes were proactively presenting the CTU message to different audiences, and Peter Harris's economic analyses were crucial to affiliates' understanding of where the organisation should be heading.

The way forward as outlined in the CTU's 'Strategies for Change' document in May 1989 identified 14 economic sectors — such as manufacturing, education, health, finance and communications — within which unions would be amalgamated, with memberships between 15,000 and 20,000. It was a bold plan which was sure to face heated opposition from those unions that felt giving up their autonomy was at odds with the common good of their members — and their office-holders. Douglas, as always, wanted to be proactive. A failure to reorganise, with industry-based coordinated composite bargaining, would mean employers might win the day with individual workplace or industry agreements. However, this proposed change ran into flak almost immediately when Martha Coleman, assistant secretary of the women-intensive Clerical Workers' Union, said the proposal would decimate the union as clerical workers were divided across all 14 of the sectors. How right she was.

Conversely, there were occasional new deals which foreshadowed change in the wage negotiation process. Late in September 1989, seven unions — representing engineers, store workers, foundry workers, clerical staff, electrical workers, cafeteria staff and an occupational nurse — jointly agreed on a composite wages and conditions deal with their employer Masport Industries. The negotiations had taken two years, but such an enterprise agreement would not have occurred without the Labour Relations Act. The workers' advocate, Bruce Fowler, said the unions involved were happy to reach an agreement which included no 'clawbacks or giveaways'. The agreement added grunt to employers' arguments that the national award system was outdated, obviating the need for Masport to work its tortuous way through seven national awards to find agreement for workers belonging to seven different unions. It was a harbinger of things to come.[330]

There had been encouraging signs from the Labour Party before it came to power that it might be interested in some sort of industrial 'accord' with the unions. There was precedent. In 1983, the Australian Council of Trade Unions had reached an agreement with the Australian Labor government of Bob Hawke (a former ACTU president) and soon afterwards the ACTU's Laurie Carmichael, a key architect of this agreement, had visited New Zealand and provided a much-needed fillip to local reformers. But the idea had lapsed as the new Minister of Labour, Stan Rodger, was opposed to it.

Following the formation of the CTU the idea was revived. There were encouraging elements at play. Left-wing trade unionists were keen to see Jim Anderton replace Rex Jones as Labour Party president, but in August 1988 deputy Prime Minister Geoffrey Palmer let it be known that the government could find an accord with the CTU if the party's left-wing could be headed off. An accommodation was reached. At the Labour Party conference the following month Jones cast all 63 of the Engineers' Union votes in favour of Labour councillor Ruth Dyson — Lange's preferred candidate — thus helping to defeat Anderton. Ken Douglas was encouraged, stating that if Labour could find the political will to forge a unity with unions, 'we are more than ready to participate'. Douglas was adamant that such a compact was important. 'We are fed up with people, including some in the union movement, talking in a pious way about unemployment and then not doing anything about it ... new jobs will only come about with economic growth ... We are going to give it our best shot.'[331]

But such an agreement was never destined to have a smooth run, and it faced intense stresses from both sides. On the right, the Business Roundtable, the Employers' Federation, Roger Douglas's supporters in Cabinet and caucus as well as the National opposition intensified their calls for removing rigidities in the labour market to allow for flexibility in wages and conditions based on work site 'realities' rather then industry awards, which included dumping compulsory unionism, arbitration and wage relativities. National Party labour spokesperson

Bill Birch had already made a start by introducing a Bill in November that would reinstate voluntary unionism and allow workers the ability to negotiate directly with an employer. In a sign of things to come, his Labour Relations (Flexible Bargaining) Amendment Bill also allowed workers to elect their own bargaining agent to negotiate on their behalf. The Bill's introduction was blocked 48 votes to 33.[332]

The Labour caucus was split between the neoliberals and the social democrats. Leaders of the latter group — notably Helen Clark and Michael Cullen — were keen on a negotiated peace with industrial labour, and saw a compact as the best way to achieve this. Despite the savage restructurings of the past six years and low inflation, for these people and others such an accord was appealing because the government still faced the twin handicaps of low business confidence and high unemployment. On the union side, Ken Douglas organised an ad hoc group of advisers from among prominent unionists who were high-profile Labour Party activists. Called the Compact Group, it comprised Rex Jones, Mark Gosche, Maryan Street, Owen Harvey and Pat Kelly.

The compact concept also faced intense opposition from the left. The 20,000-strong Maritime, Transport and General Workers' Federation (that conglomerate of watersiders, seamen and railway workers whose unions had refused to join the CTU) came out in opposition to it, believing it represented a union 'capitulation' to the forces that opposed them. Some CTU unions also were up in arms. Despite an impassioned speech by its secretary Bill Andersen, a majority among his union, the Northern Distribution Union, voted overwhelmingly against the compact at a stopwork meeting in March 1990. Other dissidents within the CTU, who formed small cabals in the main cities, also made scathing attacks on its 'corporatist' approach. In Wellington, a Trade Union Solidarity Committee believed that such an accord was not an acceptable strategy because it did not involve real wages or strengthen union organisation.

There was a bigger group of mostly lower-level union organisers, Trade Unionists Against the Compact (TUAC), based in Auckland and

Christchurch who were equally outspoken against it. When the CTU accepted the government's terms of reference for forming an accord, TUAC distributed a petition demanding that it 'not be signed by a small body of delegates attending CTU's national council or national conference but be decided by the full democracy of a direct vote by all New Zealand trade union members'. One of TUAC's activists, Terry Stuart of the Seamen's Union, likened the compact to a haemophiliac going to a vampire for a blood transfusion. By May 1989, these groups claimed 6000 names on a petition demanding unions abandon the compact. It is noteworthy, however, that while sections of union members came out against the compact, or expressed strong reservations about it, apart from the Northern Distribution Union rank and file few unions affiliated to the CTU did. The Communist Party, Douglas's bête noir, was even angrier. Running a persistent, even obsessive campaign against the accord, the *People's Voice* thundered that the CTU had capitulated to government pressure and, not for the first time, decried Douglas and 'his' Socialist Unity Party as 'capitalist collaborators'.[333]

The more prominent Douglas had become, the more he had become the target of derision for Communist Party activists. In September 1987, for example, after he had addressed a business conference on the Labour Relations Act at the Hyatt Kingsgate Hotel in Auckland, party agitators outside called him a phony unionist, a phony communist and a collaborator with big business. After his speech, Douglas left the calm interior of the hotel with his paper in hand to talk to the picketers. But when he asked one protester what his specific complaint was, the malcontent simply replied: 'You are a traitor to the working class.' Dialogue, Douglas countered, was impossible, although he did use this criticism to his advantage by informing the press that the protest underlined a few things that working people were frustrated about. 'They see economic problems facing them not being addressed and that reflects frustration that the government is not doing its job . . .'[334]

Douglas staked his reputation on the passing of the compact. It was the only way for the union movement to progress, and over the following months he fought tooth and nail to see it come to fruition. There were both pragmatic and philosophical reasons for his enthusiasm for a compact-style relationship with the state. Part of this was drawn from new developments in Marxist theory emanating from Mikhail Gorbachev's 'new' Soviet Union, which was embracing glasnost and social democracies in the West as never before. Late in 1988, Douglas circulated a paper by Dr Yuri Krasin, director of the Political Institute of Working Class Studies in Moscow, to union leaders. In his paper Krasin analysed the impact of neoconservatism on the working-class movements of the West and concluded that it had, surprisingly, been rather enduring. Neoconservatism's popularity, Krasin asserted, was 'one of the causes of the serious setbacks suffered recently by workers' parties and "crises of objectives" they experience . . . the point at issue is democratising economic relations by expanding the participation of workers and their workers in crucial decision-making and management at the level of enterprises and corporations.' This, as Douglas interpreted it, was about the reconstructed labour market in the face of, as Krasin put it, 'the realities of the current new stage of technological and cultural progress in a capitalist society'.[335]

From November 1988, in a move to try to shore up slipping electoral support, the government moved more quickly to settle on an industrial agreement with unions and employers. Lange instructed Mike Moore, then deputy Minister of Finance, to take charge of negotiating a compact agreement for the government. Moore's appointment brought more hope, because he came from a working-class background (he still paid his dues as a member of the Printers' Union) and therefore could have been expected to have more empathy with trade union aspirations. Moore was enthusiastic. He saw kudos in it, and wanted the process 'sewn up' by the following September. 'No door is locked,' he said. 'We are not shooting first; talking second,' he told the press in his idiosyncratic style. 'Nor will the compact take prisoners. Of course, there are tribal differences. But if Iraq and Iran can talk peace, so can we.'[336]

On 25 January 1989 businessmen, including Business Roundtable executive director Roger Kerr, union leaders, Moore and Douglas agreed to the compact's goals of 'jobs, fairness, security and respect'

— but that's all they agreed on. From then on the employers and the Roundtable played little role in the compact's progress. On 10 February, Douglas told the annual conference of the New Zealand Pulp and Paper Workers' Federation that despite the government's economic record of instability, contraction, retrenchment, unemployment and disinvestment, the compact was necessary as a first step to 'sort out the shambles' and bring unions in from the cold.[337]

Douglas attacked those who were out to do mischief and try to wreck it, or to use the compact for their own ends:

> Workers need to be clear about one thing. The ideologues of the new right do not want a constructive role for unions in economy and society. They want to strip away those remaining protections that workers have and to have labour markets regulated by the law of the jungle . . . But I have a message for the wide boys of the speculative economy. You have had your day. We are not going to feed your speculative greed any longer. We will confront your mischief. The compact is not on your agenda. Stop pretending that it is because you aren't fooling anyone . . . The Compact is about developing new mechanisms for consulting and negotiating changes on economic, social and industrial issues.[338]

The National opposition remained scathing. Playing the 'commo card', Bill Birch called the compact evidence of a 'secret agenda' between the unions and government. Douglas, he believed, viewed the compact as another chance to continue with the 'mindless and prehistoric class struggle so beloved of the Socialist Unity Party . . .'. Ruth Richardson, a rising star within the party, and more ruthlessly right wing, promised a high-powered group of financiers that 'union rackets' would be wiped out under National and people would be able to draw up individual wage contracts. The Labour government, she said, was a 'hostage' to the unions, with which it was trying to negotiate a 'sordid' contract: 'National will not be held to ransom by these "unemployment merchants". They are yesterday's men peddling yesterday's agenda of compulsion and centralism. We will have no part of any agreement with the trade unions . . .'[339]

There were some uncomfortable incidents. When some minions in Mike Moore's office suggested that as part of the government and the CTU's promotion of the compact they make and distribute T-shirts emblazoned with the words 'Respect Me!' across the front, Ken Douglas was far from amused. He rang Moore's office and shouted down the wire: 'No bloody T-shirts! You got that? No bloody T-shirts!' His reaction highlighted a radical difference in perception of the compact's meaning. To Moore, the shirts were another public relations gimmick, designed to try to capture the public's imagination, just as he had tried years before with his promotion of 'lamburgers'. For Moore, the internationalist, the compact was one component in a process that he hoped would propel New Zealand headlong into the 'global economy'. Douglas's focus was localised. He was clinging on to a last hope that unions might move towards a comprehensive, proactive and broad relationship with the state and employers in meaningful tripartite consultations for the benefit of workers.

While the government through Mike Moore was coming to the party, employers were not. When the Employers' Federation canvassed its members, it found a distinct lack of enthusiasm — although it was likely to join, not wishing to be left out of what promised to be a high-powered quango, especially when kindred groups such as the Manufacturers' Federation had already expressed their support. There were associated reasons why many employers were reluctant. Award settlement was becoming more difficult in some industries as employers, some desperately struggling themselves with the removal of protectionist subsidies, dug their toes in.

Progress was slow, hindered by the Labour caucus voting to restore Roger Douglas to Cabinet in July 1989. Lange's authority was savagely weakened as a consequence and he resigned as prime minister a month later in favour of Geoffrey Palmer. Ken Douglas, who once said that Roger Douglas 'wanted to obliterate the trade union movement in New

Zealand', winced at Douglas's re-emergence. However, he was no longer Minister of Finance but in charge of the lowly immigration and police portfolios, where he was unable to inflict further damage. Ken Douglas was hopeful that under Palmer and Helen Clark, his deputy and the new Minister of Labour, the deregulatory programme would take a back seat. Certainly, the political changes encouraged unions to stay affiliated with the party.[340]

In December 1989, the government outlined its plan for the compact. It foresaw the establishment of an independently funded nine-member Compact Council with members from the government (Palmer as chair, Clark and Minister of Finance David Caygill), trade unions (Douglas, Foulkes and Burgess) and employers, supported by a small secretariat. While it would remain an independent body it would be financed by the Prime Minister's office. Its stated objectives were to facilitate consultation and meaningful input into the government's economic and social policy formation, identify opportunities and barriers to growth at industry level and improve workforce participation at enterprise and workplace level.[341]

The participants waxed lyrical about the agreement. Prime Minister Geoffrey Palmer called it a significant step forward in which 'social partners' would be able to work together for a better future. It was a sign, he said, of our growing maturity as a nation. Mike Moore called it 'forward-looking', noting, 'It starts from where New Zealand is now and on how we can go forward and build a better future for all New Zealanders.' He warned, however, that there was no promise of miracles or instant solutions. Ken Douglas said that the CTU had come into the process recognising that for it to be effective unions had to be prepared to work within the system, to move past political slogans, and to deal with the hard issues and difficult decisions at all levels where the compact would operate.[342]

On 4 April 1990, 149 delegates representing 37 unions agreed by a four to one majority to adopt the compact and then, buoyed by the vote, agreed on a sweeping national campaign to create jobs, to protect New Zealand industry through tariffs, cease state asset sales and improve the living standards of the low-paid. The broad jobs programme — promoted by the Service Workers' Federation — came after a card vote of 363,481 in favour of the compact; 64,775 votes against, and 34,388 abstaining in a total of 453,418. For most, it was better the devil you knew than the devil you did not. Yet there were still worries. Never short of a word, veteran unionist Pat Kelly, who was also president of the Labour Party's affiliates' council, asserted that workers ought to prepare themselves that in the event of the Labour government falling, the compact was likely to go: 'Once Ruth Richardson and her gang get into power you will think that this government was not so bad after all.'[343]

The compact was the high point for the CTU in 1990, with agreement coming as it did after a long 18 months of haggling within the CTU, its affiliates and the government. But it had taken too long. Peter Conway, an industrial officer with the Distribution Workers' Union and one of the new breed of university-educated unionists, pointed to a truth when he commented after the April meeting that a mature union movement would have simply pocketed the concept of a compact 18 months ago. 'It's been an absurdity. We don't have to discuss for 18 months either to turn up and negotiate with employers.' It was the CTU leadership that had insisted on a slow timetable, wary of the 'quick-fix' and sometimes flaky instincts of the mercurial Mike Moore. Ken Douglas later also recognised that his judgement might have been faulty as an earlier start would have allowed the CTU to bed the compact in more firmly before the election than was now possible.[344]

Polls were now pointing to a defeat for Labour in the November election. Within days of the compact being agreed upon, the two major political parties staked opposing positions on industrial relations, which promised to be a key election issue. Apart from 'abandoning' the compact as irrelevant, National was also promising to reintroduce voluntary unionism, encourage more flexible bargaining between employer and worker, encourage enterprise rather than award bargaining, and give workers greater flexibility to decide who would represent them in dispute procedures, which did not necessarily mean unions. To wage and salary earners, National's policies did not seem to square with the Party's leader Jim Bolger's vision of a 'decent society'; nor did they accord with a statement he made in 1989: 'Industrial relations and wage fixing is an area where extremes are often argued. But extremism will not work. All it does is bring a counter reaction ... We are utterly opposed to the total domination of capital in the same way we reject the domination of labour over capital.'[345]

Ken Douglas was aware that Labour was far behind in every survey. He was hoping that an incoming National administration would continue with the compact. Rather than publicly attack National's policy on industrial relations, which looked at labour market deregulation, Douglas was conciliatory. In July 1990 he met with Bolger, Birch, Richardson, and other prominent National MPs Doug Kidd and Maurice Williamson, commenting on radio on 24 July that they had indicated a much softer position in respect to industrial relations than perhaps their policy indicated. He had told them that he had to work with them. 'We've worked with Jim Bolger when he was Minister of Labour so essentially he knows about us and we know about him. That will be a plus ...'[346]

Early in September 1990, facing electoral disaster, a panicked Labour Party dumped Palmer as Prime Minister in favour of Moore. This gave unionists hope that Moore, the architect of the compact from the government side, might lead a new post-1990 government that was more union-friendly. Douglas, however, warned that it was policy not leadership change that was important for workers. A balanced economy based on fair labour practice rather than governance based on the latest economic fad that had captured Treasury or Reserve Bank officials was what was wanted. But he was sceptical. Minister of Finance David Caygill was still committed to economic deregulation, albeit without the intensity and passion of Roger Douglas.[347]

Nonetheless, during the same month the CTU executive reached a one-year 'Agreement for Growth' with the government and the Reserve Bank. Under the agreement the CTU and unions agreed to limit wage rises to less than 2 per cent (unless justified by higher productivity) in

LEFT *Truth* cartoonist Wrathall believes that the forthcoming communist influence will be anything but gentle after Douglas takes his seat as the new FOL secretary. 26 June 1979. (*Douglas family*)

CENTRE Douglas with a New Zealand Polish delegation requesting FOL help for striking 'Solidarity' workers in Gdansk in August 1980. The Socialist Unity Party supported the Polish communist government in its conflict with these workers but Douglas put his signature on a document which supported the workers. On Douglas's right is president of the New Zealand Polish Association, Zdzislaw Lepionka, and on his left is vice-president Josef Meldrun and executive member Ztadeusz Choros. (*Alexander Turnbull Library, Wellington*)

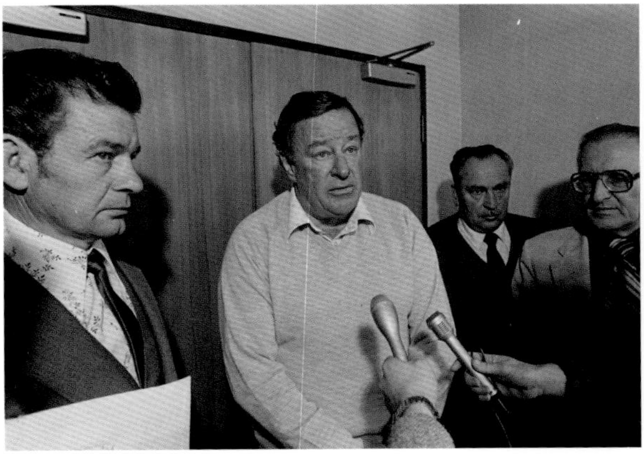

BELOW The FOL executive in discussion over the Polish Solidarity movement's call for assistance in January 1980. The Socialist Unity Party was in direct conflict with the FOL over the issue. From the left of Douglas around the table are Ashley Russ (Carpenters), Sonja Davies (Shop Employees), John Slater, partly obscured, (Clerical Workers), Bill Anton (Labourers), Wes Cameron (Meatworkers), Ted Thompson (Waterside Workers) Jim Boomer (Engineers and vice-president) and Jim Knox (president). (*Evening Post*)

RIGHT Eric Heath, *Dominion*, 19 March 1980.

CENTRE Douglas with Australian unionists Cecily and Ernie Boatswain, assistant secretary of the Australian Building Workers' Union, in the foyer of the Palace Theatre, Havana, Cuba, during the WFTU conference in February 1982. (*Douglas family*)

RIGHT Bromhead's cynical take on Muldoon's wage price freeze. (*Auckland Star*, 7 September 1982)

LEFT Douglas leading a protest against Muldoon's wage freeze regulations in Gisborne in December 1982. Walking beside him with the megaphone is Bob Taylor, secretary of the Gisborne Drivers' Union. (*Douglas family*)

LEFT Bill Anderson, c. 1982. (*Auckland Sun*)

LEFT Douglas with 'pie' all over his face at a fundraising day for a new youth club in Shannon, 3 October 1982. He spent 20 minutes in the stocks while throwers pelted him with cream sponges at $1 a throw. 'I'm used to being a target so this was nothing new,' he commented. (*Evening Post*)

ABOVE The funeral of Ernie Abbott in the Wellington Town Hall on 3 April 1984. Ron Burgess stands behind the microphone while Pat Kelly and Jim Knox are on his right. Ken Douglas, who was a pall bearer, stands fourth from left in the front row. Abbott, the Trades Hall caretaker, was killed by a bomb left in the building on 27 March. Explosives were left inside a suitcase which had sat in the foyer of the Trades Hall for seven hours before Abbott began to move it, detonating a mercury switch which caused it to explode. The perpetrator or perpetrators were never found despite the police offering $25,000 and later $50,000 for information leading to their capture, then the largest sum ever put up in New Zealand. Abbott, who lived in a flat on the premises, was a warm-hearted, genial character who was well-known and liked in the area. His dog *Patches* survived the blast. (*Evening Post*)

CENTRE *National Business Review* cartoonist Bob Brockie takes a potshot at the FOL's opposition to Muldoon's intention to outlaw compulsory unionism in July 1983. Lorraine Downes had just won the Miss Universe crown. Voluntary unionism became law on 1 February 1984. (*Bob Brockie*).

RIGHT Douglas and Knox at the Labour government's economic summit in Parliament, 13 September 1984. (*Alexander Turnbull Library, Wellington*)

LEFT Ken Douglas and his partner Marilyn Tucker at dinner, October 1985. (*Douglas family*)

CENTRE Douglas celebrated his 50th birthday with Marilyn in Moscow in November 1985. He is photographed here with friends from the Russian Communist Party. The urn in the foreground was a birthday present from Mikhail Gorbachev and the party's Central Committee. (*Douglas family*)

LEFT David Lange addresses the 1985 Federation of Labour Conference, his first as Prime Minister. (*Private collection*)

ABOVE LEFT A special edition of the *PSA Journal* in January 1986 exhorts its members to get in behind its proposal to form a Council of Trade Unions.

ABOVE RIGHT The PSA's Colin Clark, who was a principal mover and shaker in the formation of the Council of Trade Unions and later in the CTU campaign for electoral reform in the 1993 election. (*PSA*)

BELOW The CTU steering committee at the top table during an FOL meeting in March 1987 *From left:* Iris Williams (minutes secretary), Ken Douglas, Angela Foulkes, Colin Hicks (CSU chairperson), and Jim Knox (*Alexander Turnbull Library, Wellington*).

LEFT Douglas and Foulkes, foreground, face the CTU executive at their first meeting on 11 December 1987. Ron Burgess is out of shot. (*Alexander Turnbull Library, Wellington*)

CENTRE Tom Murray, secretary of the Timber Workers' Union, Douglas and Knox at the International Labour Organisation's 1988 Conference in Geneva. Murray, as convenor of the CTU's Maori Committee, was its delegate to the Indigenous People's Rights Convention which had a considerable impact on both the United Nations and the ILO. (*Douglas family*)

LEFT Richie Gillespie has the floor at the Socialist Unity Party's 1988 national conference. Douglas sits at the table alongside George Jackson. (*Douglas family*)

RIGHT Douglas launches the Fijian Trade Union Congress's new union centre in Suva on 6 October 1989, after the previous headquarters had been burnt down during the 1988 coup. To Douglas's left are Mahendra Choudry, secretary of the FTUC and later Prime Minister of Fiji, and Simon Crean, president of the Australian Council of Trade Unions. (*Douglas family*)

CENTRE Grant Morgan, general secretary of the Communist Party and leader of a campaign to stop the Compact, confronts Douglas in a Hamilton Street in August 1989, during a street debate involving several hundred workers. (*Socialist Worker*)

BELOW Delegates to the Socialist Unity Party's central committee meeting in Wellington, March 1990. *Back row from left*: Joe Te Pania, Dave Arthur, Alan Ware, Douglas, Graeme Whimp, Richie Gillespie, Dave McCallum, Jan Farr, Joe Tonner. *Front row from left*: Frank McNulty, Jack Marston, Marilyn Tucker, Robin Tait, Bruce Skilton, Bill Anderson. This was the last central committee meeting before Andersen broke away to form the Socialist Party of Aotearoa, taking more than half the Auckland SUP members with him. (*Douglas family*)

return for a cut in interest rates before the election (Douglas specified that this had to be 2 per cent although he later amended it to 0.3 per cent) and a summit of union, government, industry and business leaders on 1 November — five days after the election. The CTU affiliates adopted the proposal. Labour needed all the worker support it could muster in the coming election. It was a welcome achievement. The accord with the government and the Reserve Bank was a remarkable display of altruism given the anti-union economic policies that the government had pursued hitherto.[348]

Despite his public pragmatism, Douglas's communism remained an ideological hurdle for conservative politicians. On 19 October, Bolger demanded to see confidential Treasury papers on discussions between the government and the CTU in drawing up the Growth Agreement, saying that as Douglas was a leading figure in the Socialist Unity Party 'then the economic material would probably end up in Moscow'. Douglas smiled wryly and dismissed this slight, although it did cause consternation among other unionists. Later, Bolger apologised publicly, saying he regretted the way the 'debate' had run its course, but the 'substantive' issue was that if Mike Moore showed these papers to the CTU, then he should show them to everybody.[349]

Within days Bolger was Prime Minister as National swamped Labour at the election. The extent of the 39-seat landslide (which sent Mike Moore into political oblivion after he later lost a bitter leadership struggle to Helen Clark) surprised Douglas. However, he took some solace from Bolger's second personal apology to him on television during his victory speech — for accusing him of passing state secrets to Moscow — because it reflected a deflection from the 'huge problems' confronting the new leader: the Gulf oil crisis, a world economic recession, the country's deteriorating economy, propelled by falling agricultural returns, growing unemployment, and continued lay-offs in industry.

Douglas desperately needed Bolger to be 'friendly' to him and his constituencies. But he also understood that this National administration would be different from those of the late 1970s and early 1980s, in no small part because the personalities of the leaders were very different. He assumed, rightly, that in spite of his aberrant 19 October comment, the anti-union, red-bashing tactics used by Robert Muldoon as a diversion were not Bolger's style, and that with him in charge there would not be a return to the confrontational, personalised politics in which Muldoon had regularly pilloried Douglas for his leadership of the Socialist Unity Party. Unlike Bolger, Muldoon never apologised to anybody. Moreover, between 1978 and 1984 Bolger had been a matter-of-fact rather than an ideological Minister of Labour, and one of the very few from New Zealand to become president of the International Labour Organisation.[350]

On 9 November, Douglas was on the front foot — reflecting years of frustration — when he made a stinging attack on Labour at its party conference, calling the electoral defeat the consequences of working people deserting Labour's policies of deregulation and policies of arrogance. The party had 'torn down' existing jobs and failed to put anything in their place. It had been tough, with a split in the party, massive disunity and three parliamentary leaders, but this was not, he continued, the reason the Labour government had lost the election.

He understood the anger many delegates were feeling. Party conferences were always different beasts to meetings of its leadership oligarchy, until recently enamoured of Rogernomics. This was a very mixed collective. Some delegates supported neoliberalism, or at the very least had been swayed by its promise of economic growth. Others were anxious but remained trusting, hoping that nirvana would arrive. But many more, including many unionists, had been adamantly opposed to it, preferring the traditional values of the 'old' Labour Party — which had almost attained, even after this short time, a nostalgic romanticism. They had felt impotent to modify or redirect, let alone halt the unstoppable deregulatory winds. The recent leadership changes had come too late. For some party members it had all been too much and they had abandoned their posts and joined that other refugee, Jim Anderton, when he set up an alternative party cutely called 'New' Labour and which espoused traditional labour values.

Ken Douglas's esteem among this group was very high. Delegates listened closely as he spoke, curious to learn where he thought both the Labour Party and the trade union movement should go in these unsettling and confused times. He drew applause when he declared that belief in the ability of the deregulated and undirected markets is 'as primitive as any cargo cult can be'. He stared at his audience. 'Worse, though, in the minds of the people I spoke to was the way in which the last government didn't seem to care about anything it said in its election manifesto. That brought resentment. It brought the integrity of the political process into disrepute.'

He saved his praise for the accord the CTU had reached with Mike Moore, contrasting it with the earlier politics of Muldoonism and Rogernomics which had stomped on the unions. 'There is going to have to be a recognition that governments do not have a monopoly on political solutions and even if they think they do, they are going to have to negotiate around the implementation of what they want to do.'[351]

He ended with a warning: 'You must avoid the trap of finding excuses for why you lost the election: that it was all because of disunity, or you weren't understood, or you weren't appreciated. If you do that, you'll find yourselves marginalised in the debate on New Zealand's future . . . I stress that I bring greetings and I bring the offer to co-operate in defining the new agenda. Because we certainly need it. And soon.'[352]

Labour leaders, still in shock from their massive defeat, were humbled. Mike Moore, surprisingly, said he agreed with Douglas. Party president Ruth Dyson said Douglas's analysis of Labour's defeat was also 'part of our analysis'. Both leaders, along with Helen Clark, sat glumly at the top table with their heads aslant. It would be a long way back. For the short term at least, these people would be yesterday's politicians. Douglas was looking to negotiate proactively with the new government, which had already signalled significant labour reform that its predecessor, despite its quantum leap to the right, had not touched.

CHAPTER 12

Nadir — the Employment Contracts Act

Despite the fourth Labour government shying away from direct labour reform, Rogernomics had emasculated the union movement. As business thrived in the new, unfettered environment of deregulation, workers suffered through the weakening of protections — most notably the removal of tariffs and subsidies, allowing the country to be flooded with cheap Asian imports — and the rise in status and power of right-wing ideologues on both sides of the House. Unlike any politicians before them, these people had the ear of pressure groups such as the Business Roundtable, the Employers' Association and the metropolitan Chambers of Commerce. Notions of egalitarianism, cited by many as underpinning the 'humanity' of New Zealand society, were discarded on the trash heap once and for all.

Neoliberalism was more than just a theoretical catch-cry; it had blasted through the country like an unstoppable wind. In its most visible manifestation, the capitalist nouveau riche, particularly before the October 1987 stockmarket crash, exhibited untrammelled symbols of conspicuous consumption in the form of luxury apartments on the waterfront, expensive European cars and frequent holidays in exotic locales. For their part, all that workers wanted was a job, a liveable wage and a share of the good life. What many received was their notice. As Roger Douglas rocketed out of control, unwilling to partake of David Lange's pause for a 'cup of tea', unemployment soared to levels not seen since the worst days of the high-inflation Muldoon era. By January 1990 economic 'restructuring', and the advent of new technologies, had knocked the lid off 67,000 jobs. Between 1986 and 1991 10 multi-chain meat works were mothballed; others were downsized, collectively destroying the jobs of 17,000 freezing workers, all victims of a combination of corporate takeovers, company rationalisations and technological advance. The government was unapologetic. In February 1989 Roger Douglas told a conference in Whangarei that unemployment was an obligatory by-product of true business activity and its cause was 'fundamentally good news' — a necessary consequence of businesses rationalising to make better use of their resources.[353]

Introducing the compact, as we have seen, proved to be a last throw of the dice by a desperate government that was internally haemorrhaging in the wake of the deep acrimony of Lange's fall-out with Douglas. Following Labour's slaughter in the November election the compact quickly disappeared from view. National, in power by Christmas, soon signalled its intention not only to continue a confrontational deregulatory approach to economic management, but also to intensify it, with Minister of Labour Bill Birch its chief architect. Roger Douglas had tilled and fertilised the soil; Birch would plant the seeds, water them vigorously, and watch the resulting plants thrive with satisfaction.

Initially, the approach of the new Prime Minister, pleased Ken Douglas. On 8 November, Bolger slammed Fletcher Challenge's decision to increase the fees of its non-executive directors by 50 per cent — from $400,000 to $600,000 — as greedy and not in keeping with the spirit of sacrifice shown by wage earners. 'It is no use preaching the values of hard work and economy to the workers of New Zealand if the words are not matched by action on the part of those in positions of responsibility,' he said. Then, in a meeting with Douglas, Foulkes, Burgess and Birch, he acknowledged the need for unions to stick to the 2 per cent Growth Agreement already negotiated with Labour, and all consented that a 'moderate' wage round was essential.[354]

But Birch was soon singing a different tune, stating within days of Bolger's comments that National's industrial policy might be 'even more radical' than previously considered (such as his failed November 1987 Labour Relations Amendment Bill). At the same time, currying favour, Birch maintained publicly that he had a high opinion of Ken Douglas and his ability to be 'reasonable'. 'We believe the influence he is exercising on his affiliates for moderate wage claims is very important in the battle on inflation. We hope that will continue. We applaud the recognition that higher wages can only come through higher productivity gains.'[355]

In the meantime, and taking attention away from labour matters, Birch signalled National's intention to scrap Labour's recently passed pay equity legislation — and with it close the newly opened Employment Equity Office — which had introduced the concept of equal work for equal value for men and women. This angered many women's groups including the conservative National Council of Women, as well as most unions, the CTU and a number of newspaper editorial-writers. But it was gone by Christmas, Birch arguing that it was 'expensive, cumbersome and "trade-union captured"'. Needless to say, the numbers of unemployed kept rising. Labour Department figures showed that they grew by 6089 during November 1990 to 169,026. In addition 17,528 students were seeking holiday work and there were a further 15,000 New Zealanders on subsidised work schemes, bringing the total to 202,054, at close to 13 per cent, the highest on record.[356]

Then, on 13 December 1990, trade unionists stared down the barrel of the most devastating anti-union legislation this country had ever seen. Under the guise of 'freedom of choice' Birch introduced an

Employment Contracts Bill which aimed to abolish national awards and introduce a system of individual or collective contracts; abolish compulsory unionism; abolish unions in favour of 'bargaining units' or 'employee associations'; abolish party clauses which bound all workers in an industry to similar wages and conditions; abolish compulsory conciliation for negotiation of awards and agreements; abolish union officials' right of access to the workplace and workers' entitlement to two paid meetings a year; abolish the right to strike before an award or agreement had expired; abolish majority rule through secret ballot on union membership in favour of 'individual choice', and abolish exclusive union coverage of particular work.

In short, he sought to turn on its head the 'historic consensus' compact between capital and labour which had underpinned the structure of industrial relations in this country for close to 100 years, enshrined in the 1894 Industrial Conciliation and Arbitration Act (and left little different in the Industrial Relations Act that succeeded it in 1974) in a barely disguised move to diminish, if not smash, real or perceived union power. It was noteworthy that in the Bill's text the word 'union' appeared only once, the word 'worker' did not appear at all, and even Labour Day was not given its name — it was referred to as 'the fourth Monday in October'. In a particularly tactless act Birch chose 1 May — May Day, or 'International Workers' Day', the day on which unions and workers commemorate the historic struggles of working people throughout the world — as the date which the Bill would become law. Birch was probably not even aware of its significance. The Business Roundtable expressed its pleasure but wanted to go further and tried to persuade the government to drop its minimum wage provisions as well.[357]

Critics inside and outside the union movement were up in arms. Dr Ray Harbridge, a senior lecturer at Victoria University's Industrial Relations Centre, called the proposed legislation incoherent, inequitable and unfair. It was also unnecessary, he believed, because the Labour Relations Act was already delivering the kind of enterprise agreements so keenly sought by employers and the government. Unions had already shown a great deal of flexibility in negotiating key elements such as hours of work, penal rates and skills training packages, and wage rises through this period were well behind the rate of inflation. Long-term research at the Industrial Relations Centre had shown that enterprise agreements reached under the 1987 law had not resulted in cheaper outcomes for employers. National awards yielded smaller wage rises than regional or enterprise agreements because they served as a restraint, tempering what 'elite' workers could have received at the expense of poorer workers.

Later Harbridge would go much further. After the Bill became law he accused the government of exposing New Zealand to the worst excesses of 'gangster unionism'. The legislation had wiped away all the stringent requirements for unions to be democratic and accountable — now they had only to meet the less rigorous requirement that they be an incorporated society, which meant they did not need to be democratic at all. This scenario opened up the possibility of 'agents with muscle' from outside the movement persuading workers to cede to them the authority to bargain, charge them heavily for this, and extract similar fees from employers for keeping the workforce 'in line'. This was akin to worst-practice American experience, some of which had been deeply corrupt.

Indeed, bargaining agents were at the core of unionists' outrage. They feared that employers would exploit the new legislation by hand-picking pliable agents on behalf of their staff. Pencarrow MP Sonja Davies told the House that she understood gangs were preparing to work as bargaining agents because they saw opportunities under the Bill to stand over workers — using intimidation to enforce deals in vulnerable workplaces while acting as legitimate 'bargaining agents'. This was no idle comment. In April, Black Power officially announced it was establishing an advocacy agency in preparation for the new law, in response to which Bolger acknowledged that the Bill, as it then stood, entitled any gang to do this 'if it acted lawfully'.

However, on assessment, between the Bill's unacceptable clauses there were a handful of sections that made sense in the new deregulated economic environment. The personal grievance provisions of the Bill were a vast improvement on previous legislation where grievances were restricted to unionists working under an award. The scrapping of compulsory unionism was also sensible, although many union leaders failed to see it at the time. Many smaller unions only existed because of compulsory unionism, and many members, as we shall see, left when they no longer had to belong. Fintan Patrick Walsh had owed his power base, particularly in latter years, to his leadership of the large Clerical Workers' Union, whose members were scathingly derided by blue-collar workers as those 'compulsory unionists'. Once membership was voluntary, many clerical workers left the union, and within two years this union itself would collapse. In hindsight, and as Ken Douglas had foreseen, compulsory unionism had denuded many unions of the vitality needed to survive in a deregulated marketplace. A reluctant unionist was 'dead wood' to his union.

But appraised in toto, the Bill's radicalism was forbidding. Not all employers felt it was necessary either. Earlier, in August 1990, an Otago University Management Department survey had found employers were evenly split between those seeking change and those satisfied with the status quo. Later the same year the Manufacturers' Federation had publicly endorsed the Moore-Douglas compact. In the main, support for Birch's legislation came, strongly, from the Business Roundtable which represented big business, and the Employers' Federation which had between 10,000 and 11,000 members — but which represented just 9.6 per cent of the 115,000 business enterprises identified as employing staff by the Statistics Department in 1989. Some large concerns — such as Air New Zealand, Fisher & Paykel, McDonald's and Progressive Enterprises — were worried about how workplace agents would be chosen. In submissions to the select committee they sought provisions to prevent a multitude of competing agents emerging in the workplace and proposed majority votes by workers as the answer.[358]

Helen Clark, the Opposition's labour spokesperson, called the Bill a kick in the teeth for unions and a recipe for industrial chaos. Rather than encouraging industrial harmony she said the measure was an 'obsessive drive for ideological purity'. The most ideological aspect of the Bill was that it largely swept away legal protection for workers in the naive expectation that they and their employers would be able to negotiate their own fair deals.

The government — and employers — maintained that its formula was 'liberating' and 'emancipatory' — as if somehow workers had been 'imprisoned' by their unions. However, Patricia Herbert, a broadcaster and a writer and columnist for the *Auckland Star, Listener* and *National Business Review,* believed that while this might have been true in times of prosperity and labour shortages, in a deep recession with rising unemployment it was a recipe for exploitation:

> National has chosen the southern United States as its model. The governments of these states, anxious to attract investment, have fashioned their industrial relations policies around the need to provide a pool of cheap, pliable labour. As a consequence, large segments of the workforce — predominantly those who are black, female, young or unskilled — work for wages below the poverty line.[359]

Herbert argued that while discrimination on that level was unlikely to occur in New Zealand because the histories were different — slavery as opposed to a strong egalitarian tradition — it did not absolve National from creating a legislative environment which would allow such abuse to occur.[360]

Unions were an easy scapegoat for what the government believed was wrong with industrial relations in New Zealand, but the Bill did little more than pander to a public distaste for the unions that was the outcome of long-standing annoyance at disruptions that had occurred in the past. The Planning Council felt differently. In its 1989 paper *The Economy in Transition,* it blamed a faltering economy not on employer/union strife but on 'misdirected investment decisions and inefficient use of capital stock'. The basic underlying concept that somehow growth in productivity could only occur with market reform was also flawed. Among others, New Zealand had one of its productivity peaks through the 1950s, when both unionism and industrial arbitration were compulsory and the state apparatus was centralised and powerful. More recently, productivity in manufacturing had risen 31 per cent between 1980 and 1987; in the construction industry it had risen more than 50 per cent — despite a fall in the value of real wages.[361]

The Bill also provoked international condemnation, running foul of the conventions of the ILO, the tripartite body of governments, workers and unions which developed guidelines — or conventions — for what it believed were minimum standards for industrial legislation internationally, conventions that were established after agreement from two-thirds or more of its 160 member states, including New Zealand. The government, despite promises to do so, ratified neither convention number 87 (which dealt with the freedom of association and protection of the right to organise) nor number 98 (the right to organise and promote collective bargaining). Along with the CTU and a number of labour lawyers, the Department of Labour informed the government that it had strong misgivings about the Bill's legality, arguing in particular that a key tenet within the right to bargain collectively with employers regarding conditions of work was freedom of association. The government turned a blind eye to these conventions.[362]

From its perspective, the Employment Contracts Bill was designed to work in tandem with Ruth Richardson's benefit cuts to drive down wages. Bill Birch pointed the finger at unions for spreading disinformation but the public seemed to be able to work out the basics for themselves — that a young person on minimum wages or on the dole would now be in a very weak bargaining position with their employer or potential employer. Polling through this time consistently showed that the public believed the main aim of the Bill to be threefold: to remove or severely downgrade unions; to drive down wages, and to give employers more power. Later, in May, just before the Bill became law, just 7 per cent of respondents to one poll accepted Birch's claim that its purpose was to boost productivity and usher in a period of higher 'real' wages, more jobs and economic growth. The unflappable Birch, always quietly self-assured, was not persuaded. By January 1991, unemployment figures had reached a new high, exceeding 215,000 or 14.89 per cent of the labour force, surpassing the 12 per cent average during the worst years of the 1930s Depression. By March it had worsened further as the figure for Auckland passed the 50,000 mark, the biggest in its history.

Initially, Ken Douglas was publicly quiet on the Bill. But behind the scenes he shared the rage of his colleagues. While he had long foreseen a measure of this type — Birch had been signalling it since his November 1987 Bill — its radicalism, its all-encompassing nature, and particularly the likelihood that unions would be completely removed from the wage negotiation process was galling and shocking. But Douglas kept his feet on the ground. In a circular he sent to all affiliates following a meeting of the national executive after news of the Bill had been released on 20 December, he indicated that the executive declared it to be both inequitable and unworkable. The executive promised to expose the Bill's unworkability and to try to secure amendments that offered more effective and equitable protection to working people in line with the principles of the draft Charter of Worker and Union Rights. The latter, which had been drawn up by the CTU and was adopted by it on 21 February 1991, was based on a number of international conventions and declarations under the jurisdiction of the United Nations and the International Labour Organisation.[363]

In mid-January, the CTU turned up the heat. Head office produced an action kit for affiliates and members and advised them to lobby MPs in their areas. Delegates were told to visit MPs, and write letters or emails, and it was suggested that protests against the Bill should also target the other unfriendly legislation the government was proposing to pass, such as benefit cuts. Union organisers and delegates urged members in their workplaces to take whatever action they could, both individually and collectively.[364]

At a meeting of 200 delegates in Wellington on 21 February, the notion of a general strike was informally canvassed. There was no decision but the idea was not ruled out. Some, like Rick Barker, secretary of the Service Workers' Federation, and Don Aimer, secretary of the financial sector union Finsec, believed education should come before strike action. The meeting passed a number of key motions, including a need 'to demonstrate the unworkability and inequity of the Bill' and to seek maximum membership mobilisation in protest against its provisions through a week of action. Many were optimistically relying on the CTU and unions to persuade the select committee in their submissions that significant change was needed to make the Bill fairer for workers.[365]

Workers and their unions held protest meetings up and down the country. A finger-pointing Douglas aggressively lectured 500 Christchurch union delegates on 19 February:

> In working class history nothing has been won without fighting. Nothing was won by compliance with the law of the time. I refer to the Tolpuddle martyrs who were deported from England in the 1830s for conspiring to organise a trade union. This proposed legislation turns back the clock to those days ... The Employment Contracts Act is like the Clyde Dam project. Nice, to some, in theory but it's built on a major fault line, remedial work costs will be horrific and at the end of the day it will be yet another monument to Treasury and government incompetence.[366]

Late in February, Jim Bolger entered the fray before a friendly Te Kuiti audience, exhorting unions and the CTU to accept that they would not win the battle against the government's new industrial relations law. 'Stop grandstanding,' he called from afar. 'You will not win. If the union leaders [he was careful not to mention any names] persist in their battle it could cost their members even more jobs that those same union leaders have helped to destroy in the past with their stubborn refusal to face realities.' Birch, too, was becoming anxious about public relations fall-out over the Bill and sent a letter to every householder in the country extolling its virtues — at a nationwide distribution cost of $240,000. Helen Clark called it a 'grubby little pamphlet'; Ken Douglas called it deceptive propaganda. Birch called the attacks on his words 'a disgrace'. It caused a bitter argument in Parliament. There was also debate about whether Bolger could be trusted. Before the 1990 general election he had denied that National would abolish penal rates — 'It's a lie,' he had said when questioned by the press. Under the subsequent Bill all 'extras' — penal, overtime and weekend rates — were gone.[367]

Many unions contributed to a comprehensive and hard-hitting CTU submission to the select committee, as well as their own submissions. On 8 March, Douglas pulled no punches at the hearing. While conceding that the CTU was abandoning its opposition to voluntary unionism, describing it as a 'blue herring', he said he believed the Bill was intended to create a state of 'anarchy' and 'uncivilised behaviour'. The Bill repealed all legal recognition of unions, he said, noting that small groups of workers in key jobs would be able to disown any deal struck by a union and use their industrial muscle to win a better deal for themselves. The government was driving the whole thing by encouraging conflict and uncivilised behaviour that was quite unnecessary.[368]

Protesters now took to the streets. On 11 March, 2200 workers, beneficiaries, students and self-employed rallied in opposition to the Bill in Whangarei's Okara Park. Three days later 200 noisy protesters marched through the town of Masterton. The following day, close to 2000 strode to Parliament under the leadership of a Coalition Against Poverty. On 22 March, 5500 members of the Northern Distribution Union, including drivers, store workers and boiler attendants, debated the Bill at a mass rally at Auckland's Mt Smart Stadium and went on strike for the rest of the day. More than 1000 Hamiltonians marched in an anti-Bill rally on the same day.

This was just the beginning. During a CTU-planned week of action between 3 and 9 April a variety of unions organised rallies, stopwork meetings and public meetings throughout the country. On 3 April, 5000 workers marched in protest in the rain up Queen Street before listening to speeches by Ken Douglas and others in Aotea Square. On 4 April, CTU youth worker Robert Winters organised a National Youth 'education' day on the Bill. Seafarers planned to take indefinite strike action from 10 April to retain conditions threatened by the Bill.

More remarkably, close to 80,000 child-care workers, kindergarten, primary, secondary and area school teachers, along with school office staff, cleaners and caretakers, teacher aides and library assistants across the country walked off the job for 24 hours — thousands marched in protest down the main streets of all major centres. They were joined by thousands of others, mostly civil servants who took time off from their jobs. In Auckland, upwards of 15,000 protesters participated in a 'March of Anger', as it was dubbed, being joined by people from nearby offices and the street — yelling '1, 2, 3, 4 ... kick the Bill right out the door, 5, 6, 7, 8 ... stop the Bill, it's not too late!' The play upon the word 'Bill' was not coincidental.

In Hamilton there were 3000 protesters; in Rotorua 1000; in Whakatane 1500 — teachers, pulp and paper and timber workers, and office workers. In Whangarei a crowd of 6000 shouted down local MP John Banks when he claimed that under the new legislation 'useless' unions would 'go out the back door'. In Wellington, more than 8000 teachers and associated workers attended a rally at Parliament grounds. Hospitals came to a virtual standstill on 8 April when health sector workers in many towns and cities held stopwork protest meetings. The following day more than 1000 office workers, prison officers, council employees, dockyard workers and dental nurses marched through central Takapuna and rallied at Hurstmere Reserve. To coincide with the end of the CTU's week of action, a further 5000 marched down Queen Street in a rally organised by the PSA.

On 10 April 'blue-collar' unionists marched from Wellington Railway Station to the Trades Hall in Vivian Street, both protesting against the Bill and commemorating the death of Trades Hall caretaker Ernie Abbott, murdered in the building 10 years earlier when a bomb, left there in a suitcase, exploded. Seamen, watersiders, drivers, factory workers, hotel and hospital workers and construction workers dominated the march, alongside delegates representing the Unemployed Workers' Union. Ken Douglas marched at the head of the crowd and spoke at the end of many of these protests. The temperate became militant overnight, with many marchers taking to the streets for the first time. During one week in April alone, more than 400 state sector workers applied to join the voluntary Public Service Association.

The discontent spread. Both the Roman Catholic and the Anglican churches declared 'holy war' against the Bill and the concomitant benefit cuts. Anglicans called the measure 'a betrayal of the Christian vision of peace and justice'. The Bishop of Christchurch, the Right Reverend David Coles, said seeking economic recovery at the cost of greater poverty, pain and alienation for those who suffered the most was no recovery at all. Speaking on behalf of his church, New Zealand's Catholic leader Cardinal Thomas Williams described the Bill as 'very damaging to the social fabric of New Zealand'. The Catholic Commission for Justice, Peace and Development produced a pamphlet describing it as sinful and called for the Bill to be immediately withdrawn as 'it did not meet the basic norms of justice, social ethics and social morality'. Another Catholic group, the Network of Religious Priests, Nuns and Brothers for Justice, sent an open letter of protest to Bolger, a fellow Catholic.[369]

Birch brushed off the protests, calling them 'very crude instruments', and professed he did not take much notice of them. He continually downplayed the importance, and the potential impact, of the proposed legislation. At the end of March he had told the triennial conference of the New Zealand Harbour Board Workers' Union that the Bill did not favour individual contracts or collective bargaining. 'The Bill just gives a right of choice — but collective bargaining will remain an integral part of New Zealand working life.' But Birch was being disingenuous. The changes were radical, turning the structure of industrial relations in New Zealand on its head. He was also turning his back on pronouncements he made before National came to power. In July 1989 he had criticised Ken Douglas for spreading 'untruths and falsehoods' about National's plan for the labour market when Douglas had said that right-wing elements in the National Party intended to implement the Business Roundtable agenda for labour market deregulation. Birch had argued that there would be more flexibility in the labour market but that National would not abolish national awards — which it did.[370]

It was later revealed, in documents that were released by the Labour

Department, that the Department and the State Services Commission had warned that Birch's Bill could lead to costly and disruptive industrial action if it was not moderated. These documents — which included Cabinet papers and departmental reports — showed that both departments had sent Birch alternative drafting guidelines to those prepared for him by Paul Bell, a National policy adviser and former advocate for the Employers' Association. In a further released document, a memorandum from Birch to the Cabinet legislation committee confirmed that the government had ignored the chance to consult with the union movement in favour of the Employers' Association. It was informed of the tenor of the Bill and had held formal discussions on it with the government, whereas the CTU, workers, unions (and employers in general) were not consulted.[371]

For his part, Ken Douglas was already looking ahead, telling one of many audiences that he did not have any fears about the future of unions and workers but he did fear the huge cost of 're-fighting the same battles of the past 100 years'. He predicted that the union movement of the future, post the Employment Contracts Act, would be 'much more alive — smaller, but of much better quality'. Protest was necessary, but developing strategies to survive in the post-Employment Contracts Act period was more important. He also believed that to become stronger in this hostile environment it would be critical for kindred unions to amalgamate to develop both similar and different strategies to survive the legislation. The Harbour Board Workers' Union was one which took such action. Within months it had amalgamated with the New Zealand Seafarers' Union, although its natural ally, the Waterside Workers Federation, stayed outside, racked by internal differences and financial problems.[372]

But there was union disquiet when Douglas 'danced with the enemy' by sitting at the top table of an $895-a-head big-business seminar on the Bill at Auckland's Aotea Centre on 10 April — alongside, interestingly, former friend Rob Campbell, now a business consultant with his own company, Wheeler Campbell Labour Markets Ltd. The seminar was attended by 300 employers, and earlier in the day had been addressed by Bill Birch.

The event followed an anti-Bill march up Queen Street the same day and a rally at an overflowing Town Hall, where Douglas told the audience to tell the Business Roundtable and the Employers' Association that 'if you attack workers in any one part of the country we in the union movement will stand solid and deal with you'. It was from here that Douglas walked the 100 metres to the Aotea Centre to deliver his speech to the business seminar. Laughter filled the venue when the chairperson, Judge Paddy Finnigan, quipped, 'I'm sure I heard Ken practising his speech in another hall on the other side of the square.' 'I suppose,' Douglas replied, 'what the chairman is referring to about my speaking in the other venue is just an indication of how pluralism is alive and well in New Zealand. Certainly there are some people who are concerned about me being in this forum but that's an indication of the troubled times we live in.'[373]

Douglas's tone appeared to be different at this venue. The main theme of his address was the need for the union movement to 'collaborate' with big business; he described this collaboration as the 'central aspect we've been driving in the trade unions', adding 'and we do have an overwhelming commitment to it'. But he also said that the Bill could not be made to work while it contained the specific principle of de-recognising unions and not providing for a legal process for their activities. 'We've made this clear to the Prime Minister and the Minister of Labour and the chairman of the Select Committee. We've offered collaboration and cooperation of the CTU to develop a workable system.' Of course, the word 'collaboration' itself was like a red rag to a bull for those blue-collar workers and Communist Party agitators who believed that Douglas and the CTU were becoming too cosy with the capitalist class and their 'close mates' in government.

Continuing, Douglas stated his belief that more union amalgamation was desperately needed, and he slammed those union officials who had 'strong emotional ties' to smaller unions that were resisting amalgamation: 'We have too many kings and a few queens now, on two-pin fiefdoms in the movement who we have got to deal with. Stan Rodger [the former Minister of Labour] said that if he bought us a bucket of cyanide pills we might resolve the question pretty quickly but he wanted a more humane way so he gave us $1.5 million to try and encourage unions to amalgamate to deal with those sorts of problems that way.' Following this speech Finnigan quipped that it was his impression that Ken Douglas had been enjoying himself. He described him as a 'strong and brave man' and called for a very warm vote of thanks, at which point Douglas received loud and sustained applause.

This was Douglas at his most chameleon-like. Critics, and there were plenty of them, berated him for his apparently close connection with some business people, but much of this criticism was emotional. Yet it was also understandable, bearing in mind the mind-boggling intent, and extent, of the forthcoming legislation. On close analysis, however, his message to employers and unionists was essentially the same, even if the emphasis was different. He was telling unionists that he and the CTU leadership were going to fight the Employment Relations Act with all the energy they could muster because it was grossly unfair and discriminatory. But he also understood that because of National's determination to see it through, allied with its huge majority in the House, overturning it was an impossibility. He was also telling the unionists to pool their resources, amalgamate, become proactive and choose leaders who were prepared to look ahead — to understand and deal with the radically different world of work that massive technological advances had brought about, outside of any industrial legislation, and try to use it to their advantage. He was giving employers exactly the same message, in effect, sometimes with the same note of hectoring as he exhorted them to 'get their act together'. Some, both kindly and unkindly, were now calling him a man for all seasons.

Demand among some unionists for a general strike against the Bill grew increasingly strong, and a CTU affiliates meeting was called for 18 April to discuss the proposal. Before the meeting, outspoken CTU official Pat Kelly predicted the strike had a 60 per cent chance of going ahead. But Douglas had already signalled that he was not in favour. Any such decision, he indicated, would need to be a democratic one from affiliates to the CTU, but he made his own view very clear — he personally would not call a general strike. Few unions to date had supported a 24- or 48-hour stoppage, he said, and any such action would have to be taken on an individual basis. 'A national strike is negative because the government has the machinery to pass [the Bill] — but I believe it will be changed by this government because it is unworkable.' This was engagement with supreme optimism and most unlikely.[374]

The issue came to a head at the 18 April meeting. By then, it was clear that select committee submissions from the CTU and unions — and the fact that the majority of submissions in general were against it — were going to make very little difference to the tenor of the Bill. Douglas moved an executive resolution, which the delegates passed, stating that the government did not appear to have heeded the massive tide of resentment against the Bill's essential principles, and calling for necessary steps to ensure that no employer would be allowed to use the licence given under the Bill to exploit or victimise workers. It also promised that the CTU would organise effective responses to any employers who did seek to abuse that licence — including industrial action, boycotts, bans and pickets. Separately, and most importantly for activists, the delegates resolved to participate in a National Day of Action against the Bill on 30 April, ranging from lunchtime meetings to a 24-hour strike.[375]

Crucially, after vigorous debate, Rick Barker and Bill Andersen moved a more moderate amendment that dispensed with the 24-hour option and called on all affiliates to participate in a National Day of Action with a four-hour national stoppage and combined rallies. After further argument, sometimes heated, a further amendment was moved by Maurice Ward of the Tramways Union and Tony Wilton of the Journalists and Graphic Process Union, which read 'That the CTU will co-ordinate a campaign of mass action to oppose the Employment Contracts Act until it is withdrawn or defeated'. Andersen withdrew his amendment before a third, more militant, proposal emerged from Barker and Ray Bianchi of the Labourers' Union which called upon all unions, affiliated and otherwise, 'to participate in a nation-wide stoppage of 24 hours to commence at midnight on 29 April and that during it regional CTUs organise mass meetings against the Bill and the attacks on beneficiaries'.[376]

Loud voices, strained tempers and interjections from the floor characterised the meeting as 13 speakers then spoke for or against this amendment. Douglas effectively brought the debate to a halt when he told delegates that any success would be the outcome of what happened 'on the ground', a less than subtle reminder that all, or the vast majority of, unions would need to agree to a general strike for it to have any chance of being effective. The government's economic policy was the main target, he believed. 'We should be looking at challenging the economic policy head-on, and this means planning right through to at least the date of the budget.' He added, pointedly, that those who wanted a 24-hour strike would have the executive's total support, but 'to limit resolution to a 24-hour stoppage ran the danger of demonstrating a weakness both to the public and ourselves. We must not confuse unity for uniformity.'[377]

The 84 delegates present represented 39 unions, which in turn represented a voting strength of 448,760 workers. Ward and Wilton's amendment was put to the meeting and lost on voices. Barker and Bianchi's motion on a 24-hour stoppage was then put to the meeting and appeared to be lost on voices, but the response was close enough for Pat Brown of the Northern Drug and Chemical Workers' Union to call for a card vote. This resulted in delegates representing 190,910 members voting for the resolution, but 250,122 voted against; the measure was defeated by 59,212 votes. Thereafter 24-hour stoppages or any other union action against the Bill on 30 April, or any other day, would be the responsibility of individual unions.

The CTU's 'Big Seven' — the Engineers' Union; Public Service Association; Post Primary Teachers' Association; Nurses' Association (as opposed to the Nurses' Union, which supported the strike); Post Office Union; New Zealand Educational Institute, and Finsec, the bank workers' union — opposed a general 24-hour strike. Against them ranged the big blue-collar unions — the Service Workers' Union, the

Electrical Workers' Union and the Northern Distribution Union — and others, notably the Clerical Workers' Union which, as it was structured, was bound to lose most under the legislation. But the Hotel and Hospital Workers' Union was against, its secretary Mark Gosche calling for unity, as did many other speakers from other unions. Others, mostly blue collar, such as the Meat Workers' Union, declined to show their hand.[378]

On 30 April — 'action day', the day before the Bill was due to become law — over 50,000 workers and their supporters took to the streets in huge numbers. Marches were followed by rallies. Workers who had previously been unwilling to take protest action were now visible. In Auckland, an estimated 20,000 to 25,000 protesters marched up Queen Street in the biggest street protest in New Zealand since the 1981 Springbok tour — and the biggest ever for an industrial issue. Leaving Post Office Square at 12.30pm, and gathering thousands of additional protesters as they made their way up Queen Street, the first marchers reached Aotea Square as the last were leaving from the bottom of the street. In Wellington, 12,000 workers led by Douglas and Kelly marched on Parliament. What was noticeable in the nationwide mobilisation was that white-collar unionists hugely outnumbered blue-collar workers. For a variety of reasons, as discussed earlier, the latter simply were not visible in numbers anymore.[379]

In Auckland, Angela Foulkes was one of those who addressed the crowd, telling them that the Bill was the most obnoxious legislation introduced anywhere in the world. Jim Knox, 72 and in ill-health, rode on the back of a four-wheel-drive vehicle during this protest. He addressed the crowd with passion: 'I am very happy and very proud to be present to speak to such a massive crowd who are prepared to struggle and fight back and get rid of the National government which brought down the suppression of trade union rights of the trade union movement . . . you are getting poorer and poorer while the rich are getting richer and richer and richer . . .' He also criticised the CTU executive for not calling a general strike. 'There is no doubt in my mind that if there had been a national stoppage we'd have three to four times the number that's here today.' Auckland's May Day rally the following day was Knox's last public appearance — within eight months he was dead. Before succumbing on 1 December 1991 — just three weeks after his predecessor Tom Skinner, who died on 11 November — he would become one of the first members of the new Order of New Zealand.[380]

Through April, some 350,000 marchers had taken to New Zealand streets rallying against the Employment Contracts Bill — the largest outpouring of protest in the country's history over the shortest period of time. This figure was equivalent to one-tenth of the country's population — children included. It was noteworthy, however, that the CTU line was to 'oppose' the Bill, while marchers at all of these protests wanted more, calling for 'defeat' or to 'kill', 'stop' or 'ban' the Bill.

Birch was adamant that no matter the extent of the 30 April protests, they would make 'not one iota of difference' to the outcome of the legislation. Changes to the final form of the Bill were minor. Personal grievance provisions for workers were extended and another modification went some way towards establishing a code of employment protection for vulnerable and youth workers. In Parliament Labour fought the Bill clause by clause. Finance spokesperson Michael Cullen described it as a 'narrow, bigoted, stupid piece of legislation' and vowed that Labour would repeal it and replace it with 'sensible' industrial relations law. But the government had the numbers and voted 43 to 24 to advance the Bill into law which it did on 15 May.[381]

Birch was relying on employers' 'goodwill' not to exploit their workers after the law came into force. But some employers immediately and unilaterally lowered wages, waving contracts in front of workers and telling them to 'sign now or be sacked'. Douglas told workers to 'sign nothing until you have advice — from the union, the local district council or from the CTU'. Jim Bolger urged employers at their annual conference to 'capitalise on the new industrial relations environment' to hire more staff, implicitly at the expense of lower-paid workers. It should also be said that a few unions tried intimidatory tactics to encourage workers to remain with them and use them as their bargaining agents.[382]

At its 18 April affiliates meeting the CTU had not called for a general strike, though the margin was relatively narrow. Nonetheless, large numbers of trade unionists were angry at the perceived timidity of this reaction, and the argument for a strike remained strong, with many feeling that a symbolic gesture of defiance was necessary to demonstrate to the government that its anti-union stance would not be tolerated.

The vote against a strike had been carried on the strength of the CTU's white-collar membership. This was galling to members of those blue-collar unions that had refused to join the expanded organisation in 1987, or remained non-aligned, and whose votes would undoubtedly have swayed the wider membership to agree to a general strike. Despite the strength of the protests against the Bill, many unionists felt hamstrung by the fact that once the law was passed the CTU had seemingly accepted it as a fait accompli.

Much anger, rightly or wrongly, was directed at Douglas. He remained unapologetic. In early June, just days after the Bill had passed, he told a journalist that he was adamant he was not going to lead workers into a fight that he knew he would not be able to deliver on. 'That doesn't develop confidence in the union movement; it just bloody demoralises people,' he said. To another audience he reiterated that workers themselves wanted more flexible work practices. 'On the other hand there are thousands of employers who believe the Act is rubbish because it flies in the face of the objective needs of the economy for a stable, skilled workforce.' That was an exaggeration, but Douglas was practised at using hyperbole to get his message across to an often sceptical audience.[383]

He now believed that despite the rhetoric and the slogan-shouting, unions were powerless and meek when it came to applying political pressure. Asserting that New Zealand workers had for too long been treated like 'tap water to be turned on and off for demonstrations', he had had enough of that approach. Using a poetic analogy, he referred to himself as personifying 'the Grand Old Duke of York' who marched 10,000 men to the top of the hill and marched them down again, 'carrying slogans, yelling chants, feeling good, traipsing to the pub, having a "celebratory" beer, going home and achieving nothing' — except perhaps a venting of some frustration or anger at employer or state intolerance. What he wanted was radical in terms of trade union and worker history — a possible trade-off of wage hikes and better conditions for more genuine union input into the management of enterprises through conciliatory negotiation. But it would be a massive task to overthrow more than 100 years of inherited confrontational relationships between employer and worker. Douglas relished the challenge. Real trade unions, he believed, were about empowering workers to make relevant decisions about their lives.[384]

Douglas never wavered from this approach despite the often intense flak that he and the CTU leadership received from unionists and supporters who called for a more militant response to the Act — a 24-hour general strike at the very least. As late as 1997 he was telling a CTU audience that anyone who thought that his calling for a general strike in 1991 would have led workers everywhere to walk off the job was talking rubbish — 'and they know it'.[385]

As he was wont to do, Douglas invoked Karl Marx's 'pragmatism' in relation to dealing with the Employment Contracts Act. 'People's consciousness lags behind reality,' he stated. 'We become aware of problems after the conditions that created them have already occurred. But at the very point we become aware of those problems the process of finding the answer has already been established.'[386]

It was not only Douglas who was cautious. A CTU-commissioned survey in January showed that the public had little awareness of the impact of the Bill. In addition, many unions that had actively protested against the Bill before it was passed into law decided that they would continue to oppose it, at the same time realising, like Douglas, that it would be impossible to defeat it. These unions included those representing teachers, nurses, engineers, bank and Post Office workers and public servants. Moreover, significant numbers of rank and filers from other unions calling for a strike, such as the Clerical Workers' Union and the Service Workers' Union, were unwilling to withdraw their labour because they feared employer victimisation at a time of high unemployment. Not all workers felt this way, and there were internal disagreements. For example, on 12 and 15 April, both the Nelson and Canterbury branches of the PSA passed no-confidence motions in their national leadership, citing 'mishandling and misleading' of the campaign against the legislation. Both called for a general strike.[387]

On the ground, there was no disagreement that under the Employment Contracts Act the future for many workers was dire. Few rank and filers possessed expertise in wage negotiation, having left award negotiations in the past to union officials. They needed to understand, for example, that if they were over 20 they were entitled to at least $245 a week, and that under the Factories and Commercial Properties Act the workplace had to have basic facilities such as toilet, basin and lunch facilities. Workers would now be required to decide whether they wanted to negotiate for a collective workplace agreement or go ahead on their own with individual contracts. Then they had to hire a 'bargaining agent' to work on their behalf. This could either be a lawyer (at huge expense), the Black Power gang (who were ready and waiting to go) or a 'consultant' such as one employed by Rob Campbell's company — or they could hire a union official. All but the latter would be expensive.[388]

The employers held all the cards and could offer pay and conditions less than those the workers enjoyed currently. Even the most skilled negotiators would be powerless to effect any change, particularly in these difficult economic times when the viability of many businesses was at risk. Even Bill Birch agreed that there would be greedy employers cutting wages for short-term gain, though he asserted that the great bulk of them would see the benefit of negotiating to keep both sides happy.[389]

The tepid response to the Employments Contracts Act that many ascribed to the CTU leadership, and particularly Ken Douglas, alienated him from a significant number of left-leaning trade unionists. In July 2005, former Bakers' Union official John Stansfield recalled that he 'would have crawled over broken glass up Queen Street' for Ken Douglas before the passing of the Employment Contracts Act but now, sadly disillusioned by him — and by the timidity of the trade union leadership as a whole as he observed it — he 'would not give him the time of day'.[390]

Peter Galt, a Lyttelton-based seaman and union official, expressed views which were typical of many workers:

> The big man came to Christchurch to address a town hall full of workers. He said no, we haven't got the power to take on the government. The whole meeting was against him, screaming strike, strike, strike! Nobody could believe it. Here was this 'red-hot commo'; we thought he'll push it through for us. He didn't. He was the man who used to say 'Never give an employer an even break'. Ah Jesus, it was the saddest day of my life.[391]

These men were not alone. Many were the epithets — traitor, scab, chicken-shit, coward, class collaborator — expressed in private and in public at the mere mention of Douglas's name. It was as if a favoured son had turned his back on them and walked the other way.

There were other critics too. Newspaper columnist and self-styled guru of left-wing politics Chris Trotter was one of the most trenchant. In 1997, after Douglas suggested to the CTU conference that delegates sing a song as a means of building strength and solidarity among its members, Trotter composed one to the tune of 'Joe Hill' which savagely berated Douglas, whom he blamed entirely for not leading a fightback against the Employment Contracts Act. Trotter's comments in the song that a general strike would have 'called the bosses' bluff until they cried "enough"' was patent nonsense. At its very best, such a strike would have served as a symbol of defiance and would have gone some way to alleviate their frustration. But there was no chance that the National government, with its huge parliamentary majority and its determination to 'put unions in their place', would have backtracked on this legislation irrespective of the intensity or size of any protest.[392]

Moreover, there was no guarantee that all workers would have participated in a general strike. White-collar unionists such as nurses (wanting to settle their contract and not be sued), bank officers and teachers, among the most vigorous in protesting against the legislation during its gestation, indicated that they would not have. Engineers and their union were also opposed to such a move. Both the PSA and the Post Office Union were divided. Workers at Kinleith were also not keen. They had already taken a day off to protest when the Act was in Bill form and the management, having had enough of wildcat strikes, had issued every worker with a writ charging them for the cost of a day's production if they went on strike again.

For his part, Douglas was prepared, grittily, to be patient, waiting for a 'new' Labour Party to become government and fulfil its promise to overturn the Act and replace it with measures that were more humane. There was little else that made sense to him. Already Michael Cullen, Labour's finance spokesperson, had said that a new Labour government would repeal the Act and replace it with a system that reflected the principles of a negotiated economy. This would not, he believed, include a return to the days of 'rigid bargaining structures' — the Labour Relations Act, arbitration or labour courts, national awards or wage relativities — but it would mean a fresh new look at industrial relations without the constrictions of the Employment Contracts Act, particularly as they pertained to unions.

Douglas's estrangement from a significant number of unionists, and the bitterness that went with it, remains to this day. But his attitude to the measure was clear. Over the past few years of trying to deal with unsympathetic governments he had developed a strong belief in the need to look for new solutions to age-old problems such as the protection of workers' jobs, and issues around wages and conditions of work. Head-in-the-sand stuff was totally ineffectual, and although as a socialist Douglas regretted the changes that had broken the unions' traditional power bases, as a political realist he tried to protect his philosophical ideals by taking a different stance. In the industrial 'revolution', where the old order was not going to work any longer, unions had to pursue a radical new path. In the late 1980s, even before the Employment Contracts Act was conceived, Douglas had visualised new, more cooperative and less confrontational roles for unions as long as they could be adopted without the loss of the future rights and well-being of members. Through the previous five years the union movement had struggled because it had held on to past attitudes and actions which simply did not work in the face of savage reforms.

After the passing of the Act some of Douglas's habits changed. He stopped going into pubs and talking to workers, as had been his custom. There was anger from those who felt he had sold out, and occasional fist-fights. In the worst instance of its kind an aggrieved worker in a Porirua tavern smashed a glass into his face. But there were plenty of alternative options. At the bar of the Norths Rugby Club, Titahi Golf Club and the Porirua Club he was among friends — and protected. He may have had 'a glass too many' but he was not alone. There was also unwavering family support and that was important to him as well. He did not have time to stand still and feel sorry for himself. On the contrary, he was invigorated and stimulated by the debate. He was moving forward.

The union movement was in revolutionary transition and Douglas, and his leadership of the CTU, acted as a conduit between the old-style blue-collar traditionalists, exemplified by his immediate predecessor Jim Knox, and a new breed of university-educated, executive-type leaders such as Ross Wilson of the Harbour Board Workers' Union, soon to become the CTU's vice-president, and later Andrew Little, the high-profile head of the New Zealand Amalgamated Engineering, Printing and Manufacturing Union (EPMU), by far the largest private union in the country. These men, both trained lawyers, did not abandon the traditional grass roots struggle but they went further, looking for new, more complex solutions in a rapidly changing industrial world, rather as Rob Campbell had been trying to do in the mid-1980s. Historically, Douglas, the self-educated, cloth-capped Marxist, had been more comfortable with old-style unionism — he always enjoyed reminding journalists that the highest qualification he possessed was his heavy transport licence — but his intelligence, foresight and sense of realpolitik necessitated not only coming to terms with the new order, but also trying to use and develop it for the benefit of working people.

There is no doubt that the Employment Contracts Act sped up the enfeebling of trade unionism begun under the fourth Labour government. When the CTU was formed in 1987, it represented 660,000 unionists. By December 1994 that figure was down to 380,000, and by the end of the decade, close to Douglas's retirement from the organisation, it would hover around the 210,000 mark. Workers now on individual or site-based contracts did not need, did not want, or were discouraged from remaining within, their union. The employment of 'casuals' on short-term contracts further reduced union strength; many of these workers saw no need to join a union, even if there was one available for them to join. The restructuring and down-sizing of state-owned enterprises further sped up this process.

For workers, the consequences were dramatic. There were 15,000 redundancies at New Zealand Rail alone. Trade union training fell away. The Employment Contracts Act also made it much easier for huge international corporates to buy into New Zealand industry and take profits out of the country. All the country's trading banks and some insurance companies succumbed to Australian ownership — with the same consequence. In many cases this caused further redundancies. Local wage rates slipped behind those in other OECD countries and have continued to do so — noticeably behind those of Australia, where there were no Rogernomics or Ruthenasia 'revolutions', and whose workers were soon paid 30 per cent more on average than those in New Zealand.

The first to lose out after May 1991 were the country's 25,000 shop assistants. In December 1990, just before the Employment Contracts Bill was made public, employers had refused to settle the retail non-food award unless the union agreed to the removal of weekend penal rates and other protections. The imminence of the new law stifled any further talks. With 10,000 separate employers, the Distribution Workers' Federation then faced the near-impossible task of negotiating separate contracts with each employer. In like vein, when the General Labourers' Award expired, employers refused even to discuss a new contract. Some of them lay off staff immediately and then pressured contractors to cost jobs using cut-price labour. The Master Builders' Federation circulated a draft contract to its members with no overtime, specified hours of work, or provision for tools or travel money.[393]

Low-paid women were particularly hard hit. By the end of May 1991, just 230 out of 700 rest-home owners agreed to be covered by a collective contract, leaving more than 4000 domestic staff on individual contracts — many worse than those they had had before. For most it was a 'sign it or leave' option. The 16,000 largely female workforce who ran the cafeterias, tea rooms, coffee shops, restaurants and fast-food outlets also lost their award, with a few on collective or individual contracts — or none at all. Seeing little help coming from their union in the future, many cancelled their membership. Some remained unemployed for months, even years. Other employers actively worked to bust union presence in their workplaces altogether. Whitcoulls and Fletcher Challenge, for example, tried to deunionise their staff by stopping the deduction of union fees from their wages. This was just the beginning.

CHAPTER 13

The dark days?

For Ken Douglas the rest of 1991, on the surface at least, was an *annus horribilis*. He had grimaced when Rob Campbell launched his bargaining agency, charging individuals $5 a week just to belong. It was a 'confidential service', Campbell had written, ready for those who no longer wished to remain part of a union. He referred to it as a 'plain-vanilla contract negotiation and enforcement service'. 'Are You Protected?', the core of its advertising campaign, sounded more like a teaser for a prophylactic. As promised, the Black Power gang opened a bargaining agency service in its Wellington headquarters during the second week of June. Earlier it had received money from the Lottery Grants Board to pay for office renovation, a computer and the salary of a full-time officer.[394]

Alongside the Employment Contracts Act, Douglas watched, with disenchantment, the disappearance of the Soviet Union, whose break up swept away in one fell swoop the nourishment that had been his intellectual bedrock. 'The only thing which put 1991 into perspective,' he commented wryly, 'was the top of Mt Cook falling off.'

The new legislation did nothing for employment, as more and more New Zealanders lost their jobs. By December 1991, unemployment had increased to 205,313, up from 197,582 the previous October. There were another 17,517 who were either temporary 'vacation workers' or on Access schemes. This combined total of 222,828 represented 14.4 per cent of the labour force — about one in every seven full-time workers. A September 1991 Statistics Department household labour force survey revealed that between June 1986 and June 1991, the number of jobs in the highly unionised manufacturing sector shrank from 302,000 to 221,000. Manufacturers were increasingly putting workers on four-day working weeks to save jobs and costs, particularly in the clothing, textile and footwear industries. For young people, the situation became even more dire when in the July 1991 budget the government abandoned the long-running apprenticeship scheme in favour of a more nebulous industry skills trading system, with few specifics as to how it was going to work. Later, the government froze the minimum wage at $245 a week.[395]

Unions merged to stay alive. Close to Douglas's heart, of course, was the Wellington Drivers' Union, which in 1989 had joined with the central branch of the New Zealand Labourers' Union. In July 1991, along with its Taranaki counterpart, the mixed group absorbed the Workers' Union, which voted itself out of existence. The new Amalgamated Workers of New Zealand (AWUNZ) covered workers employed in construction, horticulture, agriculture, mining, oil exploration, rubber manufacture, local-body labouring, milling, shearing and driving in Wellington and Taranaki. It anticipated a membership of between 25,000 and 30,000; it got 14,000. Afterwards the group restructured to become three autonomous unions (Northern, Central and Southern) under an AWUNZ Federation.[396]

Many unionists fumed over the CTU's invitation to Jim Bolger to attend its biennial conference in October — the first time the FOL or CTU had ever invited a National Party Prime Minister to its conference. The CTU's executive rejected a demand from the Amalgamated Workers' Union to withdraw the invitation. That displeased the union's northern secretary, Ray Bianchi, who believed that the matter was bound to spill over onto the conference floor, causing 'seething resentment'. Others outspoken in their objection were Pat Brown, secretary of the small but militant Chemical Workers' Union; Alan O'Neill, secretary of the Building Trades Union, and Rick Barker, secretary of the 60,000-member Service Workers' Union and a CTU executive member. Bill Andersen, who had been absent from the executive meeting where the decision to invite Bolger was made, also objected to the decision — as did the CTU's Auckland District Council.[397]

Douglas's view was that the invitation provided an opportunity to leave Bolger in no doubt about the strength of union concerns over the government's attitude to workers' rights and its economic failings in a time of deep recession and high unemployment. After a card vote, the conference voted two to one that Bolger be allowed to speak — his presence being backed by the big teaching, nursing and engineers' unions and a handful of others. But he ran the gauntlet of vociferous picketers at the door when he arrived, and had to sit and listen to an hour and a half of speeches attacking the Employment Contracts Act and bemoaning the government's economic performance and its effects on workers. Many seats were empty, a significant number of delegates deciding in advance to boycott Bolger's speech.

When he did speak, he was heard out in stony silence, with Douglas drawing a finger over his lips at any sign of heckling. Defending the legislation as an established reality, Bolger told delegates that the country's social and economic woes would increase unless people cooperated in a programme of fundamental change. This programme, he believed, had the potential to make New Zealand a high-tech, high-profit, high-employment, high-wage nation — creating the 'New Zealand Way', as he described it, without articulating how this would come about. There were murmurings at the end of the speech, but no applause. It was a stark and sobering reminder to Bolger of the anger unionists felt about the most vigorously anti-union law the country had ever witnessed. Douglas was alone when he shook Bolger's hand, thanking him for 'having the guts to come'.[398]

At this conference, Douglas courted rather than antagonised the powerful and the profitable. The economic prospectus — or Growth Strategy as it came to be known — prepared by Peter Harris (with graphs and slides which some delegates had trouble understanding) was also remarkable for its emphasis on wage restraint, accepting that lower living standards were the inevitable penalty of an open economy competing poorly. The new outlook urged workers to cooperate in efforts to redesign industry for greater productivity and a role in making productive decisions. In essence this proposition extended the 'Growth Agreement' the CTU had reached with Mike Moore the previous year.

As droll as ever, Denis Welch, the *Listener*'s political columnist, reflected on Ken Douglas's contribution on the first day of this conference, contrasting his performance with one he had given at the Labour Party Conference:

> . . . his address to the Labour Party Conference was a cracker in content, exposing Mike Moore's effort as stodge with sugar on top. It incisively analysed the New Zealand situation in a global context and made out a convincing case for the 'smart, quality, negotiated economy'. But it was delivered with all the enthusiasm of someone asking for condoms in a crowded chemist's, i.e., in a low hurried manner. Nervously, he mangled words like a true successor to Jim Knox; 'authoritarian' came out like 'autharian' and 'nostalgia' mysteriously like 'nostagalia'.
>
> But Douglas was among his own people here and the more he spoke the bolder he became. By the end he was shouting, all shame cast aside. More urgently than ever, it seemed, he sought to convert his colleagues to the creed of the smart economy.

> This has been the whole thrust of his leadership: to adapt the union movement to changing times and technology. Ken's had enough of protest marches and 'postures of defiance'. He might march down Lambton Quay again, if the cause is right, but his heart just won't be in it. To him, that's knee-jerk stuff. His dream CTU will be helping to guide the destinies of the nation with unions involved in all aspects of the economy, from job creation to roadside beautification . . .[399]

Secretary Ron Burgess retired at this conference, his departure a big loss to the CTU. The son of a West Hartlepool riveter, he had escaped the grim industrial Durham town in adolescence by becoming an able seaman on cargo vessels. As he sailed the world he educated himself through reading and political debate in the ships' rank-and-file mess-rooms. Disembarking in New Zealand, and later working as a cable jointer in Timaru, he rose through the ranks of the Post Office Association (later Union) to become its general secretary. Possessing a strong awareness that the state sector unions needed organisation and cohesion, with the PSA's Barry Tucker he was in at the beginning when the Combined State Services Organisation was transformed into the Combined State Unions. Later he replicated this vision when he took a primary role with Douglas, Colin Clark and Colin Hicks (chairperson of the Combined State Unions) in the formation of the Council of Trade Unions.[400]

Calm, considered, thoughtful, understated and always well-prepared, Burgess was an ideal antidote to the sometimes unrestrained emotions of Douglas and Foulkes, and he acted as a bridge between the two when they were in conflict. In some respects Ross Wilson, who replaced him at the top table, would play a similar role. Wilson, a 45-year-old lawyer and secretary of the Harbour Board Workers' Union, was also a former deputy chairman of the Accident Compensation Corporation (ACC). He became vice-president, while Foulkes was elevated to secretary. Douglas was elected unopposed for a further four years.

Meanwhile the CTU was struggling with a broader problem, one which it had faced from its beginning and which would be exacerbated in no small measure by the Employment Contracts Act. This was the problem of size. From a starting point of 660,000 members, by the time of the 1991 conference the 180 delegates attending represented 40 affiliates and some 450,000 members. Reflecting this downward trend, there were cuts at head office too; formerly there had been three paid officials — Douglas, Foulkes and Burgess — now there were only two. Wilson's position was non-remunerative.

To combat the shrinking membership, at least in part, the CTU wanted smaller unions to continue to amalgamate with speed. From 1990, after the CTU had restructured its constitution, only unions with a membership of 15,000 or more were allowed a seat on its executive as of right. It had also dissolved regional structures with the aim of creating a leaner, more supple organisation, and as ideas of 'quality economy' and jobs superseded wage increases during the recession of this period. As the CTU continued to shrink, the membership necessary to entitle unions to a seat on the executive was reduced to 10,000.[401]

The degree, and the speed, with which Douglas was able to accommodate the 'oppression' of the Employment Contracts Act within a positive framework was remarkable. In March 1992, in an address to an international trade union audience in Caracas, Venezuela, he said that while the legislation was 'massively anti-union and anti-worker' it was not overtly oppressive in a global context. Many of the conventional union-busting interventions in other countries applied criminal conventions in the forms of fines or imprisonment to stop particular sorts of behaviour by unions, he told his audience: 'This Act is deceptively clean of overtly harsh and oppressive measures. For that reason it is much harder to rail against standards of civil and human rights. It is what could be called permissive legislation. With the exception of some critical "thou shalt not" clauses it essentially says that workers and employers can do whatever they like.'[402]

But there was a dastardly catch, he continued:

> This Act was promoted as freedom to associate and freedom to

> contract. Thirst has made it almost impossible for unions to operate. First 'unions' were removed from the statutes. There was no process for registration or recognition of unions — no specifications of their rights, roles and obligations. This may look good to anarchists or revolutionaries. In practice it is a recipe for both the fragmentation of unions and a massive contraction of their role.[403]

By early 1992 it was clear that the Employment Contracts Act was on the way to achieving one of its aims, with only half of the collective agreements settled since the Act was passed being negotiated by unions. The other half, according to the Labour Department, had been negotiated by employees themselves or by non-union bargaining agents — or (although this was never officially acknowledged) imposed by employers with no negotiation allowed. There was also evidence that some employers were not giving workers the bargaining agents they wanted. Moreover, national, multi-employer agreements had declined markedly. By the end of 1991, the department had sighted only one. Yet this began to change as time moved on. By April 1993, when the worth and expertise of union representatives as negotiating agents had become clearer to workers, 83 per cent of contracts analysed by the department had been negotiated by unions. Generally this included larger employer contracts. Unions were learning to walk again without the legal 'crutch' they had depended upon for generations.[404]

In February 1993 the CTU lodged a complaint with the International Labour Organisation, claiming the Act breached its Conventions 87 and 98, which related to freedom of association and collective bargaining. While the ILO could not formally discipline the government, if it upheld the complaint Douglas believed it would mean 'international humiliation' for the government. Around the same time, the Act attracted further international condemnation when the International Confederation of Free Trade Unions (ICFTU) declared in its 1993 report that 'the New Zealand situation represented probably the most comprehensive attack on trade union freedoms in the world'.[405]

The ILO set a 15 April deadline for the New Zealand government to respond to the complaint but it failed to do so. This came as no surprise to Ken Douglas, who he believed the government was trying to prevent the relevant ILO committee dealing with the complaint until after the election later in the year. The Committee on Freedom of Association — a tripartite group drawn from the ILO's governing body, made up of representatives of employers, governments and trade unions — found unanimously for the CTU. The ILO went further, dispatching an investigating officer, Alan Gladstone, to New Zealand. He talked to ministers, government officials, the Employers' Federation, Federated Farmers, industrial practitioners and academics as well as the CTU and a selection of union leaders. His report, endorsed by the ILO's governing body, identified a fundamentally different philosophical outlook as the root of the inconsistencies between the New Zealand Act and internationally accepted principles of freedom of association.[406]

The ILO's findings caused ructions in the House. Doug Kidd, the new Minister of Labour, condemned the 'wrong processes' of the ILO (without explaining what was wrong with the processes) and lambasted its conclusions as 'very erroneous and unjustifiable'; it was wrong that the New Zealand combined trade unions had gone 'whingeing' and 'whining' to Geneva, he said. Earlier, following the ILO's interim assessment in April, Kidd had denigrated the organisation's work as 'archaic . . . a blast from the past' and characterised its committee's procedures as 'Stalinist and kangaroo court stuff'. This contrasted markedly with Prime Minister Jim Bolger's assessment of the organisation in 1983 — after he had accepted the ILO's presidency when Minister of Labour in Robert Muldoon's government — when he called it a 'unique international forum which exerted a positive influence in all parts of this interdependent world ... its aims and purposes the most powerful statement of objectives for the international community on labour and employment matters.' Bolger went on, 'The ILO must continue to exercise its influence on a universal basis ... it cannot select which violation it will oppose and which it will ignore ...' For its part, the ILO in November 1993 expressed the hope that the New Zealand government would hold quick discussions with the CTU and the Employers' Federation as part of a process of rewriting the Employment Contracts Act, and offered technical assistance with the rewrite. It was a pipe dream.[407]

In the first months after its passing, the courts interpreted the Employment Contracts Act as meaning an employer could not unilaterally vary the essential terms and conditions of an employment contract until the next round of negotiations. Bill Birch also contended that such conditions would be safe until then — indeed, this was a key point of his controversial March 1991 letter to householders. But that belief was blown sky-high in November 1991 when Air New Zealand dismissed 159 Auckland Airport catering staff following a breakdown in pay negotiations — clearly demonstrating that employers could sack workers who failed to accept new and lesser conditions of employment. Soon afterwards in the Employment Court, Judge Castle ruled that employers could — as the New Zealand Society for the Intellectually Handicapped had done — impose a lockout or partial lockout when workers objected to employers refusing to pay previously granted allowances. The Act gave employers much greater power to use lockouts to get their way.

Birch's letter to householders, written to counter what he called 'scaremongering' by unions and the CTU, came back to haunt him as evidence accumulated of more and more employers settling new agreements with their workers always with non-union bargaining agents or on their own, with lower wages and/or penal rates and fewer conditions. Sometimes this was done unilaterally, giving employees no choice but to accept or lose their jobs.

One example, among a number, occurred at Alliance Textiles in Milton, South Otago, in January 1992 when the employer — pushing aside the union — told the workers that there would be no negotiation of their new, less advantageous contract. They were told to 'sign or starve', as one worker put it. Forty employees, some racking upwards of 30 loyal years at the mill — the town's biggest employer — refused to sign and were locked out. Many with their families, were among a group who kept a rolling picket in protest going outside the front gate for weeks. It was all to no avail. The employer remained intransigent, and slowly, as money became short, and lacking any other option during straitened economic times except probable unemployment, most reluctantly signed and returned to work. The protest split the town as tensions rose between the workers and their supporters and those who considered them 'lazy' or 'work-shy', and were not afraid to say so. The bitterness manifest in the small community still lingers today.

The Employment Court was setting a high threshold of proof of harsh and oppressive behaviour on the part of employers. It ruled that misleading information and efforts to bypass union bargaining agents by direct approaches to employees were not unlawful. This authority to bypass authorised agents — or to use non-union agents — made it very difficult for union leaders to retain credibility with workers who were no longer bound to the cause. Although the law said employers had to recognise an authorised agent, it was silent on how this was to be done and it did not require any bargaining to occur. Employers could impose what they wanted. They had all the power. The Nurses' Union was one that struggled valiantly to serve its members, but more than one private hospital served trespass notices on its officials after they attempted to enter their premises to try to persuade members not to sign pay-cutting contracts. This weakened the nurses' resolve, and having no other choice but to leave or be sacked, they signed the new deals.

It is hard to overestimate the radicalism of the change. There is little doubt that less scrupulous employers were using the Act to rid themselves of existing staff and bringing in contractors at cheaper rates. They also pressured workers to accept wages and conditions that were inferior to those they had previously received, and in some workplaces management offered workers substantial inducements to switch from union-based negotiations to individual contracts. The most notorious of these was at the Tiwai Point aluminium smelter near Bluff, where the vast majority of the 12,000 workers accepted much higher pay from Comalco on condition that they switch to individual contracts. As a consequence, unionism was virtually extinguished at the plant. Other workers, however, remained loyal to their unions despite inducements. Employees at Fletcher Challenge's Pacific Steel mill proudly sported 'collective contract' slogans on their hard-hats.

Birch acknowledged that a 'small minority' of employers was abusing the Act. In May 1992 Bolger warned the Employers' Federation's national council that its members must not abuse the spirit of the Act by pursuing a low-wage, low-reward policy against the workforce, because it was 'unjust, unsustainable, and foolish'. He called on them to enhance their management skills. In the meantime, over the previous eight months more than 3000 workers had complained about oppressive contracts or unilateral changes to their working conditions or pay rates.[408]

There were numerous examples of intolerance under the Act. In November 1991, Auckland's Yellow Bus Company foisted new individualised contracts on their drivers which cut their pay and redundancy agreements, freezed the union out of the workplace and allowed the company to 'vary' the contract at will and without notice. Despite a $10,000-bonus 'sweetener' if they accepted the new deal, many drivers refused and were locked out. They wanted a collective contract, but under the Act the Employment Court had no choice but to rule in favour of the company. In Invercargill, junior doctors at Southland Hospital went on strike for a month after refusing to sign individual contracts that the Hospital Board tried to impose upon them without negotiation.

It is true that in some workplaces, where there was longstanding goodwill on both sides and where employer-union-worker relations were positive and workers had access to bonus schemes, reasonable holidays and health care, sometimes employer-subsidised, the flexibility associated with the Act — most notably the lessening of demarcation disputes — did stimulate increased efficiencies and productivity gains. But elsewhere its misuse was constant. At Freightways, for example, freight forwarders were paid salaries of between $30,000 and $40,000, up to 40 per cent above the award rate prior to 1911. After the Act was passed new employees taken on as freight forwarders were paid $25,000. After the 1991 killing season, workers at the Richmond-Takapau Freezing Works were offered non-negotiable contracts and forced to sign them for fear of losing their jobs. They also rescinded the Meatworkers' Union as the site bargaining agent — 192 workers left the union, leaving 329 remaining.[409]

A pattern emerged. Many workers were denied union cover; there was little or no negotiation; many were required to be 'on call' for some or all of seven days — and paid for 40 hours; there was no provision for casual workers; there was no service pay or recognition for long service; there were no allowances for laundry, clothing, shoes, first-aid or transport, and 'trial' employment periods became common. Reports of young supermarket workers being paid as little as $1.50 an hour — less than the dole — were denied by the Merchants' Association but considered 'satisfactory' by Roger Kerr, executive director of the Business Roundtable. Speaking to Sharon Crosbie on National Radio's *Nine to Noon* programme in February 1993, Kerr agreed that these young people worked hard, but 'we cannot afford to pay people more than their productivity justifies . . . now the kind of wage levels you're taking about are nevertheless above the kind of social security net that we think is a reasonable floor . . .'[410]

There were also increasing delays at Employment Tribunals, with workers exhibiting high levels of frustration and bitterness about not being able to have their personal grievance cases heard — even the appointment of additional tribunal members in May 1993 failed to clear the backlog. In desperation some workers attempted redress through private mediation at exorbitant cost. Others, despite being unhappy with contracts they were being forced to sign, refused to complain fearing they would lose their job in the tight employment market. In April, Birch was forced to admit in Parliament that the number of complaints of alleged breach of statutory minimum working conditions received by the Labour Department had more than trebled — up 325 per cent — since the introduction of the Act, reaching more than 6000 a month, and the department was employing extra staff to deal with the workload.

Other unions, particularly those covering workers in low-paid work — such as in shops and supermarkets, fast-food outlets and hairdressing salons, and others such as hotels, restaurants, rest homes, childcare centres, garden centres, factories, hospitals (including nurses, midwives, nurse aids, orderlies and cleaners) and airlines (particularly flight attendants and ground staff) — complained that their members were being denied the use of the union as their bargaining agent, and that workers employed since the passing of the Act were on lower wages. These problems might have been overcome by the insertion of a good faith bargaining provision in the legislation.[411]

Moreover, individuals, mostly young people, were being hired for trial periods without pay and then sacked when they refused to sign a non-negotiable 'take it or leave it' contract. Semi-skilled and unskilled workers were worst off. This letter from a supermarket checkout supervisor to the Department of Labour spoke for many workers:

> As soon as the Employment Contracts Act came in everything changed in this place. We were told now he'd do it his way. First he got rid of the union, and we were threatened that if we belonged to any union we'd be down the road. The contracts were never negotiated. We were called in one by one and given this printed document with a place to put your signature. Some of the young ones were not allowed to take these contracts home for their parents to read. The first year all of us who worked there got penal rates. As people left or were sacked, the new ones went on to a flat rate with no set amount — we were all getting different wages. Within a year there was a 90 per cent rollover of staff.[412]

A 1992 Heylen Survey showed that overtime pay rates had been reduced or abolished in 42 per cent of enterprises, raised in just three; weekend rates had been cut in 43 per cent of cases, raised in three; special allowances had been cut in 29 per cent, increased in 12; sick leave reduced in 15 per cent of cases, raised in six; long service leave cut in 16, raised in four; and ability to accumulate leave reduced in 29 per cent of cases and improved in two.[413]

Sometimes the animosity rebounded on employers. In September 1992, the Employment Court's Chief Judge Tom Goddard lambasted Talleys Fisheries for the 'tyrannical arrogance' it showed after it had broken agreements with its workers and defied the Labour Court. The company had set out to deprive its employees of the freedom guaranteed them under the Employment Contracts and Bill of Rights Acts by refusing to grant officials of their union, the United Food and Chemical Workers' Union, access to Talleys' premises, stopping the union's right to collect fees through deductions from employees' pay packets, and denying employees the right to attend union meetings in their working hours without loss of pay.[414]

Goddard fined the company $5500 and joint managing director Michael Talley a further $800 for breaking the law under the 1987 Labour Relations Act, and later ordered the company to hand over a cheque to the union for $24,812.98 for union fees plus a further $20,000 in costs. Goddard warned he would consider further action if the company failed to comply, which was likely because 'they could not be trusted to comply by themselves'. He ended his criticism of the 'arrogant, condescending and patronising' company by quoting from Shakespeare's *Measure for Measure*: 'Oh, it is excellent to have a giant's strength; but it is tyrannous to use it like a giant.' Ken Douglas knew Goddard. Their professional paths had crossed and they had been classmates in '5 Special' at Wellington College in 1951.[415]

In May 1992, just a year after the enactment of the Employment Contracts Bill, the government had scrapped the union-organised Trade Union Education Authority (TUEA), Bill Birch saying its repeal would 'end the nonsense' by which employers were compelled to pay staff to take time off for union education. Yet remarkably, even for this government, it ignored the report of a specially appointed review committee (hand-picked by Birch) that showed the authority had performed a first-class function. Recently, as the report noted, the provision of such leave had been successful in helping workers and employers deal with the changes that had occurred over the previous five years.

Helen Clark, Labour's deputy leader and labour spokesperson, called the act 'mean-spirited and vindictive' — and completely out of line with ILO conventions. Ken Douglas — who chaired the authority's board — called its demise a victory for 'ignorance and prejudice', claiming it was further evidence that Birch was a puppet of the Business Roundtable and the Employers' Federation, which had long pushed for its abandonment. Even Birch agreed that the review team had found the authority to be well-managed and that it had contributed to the objectives set out in the union leave legislation. 'But those objectives related to a very different industrial relations environment,' he said, without explaining what that meant. An institution such as the TUEA was now needed by unions and workers more than ever before. Australia, Sweden, the Netherlands, Germany, France, Spain, Denmark, Finland and even Margaret Thatcher's United Kingdom all retained schemes similar to the TUEA. But that was of no relevance to this government. It had the numbers and the authority was gone by November.[416]

In June, Ken Douglas visited Australian cities on a whirlwind tour, addressing meetings of the Trades and Labour Councils on the Employment Contracts Act. Australian workers and their unions feared similar legislation might be in the pipeline for them, and had invited him to talk to them in order to prepare for that possibility. Douglas's energy was prodigious. During the latter months of 1991 and the first six months of 1992 he stumped around New Zealand talking to union, employer and any other interested groups about good capitalism and bad capitalism. On one day, 7 April, he spoke to three separate and disparate groups in different parts of the country — a New Zealand investment conference in the morning, the Auckland Rotary Club at midday, and a Victoria University chief executive action Group at 9pm. The 'bad', or 'Anglo-American model', he would say, was authoritarian in its management structures, conflict-based between worker and boss, jealous of containing production secrets within separate enterprises and, according to Douglas, doomed. It was this model that New Zealand had adopted through the Employment Contracts Act.[417]

As an indication of the inequity of the law, this period saw industrial unrest on a scale not experienced since the days of Robert Muldoon. Among the more than 130,000 workers involved in disputes during August 1992 were pulp and paper and meat workers at a number of plants, members of the PSA, nurses belonging to the Nurses' Union and the great bulk of secondary school teachers belonging to the PPTA, who had been locked out over a bitter pay dispute. Official figures from the Department of Labour late in August showed that during the first year under the Employment Contracts Act penal payments for overtime and weekend work had plunged. Women were mostly disadvantaged, their overtime earnings dropping 16 per cent between May 1991 and May 1992. For many workers, working late now meant being paid more at ordinary time rates. The survey also showed that employment had grown most strongly where the loss of penal rates had been greatest. Full-time jobs were declining, whereas part-time work was increasing — 2.6 per cent for women and 5.5 per cent for men. Moreover, many negotiations under the Act were still not being settled for months, the affected unions victims of a serious backlog of cases at the Employment Tribunals.[418]

There was a significant shifting of the sands at a July 1992 meeting of CTU affiliates. By the narrowest of margins, 51 to 49 per cent, the meeting rejected agitating for a return to compulsory unionism, national awards, wage relativities and obligatory arbitration. Discarding the traditional compulsory system as 'too narrow' for the rapidly changing economy and world of work in New Zealand, it was argued in papers released on the eve of the conference that there should be a new system of free collective bargaining which would give workers an unlimited agenda of industrial, economic and social issues for bargaining — including an 'unfettered' right to strike.[419]

Representing the 'new order', the CTU produced and distributed a booklet entitled 'Workplace Reform' which argued that successful reform depended on the integration of skills, training, work organisation, industrial relations, new technologies, production, service delivery and systems, and quality programmes in one cohesive package. This would be brought together and coordinated through joint union/management consultative committees at work and company/industry levels. As Douglas implored in the introduction to the booklet, '. . . please use it. As I have said before — management is too important to be left to managers.'[420]

The proposed changes were revolutionary. No longer would the wider trade union movement be solely concerned with pay, conditions of work and compulsion within a system that had become ritualistic and often ineffective over many decades. The CTU was breaking free, metaphorically, from the ties that had traditionally bound union leadership and membership to a narrowly prescribed formula that related directly and only to workers' jobs. In doing so it was largely reacting against government policies and/or employer activities which mitigated against these. Now, following Douglas's lead and strong urgings, it was opening itself proactively to organising new, more flexible strategies to try to improve workers' lives, depending on the circumstances of the worker, groups of workers, companies or groups of companies.[421]

The CTU now needed to tie itself to the political opposition, which had been developing industrial policies along the same lines. Discussion had begun immediately following the implementation of the Employment Contracts Act, in the form of a number of heavyweight policy discussions between Douglas, Foulkes and Harris representing the CTU and politicians Mike Moore, Helen Clark and finance spokesperson Michael Cullen. Both organisations looked forward to the day when Labour would return to power — for the moment at least, the two were instinctive bedfellows.[422]

The outcome of this collaboration was the introduction by Labour of an Employment Law Council Bill in June 1994. Aiming to repeal the Employment Contracts Act and replace it with 'fair and just' labour relations, the Bill proposed setting up a body consisting of two representatives each from employers, unions, the National

Party and the Labour Party and one representative from the Alliance and New Zealand First parties. For its terms of reference it would establish an employment relations framework that provided for the orderly conduct of relations between employers and employees in the negotiation of wages and conditions. There would also be consultation on and development of training, health and safety, equal employment opportunities and employment-related education and reform policies in the workplace.[423]

Introducing the Bill in Parliament, Steve Maharey, the party's new labour spokesperson, indicated that the proposed legislation would be consistent with ILO frameworks and would allow the country to ratify its core conventions. It would also promote collective bargaining between employers and unions; give legal recognition to unions and endorse principles of freedom of association; ensure unions had a fair and reasonable right of access to the workplace; require negotiations for wages and conditions to be conducted in good faith; provide a safe framework for ensuring that working people were guaranteed protection from unfair treatment within the workplace and a fair minimum set of working conditions; eliminate destructive wages competition; create no legal barriers to multi-party bargaining, and provide expedient resolution of disputes and personal grievances. Maharey hoped the Bill would expedite the repeal of the Employment Contracts Act and be law by 1 January 1995.[424]

It was not revolutionary, but rather a fair and considered response to the inequities of the current legislation. Its provisions sat somewhere between the current law and the former culture of compulsion in union membership and arbitration which Labour, like National, wanted to replace. But Minister of Labour Doug Kidd derided the Bill as a 'quick whip-round' by a hopelessly stacked committee set up to ram through a Bill to replace legislation that was working 'excellently' and did not need fixing. Maharey's belief that the Bill would pass was optimistic, of course; it was never going to succeed along party lines. The Labour Party's real aim was to fix a stake firmly in the sand, not just about its long-held views on the Employment Contracts Act and its consequences, but also to make it clear that it was going to expedite new and fairer industrial relations legislation when it came to power and that this was what it was going to look like. In the meantime, increased casualisation of work, contracting out, and the bypassing of union involvement in wage and salary negotiations were here to stay in the short term, and there was nothing the unions, the CTU or the Labour Party could do about it.[425]

By this time Douglas and the CTU were facing more flak from the left than from the right. In July 1992, there had emerged a first sign that some unions and their leaders — upset and annoyed at the CTU leadership's perceived timidity over to the passing of the Employment Contracts Act — were about to organise a union collective in opposition to the CTU. Drawing strength from those blue-collar unions that had refused to join the expanded CTU when it formed in 1987 out of the ashes of the Federation of Labour, the initial impetus was the brainchild of Graeme Clarke, secretary of the Manufacturing and Construction Workers' Union. It was Clarke who led the organisation of a Wellington meeting of 'like minds' on 26 August. These 'like minds', according to the *Workers' Voice* (the successor to the Communist Party's *People's Voice*), were responding to 'widespread dissatisfaction with the line of class collaboration promoted by top CTU leaders like Douglas and Foulkes, reflecting a general feeling within the union movement that the CTU was doing worse than nothing to organise against the increasingly oppressive big business onslaught on working-class living standards and political rights.'[426]

At this meeting, representatives from 14 blue-collar unions — representing some 35,000 workers — established a Trade Union Federation (TUF) with an interim committee comprising Clarke and Con Devitt (also from the Manufacturing and Construction Workers' Union), Dave Morgan (president of the Seafarers' Union), Garth Fraser (secretary of the United Food and Chemical Workers' Union) and Murray Reed (secretary of the Building Trades' Union). It was a move to a cloth-cap past yet, ironically, their aims for the most part were synonymous with those of the CTU — immediate repeal of the

Employment Contracts Act, support for electoral reform through a mixed member proportional representation system, defeat of the National government, support for the return of a Labour government, and support for industry training modelled on the principles of the old Apprenticeship Act.[427]

Then, as later, the group failed to explain how it was going to fulfil its agenda. Adrift from the main union conglomerate and refusing to cooperate with them, their pleas were easily ignored by the body politic. Some in the press called them Luddites. Given the direction in which trade unionism and the world of work was headed in the 1990s, not to mention the political realities, this was not far from the truth. Wry observers noted that while the CTU was housed in new state-of-the art premises in the Tasman Hotel, the TUF headquartered itself in the old Trades Hall in Vivian Street, the traditional home of trade union administration for decades (and where Douglas had begun his career in the dusty and cramped second-floor office of the Wellington Drivers' Union). It was a fitting allegory for the new and the old.[428]

In 1995 Maxine Gay, the TUF's inaugural secretary, said that its members were still bitter over the 'betrayal' by the union leadership over the Employment Contracts Act. The unions that formed the TUF had agitated for strike action against the legislation — not necessarily a general strike, but strategic action using a few key unions such as the seafarers, whose members had the power to paralyse important sectors of the economy and were sufficiently well-paid to hold out for a long time.[429]

The TUF unions were also deeply suspicious of workplace reform, begun by Douglas and the CTU's other leaders and sustained by its membership which hung its hat on management-worker collaboration. A further objection was that under the CTU's constitution a union's voting power was determined by the strength of its membership. That gave power to big unions like the PSA and the Engineers at the expense of smaller, more militant unions that were now more likely to be found in the TUF where it was one union, one vote. There were further accusations that under the 'dog eat dog' mentality that permeated the

Employment Contracts Act, bigger unions were 'poaching' members from smaller unions, exacerbating tensions between the two groups.

The relationship between the two groups was patchy at best. Often it was non-existent, reflecting the differing cultures and constituencies as well as personal antagonisms which did not lessen as time wore on. The CTU had the size to 'stand solid' apart from the TUF if it wanted to. The TUF, bereft of this advantage, occasionally wanted assistance from the CTU. At the time of the TUF's formation in August 1992, Dave Morgan had claimed he 'would never forgive the lack of leadership' within the CTU in relation to the Employment Contracts Act. By May 1994 he was requesting its help as his union faced possible annihilation at the hands of the new owners of New Zealand Rail, a union-busting consortium comprising Wisconsin Central Transportation (26.7 per cent), Boston-based Berkshire Partners (26.7 per cent), Auckland merchant bank Fay Richwhite (31.1 per cent) and a handful of others. Buoyed by the effects of the Employment Contracts Act, this conglomerate wanted to smash the union wide open and use cheaper non-union labour to crew its inter-island ferries. After negotiations broke down Douglas called a crisis meeting of CTU affiliates on 18 May, met Morgan and his executive, and offered unconditional support.

As Douglas and Morgan, former friends, joked, shook hands and smiled for the cameras, a tense division that had been manifest since 1987 was bridged in a moment. Douglas had reacted positively to Morgan's request because the ship-owners' stance had arisen directly from the Employment Contracts Act and was not specific to the maritime industry. He stressed that the CTU's support for the unions and workers concerned was based around the need to maximise opposition to the legislation and to deliver effective solidarity to the unions. The CTU executive and council subsequently encouraged its affiliated members to boycott New Zealand Rail's services if it employed scab labour, to put pressure on employers to avoid these services, and give financial support and allow protest activity in support of the union's legitimate worker claims. Douglas did not, it should be stressed, activate or encourage direct action in support of the seafarers. For his part, Morgan expressed gratitude for the CTU's support. The Seafarers' Union fought hard and the two warring parties compromised on pay and redundancies. The union survived.[430]

Aside from TUF malcontents, Douglas's other antagonists from the left were Communist Party activists. He had continual run-ins with reporters from the *People's Voice*. At the end of one seminar speech in 1991, Douglas was in conversation with *New Zealand Herald* journalist Matthew Dearnaley when a *People's Voice* reporter approached him. Douglas saw red, waved his arms and ordered the reporter away, claiming his rag was 'gutter press' which 'told lies'. This made little difference. Party members — often trade unionists — and *People's Voice* reporters and photographers continued to hound him and other CTU leaders before and after public functions.

One such occasion was a major Workplace New Zealand conference in Rotorua in September 1992. The conference brought together 660 employers and unionists keen to find ways to reform their workplaces to better adapt to the working conditions and industrial legislation of the 1990s, to find consensus, and at the same time develop a more stimulating and productive working environment. The brainchild of former union leader Owen Harvey, the conference had taken as its theme 'working smarter' — appealing to many employers and workers (many companies sent both), who saw the advantages of learning about each other and making the most of new technology and workplace practices.[431]

While the conference was deemed a success by participants (Harvey ostentatiously told Radio New Zealand that it was a 'turning point in labour relations in New Zealand'), Douglas and his friends had to face 80 or so noisy picketers outside the conference. Verbal blasts from both party activists and members of the TUF were interspersed with attempts by the more moderate among them to engage in debate with some of the union leaders. Douglas, large and visible, was always a primary target of invective from his adversaries. Chants of 'Douglas — Out! Douglas — Out!' reverberated around the entrance door.[432]

Douglas was unfazed, returning barbs as quickly as he received them as he entered the hall. Journalist Denis Welch later commented that the 'split' he observed between the 'moderates' inside the hall and the 'militants' outside reminded him of the division in Russia early in the century between the Bolsheviks ('Leninist hardliners') and the Mensheviks ('moderates prepared to try to work with the existing order'). Those inside, he suggested, tongue-in-cheek, and making a play on Douglas's name, should be called 'Kensheviks' since they were mixing it with business instead of indulging in 'boss bashing'.[433]

The CTU's third biennial conference was held in the Wellington Town Hall between 20 and 22 September 1993. Implicitly admitting that a nadir had been reached over the Employment Contracts Act, Douglas argued, again, that it was time to look ahead:

> It is easy in times of crisis to accentuate the negatives and to concentrate on what we have not been able to achieve. Of course we recognise what still has to be done. But do not sell yourselves short. Every delegate to this conference is testimony to the dignity of labour and the spirit of working people. Workers are not going to be converted into commodities and mangled on a production line. Workers will assert their comradeship and collective unity. Workers will keep their unions no matter what Birch does with the law, no matter how Shipley [Jenny Shipley, then the Minister of Social Welfare] uses the welfare system to starve workers back to work on the bosses' terms, no matter what the ideologues on the Business Roundtable might do with their corporate strength . . . We are still here. We may be tired. We may be frustrated . . . but we are still here and we won't go away . . .[434]

Early in 1992, Rosanne Meo had become president of the Employers' Federation, the first woman to hold this position. Meo and Douglas had known and worked with each other for some time, and in his discussions with her Douglas had found her 'a receptive mind — not an ideologue although her natural instinct was always to take a conservative, right-wing position'. As the Federation's representative Meo spoke at the June 1992 ILO conference at Geneva on the need for more labour reform in New Zealand, after which Douglas sought her out to berate her for her comments. She countered by telling him that she would never have insulted him 'like this', by deprecating his views and values, and angrily stormed off. Impressed, Douglas later returned and apologised. Communication intensified, intellectual discussion deepened, and befitting Meo's inheritance of a sense of 'social good' from her Irish Catholic forbears they sometimes found consensus, albeit from contrasting angles. 'Electricity' sparked and, later that year, after they had both attended a function at Parliament hosting a Japanese trade delegation, a relationship began which continued for the following 18 months. Meo had separated from her husband and was raising two girls, aged 15 and 12.[435]

Douglas confided in a select few of his union colleagues about the affair, as well as his family and, after a few months, when it was developing into a serious and loving relationship, his partner Marilyn. His children were not comfortable about the affair and were concerned about its implications, although they did meet Rosanne and her family. Marilyn, understandably, was very hurt, and Douglas felt guilty about that. But his connection with Meo was intense, and there was talk of marriage. It was soon known publicly and discussed in the gossip columns, although as Douglas recalled, the press 'did not seem to be making a meal of it'.

Douglas contends that there was nothing sordid about the affair — nor did he regret it. The relationship was out in the open. He stayed with Meo in Auckland and they attended social functions and concerts by the Auckland Philharmonia, whose board Meo chaired. The relationship finally broke up after Meo accepted an invitation to join the Business Roundtable. Douglas felt her reasons for joining were self-serving rather than collaborative — advancing a personal agenda rather than exercising a wish to offer her undoubted skill to the wider business community. This, he felt, was intellectually dishonest. It was a bridge too far. Both were very hurt by the fracture.

Meo again created a precedent by being the first woman to be invited to join the Roundtable. She was also a member of the board of directors of the Forestry Corporation of New Zealand, a state owned enterprise, and later chaired its successor, Forestcorp — the first woman to chair an SOE in New Zealand. Her involvement in the Roundtable was relatively shortlived, however. She resigned when, as she put it, it seemed to her that the organisation was becoming more like a branch of the ACT Party.[436]

Like Douglas, Meo was and has continued to be a high-flyer. Her entrepreneurial acumen led to an OBE for services to business in 1993, the same year in which she was awarded a Women's Suffrage Medal. When she left Forest Products after 20 years she initially ran her own business consultancy but is now a full-time director on various boards. She has chaired, and in some cases still chairs, the boards of Television New Zealand, AMP Services NZ, Baycorp Advantage and Briscoes Group, and has been, or is, a director on the boards of AMP Life (Australia), Ports of Auckland, Ceramco, Mercury Energy, Sky Television, Clear Communications and Overland Footwear. She has been a trustee of the Arts Foundation of New Zealand, the Kelliher Charitable Trust, the Liggins Institute, the University of Auckland School of Medicine and the South Auckland Health Federation, and was a member of the Todd Task Force on Tertiary Funding. She continues to chair the board of the Auckland Philharmonia and is active in a number of volunteer organisations.[437]

In hindsight, the relationship was not so politically surprising. Befitting his sense of realpolitik, Douglas was in constant communication with a wide range of people across the labour spectrum, irrespective of political persuasion, and Meo's role as head of the Employers' Federation (and the fact that she is a 'consensus' person by nature) also brought her into contact with trade union leaders, Ken Douglas most of all. Love is an immutable sensation which transcends all boundaries.

CHAPTER 14

Here, there and everywhere

As the decade rolled on with the Employment Contracts Act a fait accompli, Ken Douglas began to worry that some unions were failing to accommodate the new realities. He believed that all unions had to set goals for the following 10 years or they 'might not make it'. They had to find new ways to recruit members, and work hard to figure out how to become advocates for workers whom employers wanted to hire under the new legislation. Amalgamation between unions had sometimes been problematic, being foisted upon the parties through necessity rather than choice. Some were hampered by petty jealousies among leaders and their operation was far from smooth.

Late in 1995, Douglas even questioned whether the Council of Trade Unions could continue to be a viable organisation. The next 12 months, he said, would be a huge test of whether the restructuring and cost-saving initiatives were enough to sustain a national union centre. Douglas always believed that the CTU was not just the sum of its affiliates: 'It's not just one big union. There are differences between affiliates or else we would just have one big union. There are some things the CTU does in conjunction with its affiliates and there are some things the affiliates do themselves. It is important to know the difference and to avoid blaming one for defects of delivery that is not in its patch.'[438]

The statistics were damning. Between December 1991 and December 1994, according to a Victoria University Industrial Relations Centre survey, numbers of workers in agriculture, fishing and hunting suffered a devastating 64 per cent decline (14,234 to 5110); in construction, 63 per cent (14,596 to 5338); and in retail, wholesale and accommodation, 69 per cent (64,335 to 19,778). There were smaller declines in manufacturing, 24 per cent (114,564 to 86,654); in transport and communication, 22 per cent (52,592 to 41,738); in finance and business, 25 per cent (32,219 to 24,107); and in public and community services, 13 per cent (205,925 to 179,167). In many businesses, the recruitment of new members was slower than the attrition rate. Contiguously, CTU membership continued to retreat. In October 1991, 43 unions representing 445,116 workers were affiliated; by December 1994 this had constricted to 27 unions and 296,959 workers. Since 1987, staff numbers had been cut from 30 to 12. The CTU itself 'downsized', shifting its head office from the state-of-the-art premises in the Tasman Hotel to smaller offices in Education House further up Willis Street.[439]

Many unions faced extreme financial pressure. The big Service Workers' Union was one of the hardest hit, its membership halving between 1991 and 1994 to around 25,000 members; many of these were 'casuals' who left their temporary workplace, and often the union, when they secured another job. According to regional secretary John Ryall, a large number of his members had no set hours, no set pay and no set minimum standards: 'They work all hours of the day and night so our organisers have to be available 24 hours a day. It's tough as hell.'[440]

Other unions were accused of poaching members from fellow unions. Maxine Gay, secretary of the Trade Union Federation, accused the CTU's Engineers' Union of 'borrowing' workers from the TUF-aligned United Food, Beverage and General Workers Union, a claim which the Engineers denied. She also blamed poaching for the demise of the Timber Workers' Union, whose membership fell when the wood industries unions merged. The wider problem for unions was that workers were free to choose their own bargaining agents, which made swapping unions relatively easy, or they left the union altogether and used non-union personnel as their representatives.[441]

In February 1994, Douglas led a CTU affiliates 'Search' Conference from which the executive determined to promote unionism and collectivism; manage the transition from occupationally based general unions to well-resourced, industry-focused unions; coordinate affiliates around agreed issues and programmes, and actively campaign on an agreed political programme. From the conference, the CTU appointed Sue Christie in the new role of union education and organising coordinator, which resulted in the CTU campaign to help affiliates to adopt an 'organising model' of unionism. This, in essence, meant 'organising workers to do it by themselves proactively' — helping to build a union into a force of many rather than a service organisation of just a few leaders and their staff. At the same time, it campaigned to reorganise and strengthen unions. For example, it facilitated a series of meetings of members which assisted the amalgamation process between the National Union of Railway Workers (which was not in the CTU), the Combined Union of Railway Employees and the Harbour Board Workers' Union which resulted in a larger and more powerful body — the Rail and Maritime Transport Union — emerging on 1 May 1995.[442]

More CTU energy was expended at the sector level. For example, it assisted Finsec in mobilising members to resist another round of cuts to jobs and conditions imposed in an effort to 'reduce costs' by the foreign banks which then owned 90 per cent of the New Zealand industry. It participated in a steering committee to coordinate debate around the threats facing the agricultural sector following settlement of the Uruguay round of GATT. Company failures in the struggling meat industry owing to declining profitability and inefficient and corrupt management at Fortex, the Weddel chain and the Waitaki Companies — and the radical restructuring of AFFCO and Alliance (which collectively underpinned 10 per cent of the country's employment base and 20 per cent of its export earnings) — led to extensive CTU involvement in crisis management in the affected firms to help stabilise the industry. The CTU also worked with the health unions to develop a critique of new structures for more efficient delivery of health services, at the same time trying to save as many jobs in the health sector as possible.[443]

The organisation was busy in other areas too. In June 1994, the CTU received money from the Employment Related Education Fund — which had replaced the TUEA — for projects on the extension of workplace reform and skills development for the workplace. In May the same year it had established an occupational safety and health committee composed of affiliate representatives, its main object being to build up health and safety activity in unions. Partly in response to CTU pressure, the government made marginal improvements to the adult minimum wage and introduced a minimum wage for young workers where previously there had been none.[444]

Douglas's responsibilities were also expanding. In 1997 he became a member of the Prime Ministerial Employment Task Force chaired by Sir John Anderson. The task force was an initiative of Winston Peters when his party New Zealand First was in coalition with National. Douglas and the other members traversed the country off and on for nine months, receiving submissions about rationalising resources relating to employment opportunities for young people.

They found a massive disproportion between training and industry needs. Northland Polytechnic in Whangarei, for example, had 14 courses for hairdressers but none for welders, of whom there were drastic shortages at Marsden Point oil refinery and in the local shipbuilding yards. Skills development in tertiary institutions was often unrelated to the economic needs of a region, a situation Douglas blamed on both Roger Douglas's deregulation and Bill Birch's destruction of the apprenticeship system. The task force had been established to appease

Peters, and while the recommendations for change and rationalisation were sound, very few of them were taken up. Nonetheless Douglas found his involvement in the task force stimulating, among other things coming face to face with the reality of the importance of the Treaty of Waitangi settlement process in generating wealth for deprived rural Maori communities.

Douglas also led the CTU in joining the Coalition on Accident Compensation (COAC) in a strong campaign against the 1992 Accident Rehabilitation and Compensation Insurance Act. The coalition lodged three complaints with the ILO over this legislation, relating to breaches of three ILO Conventions. In December 1993 Doug Kidd acknowledged to the ILO that New Zealand was in breach of one of these, and promised to remedy the situation by legislative amendment. This was not done, and the CTU complaints were again considered by the ILO in 1996.

He remained a long-term member of the Prime Minister's Enterprise Council, a structure established out of the 1984 economic summit whereby the FOL and unions worked with the government, Treasury and business on 'where to take' New Zealand industry. Little was achieved, according to Douglas, who viewed it as a showcase for speechmakers. At Victoria University, he was active on the council of the Industrial Relations Centre, the only organisation in New Zealand dedicated to researching and publishing on labour/capital/state relationships. For many years, academics such as John Young, Pat Walsh and Raymond Harbridge researched issues associated with employee rights, among others, and after the passing of the Employment Contracts Act (which had abolished the office of the Registrar of Unions) Douglas and the CTU relied heavily on their analyses of wage movements. Such information was vital to the CTU, aiding the work of Peter Harris in particular. 'It was like a Bible to us,' recalled Douglas.

He was also on the councils of the university's Institute of Policy Studies and its successor, the Institute of Strategic Studies, which analysed New Zealand's international roles, including trade and industry. This organisation had close links with the ILO, and Douglas found it useful to be in on the ground floor through his links with the ICFTU and APRO, the Asia Pacific Regional Organisation of the ICFTU. Douglas continued to work on the New Zealand Trade and Enterprise Board, a merger between the Trade and Development Board and Investment New Zealand, which had been set up to attract foreign investment into New Zealand.[445]

From 1991 onwards Ken Douglas had been spending more time overseas on international trade union business, to the chagrin of some within the movement who accused him of 'escaping the fallout' for workers suffering in the wake of the Employment Contracts Act. Theirs was a short-sighted perspective, and one which annoyed him. Trade barriers were coming down with ever more rapidity, and in the wake of increasing globalisation, without water-tight protections in place, workers were becoming more and more an exploited commodity. International unionism had been one of his long-term interests, and he always welcomed opportunities to use his expertise and knowledge to assist workers anywhere. He also sought — or was appointed to — a raft of positions in the broader movement's engine room.

As CTU president, for example, Douglas was a long-term substitute member of the governing body of the International Labour Organisation, a member of its 17-member steering committee and, as a consequence, on the executive of the International Confederation of Free Trade Unions (ICFTU). Throughout the 1990s, again as CTU president, he was the worker's delegate to the ILO conference. He was also involved in a number of spin-off committees such as a special ILO apartheid committee, and he became president of the administrative Council of the International Centre for Trade Union Rights (ICTUR), recognised by both the UN and the ILO as an accredited NGO campaigning for both workers' rights and the existence of 'free' trade unions internationally. This committee had been established by left-wing unionists from socialist countries in Europe and South America primarily; they were concerned that under increased globalisation there was no effective mechanism for union leaders to develop the economic and political skills to be effective participants in real issues of wealth creation so that workers might benefit. The committee was also designed to bring the two international trade union organisations — the left-leaning WFTU and the more moderate ICFTU — closer together. Worker democracies were not developing in socialist countries and the committee was charged with designing structures and processes to facilitate trade union democracies among workers. Chairing this important group was one of Douglas's more positive experiences within the ILO structure.[446]

In April 1993 he became vice-president, and in August 1994 president, of the Asia Pacific Regional Organisation of the ICFTU (ICFTU-APRO) which comprised 40 national trade unions in 28 countries, its membership stretching from Turkey to the Cook Islands. By this time Douglas was a respected and widely known figure in the broader movement, and following his ICFTU-APRO vice-presidential appointment, ICFTU general secretary Enzo Freso told the press that he was sure Douglas's long involvement both in the ICFTU and in APRO would 'greatly contribute towards a further strengthening of our organisation'. For three years, he also chaired the South Pacific and Oceanic Council of Trade Unions (SPOCTU), and he remained on its committee until he retired.[447]

Late in 1994, as president of the ICFTU-APRO, Douglas was instrumental in developing a Social Charter for Democratic Development. This was intended to put unions on the front foot in the fight-back against free market ideologists who were gaining political influence in 'capital-heavy' countries like Singapore and Taiwan and would soon do so in Indonesia, South Korea and Malaysia. The charter recognised that the global economy could only run successfully on the basis of a new international order founded on democratic principles, and it rejected an argument from some Asian states that successful economic development could ever work under totalitarian government. It stated unequivocally that unless strong rules were set to govern behaviour in the global market and governments created mechanisms of social solidarity to protect the weak and vulnerable, the turbulence of market forces would destroy international cooperation — and it asserted that workers' rights must be included among the rules for the new world economic and political order.[448]

The charter was clear on what these minimum basic rights were. They were set out in seven key ILO Conventions: freedom of association (No. 87); the right to organise and collectively bargain (No. 98); the right to agitate for freedom from and abolish forced labour (Nos 29 and 105); the right to agitate for freedom from child labour (No. 138); the right to promote and enforce equal remuneration for men and women (No. 100), and the right to always allow freedom from discrimination in respect of employment and occupation (No. 111). The charter campaign faced strong opposition from employers and governments in the Third World and Asia/Pacific especially — but also in New Zealand, where the Bolger government refused to accede to it, one of only two OECD countries to do so, the other being Great Britain. At the United Nations Summit for Social Development in March 1995, the ICFTU was effective in countering a New Zealand government move to prevent reference being made to the core ILO conventions in the summit's final declaration.

Throughout the mid- to late 1990s, union amalgamations continued apace. In a key development, in 1996, the Engineers' Union absorbed the smaller and struggling Communication and Energy Workers' Union (CEWU) as well as the Printing, Packaging and Manufacturing Union (PPMU). It made sense. They were all losing members, and around 70 per cent of the CEWU membership were sharing common employers with Engineers' Union members. The CEWU — itself the consequence of a 1991 merger between the Electrical Workers' and Post Office Unions — had lost over $1 million in fees, two years running.

The new assemblage, the Engineering, Printing and Manufacturing Union (EPMU), was, then as now, the biggest private sector union in the country and the second overall biggest behind the PSA. (Today the EPMU represents around 50,000 workers in 11 industries — engineering, print and media, manufacturing, telecommunications, timber, aviation, plastics, energy and mining, postal and logistics, public service and infrastructure, and food.) In April 2000, Andrew Little — a trained lawyer and the current Labour Party president — would replace Rex Jones as EPMU's national secretary. Along with Helen Kelly, the current CTU president, the big-picture-oriented, media-savvy and politically vigorous Little has become New Zealand trade unionism's most prominent voice.[449]

On 19 March 1996, addressing an industrial relations conference in Auckland, Douglas spelled out the future shape of employment relations and the Employment Contracts Act as the CTU saw it. He restated its economic limitations — that it was a conflict model of industrial relations, had a short-term focus, and did not promote industrial-level coordination and cooperation on matters such as skills development, quality standards and work practices. He believed that while the coming election would be fought on a number of issues, such as health and education, tax cuts, the shape of the Accident Compensation Corporation, immigration and superannuation, it was quite clear that industrial relations in general and the Employment Contracts Act in particular were seen by many 'as the ultimate trophy that the contestants will be fighting for'.[450]

This seemed an optimistic assessment, as was the prediction that the pre-election debate on the Employment Contracts Act would be long and hard, particularly under the new mixed member proportional electoral system which brought a new dynamic into the industrial relations debate. The National Party was adamant that the Act was essential to the campaign it was running. The reality, however, for workers, was that over the first 18 months of the Act there had been a virtual wage freeze. In 1992, for example, around two-thirds of wage rates did not move and a total of more than three-quarters had movements of nil or less than 2 per cent. There was a 'drafting gate' operating by now. While many wage rates were not moving, 20 per cent had increased by 3 per cent or more. This was despite the economy growing by 17 per cent and employment expanding by 12 per cent over three years. Conversely, capital income share had risen by about 6 per cent over the same period. According to OECD figures this was the third highest in the developed world, behind only Mexico and Greece.

By this time, the growth in labour productivity which the government promised after the passing of the Employment Contracts Act was proving mythical. In fact, as Bryan Philpott, Professor of Economics at Victoria University, recorded in December 1996, such growth had slowed considerably. 'We must wonder,' he said, 'whether the Employment Contracts Act and the downward pressure on wages associated with it, has led to greater accent on labour intensive techniques of production and to favour those sectors which, by their very nature, tend to be more labour intensive than others. The ECA has encouraged low-skill labour intensive activity rather than displaying skill and capital intensity.'[451]

There was also by this time a growing feeling among many apolitical New Zealanders, who might have viewed trade unions and their leadership as bully boys in the past, that the tables had turned and that the unions were now the underdogs and deserving of some sympathy. The particular bogeyman appeared to be the Employment Court, which came to be blamed for continuing low wages despite an economy that was beginning to bounce back. Paradoxically this court, and its chief judge Tom Goddard, also got it in the neck from employers. In 1996, the Business Roundtable commissioned a report on the Employment Contracts Act. Its author, Australian lawyer Colin Howard, focused much criticism on the working of the court, calling its interpretations 'improbable', reflecting an 'unwillingness to adapt'. Howard recommended that the court be abolished.[452]

On 15 May 1996, at the Ellerslie Conference Centre in Auckland, the Employers' Federation, along with farming and manufacturing leaders, members of the Business Roundtable and a gaggle of Cabinet ministers — including Bill Birch — celebrated the Employment Contracts Act's fifth birthday. Labour leader Helen Clark called it 'a day of shame'. Steve Maharey, Labour's industrial relations spokesperson, produced figures that showed that average weekly earnings between February 1991 and November 1995 had risen by just $11.35 — less than 2 per cent. Women's weekly earnings had risen by $7.56 (just 1.5 per cent) and men's by $16.67 (2.5 per cent), from $644.12 to $660.79. On the other hand, Bill Birch told his audience that unemployment had dropped from 10.9 to

6.1 per cent, that 202,900 jobs had been created, and economic growth had averaged 4 per cent per annum. Others at the celebrations called for more labour reform, focusing their attention specifically on the Employment Court. Business Roundtable chairman Douglas Myers called the court the most harmful feature of New Zealand's current freemarket arrangements; an outspoken Australian mining executive who was present dubbed it the 'Unemployment Court'. The distance between the two sides was greater than ever.[453]

There was also a vast gap in attitudes between New Zealand and Australia. As already noted, the 1984 Economic Summit had delivered little; the fourth Labour government had not been genuinely interested in bringing unions and the CTU into an economic decision-making mix until Mike Moore's compact, and then it was too late. In contrast, the Labor government of Bob Hawke reached an accord with its trade union leadership which allowed that country to pursue a much more expansionary economic policy, which in turn created a far greater number of new jobs than in New Zealand. Subsequently Australia introduced some measure of enterprise-level bargaining that was far less disruptive than the Employment Contracts Act, and in 1996 Paul Keating's Labor government signed a further accord with its country's unions, with similar results. It was based around working together on job targets and a 2 to 3 per cent inflation rate. There was no thought of even considering a commensurate move in New Zealand.[454]

In the latter 1990s, union membership continued to fall. A Victoria University survey in November 1996 showed that just one in five workplaces — or 20 per cent — had union members. It was not an even spread — the contrasts were dramatic. The survey showed that 90 per cent of public sector workplaces were unionised, with some white-collar sectors such as teachers and nurses almost completely so. By contrast, an average of just 12 per cent of private sector firms employed union members, a cheerless figure in comparison with CTU membership at the organisation's inception. The actuality was that thousands of workers either were not interested in unions, seeing no benefit to themselves in membership, or they were unable or unwilling to join a union because of management antipathy.[455]

After the 1996 election, the CTU executive put together a Bill which presented its policies for fair labour law in draft legislation. This involved long discussions with member unions, after which the CTU contracted Gordon Anderson, then a senior lecturer in commercial law at Victoria University, to compose a draft along CTU guidelines. Completed on 10 December 1996, its objectives were to create a new law to cover both collective agreements and individual employment contracts; promote collective bargaining; recognise the peculiarity of state sector unionism and provide incentives for employers to engage in good behaviour.[456]

The Workplace Relations Bill, a coherent alternative to the Employment Contracts Act, was made public in October 1997. Its underlying principles were based on ILO Conventions 87 and 98 — the right to 'freely associate' and the right to organise and bargain collectively. The Bill required access to the workplace for recruitment purposes; rights to hold stopwork meetings; rights for workers to have time off for union business; the requirement for both parties to act in good faith, including an obligation to meet, not to undermine the other party, not to use undue stalling tactics, and to use mediation if necessary. It also assumed that workers needed to be organised to be represented — a principle of worker self-help. The needs of all workers would be achieved not through this Bill alone but by a combination of strong legislation determining their minimum rights.[457]

It is important to acknowledge what this Bill was not. Firstly, it was not drafted as utopian law or even as legislation that the union movement might consider ideal. Rather, it was designed as an alternative to the Employment Contracts Act, one which was likely to be perceived as acceptable to a Labour or Labour-dominated government. Neither did the Bill signal a return to the industrial relations system before 1991. It was a charter of 'worker rights', not a re-establishment of union monopolies. There would be no return to compulsory unionism, relativities regulation, union monopolies and demarcation of the workforce, compulsory arbitration or restrictions on access to personnel, or grievance rights and procedures for workers who did not belong to unions.[458]

Indeed, much of the Bill replicated the Employment Contracts Act. The personal grievance and enforcement provisions, for example, remained substantially unchanged, and the Employment Court was kept, as were provisions regarding freedom of association. The main differences related to the role of unions in the process — in that they needed to conform to the requirements of ILO Convention 98 — most fundamentally, that a collective agreement becomes an agreement between an employer and a union only; that unions return to a central legal role in negotiations and that their unique role as a workers' collective is recognised. Just as importantly, the tough restrictions on the right to strike would be set aside.[459]

The Workplace Relations Bill was prominent in Helen Clark's thoughts when she addressed the national affiliate council on 20 October 1998. She told delegates that the CTU measure was 'very, very close' to Labour's policy, and that her party would not resile from it despite the expectation that it would meet very strong opposition. She also said that in replacing the Employment Contracts Act a Labour-led government would provide a route for collective bargaining beyond the level of enterprise and that unions had the inalienable right to take industrial action in pursuit of a multi-employer collective agreement.[460]

The CTU always had a high public profile and a major presence in the country's media. For example, both the CTU and unions — although initially led by the PSA's Colin Clark — had been leading participants from the early 1990s in the electoral reform process as they argued that proportional representation was more democratic than the first-past-the-post system. For years the CTU had met emotion with logic to stall employer moves to revamp or dismiss altogether the Employment Court. The CTU and its affiliates were the only advocates for minimum provisions for workers as the cornerstone of a fair collective bargaining system. The organisation also highlighted — persistently — the disadvantages women faced under existing laws and policies, and developed strategies to close the gender pay gap. It also led the consumer cause for a decent ACC system and for safe workplace practices, with industry training and retraining.[461]

This was the macro picture, but by 1997 the organisation itself was at the crossroads. While it still faced sometimes intense opposition from right-wing politicians, employer groups and the Business Roundtable, more vitriolic attacks kept coming from the left. Many unions and their members still felt bitter about what they perceived as the CTU's lack of aggression after the Employment Contracts Act was passed. The perception that since that time the organisation had become too close to the 'bosses' and politicians — both National and Labour, the latter still damned as the abetter of Rogernomics — deepened these tensions.

The divide was graphically illustrated just before the CTU's October 1997 conference when the 19,000-member National Distribution Union — the second-biggest blue-collar union still in the organisation — disaffiliated. President Bill Andersen said the withdrawal had been coming for some time as his members had become increasingly disenchanted with the CTU's direction. They felt it lacked the will for collective action, and decried its lack of campaigning about specific issues such as the Employment Contracts Act. Andersen further alleged that the organisation had become a mere union resource provider rather than a meaningful organising centre, and he also asserted that unions should be protected against others poaching their members, with clear definitions of which unions had coverage over particular workers.[462]

Douglas retorted that under voluntary unionism — with which he agreed, since it freed up union officials who might otherwise spend 'wasted' hours chasing up union fees from workers who did not want to pay — it was not possible to dictate to workers which unions they should belong to. He insisted that Andersen's dissatisfaction with the CTU was the result of his increasing isolation within it, in that his ideological mantras were now being gleaned from the Workers' Communist League with its vows to continue to fight the 'class war' despite international communism being a spent force. It may have been an unkind judgement, but since their fallout in 1990 over the future direction of the Socialist Unity Party, the two men had barely been on speaking terms.[463]

There were other grumblings among affiliates about the CTU's state of health and future direction. This led the conference to agree to a major review of its role, functions and direction over the next five years. To facilitate this, it set up a review committee which employed Nigel Haworth, Professor of International Business at Auckland University, to undertake an extensive information-gathering process. Haworth saw a lot that he liked. Within the CTU, he identified a powerful and respected public presence; a leadership recognised by policy-makers and the wider public; highly competent staff; coherent policy recommendations informed by a clear understanding of the environment and a strong international dimension; agreement among affiliates about the fundamental rationale for the CTU; a commitment by the affiliates to act together; a responsiveness to changing circumstances; strong traditions of research, information dissemination, lobbying, campaign organisation, gender and equity activities and excellent linkages with political parties.[464]

But there were weaknesses. Obliquely calling it 'future development', Haworth suggested that the CTU work towards removing differences between affiliates in responding to shrinking union membership; recruit more workers to unions, especially Maori, Pacific Island and women; refocus CTU activity within a limited financial resource base; develop appropriate regional institutions and activities in the alignment of affiliates with the CTU; resolve tensions between affiliates, and between affiliates and the CTU; repair a lack of commitment by affiliates to decisions linked to a tendency for 'scapegoating'; address inadequate integration of union memberships into CTU activities, and focus on unresolved debates about appropriate strategies to respond to Maori and Pacific Islanders' concerns.

From Haworth's report, a new CTU constitution emerged on 1 October 1998. It included significant structural changes. The national executive disappeared and was replaced by a national affiliate council that had a clear strategic role, with representation from the women's committee, runanga and Pacific Island fono, all with full voting rights, a charter of affiliation for all members, and a work programme to advance the participation and representation of Maori on the CTU and affiliated unions. The plan was that the CTU would be a much more interactive organisation, developing plans and policies for implementation rather than passing resolutions. Douglas's role as president was reconfirmed, including his responsibilities as chair of meetings of the affiliate council, biennial and special conferences and other meetings, with the power to make casting votes when necessary and to delegate meeting facilitation. He was entrusted to see that the constitution was observed and promoted by officers and affiliated members.[465]

In November 1997, the CTU established an international committee to support Ken Douglas in carrying out the organisation's international work, which was now taking up much of his time. The Asia-Pacific Economic Cooperation group (APEC), a powerful grouping of 24 Asian and Pacific Rim countries, became its first focus of attention, mostly because the 1999 APEC Heads of Government meeting was to be held in Auckland. APEC was important for New Zealand because 70 per cent of its exports and imports were to and from APEC countries; 80 per cent of the country's investment came from these countries, as did most of its tourists.[466]

But APEC's activities and goals were anathema to trade unionists. It stood for liberalisation of trade, globalisation, free movement of capital and promotion of new-right political ideology, all of which were at odds with workers' rights. The CTU's objectives were to influence APEC to develop a social dimension and social partnership through a trade union presence at all levels, to introduce and protect minimum labour standards as established by ILO conventions, and to try to moderate APEC's economic objectives by engaging with, rather than opposing, the organisation. The CTU advised unions to pursue these objectives by raising members' awareness of APEC and the issues for workers, to work with APRO and other international union organisations to put pressure on it to modify its philosophy, and to develop networks with academics and other organisations interested in worker and human rights.[467]

In 1998, a financial and economic crisis reverberated throughout Asia and brought renewed and increased poverty to hundreds of millions of workers and their families, seriously undermining progress achieved through several decades of economic development. The fourth conference of the ICFTU's Asia Pacific Labour Network (APLN), held in Kuala Lumpur in September 1998, just prior to the APEC leaders' meeting there, produced a hard-hitting statement decrying the self-congratulatory approach shown at the APEC leaders' conference in Vancouver in 1997.[468]

Douglas played a leading role in the APLN, urging APEC leaders to develop regulatory mechanisms to control hedge funds, prevent speculation and stop the undermining of local currencies, encourage fresh investment in human and capital resources, establish social safety nets, restore high levels of economic growth and include a social dimension in the development process to ensure that the benefits of economic growth were distributed fairly. He also wanted APEC to prioritise fundamental workers' rights, health care, food security, education and the needs of the most vulnerable sectors, especially women and children. Further, he wanted APEC forums to include trade union and employer input to develop policy recommendations to overcome the current crisis.[469]

In combating APEC's philosophies the CTU had been encouraged by the ILO's 22 June 1998 Declaration on Fundamental Principles and Rights at Work which pointed out that economic growth itself was not sufficient to ensure equity, social progress and the eradication of poverty. It argued that strong social policies, justice and democratic institutions were also needed. There was major controversy in October 1998, however, after Prime Minister Jenny Shipley invited Angela Foulkes to join a government APEC advisory council. Shipley's intention was to bring together a small but broadly representative group of New Zealanders who could 'lend their experience and insights through providing direct advice to her, on the overall policy planning for and carriage of New Zealand's year of chairing APEC and play an active role in the domestic debate around the issues that will emerge as we seek to craft a positive set of outcomes for our year'. She stressed that Foulkes would be appointed in a personal capacity and would not be expected to be a defender of the government's policy positions.[470]

Nonetheless, Foulkes's acceptance of the appointment was seen by some as the trade union movement backtracking on its opposition to APEC's policies. Darien Fenton, general secretary of the Service and Food Workers' Union, wrote to Foulkes saying that her union was very concerned about the appointment, for which there was no mandate from the affiliates despite concerns raised by the national affiliates council about CTU officers accepting appointment to controversial government bodies. It was not CTU policy to 'promote' APEC, Fenton understood. Jane Kelsey, national secretary of the Association of University Staff, had similar concerns, particularly since Shipley's press release indicated that the role of the committee was 'to help communicate the benefits of APEC and advise the government on its plans for the year'. Both women wanted answers at the forthcoming International Committee meeting.[471]

This meeting, too, was testy. Douglas reiterated that Foulkes had been appointed in a personal capacity, and that the CTU had not been asked to appoint a representative. But John Ryall of the Service Workers' Union said he believed that even if a CTU member was appointed as an individual she was still an officer of the organisation, one that existed to promote workers' rights, unlike APEC and this advisory council, which promoted trade liberalisation. Kelsey believed it was clear that the government viewed the council as a 'cheer team' for APEC. 'You can get co-opted without changing anything in the organisation,' Ryall said. 'This seems like an innocent way of being hooked into a consultative process but it seems very much like a committee that is promoting APEC.' He thought the committee was a cynical marketing exercise.

An annoyed Foulkes countered that 'we regularly accept invitations to a whole lot of things that were reported without all this fuss'. Affiliates should be consistent, she counselled. Douglas, too, was irritated, saying that people get 'hooked in' if they want to get hooked in. There was no abrogation of CTU policy, he said. 'We champion the rights of workers to be heard in every forum. We seek to influence wherever possible.' In this he was not being inconsistent; this was the kind of inclusivity — between union, state and, where relevant, business — for which Douglas had been agitating for years.[472]

The 1998 review also determined that the organisation would develop a strategic plan to're-unionise' workers. Thus far this had been unsuccessful and the problem was stark — CTU membership had now dropped to close to 200,000. Many unions had disappeared. Others had left the CTU. More were members of the rival Trade Union Federation. Still more were unaligned with either body. Mergers had kept others alive, some only just. Just four — the state sector's PSA, NZEI and Nurses' Organisation, and the private sector EPMU — had more than 20,000 members. By October 1999, the situation had further deteriorated. The CTU had an operating deficit of $49,286 from 17 financial affiliates representing 189,761 members.[473]

In July 1998 the National Cabinet reviewed the Employment Contracts Act and pronounced it to be working well, saying that little change was necessary. But this government was living on borrowed time. Through the rest of that year Labour surged ahead in the polls.[474]

Knowing that a new Labour government intended to dispense with the legislation and replace it with something akin to its own Workplace Relations Bill, during the 1999 election campaign the CTU worked harder than ever to return the party to power, possibly in coalition with the Alliance Party. It appointed election coordinators throughout the country, and compiled and distributed election kits, overhead transparency packs, weekly political backgrounders, a 'Time To Win' logo, posters and T-shirts. Many CTU activists from various unions — sometimes in combination with unionists from non-CTU-affiliated unions — formed groups in specific electorates to agitate for these candidates.[475]

By this time Douglas had let it be known that he would be retiring at the end of the forthcoming 67th biennial conference of the CTU in November 1999. He was not tired but he was 64 years old and had had enough. Partly his decision was driven by frustration. After persistently addressing unions about the 'new way', receiving applause and promises, he would discover that officials were continuing in their old 'reactive' behaviours. Moreover, he was conscious that both Tom Skinner and Jim Knox had stayed in their positions too long and had become ineffective. At a national affiliate council meeting on 5 October, PPTA secretary Kevin Bunker placed on record the council's appreciation of the energy, commitment and vision that Douglas had brought to the CTU during a very difficult time for trade unions and working people in New Zealand.[476]

But others welcomed Douglas's imminent departure. Graham Speden, *The Independent*'s political commentator, believed there would be 'relief on all sides' when Douglas and Foulkes (who had resigned six months earlier) departed, calling them 'tired' and contending that other senior unionists believed it was time for a change. They would farewell the pair with gratitude, but with high hopes for a renewal of unionism and of the CTU itself. Much expectation would fall on Ross Wilson, the CTU's vice-president and secretary of the Rail and Maritime Transport Union, Douglas's likely successor. Around him was a group of younger union leaders, many, like Wilson, university graduates — EPMU secretary Rex Jones, Service Workers' Union secretary Darien Fenton, NZEI secretary Joanna Beresford and the National Distribution Union's Peter Conway.[477]

There was also likely to be a change in philosophy at the top. No longer would Douglas's 'partnership' model with employers be predominant; instead, as Wilson had already indicated, there would be greater priority on developing a more campaigning approach, not just on behalf of unions but also on behalf of workers generally. It was about reorganising and recruitment, putting emphasis on and allocating resources towards developing strategies to recruit members who had never been unionists.[478]

Trade Union Federation leaders were also keen to see Douglas go. The myth persisted among many of them that he was still 'too close to the bosses'. There were, however, more pragmatic reasons for TUF unions to return to the mainstream. They too had lost hundreds of members from their constituency, they were struggling financially, and had no political influence. In October 2000, just before his union voted for the TUF to disband and for the Seafarers' Union to join the CTU, office-holder Garry Parsloe described the CTU's main benefit to the unions as providing support for each other — 'a place of unity'. For his part, Wilson was keen to unify trade unionism by bringing the federation and other non-affiliated unions, such as the big National Distribution Union, back into the fold. He was more acceptable to the TUF than Douglas had been, and there was no doubt that unification would provide trade unionism with much-needed strength in difficult times.[479]

In September 1998, Douglas accepted a nomination to stand as an independent in the Porirua City Council local body elections, and he was elected the following month. At the end of that year Jenny Shipley's National government awarded him the Order of New Zealand (ONZ), the country's highest accolade, restricted to just 20 living New Zealanders at any one time. Douglas had turned down a 1990 Commemoration Medal, and in 1994 a knighthood for services to the trade union movement. He both disapproved of the 'pseudo-colonial' honours system and was most uneasy that working union leaders should be rewarded for what was a collaborative task, at that time in particular, under difficult conditions. The ONZ was an indigenous recognition, and as a consequence acceptable. He accepted the award for a 'long and outstanding contribution to the trade union movement in New Zealand and overseas'. It was long indeed; just on 40 years since he had been elected to the presidency of the Wellington Drivers' Union.[480]

Yet the honour came at a time when many people would have described Douglas as a failure. Under his trusteeship the trade union movement had declined more sharply than at any other time in its history — a decline in membership from more than 70 to 20 per cent of all wage and salary earners — and he still attracted the ire of many both within and without the movement for his perceived diffidence in the face of the Employment Contracts Act. Douglas understood the irony, rightly interpreting that the economic and legal assaults on workers over the past 15 years had been a primary factor in creating this conundrum. 'I suppose I'm surprised in a sense that you get an order for representing men and women the best you can in an anti-worker massively deregulated economy,' he told the press. Interestingly, he credited his achievements, and by implication the award, to the socialist values instilled in him from his mother's and his father's families.[481]

The Order of New Zealand was the first of two major awards. The following April, Victoria University's honorary degrees committee bestowed on Douglas a Doctor of Laws, *honoris causa*, in part to celebrate the university's centenary year. This caused him some mirth; in anger he had sometimes described capitalists and others as 'escapees from the university'. Like many school failures he had found a more appropriate niche beyond it.[482]

The citation acknowledged his 'tireless service on behalf of ordinary New Zealanders', one that had vital and beneficial effects on New Zealand's systems of industrial laws, its industrial relations, its political processes and its international policies and reputation. It continued:

> Of course this work has brought its share of conflict and criticism. Ken Douglas held fearlessly and publicly to principles that often brought censure. When one Prime Minister revealed to the country that Douglas was a communist and member of the Socialist Unity party it surprised only those who had not read the material he himself had supplied for his entry in *Who's Who*! . . . His high standing in the international trade union movement and his strong advocacy of human and civil rights especially in the Asia-Pacific region, exemplify his sustained commitment to his principles.[483]

Douglas's hard work, energy and foresight were never in dispute. As well as his presidency of the Council of Trade Unions, at the time of this award he was also president of the Asia-Pacific Regional Organisation of the ICFTU, a member of the executive board of the ICFTU, and on its 17-member steering committee. He had retained the presidency of the International Centre for Trade Union Rights and was still the worker representative on the ILO. He remained a member of SPOCTU's steering committee and retained the presidency of the Asian and Regional Organisation of the ICFTU until September 2000. He was still a leader of the Asia-Pacific Labour Network fighting APEC's agenda of economic liberalisation.

On 18 October 1999 Douglas retired as president of the Council of Trade Unions and was replaced by Ross Wilson. Wilson was the ideal replacement for Douglas, having already won widespread respect as an astute, personable and hard-working lawyer who had dedicated his career to trade union administration. He was quieter than his predecessor, considered, thorough and conciliatory. He was also experienced, having served a long apprenticeship firstly with the Amalgamated Society of Railway Servants, then with the Harbour Board Workers' Union, leading the facilitation of the merger of the two in 1995 to become national secretary of the Rail and Maritime Transport Union. Wilson's ability to quickly grasp all sides of an argument and close all loopholes would stand him in good stead in future years. Darien Fenton of the Service and Food Workers' Union replaced him as the CTU's new vice-president.

Foulkes was gone too. She had played an important role as the highest-profile woman in a leadership role within the trade union movement, the Federation of Labour in particular, and unions in general, which had traditionally not been sympathetic to women's aspirations. Only Sonja Davies in her latter days in the FOL had achieved the kind of prominence for women that Foulkes attained. (In 1978, Davies, then an advisory officer with the Shop Employees' Union, had become the first woman to be elected to the FOL executive — on her fourth try. Her election had been a breakthrough. Davies recalled that when she first attended an FOL conference in 1968, delegates 'sighed heavily or pointedly unfolded newspapers' when she rose to speak.)[484]

Foulkes was a good thinker and a diligent worker but she could be loud, belligerent and unwilling or unable to acknowledge opposing viewpoints. She had clashed with Douglas over style. Foulkes was a technocrat; Douglas was often less organised, and more passionate in public — often wearing his heart on his sleeve. Douglas analysed issues in terms of class. Foulkes did not, Finsec being primarily a union of managers, sub-managers and clerks. It should be stressed, however, that the differences in style between the two were kept professional and were never a barrier to effective policy decisions and the outside work of the CTU. Finsec secretary Paul Goulter replaced Foulkes as the CTU's secretary on her retirement from the position.[485]

Economist Peter Harris also resigned when Douglas retired. His economic analyses had brought a vital new dimension to the development of trade unionism and he was soon missed. He had provided an intellectual foundation for the leadership and the firepower that enabled the CTU to compete with the best economists in the land — in Treasury, the Reserve Bank, the trading banks, Federated Farmers and the Employers' and Manufacturers' Federations. The possessor of an able mind, and an instinctive empathy with the 'underdog' allied with a skilled communication ethos, Harris, most of all, represented a 'new face' for the movement. Douglas was in no doubt that without his input and analysis the CTU would not have gained the respect it did through the 1990s. Harris became an economic adviser to the newly elected Labour government's Minister of Finance, Michael Cullen. He was replaced by Peter Conway, who had been an economist with the National Distribution Union.[486]

Douglas's departure from the CTU was bitter-sweet and he cogitated on the highs and lows of his union career before addressing his last conference. There would be no slipping out the back door wiping a nostalgic tear from his eye. Neither would there be sadness, regret or apology. He knew it would be a long hard road back from the attempts of Birch and Bolger's government to eliminate unions altogether. As it would to 'reconvert' workers from being production units with no rights back to being 'real' citizens with civil rights. 'But the movement had to try its damndest.'

In a tub-thumping speech in the best traditions of Fintan Walsh at his most fiery, he passionately called for unity in the union movement. 'The way forward,' he intoned, drawing an analogy with the All Blacks' recent loss to France in the World Cup semi-final, 'was to be heard, be effective and change the game plan when you have to . . . If you are serious about the appreciations you have given me and Angela, think about where this movement is going. If you want to give us thanks deliver it by action. Don't sit on your bums and wait for things to come to you.' As Bob Dylan, a poet from a kinder time, had summed it up: 'You'd better start swimming or you'll sink like a stone, for the times they are a-changing.'[487]

Taking his next cue from the direction in which he had been taking the movement, and implicitly acknowledging that in some senses he had failed, Douglas hectored his audience: 'The way forward has to involve a radical departure from the narrow, reactive, short-term occupational wages-only focus of our trade union traditions. You've got to take it to them. Thank me for carrying out my class obligations? Thanks but no thanks.' And with that he raised his fist above his head as the assembled delegates burst into 'Solidarity Forever'.

Ross Wilson told the audience that following Douglas would be an impossible task. 'He is the union leader of our time and many will recall no other,' he asserted. Douglas had other, more surprising admirers. Former Minister of Labour Max Bradford praised Douglas's commitment to workers. 'I have a great deal of respect for his integrity and the passions with which he has pursued the interests of working people,' he told the press. 'He has the skills of a diplomat, orator and activist rolled into one.' Employers' Federation president Steve Marshall, with whom Douglas had consulted closely and argued frequently, understood his abilities more than most; he believed you underestimated him 'at your own risk' — 'Ken won't die in a ditch,' he said.[488]

Fittingly, Douglas's final task as CTU leader was to participate as an adviser to the New Zealand ministerial delegation to the World Trade Organization's biennial conference in Seattle, in December 1999. The WTO, established among 153 member countries in January

1995 to supervise and liberalise trade, had evolved out of the General Agreement on Tariffs and Trade (GATT) which was begun in 1947 to stimulate world trade. But for many concerned citizens the WTO represented the pursuit of an international free trading system with little or no protection for workers, particularly those in third world countries where many lived in abject poverty. In Seattle, Douglas along with all the other participants faced thousands of protesters who tried to hold up or disrupt the conference.[489]

The aggression and the size of the protest impressed Douglas, who described the protesters' presence, and the conference itself, as a watershed in future trade negotiations. He believed that no future WTO conference would be able to ignore the huge public pressure and expectation that the world trading system had to be comprehensive, coherent and integrated with other global issues such as the environment, human rights and trade union rights. He insisted that the protesters were 'not anti-WTO' but people imbued with humanitarian concerns about all the world's peoples, who all needed labour standards, not labour exploitation.

'World trade should have a dynamic effect with the goal of expanding opportunities, improving working conditions and raising wage levels within developing countries,' he reflected at the conference's conclusion. 'We must recognise that developing countries have a competitive advantage with lower labour costs and trade barriers must not be invoked to counteract this advantage . . . the WTO should cooperate with the ILO in dealing with labour standards. The ILO has the necessary competence in this area while the WTO has the necessary rule enforcement ability.' In this speech at the end of his working life Douglas nailed his colours to the mast, just as he had at the beginning. He was a trade unionist through and through. Despite the revolutions that had whirled around him over close to 40 years, and the accusations from some trade unionists that he had long since 'lost his way', he had remained loyal to the core essence of his character.[490]

At the time of Douglas's retirement it was clear that limitations of new-right ideology had been exposed. The economy was stagnant, the rate of growth in labour productivity had slumped, there was a chronic deficit in the balance of payments, and numbers on benefits were higher than in May 1991 when the Employment Contracts Act came into being. But as Douglas piled the detritus from his office into two battered suitcases before handing over to his successor he was in characteristic good humour, refusing to berate the CTU's adversaries, as Angela Foulkes had done when she retired the previous July. He revealed to journalists that he was about to undergo a knee operation. 'That's what you get when you do a lot of praying as a young man,' the deeply irreligious Douglas joked to his audience.[491]

Far from being gloomy about where he had come from and the parlous state of trade unionism in New Zealand, he eagerly looked forward to new challenges. These included his role as a Porirua City councillor, which had already introduced him to a whole new world of arcane bureaucracy; new challenges in sports administration in Titahi Bay as well as playing more golf; continuing his service on a variety of public and private boards — an activity that would increase considerably in the coming years — and spending more time with his sons and daughters, and his seven grandchildren.

During this 'bend in the road' he mused on his memories of his beloved grandmother Carrie Douglas, his principal caregiver as a child and the source of many sensible homilies. She had told him: 'Trust everybody once. Never ascribe a bad motive to someone until they give you a reason to.' On reflection, he hoped he had lived up to that creed as a trade union leader. He would have loved to have believed that Carrie was smiling down upon him as he took his last steps from his CTU office.

CHAPTER 15

Poacher turned gamekeeper?

At 63, Douglas was still a relatively youthful man when he retired from the union movement in November 1999. But 'retirement' was a misnomer — the word meant little to Douglas. His mind was still active and he was not the type of bloke to relax by rising late, putting his feet up and reading a book. Indeed, his sleeping habits did not change — he still went to bed late, often, and only needed five hours' sleep to sustain himself. Clearly, he needed to find outlets for his prodigious energy and instinctive altruism.

He was given an important role, early in 2000, as a special adviser to the select committee hearings on the new Labour government Bill that would replace the Employment Contracts Act. The Bill was largely based on the CTU's Workplace Relations Bill and to a lesser extent on Labour's earlier Employment Law Council Bill. The legislation that evolved returned industrial relations to a more collectivist approach, its primary objective being building productive employment relationships through the promotion of mutual trust and confidence based on long-held ILO conventions. Collective bargaining meant a recognition of unions in wage and condition negotiations, and multi-employer contracts allowing unions to negotiate contracts over several work sites. Unions were in, bargaining agents were out. Yet more was retained from its predecessor than was removed. There was no return to compulsion, to national awards or to fixed conciliation, arbitration and relativity procedures. However, there were further changes in an amendment in 2004 pertaining to 'good faith', the application of collective bargaining and transfer of undertakings — most of which favoured the unions. The Employment Relations Act (2000) and its succeeding amendment brought New Zealand closer to the international mainstream of industrial law, and has remained uncontroversial ever since.[492]

Ken Douglas had won a seat as an independent councillor for Porirua City Council's Western ward in 1998. He did not consider the switch of interest from national and international trade unionism to community concerns a backward step. He had always been proud of being a 'Bay boy', and been extensively involved in local sports clubs both as a player and as an administrator. Election to the local council was just a further step in that process. A strong advocate of the concept of the public good, his main motivation initially was to help the city develop an infrastructure that suited the needs of its young people, keeping them there for sport and recreation rather than having them move away. He believed the council should not be driven by political ideologies but by pragmatic responses that met people's real needs.

On his election as a councillor he had been shocked by the low skill-set of several of his fellow councillors, many of whom, he felt, did not understand the difference between governance and management. Some seemed to believe their responsibilities rested with repairing potholes and little else. The political climate was defensive and parochial, with councillors forever accusing the Wellington Regional Council or other neighbouring councils of shortcomings rather than looking to themselves, and their communities, for answers. There was no sign of an economic framework in the council's planning for growth. The biggest driver of their decision-making was populist sentiment, most clearly expressed in editorials or letters to the editor in the local *Kapi Mana* newspaper. There seemed to be a climate of apologetic negativity, whose roots appeared to lie in Porirua's large concentration of low-income earners. That was galling to Douglas, and he soon came to see himself primarily as a 'change agent' within the council, wishing to expand its horizons beyond minutiae and to use his national and international experience to revitalise the organisation, giving it an important and visible leadership role in the community's life.

He found some allies, among them Helen Smith, a former Values Party activist whose outspokenness had seen her persistently overlooked for the deputy mayor's position. Smith had been primarily responsible for the establishment of Pataka, the local museum and art gallery. Douglas formed an informal alliance with Smith, and Labour members Kevin Watson and Naureen Palmer in the eastern ward, and together they presented a formidable cabal around the council table. Even more important was the appointment of Roger Blakeley as the city's new chief executive.

Blakeley had had an impressive public service career as the country's first Secretary for the Environment under David Lange before being appointed chief executive of the Department of Internal Affairs. During the late 1990s he had overseen some important and much-needed local body reform, and he wanted to see how these policies were working. Blakeley brought to the council a clear understanding of where he wanted to take it in terms of transparency and accountability. With support from Douglas, he encouraged the council to help establish a regional economic development agency, and the two lobbied other councils — Wellington, Lower Hutt, Upper Hutt and Kapiti — to do the same. Their work took shape in September 2001 as the Wellington Economic Development Trust, aka Positively Wellington Business, an umbrella group charged with promoting, fostering and developing an innovative economy in Wellington. It would use council money and tap into local business expertise to assist the establishment of new, sustainable business enterprises, bringing growth, development and employment to communities in the broader Wellington region. Representing the Porirua Council, Douglas was a founding trustee, and was its chair between 2003 and 2007.[493]

The headlines he created in his role as a councillor, however, focused on parochial issues, of which humanitarian concerns were uppermost. In April 2000, for example, he won a battle with fellow councillors to reduce a projected $20-a-week rent increase for the tenants of its Moana Court flats to $12. This followed a petition signed by the flats' residents, which was presented by Douglas to the council's March meeting. In 2003 he argued that instead of a rejigging of councillors' salaries, which would result in some getting more under a new remuneration system based on leadership of standing committees, pay should be tied to performance. He argued that in order to receive their full remuneration they should be available for council duties for 25 hours a month: 'If not they should be docked 50 per cent,' he declared. This was a new radicalism, calls for performance pay being hitherto the preoccupation of right-wingers. Douglas believed his motion to introduce performance pay was a means of stretching the thinking of the Remuneration Authority, the body that had oversight of councillors' pay. The motion was lost, by six votes to eight, some opponents questioning how it could be monitored while others believed accountability should be measured by performance per se, not attendance at meetings.[494]

Since 1998, Douglas has topped the poll in the Western ward. In 2004, he joined the Labour Party and contested both the council and Capital and Coast District Health Board elections on its ticket. In 2007, however, he quit the Labour Party when it refused to select him to contest the ward and instead chose Bud Lavery — a former councillor and Porirua Trust president. In this election, as 'independent' Labour he again topped the poll. Following the suggestion of councillors, Blakeley established a democratic procedure whereby residents could approach councillors about specific issues or problems. This prompted

Douglas and his fellow ward representatives Liz Kelly and Helen Smith, collectively known locally as 'The Three Musketeers', to establish their own monthly forums or clinics at Pataka (usually), in their ward.

Citizens come to listen and talk to the councillors and record their concerns, whether they be general or specific. Issues are taken up as a collective, with each councillor responsible for a specific task. Smith organises the venue; Douglas writes a summary report for presentation to Blakeley, and the ebullient Kelly is the front-of-house person. The councillors, and Blakeley, guarantee that all problems will be actioned within a week — a report from Blakeley or his officers acknowledging the complaint and the steps taken, or about to be taken, to remedy it. Douglas, Kelly and Smith pride themselves on representing the only Porirua ward to provide that guarantee, and Blakeley has been impressed by the Musketeers' achievements, saying their energy and enthusiasm has resulted in a vibrant interaction between them and their constituents.[495]

Currently, Douglas is the council's alternative representative on the Wellington Regional Strategy committee working under the auspices of the Wellington Regional Council. He has invested considerable energy in developing a framework of economic coherency across the wider region. Until 2007, he chaired the council's strategy, finance and regulatory committee, one of its two standing committees. He also chairs the audit and risk management committee and has stamped his imprimatur on both. Specifically, he has taken a leading role in economic strategy and policy development in the city. Partly as a consequence, Porirua City has gone from being a dismal, run-down suburb, whose unemployment figures ballooned with the 1998 closure of the Todd Motors plant, to a thriving community. In 2007, according to economic research group BERL, it became the fastest growing city in New Zealand with a 12.7 per cent growth in GDP and significant developments in the employment, finance, communication, retail and accommodation sectors. Douglas's strong sense of social equity has found expression in overt support for the Porirua Health Centre of Excellence, which he helped to establish, and the Midnight Express programme in which volunteer youth workers patrol the streets of East Porirua on Friday and Saturday nights ensuring that young people are safe.[496]

Further challenges await. Douglas would like to see high-speed fibre access to Porirua City to further develop its economic infrastructure and for use in homes, schools and business. He would also welcome centres of health excellence with connections to Wellington Hospital and Otago University's medical school in the city, and centres of educational excellence with links to Victoria University, Whitireia Polytechnic — on whose board he has also sat — and iwi centres of learning.

Blakeley is impressed by Douglas. He is, he says, careful to differentiate between governance and management, and to educate other councillors and board members about that difference. Blakeley says his message that operational detail needs to be left to the appropriate person on council rather than being up for discussion at the council table is gradually being taken on board. At the council table, as in other meetings, he can be critical of others, but Blakeley contends that criticism is expressed in a way that engenders mutual respect. 'He is literate, articulate and always very well-prepared before he enters any discussion.' He also praises Douglas's ability to present an argument logically and coherently, saying, 'I've seen colleagues applaud his speeches, something I've hardly ever seen before in a council chamber. His ability to make strategic analyses about complex regional, national and global issues demonstrates an extraordinary intelligence.'[497]

In 'retirement', Douglas was able to play more golf at Titahi Golf Club both as an interclub player and as a manager for junior teams. He was also able to put more time into assisting Michael Campbell's professional career. He had known Campbell since he was a boy, and as a friend and mentor Campbell's international success brought him huge joy. In April 2006 Douglas was a caddy for Campbell for a light-hearted, par-three championship on the day before the Masters Championship in Augusta, Georgia. During the day where, by tradition, the caddy putts on the final green, Douglas two-putted down a slippery slope very close to the hole from 8 metres away. 'No sweat. I've had bigger crowds watching me at Titahi Bay,' he insisted, tongue firmly in cheek. Campbell was impressed, indicating that Douglas had putted better than major winner Ray Floyd, who was his partner on the day. 'On the other hand he struggled to keep up and his club selection was hopeless. Michael Waite [Campbell's regular caddy] has still got the job for the next ten years.'[498]

After Campbell turned professional in 2003 he attracted a range of managers, some of whom were competent, some of whom were not. Douglas and others saw a need for Campbell to have his non-playing life disciplined and his taxation, investments and travel arrangements taken care of so that he could focus on just his sport. In order to do that Grant Duncan, a talented amateur player with whom Campbell had played at Manor Park, where he had developed his game, and who was a tax inspector at the Inland Revenue Department, chaired the board of a company called Cambo Enterprise Investments with Douglas and representatives of Campbell's management company, Stonehage.

After Campbell and his family returned to Australia as their principal home, Cambo Enterprises took a back seat to a more recent venture, the Michael Campbell Foundation, which Campbell established with his wife Julie in 2006. It has three aims based around a talent pyramid. At the top it identifies elite performers, provides them with inspiration and helps them to realise their dreams. The second aim is to ensure more children are given the chance to pursue and develop their talent. The third aim is to reduce 'talent wastage', by giving children access to the necessary 'building blocks' to success. Campbell asked Douglas to chair and guide the foundation, whose trustees include Julie Campbell, former National MP Philip Burdon, businesswoman Liz Read, lawyer John Allen and entrepreneur Craig Heatley. Recently the foundation selected three talented young New Zealand golfers to spend a week with Campbell and his coach Jonathan Yarwood at their English base for one-on-one tuition.[499]

One of Douglas's most rewarding experiences has been his work as a member of the Department of Corrections inmate employment board, in which he represented the CTU between 1997 and 2007. Douglas's aim on joining this committee, which reports to the department's chief executive on all aspects of the operation of inmate employment programmes, was to focus on helping inmates to better themselves and not be a burden on the state on their release. He believed in restorative justice, and despite scepticism from within the CTU executive, teamed up with a Corrections Department psychologist, Phillipa Rush, to develop a pre-release skills programme. John Banks, Minister of Police at the time, was sceptical about prisoner education and rehabilitation but he gave the programme the green light on condition that Douglas and Rush produce a business plan to guarantee a return to Treasury. The scheme is now showing the benefits, with skills trainers in a number of areas working with ever larger numbers of prisoners in preparation for life after incarceration. It is a key business group within the Department of Corrections.

Associated with this work, between May 2000 and September 2004 Douglas also chaired the board of Instep Limited, a company established by Matthew Beattie in September 1998 as a behavioural healthcare company offering workplace programmes to counter stress, and alcohol and drug abuse. Today the organisation either employs or contracts more than 300 psychologists and counsellors, providing round-the-clock call centres in 90 New Zealand and Pacific Island locations.[500]

Douglas's longest-serving activity outside his union work had been his commitment to what was originally Mike Moore's Market Development Board, which was established in 1985. Douglas joined the board the following year, replacing Jim Knox. In 1988 it expanded into the Trade Development Board, or TRADENZ, then under the 1990s National government it evolved into Trade New Zealand. Later it changed again, merging with Industry New Zealand on 1 July 2003 to become the New Zealand Trade Development Board. Douglas continued to serve throughout this time.

After Labour's re-election in 2005, Economic Development Minister Jim Anderton — whose brainchild it was — and Trade Negotiations Minister Jim Sutton established a new investment board — Investment New Zealand. Douglas and the CTU lobbied the government to merge the Trade Development Board and Investment New Zealand into one body — New Zealand Trade and Enterprise. It offered similar services to its predecessors, designed to assist young companies and entrepreneurs, accelerate the development of potentially high-growth business at home and abroad, and boost the country's regional development programmes, sector development and trade and investment promotions. Douglas served on the Trade and Enterprise Board until 2007 when he resigned and was replaced by CTU economist Peter Conway.

It was through his work on this board that Douglas met Philip Burdon, up until 1996 Minister of Trade in Jim Bolger's National government. Burdon was instrumental in appointing Douglas to the board of Asia 2000, established by Burdon and Don McKinnon, the Minister of Foreign Affairs, in 1994 to promote New Zealanders' awareness of Asia and Asian people. Increasing trade with Asia was a significant factor in its establishment but Burdon believed that New Zealanders had to develop a deeper understanding of Asian culture. He was also concerned about increasing levels of anti-Asian sentiment.

As president of the ICFTU's Asia Pacific Regional Organisation Douglas was cognisant of the problems of Asian workers and their unions, and was instrumental in persuading APRO to develop unilateral relationships with China and the Chinese trade unions alongside former communist Asian countries Vietnam, Laos and Mongolia. By 2000, with these relationships bedded down and business between New Zealand and these countries growing, the emphasis shifted from business to a more 'people-to-people relationship'. The name changed to Asia: New Zealand and thereafter, through diplomatic manoeuvrings, there was more emphasis on cultural and educational exchanges designed to benefit all countries. Asia: NZ is mostly government funded, and as a non-profit and non-partisan organisation it enjoys strong cross-party support in Parliament along with the patronage of Governor-General Sir Anand Satyanand, a former deputy chairman. Some of its most public events — notably the Lantern and Diwali festivals — are funded by corporate sponsorship, while philanthropic sources within Asia provide funding for scholarships and other work.

Its corporate partners are the New Zealand Ministry of Foreign Affairs and Trade, Fonterra and New Zealand Trade and Enterprise.[501]

Douglas has continued as a trustee since 1994, and in 2007 became deputy chair, a role he currently shares with Richard Nottage, a former Secretary of Foreign Affairs and Trade. Burdon is the current chairman. The board has a research focus, and has a research advisory group comprising of scholars from New Zealand and Australia alongside business people and top public servants. Douglas argues that the organisation is even more important today than when it was established. In 2006, 10 per cent of New Zealand's population was Asian; it is predicted to grow to 16 per cent by 2025. Asia is also home to 10 of New Zealand's top 20 markets for goods and exports and is becoming increasingly important for tourism and education; India and China are the world's two fastest growing economies. New Zealand has beaten Australia in already signing a free-trade deal with China, and as this book goes to print is in deep discussion with India's leaders for something similar.[502]

Douglas holds Burdon in high esteem. 'He was the only Minister of Trade in the last 20 years to have attended, in his lunch times, full meetings of the Trade Development Board and to ask questions and provide answers on trade — not only Asia but to the rest of the world. The others would sit in their offices and we'd have to go and see them at their convenience ... Unlike some of his colleagues, Burdon was never anti-union, always open to new ideas and able to absorb important political nuances in our work ... Other politicians get corrupted by the job and its lifestyle, unwilling to rock boats. Burdon was not dependent on politics. He was a self-made millionaire and could have walked away.' He did eventually, resigning from Parliament in 1996.[503]

Burdon, conversely, has great respect for Douglas's abilities and expertise, believing he combines valuable worldly experience and wisdom with an all-embracing overview of issues that is neither judgemental nor insular. 'He is always seriously informed and well-briefed, and makes realistic and measured appraisals of the issues and is too astute to be taken in by the usual combination of pretension and self-importance that one often comes across ...'[504]

ABOVE Douglas at a working bee. In March 1990, SUP member Alan Ware was national secretary of the Pulp and Paper Workers' Union and arranged for SUP members to work on their new union building in Tokoroa as a fundraising exercise for the party. (*Douglas family*)

BELOW Douglas addresses 4000 workers and supporters at Parliament protesting Roger Douglas's tariff-slashing agenda in March 1990. (*Douglas family*)

Reflections from cartoonists Tom Scott (top and bottom), Anthony Ellison (centre left) and Bob Brockie (centre right) on the Employment Contracts Bill.

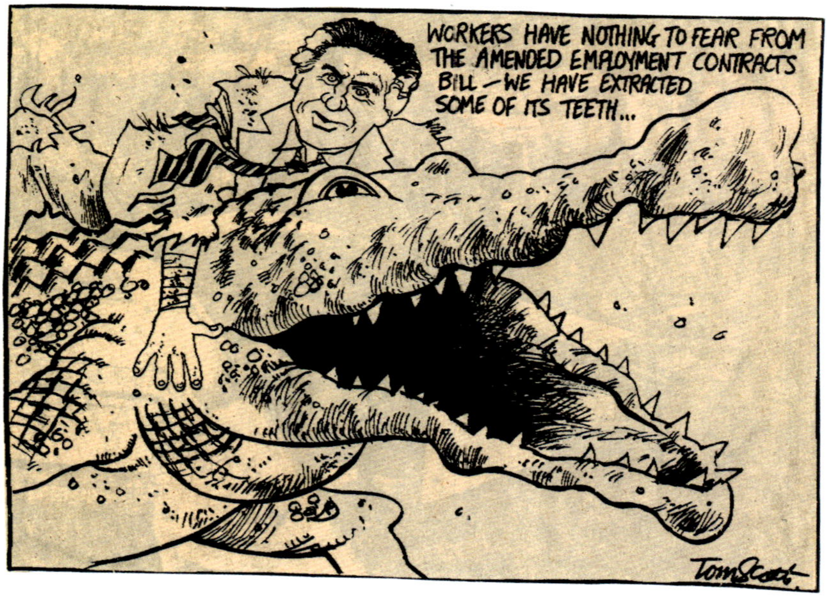

LEFT Douglas before teeing off with, *from left*, Ong Teng Cheung, Singapore's president and former general secretary of Singapore's National Trade Union Congress, Takashi Isumi, of Japan, secretary-general of APRO-ICTFU and Ashida, president of the All Japan Trade Union Organisation, in June 1991. At the tee on the second hole Ong received an 'urgent' phone call from American President Bill Clinton pleading with him to pardon a young American caught tagging in Singapore and sentenced to six strokes of the rattan. Ong asked him if he would do the same if a Singaporese lad was in trouble in the United States. Ong refused to intervene. The sentence was carried out. (*Douglas family*)

CENTRE Ken Douglas accompanies Prime Minister Jim Bolger to the stage at the October 1991 CTU conference. Note the empty seats; many delegates boycotted Bolger's speech in protest at the Employment Contracts Act. (*Socialist Worker*)

LEFT Douglas addresses the ILO's June 1991 Conference. (*Douglas family*)

RIGHT Rosanne Meo representing the Employers Federation, and Ken Douglas representing the CTU, relaxing while attending the ILO conference in Geneva in 1993. (*Douglas family*)

CENTRE Douglas applauds Michael Campbell's shot in an overseas tournament at the Titahi Golf Club on 24 July 1995. Beside him watching the match on television sits Neil Tuffery, the club's secretary. Observing Campbell win the US Open in 2005 was one of the happiest moments of his life. (*Alexander Turnbull Library, Wellington*)

RIGHT Peter, Helen, John and Jane Douglas (holding microphone) share their father's 60th birthday celebrations at the Titahi Golf Club, 18 November 1995. (*Douglas family*)

LEFT Douglas greets Juan Samania, the Chilean director-general of the International Labour Organisation in June 1998. (*Douglas family*)

CENTRE Douglas and Marilyn Tucker in Red Square, Moscow, on a private visit in September 1998. (*Douglas family*)

LEFT The old and the new. CTU headquarters, 29 October 1999. From left: Ross Wilson, Paul Goulter, Angela Foulkes, Ken Douglas. (*Douglas family*)

RIGHT Ron Burgess addresses the audience at Douglas's CTU retirement function in December 1999. Marilyn Tucker sits beside Douglas. (*Douglas family*)

RIGHT The Governor-General, the Rt Hon Sir Michael Hardie-Boys, presents Ken Douglas with the Order of New Zealand at Government House, Wellington, January 1999. (*Douglas family*)

RIGHT Douglas celebrates the award of the ONZ with his family at Government House. *Back row from left:* Helen, Peter and John Douglas. *Front row from left:* Jane Douglas, Marilyn Tucker, Ken Douglas, and Elizabeth Knox, Jim Knox's widow, who was present to hand over her late husband's ONZ to Douglas. (*Douglas family*)

LEFT Many New Zealanders would have agreed with the sentiments expressed by Jim Hubbard in this *Bay of Plenty Times* cartoon. Jim Knox and Sonja Davies were also recipients of the Order of New Zealand. (*Jim Hubbard*)

ABOVE Informal congratulation at the Titahi Golf Club on 31 December 1998. Congratulating Ken, *from left:* his cousin Terry Farrow, Harold Paul, daughter Jane Douglas and Dan Hunia. (*Titahi Golf Club*)

LEFT Douglas was awarded his honorary Doctor of Laws at Victoria University with arch-capitalist and Business Roundtable member Rod Deane. Douglas joked with Deane that he had 'got him at last' as they both wore red gowns to the ceremony. (*Douglas family*)

LEFT Douglas in Mongolia in September 2005 on his mission for the International Labour Organisation. (*Douglas family*)

BELOW The New Zealand Rugby Union Board 2008-09. *Back row from left:* Gerard van Tilborg, Bill Thurston, Graham Mourie, Steve Tew (CEO), Mike Eagle, Ivan Haines, Paul Quinn. *Front row from left:* Mark Peters, Andy Leslie, Jock Hobbs (chairman), John Sturgeon, Ken Douglas. (*NZRU*)

BELOW Porirua City Council 2007-2010. *Backrow from left:* Timothy Manu, Denys Latham, Euon Murrell, Taima Fagaloa, Nick Leggett, Tim Sheppard, Robert Shaw. *Front row from left:* Hemi Matenga, Ken Douglas, Liz Kelly, Jenny Brash (Mayor), Sue Dow, Litea Ah Hoi, Henry Smith. (*Douglas family*)

Through his leadership of both the FOL and the CTU, Douglas has had dealings with Air New Zealand through industrial disputes over many years. When the airline was privatised in 1989, wage bargaining was fragmented and difficult to conclude. The bureaucracy was cumbersome and leadership seemed to be fixated on the traditional 'public service' model whereby length of service determined seniority, and talent and ability were pushed aside. Through the 1990s industrial relationships worsened and Douglas realised that something needed to be done or Air New Zealand would, in his words, collapse under its own weight.

There were jealousies between the myriad unions active in the organisation. Traditionally, representing the worst type of the relativity ethos concomitant with arbitration, when one group received a pay rise, others would demand it too, to maintain margins. This was particularly true among the organisation's 'elite' — the Salaried Officers Guild and the Institute of Licensed Engineers in particular. Conversely, with Rex Jones, who represented the 'working engineers', Mike Jackson in the Storemen and Packers' Union and Tom Downey, secretary of the Flight Attendants' Union, the CTU developed an Air New Zealand Agreement whereby individual skills were recognised because of the uniqueness of some of the functions they undertook. The Hotel Workers' Union, which represented the airline's kitchen staff, was part of the agreement too, although for a different reason — survival — with the airline threatening to outsource their work. Collectively, these unions developed a 'tie-rack' arrangement with each union hanging down off it, all part of a composite agreement but with individual clauses pertaining to their work.

But 'elite' workers were abusing the system. Licensed engineers' responsibilities included going out onto the tarmac and handing a piece of paper to the pilots with calculations on the tonnage, passenger numbers and fuel preparatory to take-off. When one of these men took sick leave, union rules meant that nobody else could do the job, which sometimes meant that off-duty men had to return and complete the task for five times their regular salary. Douglas called this behaviour criminal. 'These men had plenty of down-time to run supplementary money-making ventures such as orchards and other small businesses. Their selfishness meant there was less money for other workers and was one factor which contributed to the airline's financial problems. I took them on through the CTU. We didn't win that fight but we did get rid of some of the rorts.'[505]

But just as that was becoming sorted, Air New Zealand collapsed. In 1999 the airline had become involved in a battle over Ansett which it owned in partnership with News Corp Ltd. The two had been pursuing a sale of the underperforming carrier to Singapore Airlines but in 2000 the airline announced that instead it would be increasing its 50 per cent stake in Ansett Australia to 100 per cent, at a cost of $680 million. It was a critical mistake as Ansett's fleet staffing levels and infrastructure far outweighed those of Air New Zealand. From his CTU perch, Douglas was scathing of both airlines' governance and management, claiming Air New Zealand had not carried out proper due diligence before the purchase. He predicted the worst.

He was right. By September 2001, plagued by costs it could not afford, Air New Zealand/Ansett was nearing collapse. A failed attempt to buy Virgin Blue was the final straw and on 12 September, out of both time and cash, Air New Zealand placed Ansett Australia into voluntary administration, following which Ansett was forced to cease operations. In the wake, Air New Zealand suffered a $NZ1.425 billion loss. In October, the Labour government bailed it out by renationalising it for $NZ885 million (with the government taking a 76.5 per cent stake), appointing John Palmer, a Brightwater farmer, Lincoln College graduate and successful businessman, to chair a new board of directors. It would take until 2003 before the airline returned a profit.

Palmer, who also chaired the board of AMP, insisted as a condition of his appointment that he would pick his own board members — not the government. Through Rosanne Meo, he met Douglas in the AMP tent at the 2002 New Zealand Golf Open in which Tiger Woods was playing. 'He approached and asked me some searching questions as to what I thought of the airline,' recalled Douglas. 'I bent his ears back for two hours. Four months later he asked me how I would feel about being on Air New Zealand's board. I said, what for? He told me that I had a lot of knowledge about its operations — and its industrial history, and saw me as a change agent to effect radical transformation as it was still wallowing in the wake of the Ansett debacle and there was no guarantee that it would survive.'

Palmer understood there were people/union issues in Air New Zealand in critical need of improvement; and Douglas was likely to be very valuable. 'As I talked to him in the tent I was impressed by his sharp intellect and open personality. I needed people who were team players and my quick assessment of him was very encouraging.'[506]

Douglas responded to Palmer's challenge with alacrity, joining other new faces — Jane Freeman, Ron Carter, Warren Larsen and John McDonald. Ralph Norris, formerly chief executive of the ASB and head of the Business Roundtable, was involved in the selection of a new chief executive when he excused himself from the process and successfully applied for the position himself. Douglas considered the move an abrogation of fair practice; nonetheless he respected Norris's talent-spotting ability.

Douglas served on the Air New Zealand board from 2002 to 2008. During that time the airline focused on developing new markets in Asia, notably China, a move which Douglas championed and which had an obvious crossover with his work in Asia: New Zealand. It also revamped its pricing structure to make it more competitive with other airlines flying in and out of New Zealand, made scheduling more friendly for local and overseas tourists, and paid more attention to its business-class passengers. It also developed its cargo-carrying capacity through its own direct flights and by establishing alliances with other carriers, rushing high-value but perishable cargoes to all parts of the world, such as flowers to Europe, and crayfish to Hong Kong.

During his time on the board Douglas was the leading voice on employment matters and, according to Palmer, was universally respected for his advocacy. There were aspects of Air New Zealand's operations that Douglas did not like, however: 'over the top' bonus structure, excessively subsidised share options for senior management, and the practice of chief executives demanding more money and better conditions once they had been selected, as a condition of accepting the job. More importantly, Douglas, in opposition to some on the board — and Norris — fought hard to win decent redundancy payments for older employees who had been dismissed when some of the company's operations were contracted out. Douglas understood that the airline was overstaffed and that it needed restructuring to make it more internationally competitive, but he also believed it was important to treat workers fairly.[507]

Understandably, the unions resisted these lay-offs. Norris wanted Douglas to talk to the workers but he refused, saying that was the chief executive's job. So Norris went to the workers, explained his salary structure and the reasons behind it, and gave a justification for theirs. He received a hostile reception. Douglas won that battle — the employees, some of whom had loyally served the organisation for 30 years or more, were looked after. These changes were overseen by Norris's successor, Rob Fyfe, who came to Air New Zealand in 2005 from a role as special projects manager with Telecom. Fyfe, who was smart and accessible, was more acceptable to the company's workers than his predecessor.

Douglas did not seek re-election at the company's AGM in September 2008. He felt that there needed to be new blood on the Air New Zealand board, with more specific skills, and with the share price healthy and industrial relations settled, meaning that in a sense his primary task was completed. There was a strong desire for the airline to become more closely associated with the tourism industry and Paul Bingham, a Banks Peninsula eco-tourism operator, was appointed in Douglas's place.

John Palmer contends that Douglas made an outstanding contribution to Air New Zealand. 'That he came as a highly respected figure both in New Zealand business and among trade unions internationally meant his experiences and insights were unique and immensely valuable ... Of the appointments that were made post-Ansett, my own included, it was soon evident that he brought to the table a much better understanding of the business than the rest of us. That was truly a bonus I had not anticipated.'[508]

Douglas's involvement with Healthcare New Zealand began after a conversation in the street with his schoolfriend Doug Catley early in 2002. Fourteen years earlier, in 1988, Catley and Peter Cottier had founded the company as a healthcare service initially based at a small hospital, Johnswood, in Upper Hutt. They went on to own or lease three other hospitals — Bloomfield, Elderslea and Kairangi. In the early 1990s, Catley realised that healthcare services were moving towards looking after people in their homes rather than in institutions. Healthcare purchased the firm Duty Calls, and a strong presence in the home and community sector was cemented. In 1995 it expanded its services to provide for those with disabilities. In 2004, it established a joint venture with Wellington Free Ambulance. Today it is the largest provider of home- and community-based health and disability services in New Zealand.

The essence of the initial conversation between Douglas and Catley was that there seemed to be no skills recognition for the carers — the nurses, nurse-aids, counsellors and therapists who worked in the sector. Catley wanted to use Douglas's industrial expertise to expedite such recognition in their remuneration and conditions of work. Douglas agreed. After Healthcare New Zealand had shifted its focus to the home it had begun competing for district health board contracts with NGOs, religious organisations (the Presbyterians and Anglicans both had long traditions of service in this area) and other private providers. Competition was tough, and there was a perception that private companies were ripping off the system as they did not possess the moral authority of the churches. The religious organisations had another advantage too — as charities they did not pay tax. In addition, the Presbyterians were in the process of selling all their commercial properties and putting the profits into home-care services because they offered a better return.

Soon after he joined the board of Healthcare, Douglas suggested a radical move. In order to be seen as operating with transparency the company should publicly announce that it would make no more than an 8 per cent return on its investments. If the profit was more, it would return it to the funder. Catley was gobsmacked. But Douglas was adamant that Healthcare needed to demonstrate its integrity as openly as possible. 'If we don't we'll get beaten up by the media and the unions as just being an outfit that turns people's misery into a profit.'

Douglas persuaded Catley that Healthcare needed to be completely transparent in its tendering process and in its negotiations with workers and unions in order to demonstrate that as a privately owned company it was not making exorbitant profits at the expense of clients, staff and the government as funder. The company's books would be shown to contractors and unions. Healthcare subsequently paid $2.2 million back to the Ministry of Health — the amount it had been paid over and above the level was stipulated in its contracts. 'It gave us integrity that was visible and showed up the competitors who were pillaging the system and the health boards themselves who were letting out their own contracts in the system but not knowing, nor caring, whether the providers were delivering a decent service or not,' Douglas said.

Douglas also understood that Healthcare had to reassure itself, and its client-base, that its recruitment, training and the quality of its ongoing care was top-notch. He persuaded the board to bring on a clinical expert to ensure these standards were met, and Dr John Wellingham, chair of the College of GPs' quality management group was invited to join the board. It was also opportune for Healthcare to have some political and business influence so Wyatt Creech, formerly Minister of Health in the National Cabinet, and a politician for whom Douglas had some respect, was brought on board. Originally Douglas told Catley he would work with him for two years, but in 2006 he became vice-chairman, and in July 2009 chairman. Douglas enjoys the work — and sparring with Catley.[509]

Catley had been in a class behind Douglas at Northland Primary School and later attended Wellington College. They were close friends, though their politics in adulthood could not have been more different. Catley labels himself, proudly, a 'Ronald Reagan conservative'. In 1981, when he stood for National in the general election, he told an Island Bay electorate meeting, not completely in jest, that when he became emperor, 'I am going to hang all of those bloody unionists in Vivian

Street from the nearest lamp post but because Ken Douglas is a mate of mine, I will only send him to a concentration camp!'[510]

Catley put politics aside when he invited Douglas onto the Healthcare board. It was the first outside appointment he had made.

> I trusted him, I knew he possessed sound judgement; his integrity as I observed it over the years, both personally and as a communist trade unionist, was impeccable — I respected that he always stuck to his guns through thick and thin through the flak he sometimes received in both his working and sporting life because of his communism ... actually I thought he was past his 'use-by' date when he came on to the Healthcare board but how wrong I was — the honesty, unselfishness and humanity was still there and that has been a wonderful asset to the company as he has concentrated on the 'people' aspect of the job — concerned about our stakeholders, our employees, and our patients in the hospitals and now their homes whereas I was the business person first and foremost, looking after the dollars and cents.

Gaining a seat on the Capital and Coast District Health Board was a natural progression for Douglas following his involvement with Healthcare. His interest in public health administration had begun when he was part of a local pressure group trying to persuade the National government to build the new Wellington hospital at Kenepuru (Porirua) rather than develop the existing Newtown site. There were concerns that in a major earthquake everybody living west of the faultline that runs through Wellington could be cut off from the hospital. In addition, thousands of people in Porirua and further west had a long-time connection with the existing Kenepuru Hospital and it was also accessible to the thousands of retirees who lived on the Kapiti Coast. He lost that battle, however, and the new hospital was built at Newtown.

After standing successfully for the district health board on a Labour ticket in 2004, Douglas found, once again, many board members confusing governance with management. In his opinion they had taken their eyes off the ball as far as the quality, quantity and efficiency of delivery of health services was concerned. On 1 May 2007, Health Minister Pete Hodgson appointed Douglas deputy chair of the board and he worked productively with Sir John Anderson when he became chair in December that year. However, Douglas's tenure proved to be a short one. Although his term was due to run until 2010, as early as June 2007 he faced questions about his suitability as a board member because of his involvement with Healthcare. Both Douglas and the board, under chair Judith Aitken at that time, took legal advice over a potential conflict of interest.[511]

The debate was raised in Parliament on 13 June when Tony Ryall, the Opposition spokesperson on health, questioned Douglas's dual roles. Hodgson was unperturbed, expressing confidence in Douglas's professionalism. Yet Douglas himself foresaw a problem given that Capital and Coast Health was due to consider the transfer of many its community services to external agencies. Healthcare was likely to seek a contract for those services. He sought guidance from the chairs of both boards on 'what level of abstention' to exercise, and believed that it 'might be prudent to withdraw from both boards during such a contracting process'. It was a wise decision. In March that year the High Court had ruled that the tendering process for Auckland's laboratory services had been unfair because Tony Bierre, an Auckland District Health Board member at the time, was involved in the Labtests bid which eventually won the contract. The contract was subsequently overturned.

Nonetheless, Douglas remained until 2009, by which time National was back in power and Ryall was Minister of Health. An official from the ministry, David Pannett, contacted Douglas and informed him that Ryall was going to sack him in the interests of 'structural reform'. Douglas told Pannett not to be stupid. He understood the political appointments process and would resign. The government wanted to reduce both the size and the number of boards, and that made sense to Douglas.[512]

Nonetheless, in his letter of resignation to Ryall, Douglas expressed his frustration at the historical practices whereby the country's health services had been poorly delivered, lacked national coherency in design and were inaccurately measured. Successful organisations needed a sequence of planning, he said — first a purpose, secondly a structure, and thirdly a process. This was not happening. He challenged Ryall to attack the core issues of lack of public transparency and accountability in service provision, and to refocus the professional health service on communities, thereby unclogging the hospital system.[513]

Ken Douglas also made a considerable impact at New Zealand Post. Mark Burton, the Minister of State Owned Enterprises first asked him to join its board, after Labour returned to power in 1999. Douglas liked the idea. There was a family connection, since both his mother and his mother-in-law had been posties, and he recalled with pride their involvement in the 1963 'Surf' strike. He was also a supporter of the development of state-owned enterprises as organisations that were not purely capitalist but a pragmatic alternative to privatisation, coming at a time when state agencies were atrophying in the face of the demands of a modern and continually changing economy. They allowed for enhanced productivity, the adoption of new technology and the improvement and widening of a skills base without exposure to the vagaries of untrammelled capitalism. Douglas was appointed to the board of New Zealand Post in October 2000, seen as something of a 'change agent'.

It was a time of significant change and challenge in the industry, with New Zealand Post's core postal business coming under increasing threat from electronic communication. As a result it was looking to expand its operations in other areas. The biggest and most important development was Kiwibank. Alliance MP and former Labour Party president Jim Anderton had long proposed the establishment of a New Zealand-owned bank, and it became part of Alliance Party policy in the Labour-Alliance coalition of 1999–2002.

Separately, New Zealand Post was developing a business case for a bank as a way of diversifying its business. Its proposal was for a New Zealand-owned, low-cost bank where 'young and old' New Zealanders could deposit their savings at competitive rates, with the profits accruing to the New Zealand government rather than overseas-based shareholders, who controlled all of the country's other trading banks. The two developments intersected, and the bank was established in 2002 as a wholly owned subsidiary of New Zealand Post. John Allen, New Zealand Post's CEO through this period, has said that Anderton was important in delivering Kiwibank. 'Politically, we would not have received government support, not as easily, and possibly not at all without Jim's active engagement.'[514]

Douglas did not agree with Anderton's initial plan for a 'small time' bank. Returns would not match expenditure, and he believed it would soon fold. He argued, and the board agreed, that Kiwibank needed to be a full trading bank with all the facilities the other banks enjoyed. It therefore had to be a bank that would assist, nurture and protect New Zealand industries and businesses, and be viable in a volatile global economy. 'Banks make money out of exchanges of capital, not out of individuals' deposits. I had been a strong opponent of the sale of our major banks to Australia so it was hugely important to have a nationally owned bank controlled by the state, influenced by an understanding of financial markets but operating uniquely on what was best for New Zealand business — not shareholders' profits — but with sufficient grunt to survive in a global marketplace with its penchant for crises . . .'[515]

When Douglas was appointed to the board of New Zealand Post its chair was Dr Ross Armstrong, a prominent Auckland-based National Party office-holder and fish exporter. With his term about to expire, he convinced Prime Minister Helen Clark to get Jim Bolger onto the New Zealand Post board. It was an astute political move as the National Party had opposed Kiwibank and was threatening to dismantle it once in power. But Bolger, who was coming to the end of his time as New Zealand Ambassador to the United States, was keen to participate, and would sweep the carpet from under National's feet. There was some intrigue in the process. Unbeknown to Clark, Armstrong had earlier sounded Bolger out about replacing him after his term expired, so when Bolger accepted Clark's offer he insisted that he become chair of both New Zealand Post and Kiwibank. This was at the expense of Sid Bradley, a Labour Party insider and former secretary of the Post Office Union, who had been on the board from the beginning and seemed the obvious successor to Armstrong as chair. Notwithstanding, Douglas worked amicably with Bolger as deputy chair from 2004 until the expiry of his term in October 2009, and came to respect him as an able and consensual chair of both bodies. A decent man is his assessment, past political differences long since thrust aside.[516]

Douglas took a leading role in all of New Zealand Post's major developments through that period — the launching of Kiwibank, the complete reorganisation of the postal business, the construction and launch of new IT companies, and the development of a joint venture with DHL, the world's largest courier company. John Allen says he could not think of a better person to have been alongside him in this crucial time of change. The pair also had an excellent working relationship, and Douglas had a high regard for Allen's business skills. Conversely, Allen learnt a lot from Douglas, describing his fierce intellectualism, wisdom, keen and deep engagement with all the issues, strong humanity and clearly defined sense of independence. 'He brought with him a "mana" that was unusual in its potency. His knowledge, integrity and vigour illuminated board discussions, especially when he brought forward propositions that others found challenging.'[517]

Ken Douglas has never lost his love of rugby, maintaining close administrative and player links with the Northern United Rugby Club in Porirua. During 2003, while the New Zealand Rugby Union was in the process of being restructured, chairman Jock Hobbs approached him on behalf of chief executive Chris Moller. They wanted him to join a sub-committee of the board which was in the process, among other tasks, of negotiating a new collective with the players. Moller and Hobbs believed that Douglas was an ideal candidate, with his experience in industrial relations and because, in his own words, he was a rugby 'fanatic'. He knew Hobbs through their joint connection with the Wellington College Old Boys/University Rugby Clubs.

Douglas agreed to join the sub-committee, refusing remuneration and undertaking the work because of his 'love of the game'. The sub-committee's competition review was a wide-ranging review that took several months, covering discussions on all issues pertaining to the shape of both the professional and the amateur game — the competition structure, selection policies, players' salaries and their movements, and salary caps. While the game had been professional in New Zealand since 1996, there was continual pressure on the union from players and their agents and the Players Association, led by Rob Nichol. During the Review, Douglas argued persuasively that the union had to set a salary cap to keep the payment system under control, and that good New Zealand players chasing huge remuneration in England, France and Japan should not be allowed to continue to represent New Zealand as the professional game in this country would soon be devastated. He also argued that provinces needed to develop their own game to a high level, in part by preventing major unions pilfering talented young players.

The Players Association had difficulty accepting the salary cap but the union was determined to see it through. 'We weren't going to let Rob Nichol take over the world,' is how current CEO Steve Tew remembers it. In a new constitution, the NZRU made provision for an appointments and remuneration committee to nominate and vet applicants representing the northern, central and southern zones who would sit on the board for a maximum of three years, and for two further independent board members chosen by the same committee. Independent board members would need to apply for these positions. The appointments committee was about to meet when one of its members pulled out and Hobbs, impressed with Douglas's work on the competition review process, asked if he would replace him. Collectively, they interviewed Mike Eagle and Warwick Syers for the central and northern zones respectively. Douglas was impressed with what he heard, including their strategies for the union to grow and promote rugby on their catchments. They were selected. The large number of applicants for the independent position was whittled down to five, but the only applicant to impress the committee, and Douglas, at interview was Paul Collins, a former Brierley manager. After some debate, however, Collins was deemed ineligible as he already sat on the boards of the Wellington Rugby Union and the Hurricanes franchise.

Two weeks later, when the appointments committee was trying to find consensus as to who they should appoint, Douglas arrived late to hear the men arguing over Collins' eligibility. When he left to visit the bathroom Hobbs followed, caught up with him and told him that the committee had rejected Collins. Instead, they had been talking among themselves before his arrival and agreed that they wanted him to withdraw from the committee and apply himself to become an independent board member. Douglas was uneasy. He had seen this before when Ralph Norris withdrew from a chief executive appointments committee at Air New Zealand in order to stand for the position himself. He had felt there that the process had been compromised.

This comment caused mirth among the others on the committee, but had the effect of reinforcing their determination to persuade Douglas. They wanted an immediate decision. There was another part of Douglas that was secretly delighted at the thought of being so close to the engine-room of rugby administration in New Zealand, so he consented with the proviso that they interview him as vigorously as the other candidates. Hobbs was impressed with Douglas's integrity. For his part, Douglas saw challenges in the implementation of the strategies articulated by Syers and Eagle, and combatting Rob Nichol and his association, which had already been to the Commerce Commission complaining that the union was indulging in anti-competitive behaviour over the salary cap issue.

The interview process was uncomfortable because Douglas knew that the committee was going to pick him no matter what he said. He told them they would need to be prepared for some flak given his politics. They were unfazed. The full board signed the appointment off at the subsequent annual general meeting. He is now in his second term as an independent councillor. In 2008 he survived 27 challenges, and in 2010 there were 39 applications for the independent positions, his colleague

Bill Thurston missing out in the last election to Chris Doig, a former opera singer and chief executive of New Zealand Cricket.

A member of the union's business and finance committee, Douglas's biggest achievement to date has been resolution of player contracts, with players mostly on three-year contracts, and ineligible to play for New Zealand if they ply their trade overseas. One of his aims has been bringing revenue stability that would increase the talent pool of professional rugby players, at the same time maintaining a strong and healthy environment for the amateur game, especially at the club level.

Steve Tew, who was raised in a state house in the Hutt , says his respect for Douglas's leadership of the union movement dates from Tew's own adolescence. He observed that Douglas seemed to bring integrity and common sense in an industrial relations scene that was often volatile.

> My initial view has proved spot on. He brings a knowledge, a level of integrity, an honesty and a passion for the game, and for its community, that is unsurpassed. As a director he's smart, always well-prepared and others always listen intently to what he has to say. He always sees the bigger picture, constantly lifting the discussion out of the detail into the strategy . . . He always challenges you. He doesn't make it easy for us. You have to earn his respect and his support. He has never been a 'yes' man. He has alternative arguments — often alone — which he expresses forcefully with passion and intellect but always accepts majority decisions. This loyalty makes him the ideal team man . . .[518]

Hobbs concurs, describing Douglas as an 'excellent' appointment to the rugby union board, and praising his 'big picture' analyses, his strategic approach and his 'courage' in raising issues that are not always popular. Hobbs is also astounded at his work rate, describing how he arrives at board meetings before the other members, goes over his notes and is persistently scribbling into oversized notebooks.[519]

Throughout the 1990s and the early 2000s, ironically perhaps in light of his work in health administration, Douglas's increasing weight was threatening his life. It had long been a problem. When he had first become a union official he had weighed just over 70 kg. A year later he was 78 kg, partly as a result of the weight-lifting he undertook to increase his size for rugby. Despite his involvement in sport he continued to put on weight, one year rising from 82 to 95 kg. A continuously poor diet, often eaten on the run, saw his weight balloon to 97 kg by 1959. In 1994, using a Jenny Craig weight reduction programme, he managed to reduce it from 135 to 108 kg, but it did not last and he bounced back to become even heavier. In 2001 he had reconstructive surgery on both knees which led him to be less mobile and resulted in more weight gain. Further knee surgery was not possible and other diets did not help. By this time he weighed 151 kg and was struggling to walk, let alone play golf. His doctors warned that his morbid obesity would shorten his life, and in December 2003 he underwent a radical stomach severance operation — or stomach stapling — the fobi-pouch. It was a success; he lost 68 kg.

After this operation, done privately at Wakefield Hospital at a cost of $20,000, Douglas became an advocate for the cause. He spoke out frequently, saying that the government should fund operations for the grossly obese as it made economic sense in the long run. 'This intervention is going to get a person back to full productive work and no subsequent hospitalisation — it's got to be money in the bank for the government,' he said. '. . . Preventing diabetes is a critical issue as the country becomes more obese . . . I see this coming out of the State's purse more in the context of an economic rationing than even a quality of life prospect.'[520]

After the 2003 operation, Douglas's dietary habits changed overnight as his small stomach and 92-kg frame can only hold small amounts of food and little alcohol. Steaks are out, as is the Sunday roast. Since then 'Retro Ken,' never a fashion aficionado, has been able to fit into his 30-year-old suits, which he never discarded. 'That's the thing about fashion,' he says, trying to find an excuse for his parsimony. 'You hold on to it long enough and it comes around again.'[521]

CHAPTER 16

Man for all seasons

Ken Douglas has many supporters and detractors, although not in equal measure — the former outnumber the latter. The most antagonistic of his critics still grit their teeth in anger when they recall his response to the Employment Contracts Act. In contrast, a handful of people from different strands of his working and sporting lives have told me that Ken Douglas is the most impressive person they have ever met. Douglas would laugh at this accolade, as he should. Like most people, his life and work reflect the best and worst in him. Nonetheless, his prominent position as the outspoken and often obdurate head of the New Zealand trade union movement through the period of its most radical changes made him as visible as the controversial politicians who shared the stage with him — ideologues Roger Douglas and Ruth Richardson and the idiosyncratic Winston Peters the most noteworthy.

His post-union working life was not an 'add on', but represented a 'full steam ahead' involvement as he brought the same intensity, energy and expertise into new, different and challenging contexts. His history here is one of outstanding success. The high, almost obsequious regard with which Douglas is held by those local body and business leaders who have worked closely with him over the past 10 years is astonishing. Porirua City's Roger Blakeley describes him as one of the most remarkable people he has ever met. Like many others, Blakeley is impressed by Douglas's single-minded ability to think strategically. 'When other councillors are bogged down in the morass of council minutiae, arguing matters of detail, Ken will challenge them to consider what the fundamental principles are and once these have been ascertained, then with his guidance the detail will sort itself out logically. He has done that time and time again.'[522]

Air New Zealand's John Palmer saw no contradiction between Douglas's communism and his work on the airline's board, understanding that his personal politics gave him a broad and uncompromising humanity. Strategic and pragmatic, he was able to influence business to give better worker (and profit) outcomes. 'Had he used the board to preach and divide, he would not have been effective. While he did not agree with all decisions made, sometimes forcefully so, he always upheld the team resolutions.' Douglas was consistent in this respect: in his union days he had accepted FOL executive and council decisions even if they conflicted with his personal politics.[523]

Philip Burdon is particularly struck by Douglas's 'very generous' humanity, his sympathy for the 'trials and tribulations' of the human condition and his genuine desire to help, combined with a serious contempt for the cant, hypocrisy, pretensions and prejudices of life — 'which is quite rare'. Union leaders have proffered similar observations. Ron Burgess among others has commented that one of Douglas's most noteworthy characteristics was his ability to cut quickly through any hypocrisy to get to the core of an issue. Rob Campbell recalled that he speedily exposed people who were following a personal or selfish agenda, and that cant and posturing always made him angry.'[524]

New Zealand Post's John Allen found that Douglas brought to the table deeply held socialist views which he never compromised:

> This was most clearly expressed in his leading the charge to upskill employees of New Zealand Post to provide them with new opportunities but at the same time trying to create those opportunities by looking dynamically at how the organisation needed to change to accommodate them. He wanted always to create a future. He was always prepared to shoot sacred cows . . . He also had an unbelievable world view, always thinking about New Zealand — and our business — in an international context which I had not expected . . .[525]

The Rugby Union's Steve Tew also acknowledges Douglas's humanitarianism. 'He has a great sense of what's important around people. Everybody here, from board member to the most lowly employee — he is always concerned with their welfare. He has a very broad scope around industrial relations issues, seeing both sides of the picture. This balance makes for more consensual decision-making.'[526]

The most astute of Douglas's former union colleagues were unanimous that his acceptance of board roles was not a sell-out. They were more, they contended, an acknowledgement of his abilities — his analytical brain and the breadth of his perspective. Pragmatically, they knew that he understood decision-making; how these organisations related to unions, government, and the global economy, and their impact on the people who worked for them. Douglas's understanding of business is not a recent thing. When leading the Drivers' Union and Drivers' Federation he learned to understand the motivations and aspirations of the 'raw-boned' transport industry in order to be one step ahead. He found tension inherent in the tough negotiations stimulating, and more often than not he won the battle of wills. Rarely did he leave the room with less than he went in with — usually it was more.

Yet Douglas is disconcerted by this recent praise. He worries that some might argue that he had forsaken his values and politics for some kind of 'collaborationist capitalist transformation'. He is at pains to point out that even though many of his post-union activities have largely been within business enterprises, he remains a Marxist. That is still his intellectual bedrock. The difference is that now he exercises this either privately or in a very different arena. He has learned to combine his socialist heart with the wisdom and expertise he has gained from working over the years with a wide range of people in often radically different circumstances.

Douglas doesn't do it for the money, and has turned down at least five other board appointments. He has been quoted in the press as earning too much money. In itself, money is not important to him and he gives much of it away to family members and sports clubs. He is concerned about equity, however. Recently, when the Rugby Union refused to give their staff a pay rise because of the recession he argued strongly against board members receiving a pay increase even though analysis showed the NZRU board was recieving less remuneration than the boards of organisations of a similar size. He won that battle.

Douglas argues the tools he used to assist unions and unionists to confront and adapt to economic, financial and technological change can also be used to develop wealth creation in the New Zealand economy.

> All governments, no matter what colour, have always had the FOL or CTU phone number close by — and they used it when they were in trouble — they relied on us. Over many years, I observed a whole lot of businesses, and western world economies being sold a fallacy and that was the market was always 'self-cleansing'. I used to put it to Roger Douglas that if market forces were so positive for New Zealand why did they enjoy legal protection behind limited liability. He could not answer that one.[527]

What purist ideologues did not understand, he believed, was that when workers invest in their job or in their family, they are investing in their future lives. For many that is all they have. But in capitalist crises, the forces of capital absorb the forces of labour, a process that has accelerated in recent years with the demise of international socialism. The answer to retaining or returning to social equity lies somewhere else. A communist society, according to Marx, was in essence a governance structure run by the people as a whole within which classes disappeared and where relations among individuals were governed by integrity and mutual respect.

At every stage of history, Douglas says, political and economic pressures within societies have had to accommodate the aspirations of the people through democratic structures. If they did not have those structures they would not survive. 'I see every step that is being taken today being a compromise with the principles of market forces. It's retreating in the face of a requirement to be regulated and accountable to society.'

There is no dichotomy between these views and his work as a board member. 'I can relate it to my board work because it is an important part of that analysis; it's a sum total of those experiences. It's not about becoming communist or socialist next week; not specific features of change but the direction of change . . . it might take 100 years. There is going to be more and more a conscription of capital and the wealthy to meet those needs . . .' As with his union endeavours, Douglas finds much intellectual stimulation in this work. The debates are vigorous as the collective looks for solutions to problems. 'My perspective or stance is clear, although it's not a question of my fellow board members agreeing with me. The challenge is always to find a common solution. You sometimes form alliances, just as you do in trade union work. As part of this process you learn from other people's experiences and they grow out of yours . . . You invest your own values into the integrity of the process . . .'[528]

It does not always work for him, however, and there have been one or two times when he has thought that 'enough was enough'. He has encountered a handful of exploiters who were there mostly for the perks. But those few people have never been able to dominate boards. They are an aberration and don't last long. To change their behaviour to accommodate more altruistic mores is a very strong pressure.

Most board members are exercising their desire to achieve a 'public good', he says. 'Apart from Air New Zealand I have not been well paid commensurate with the level of responsibility and the time and energy invested. That was one reason I came off Air New Zealand in the end. Once the industrial relations mess was sorted I had nothing left to contribute . . .' He believes an organisation is only successful when it overcomes the contradictions of marrying capital, technology and labour. 'It's not an accommodation of one over another. We are all there for a shared purpose. Nothing is black and white.'[529]

Douglas believes that economic, social and political change does not come from violent revolution but from the social pressures of the population that press for such reforms. 'We've got a long way to go. I want to live in a society where my grandkids have aspirations and real chances for highly skilled, meaningful jobs that add value to the country's economy, and this comes from a merging of trade and investment . . . we need to import overseas skill like we did with the frigate-building programme. We inherited this technology from Germany and now we have a billion-dollar industry where all the profits remain with us.' He also foresees that Maori investment will be huge for this country. 'Unlike the forces of capital aided by sympathetic governments, Maori have not sold the family silver. Iwi throughout the country are holding it in trust for future generations. It is labour (and science) that creates value and wealth,' he contends, 'not capital which devours capital and wealth.'

Yet it is his trade union leadership for which Douglas will be best remembered. His retirement from the presidency of the Council of Trade Unions on 1 November 1999 marked more than a routine passing of the baton. It marked a critical phase in the evolution of New Zealand trade unionism. Unlike his predecessors, Douglas had to contend with a revolution, albeit bloodless, in which economic restructuring was paramount and radical changes denuded workplaces of thousands of employees, and their unions of much of their life force. There were ructions over the formation of the CTU and many FOL traditionalists resented the development, many of them going on to form a rival organisation with a very different, confrontational agenda. The king-hit which superseded all of these shocks, the Employment Contracts Act, sped up the process. As a consequence of all this, CTU membership more than halved under Douglas's trusteeship and its bargaining strength was greatly reduced.

Assessed on this agenda, many argued that Douglas was a failure. But that is short-sighted. The key factors at play here were outside his control — the reduction in numbers of unskilled and semi-skilled labour; the vanishing, either by merger or disappearance altogether, of the unions that represented them; a long-entrenched 'compulsion-dominated' industrial relations system that had become increasingly irrelevant in a new world of work, and the reintroduction of voluntary unionism after which many 'indifferent' unionists flew the coop.

In evolutionary terms, Douglas was the ideal man for the times — with the ability, perspicacity and thick skin needed to act as the conduit between the old-style 'factory floor' unionism of Skinner and Knox and the more complex requirements of his university-educated successors in a more sophisticated technology-based workplace and deregulated labour market. Despite his working-class roots and devotion to communism (or Marxist/Leninism, as he defined the ethos of the Socialist Unity Party's philosophy), Douglas was a quick and perceptive learner. He understood that for unionism to be effective in the new dawn it needed to reach beyond simply reacting, often negatively, to the bread-and-butter issues of wages and conditions. Rather, it had to be proactive, taking a more prominent and meaningful role in the country's economic and political life. He tried to encourage the evolution of trade unionism beyond the inherited British model — largely based on a confrontational class system of us (the workers) and them (the capitalists) — into a more consensual European or Japanese model, where unions and their leaders were involved more fully in capitalist and governmental decision-making processes.[530]

But the road was hard. There were outspoken union leaders and rank and file who resisted him, wanting to hark back to an era of state-directed compulsion and its concomitant industrial disruption ethos. With many blue-collar unions refusing to join the CTU after its formation in 1987, and others coming and going since — alongside the bitter debates that accompanied the passing of the Employment Contracts Act — Douglas presided over the deepest schism in the trade union movement since the 1951 waterfront lockout. In this context, one could argue that he stood alongside Fintan Patrick Walsh as the most divisive and controversial trade union leader that New Zealand has seen.

Yet there were deep differences. Walsh was aggressive, autocratic when it suited him, bent his ideology when it suited him, and ruled largely by fear, intimidation and violence. He also operated in a settled industrial world. In contrast, Douglas was caught up in an industrial revolution that was beyond his control. And alongside the massive impact that technology had on the world of work, he found himself caught in a deep chasm between the progressivists — who he championed — and the traditionalists whose adherents continued to view industrial relations through an ideological prism and who were bitter and angry, sidelined and disenfranchised.

There was a dynamism in trade union politics from the late 1980s, and particularly during the early 1990s, that the country had never before experienced. Change was both omnipresent and sometimes unexpected. On 25 May 1996, Douglas told the Labour Party Congress in Wellington that he found discussing industrial relations difficult because its reformation was so volatile; it was distinctly possible, he told his audience, which included party president Michael Hirschfeld and newly appointed leader Helen Clark, that his speech might 'become obsolete and irrelevant even as it was presented'.[531]

History seemed to validate his view. There was certainty in the past as to who union members were. They were overwhelmingly men. They were overwhelmingly working class. They were overwhelmingly tradesmen, labourers or processers of raw materials into manufactured goods. They worked full-time. For some, only overtime — at double time — made the grind worthwhile. Most lived in nuclear-family structures where fathers were the breadwinners and mothers the homemakers.

They played sport on Saturdays, often with and against each other, attended church on Sundays and went on holiday for short periods — usually at Christmas during their two-week annual leave and, befitting their 'modest' pay packets, not far from home in cabin or tent. They worked hard to buy a house and had a reasonable expectation that their children would be better educated and qualified than they were, opening up more choices for them in an expanded world of work. Life was predictable, expectations modest. For them, the election of the first Labour government in 1935 was a godsend. Unions expanded; a new Federation of Labour was formed. This government invested heavily in infrastructure as the economy grew. The lives of workers improved; the health system became affordable, and under Peter Fraser's direction education became egalitarian. Workers' children attended secondary school and university for the first time. Contiguously, many working people moved out of inner-city slums into low-rent state houses in outlying suburbs.

Through the 1940s, '50s and '60s, they and their families were proud to live in a decent society where unemployment was non-existent, inflation was low, real wages grew steadily and the welfare state was in full swing. Life became easier, too, when machines slowly replaced the toughest of the back-breaking and dangerous tasks of manual labour. Yet there was a downside. Through these decades industrial relations developed into a highly regulated pattern of vertical and horizontal relativities managed through a highly centralised wage-fixing system. Essentially wages were raised in response to increases in national productivity. It could only work because the country had a ready and reliable market for its primary produce where the terms of trade were favourable. New Zealand and New Zealanders were shaken out of this somnolence during the early 1970s in the wake of the oil shocks and Great Britain 'abandoning us' by joining the European Economic Community. Henceforth the country fought hard to find alternative markets for its primary produce. On top of this, workers faced mushrooming inflation, high prices, Robert Muldoon's wage freezes and a raft of anti-union legislation.

But this was a mere aperitif. The deregulatory economic transformations from 1984 were even more dramatic. Accompanied by deepening recession and continuing high inflation into the early 1990s, companies rationalised, merged, fell away or were taken over by foreign conglomerates — nearly all of the country's trading banks, for example, soon had Australian owners. Successive Labour and National governments sold assets they claimed were underperforming to the private sector. Once again profits flowed overseas to new owners and stockholders. In contrast, hundreds of community assets — schools, hospitals, Post Offices and railway lines — were downsized or shut down altogether. Workers lost their jobs. Some manufacturers took their factories overseas where labour was cheap, leaving even more local workers lingering in dole queues. Conjointly, the technological impact quickened pace. In the wash, many were cast adrift in the wake of the introduction of new plant, machine and computerised systems.

Then came the legislation which destroyed the long-held state-employer-worker nexus. From 1991 on, the first two called the shots. In the crucial areas of wage and condition negotiations unions were hung out to dry. When voluntarism replaced compulsion thousands of workers left their unions, either because they had been uninterested in the first place or because a recession and their displacement by technology put many of them out of work — or because the Employment Contracts Act was simply too hard to fight. A new union constituency of middle-class, white-collar workers whose numbers remained stable become more prominent. Some, such as nurses, struggled but blue-collar workers struggled even more. Jobs continued to disappear. 'Redundancy' and 'retraining' became new buzz words, though often neither was available. Many workers fled to Australia, where there was more sustained economic growth, and as a consequence more work and higher wages, and where unions had not been hung out to dry by successive governments.

Locally, working people were bewildered by the speed and extent of the changes. The introduction of technology and new practices such as 'contracting out' was radically changing the world of work and they observed with mounting anger the restructuring of capital as more and more profit disappeared into secretive, expanding corporates or overseas-owned multinationals. More than at any time since 1935, they felt disenfranchised. They were not part of the change, which was crude and brutal, flouting workers' expectations that had been built up over decades. A decent society, they thought, was decent because it invested in its people. The 1990s National government did anything but.

Contiguously, throughout the late 1980s and the 1990s, the rich got richer and the poor got poorer. Economics professor Srikanta Chatterjee of Massey University interpreted a 1998 study of the Household Economic Survey to show that between 1984 and 1996 the top 10 per cent of New Zealanders increased their total share of income at the expense of the rest of the country. The bottom 40 per cent showed a fall in their spending power of more than 3 per cent; for the bottom 10 per cent of income earners the decrease was a staggering 8.7 per cent. In 1999, fellow economist Paul Dalziel of Canterbury University showed statistically that between 1984 and 1999 New Zealand experienced lower relative economic growth in comparison with Australia, where there was far less deregulation, less poverty and less unemployment overall.[532]

The trade union movement had a new mission, but there was no going back to the old ways, which were irrelevant and counter-productive. 'We have to resist a false reconstruction of a better yesterday,' Douglas had told the 1996 Congress.

> We need to protect choice and make space for different forms of engagement at work, but resist that becoming a licence to exploit. We need to rebuild a confidence that economic growth will be shared between those who contribute to it. We need to leave each generation with the expectation that their lot will be a little better than that of the one before. The new 'decent society' cannot be constructed by reliance on rugged individualism, speculation, victim bashing or the lure of political popularism and opportunism. It can be achieved only by a collectivist society that gives equal weight to rights and obligations.[533]

Yet if there was an upside to the Employment Contracts Act it was that union networks tightened, internal conflicts fell away, factionalism disappeared and cooperation intensified in the struggle to combat a single issue on which all workers could focus their anxieties.

Douglas had long seen pitfalls in compulsory unionism. While it gave the movement numbers, this did not necessarily translate into strength because many members were reluctant to belong. When unionism became voluntary the sad truth was that many workers pulled out of the movement, seeing — selfishly in many cases — no benefit to them of an affiliation fee. Douglas viewed voluntarism as liberating, forcing unions not to rely, lazily, on a hitherto ready-made constituency but to seek a new, more proactive role. To this end he was frustrated when unions and their leaders continued to pursue parochial paths and refused to amalgamate for more grunt and efficiency. Douglas was not a militant. Even when the heat was intense he was more often responsible for stopping strikes than starting them. By instinct a democrat, he could argue or cajole but he never enforced 'by decree' as had been Fintan Walsh's modus operandi in different times — a hat that also fitted his successor Tom Skinner, whose Sunday chats with Robert Muldoon to 'sort out' the country's industrial troubles have became the source of legend. Despite the Federation of Labour and its constituents acquiescing in this behaviour, viewed today such autocratic conduct would be regarded as both contemptible and farcical.

Not all reflections on Ken Douglas have been positive. Roger Kerr, chief executive of the Business Roundtable, holds that Douglas was responsible for tens of thousands of workers losing their jobs for failing to adapt to the new freedoms in the labour market from the 1980s. Relying on his own idiosyncratic version of history, Kerr criticises Douglas for constantly arguing for compulsory unionism, compulsory arbitration and national awards. 'I hold Ken responsible for holding up market deregulation in the 1980s which stopped workers from finding jobs,' he said in 2005. 'To this day he does not understand how the market economy works given his role in the Socialist Unity Party and trade union movement. I've never heard him say sorry for promoting those ideas!'[534]

There have been more serious criticisms. Some women have complained that he is misogynistic and that his commitment to women's aspirations in the union movement was lukewarm at best. Therese O'Connell was a feminist pioneer in trade unionism who was prominent in the Clerical Workers' Union, vice-president of the Wellington Trades Council and responsible for establishing, principally with Sonja Davies, an FOL Women's Sub-Committee and later the CTU Women's Committee.

Coming within Douglas's orbit between 1975 and 1990, O'Connell acknowledges his intelligent, even 'inspirational' leadership, but she found him, like most men in the male-dominated movement at the time, paternalistic and patronising. Women were expected to be part of an auxiliary operating under the leadership of men. She believed the real power, particularly in the earlier years, was in the hands of the trusted comrades stitching up deals in the backrooms and that democracy was not transparent.[535]

O'Connell, a socialist, although not a card-carrying one, felt Douglas's wrath most noticeably when, after many years, women engineered a successful remit on the floor of the FOL conference that the convener of the Women's Committee automatically become a member of the national executive. O'Connell felt she needed to attend the executive's first meeting after the conference — without invitation, but as a right decreed by the organisation's national council. 'As I walked up those steps of the FOL building in Lukes Lane with the giant mural of the male worker's pumped-up arm my heart was nearly banging out of my body . . . but I felt I was accompanied by the spirits of many women who had previously been denied a voice by the structures and politics of the trade union movement.'[536]

She greeted Jim Knox and entered the room. When Douglas came in and saw her seated there he called her out to his office where he vented his anger upon her. 'I knew how Ken operated — he would not want me to attend an executive meeting without him talking about it with his lieutenants to discuss how to deal with the situation . . . he yelled and bullied me — I was pretty incoherent with nerves and anger myself but stuck to my viewpoint and returned to the meeting to be once again welcomed by Jim Knox. I spent most of that meeting struggling to calm down.'

Today O'Connell is pleased about the small part she played in making the FOL and the CTU more relevant for women workers. 'From 20 years distant I can be more tolerant and understanding of the context from which we were all working . . .' she says. She accepts that in the context of the time many men from traditional backgrounds had difficulty coping with the feminist movement of the early 1970s, and Douglas was reflecting attitudes common to his generation.[537]

Among politicians, Douglas most loved to engage intellectually with his namesake Roger Douglas. Part of the attraction was the politician's immovability. Ken, who sometimes lampooned his 'illegitimate half-brother', says he was like an Old Testament prophet thundering on about eternal damnation unless you followed him. Roger met his match in jousts with Ken. The arguments were always emotive. During one conversation in the late 1980s Roger told him, 'Ken, you don't understand but the economy is like a rubber ball. If you hold it out and let it fall on the floor its speed of bounce is determined by the law of gravity. If you take the ball again and smash it down with great force the height of the bounce will be even greater . . .' He was indicating that a radical change to the economy would result in higher production. Ken replied that that was his assumption. 'What if,' he asked, 'the economy is a handful of shit and when you drop the ball all it will do is splash over your shoes and trousers?' Roger looked at him in disbelief. Ken surmised that Roger was really hurt that he had responded like this. 'Roger had one simple belief and he could not countenance any alternative.'[538]

Douglas is not one to dwell on the past, yet it is remarkable where his life has taken him. It could all have been very different. Had he been raised in a middle-class milieu where there was more money, opportunity and choice he might have had a successful career in business or politics, or even in academia. At school he had wanted to become an army officer. There were two main reasons for his early failure. The first was that there was no culture of book learning in the Northland Road home of his grandmother. Further, creative, lateral thinkers like Douglas were not well served by the education system of the day, where instruction was teacher dominated and learning was often by rote, its sole purpose to be regurgitated at examination time.

Evidence of Douglas's leadership qualities during his adolescence and soon after was expressed in very different ways, sometimes violently. Marxism came to him later in many forms — discussion on the wharf; involvement in the 1959 'No Maoris — No Tour' protests, and meeting thinkers Chip Bailey (most importantly), George Goddard and George Jackson among others. These experiences gave him the hook on which to hang and consolidate his humanist but disparate thoughts. The philosophy captured the void and its deeper understanding of class gave him the sustenance to succeed in his union career. Only the 1991 fall of the Soviet Union shook his feelings of invulnerability. Nonetheless, sometimes his unschooled intellect took him to places where other people could not go. Sometimes, as Peter Harris recorded, he came up with flashes of sheer genius. 'Equally he could be completely off the planet. The challenge was how to bring him back ...'[539]

Douglas has never forsaken his union roots. Sometimes friends, or friends of friends, usually workers, seek his counsel over an industrial problem they are having with their employer. He willingly dispenses advice gratis. Less frequently, he has been brought in as a mediator in in-house union disputes or to give advice to different parties on union matters. Even more occasionally, he has been called in by the International Labour Organisation to assess and give advice and help to overseas trade union groups or national organisations. In September 2005, for instance, he travelled to Mongolia for a week to assess the impact of free-market deregulation of the Mongolian economy. He was unhappy with what he saw: many skilled workers had been lost to China and Korea, education standards had dropped because the system lacked controls, many people were being forced out of their apartments and back living hand to mouth in traditional tents in the country. He also observed high unemployment and a corrupt bureaucracy. On top of this, many of Mongolia's people were nomadic and depended on their livestock, but a recent outbreak of foot and mouth disease had cost them many cattle herds. Douglas suggested unionists help farmers fight for compensation and then look at ways of improving the livestock industry. For example, he said, instead of sending unprocessed cattle hides to China, establishing a processing industry in Mongolia would add a lot of value.[540]

There are many Ken Douglases. There is Douglas the school failure turned intellectual who became widely read and able to expound on a wide range of political philosophies. There is Douglas the diehard Marxist, leader of the small Socialist Unity Party, who witnessed the collapse of Soviet-style communism with deep sadness. There is the Douglas who some party members believed was the centre of a 'cult of personality' in Wellington — like Bill Andersen in Auckland. There's Douglas the respected community man, the 'Bay' boy involved as a player, coach and administrator in local rugby, softball, golf and surf life-saving clubs and later as a councillor on the Porirua City Council. There's Douglas the well-travelled internationalist, a respected voice at world union forums. There is Douglas the humanitarian who successfully took his skills to a new stage after his union career had reached its conclusion.[541]

More fundamentally, there is Douglas the ordinary bloke, who despite his high office never succumbed to the trappings of power, only in latter years trading his unkempt hair and V-necked jersey — always one size too small as he grew bigger — for a tidier hairdo and more stylish windbreaker. There is the Douglas who often had no concept of time; his continual unpunctuality at meetings — particularly in his union days — causing embarrassment to colleagues and annoyance to those he was meeting. There is Douglas the husband, who sometimes abused that commitment by indulging in extra-marital affairs. There is the Douglas who encouraged young unionists when they needed it, or growled when he felt they deserved it. There is the Douglas whose diligence and energy was legendary, working day and night, relying on little sleep and expecting his closest colleagues to do the same. There is the Douglas who called a spade a spade, did not suffer fools easily, had a relatively short fuse in negotiations and would sometimes snap, stand up, bang the table, abuse and sometimes tussle with opponents — although he never held a grudge and was never dictatorial, despite an expectation from some that he needed to be.

There is the Douglas who always left the negotiation table stronger not weaker — often by working hard at understanding his opponents' views and exploiting them to his advantage. There is Douglas the humorist, who laughs a lot, often in self-deprecatory fashion. Hidden from public view, there is Douglas the man of sentiment who wept as he watched the television series *The Waltons* and later more close-to-home features such as the film *Brassed Off*, about a union brass band in a dying colliery town — his joy in 'happy ever after' endings a reaction to the dysfunctional nature of his upbringing.

Then there is the charismatic, passionate, inspiring, challenging, gregarious, stimulating, sometimes intolerant Douglas who really broke the mould of grey-suited, grey-faced old men in the union movement — the man who, as Rob Campbell recalled, encouraged energetic left-wingers into the unions and became like a father to many of them. The penultimate paragraph of Douglas's 1999 Doctor of Laws citation reflected the sentiments of many New Zealanders who understood his foresight and accomplishments as a union leader, acknowledging the way he had broadened of the area trade union engagement, and made the unions significant players during difficult and contentious times: 'In personal terms, in trade unionism Douglas has moved from being a powerful partisan to a widely respected national and international leader.' Truly, a man for all seasons.[542]

Bibliography

PRIMARY SOURCES

Wellington Drivers' Union. Minute Books, 1951-1978, Wellington Central Amalgamated Union of Workers Archives, Wellington.

Wellington Drivers' Union. Assorted Scrapbooks and Correspondence, Wellington 1955-1981, Wellington Central Amalgamated Union of Workers Archives, Wellington.

Douglas, Kenneth George. MS Groups 1619. Alexander Turnbull Library, Wellington.

Jackson, George. MS Group 90-234. Alexander Turnbull Library, Wellington.

Mitchell, John James. MS Group 0461. Alexander Turnbull Library, Wellington.

New Zealand Federation of Labour Records 1960-1989. MS Group 0049. Alexander Turnbull Library, Wellington.

New Zealand Combined State Union Records. MS Group 1417. Alexander Turnbull Library, Wellington.

New Zealand Council of Trade Union Records. MS Groups 96-270; 98-327; 2003-361; 2008-119; 2008-184; 2008-245. Alexander Turnbull Library, Wellington.

Roth, Bert. New Zealand Federation of Labour, Records and Research Notes. MS Group 94. Alexander Turnbull Library, Wellington.

Roth, Bert. New Zealand Council of Trade Unions, Records and Research Notes. MS Group 94. Alexander Turnbull Library, Wellington.

Socialist Unity Party Records. MS Group 91. Alexander Turnbull Library, Wellington.

SECONDARY SOURCES

ARTICLES

Ken Douglas, 'Valuable Lessons for the Workers,' 'Socialist Politics,' No 1/85, reprinted in *World Trade Union Movement*, Journal of the World Federation of Trade Unions, No 10/85, pp. 30-33.

BOOKS

Andersen, G H., *The Job Delegate*, Old Mole Publications, Auckland 1972.

Beasley, A. W., *The Light Accepted: 125 Years of Wellington College*, Board of Trustees of Wellington College, Wellington, 1992.

Bolger, Jim, Bolger: *A View From The Top. My Seven Years as Prime Minister*, Viking, Auckland, 1998.

Calder, Mick and Tyson, Janet, *Meat Acts: The New Zealand Meat Industry 1972-1997*, Fraser Books, Masterton, 1999.

Campbell, Rob, *The Only Weapon, The History of the Wellington Drivers' Union*, Wellington Drivers' Union, Wellington 1976.

Campbell, Rob, Kirk Alf, *After the Freeze*, Wellington, 1983.

Clark, Margaret (ed.) *The Bolger Years*, Wellington 2008.

Douglas, Roger and Callan, Louise, *Toward Prosperity: People and Politics in the 1980s. A Personal View*, David Bateman, Auckland 1987.

Easton, Brian (ed), *The Making of Rogernomics*, Auckland 1989.

Grant, David, *Drivers, Divots and Dongas: The Story of Titahi Golf Club 1958-2008*, Wellington 2008.

—— (ed.), *The Big Blue: Snapshots of the 1951 Waterfront Lockout*, Canterbury University Press, Christchurch, 2004.

Evans, Gerry, *Where Giants Dwell: A Sailor's Tale*, David Ling Publishing, Auckland, 1999.

Fordyce, Linda and Maclean, Kirsten, *The Bay:A History of Community in Titahi Bay*, Titahi Bay, 2000.

Harbridge, Raymond (ed.), *Employment Contracts: New Zealand Experiences*, Victoria University Press, Wellington, 1993.

Hayward, Dai, *Follow Up: Wellington College Old Boys' Rugby Football Club, 1898-1998*, W.C.O.R.F.C. Centennial Committee, Wellington, 1998.

Heron H. A., *The Centennial History of Wellington College*, Wellington College Centennial Committee, Wellington, 1967.

Johansson, Jan, *The Politics of Possibility: Leadership in Changing Times*, Wellington, 2009.

Kelsey, Jane, *The New Zealand Experiment*, Auckland University Press, Auckland 1995.

Moore, Mike (ed.), *New Zealand. A Nation That Can Work Again: Proceedings of the Waipuna Seminar*, MMSC Ltd, Wellington, 1993.

Phillips, Jock (ed.) *Biography in New Zealand*, Wellington 1985.

Roth, H., *Trade Unions in New Zealand:Past and Present*, Wellington 1973.

Russell, Marcia, *Revolution: New Zealand From Fortress to Free Market*, Auckland 1996.

Smith, Ron, *Working Class Son: My Fight Against Capitalism and War*, Wellington 1994.

Skinner, Tom, (with John Berry), *Man to Man*, Christchurch 1980.

Smith, Vivienne, *Reining in the Dinosaur: The Story of the Remarkable Turnaround of New Zealand Post*, Wellington 1997.

Stannard, L; Wickens A S , *Northland School, Wellington: The First Fifty Years*, Wellington 1954.

Thomson, Allan, (comp.) *What I Believe: The Personal Philosophies of Twenty-Two New Zealanders*, Wellington, 1993.

Urlich, John, *Journey Towards World Peace: A History of the New Zealand Peace Council*, Wellington, 1998.

Walsh, Pat (ed), *Trade Unions, Work and Society: The Centenary of the Arbitration System*, Palmerston North 1994.

Williams, Alan; Owen, Bruce, Emerson, Alan., *The Nissan Way*, Auckland 1991.

Wilson, A. C., *New Zealand and the Soviet Union 1950-1991: A Brittle Relationship*, Wellington, 2004.

Wilson, Margaret, *Labour in Government 1984-1987*, Allen and Unwin, Port Nicholson Press, Wellington 1989.

Woods, Noel, *Industrial Conciliation and Industrial Arbitration in New Zealand*, Wellington 1963.

—, (ed.) *Labour and Industrial Relations in New Zealand*, Wellington 1974.

THESES AND LONG ESSAYS

Oomen, Monique, 'The Socialist Unity Party of New Zealand: A Study of the Incentives, Ideology and Organisation of a Small Communist Party', MA Thesis, Department of Political Science, University of Canterbury, 1981.

McConnell. N, 'Why the Employment Contracts Act?' BA (Hons) Dissertation, Department of Political Studies, University of Otago, 1991.

Wilson, Andrew M., 'The New Zealand Council of Trade Unions:Formation, Role and Structure', BA (Hons) Dissertation, Department of Political Studies, University of Otago, 1991.

NEWSPAPERS AND MAGAZINES

Auckland Star

Dominion

Dominion Post

Evening Post

Management

New Zealand Herald

New Zealand Listener

People's Voice (Organ of the New Zealand Communist Party.)

Press

Tribune (Organ of the Socialist Unity Party)

Workers' Voice (Organ of the New Zealand Communist Party)

INTERVIEWS, PERSONAL CORRESPONDENCE AND THE PROVISION OF ARCHIVAL MATERIAL

John Allen
Kathleen Angel
Terree Barrymore
Matthew Beattie
Roger Blakeley
Peter Bromhead
Bob Brockie
Philip Burdon
Ron Burgess
Douglas Catley
Hannah Douglas
Helen Douglas
Ken Douglas
Jane Douglas
John Douglas
Peter Douglas
Gerald Dowthwaite
Kieran Elvy
Brian Fitzwater
Richie Gillespie
Peter Harris
Eric Heath
Jock Hobbs
June Hoskin
Jim Hubbard
Rosanne Meo
Grant Morgan
John McCormick
John Miller
Paddianne Neely
Therese O'Connell
Monique Oomen
John Palmer
Dean Parker
Len Parker
Susan Richards
Gladys Robson
Tom Scott
Steve Tew
Alan Thomas
Paul Tolich
Marilyn Tucker
Betty Walton
Ross Wilson

Abbreviations

AFL-CIO	American Federation of Labour-Congress of Industrial Organisations
APEC	Asia-Pacific Economic Co-operation
APLN	Asia-Pacific Labour Network
ATL	Alexander Turnbull Library.
AWUNZ	Amalgamated Workers Union of New Zealand
BERL	Business and Economic Research Limited
CEWU	Communication and Energy Workers Union
CSSO	Combined State Services Association
CSU	Combined State Unions
CTU	Council of Trade Unions
ECA	Employment Contracts Act
EPMU	Engineering, Printing and Manufacturing Union.
FOL	Federation of Labour
GATT	General Agreement on Tariffs and Trade
ICTFU	International Confederation of Free Trade Unions
ICTFU-APRO	International Confederation of Free Trade Unions-Asia Pacific Regional Organisation
ICTUR	International Centre for Trade Union Rights
ILO	International Labour Organisation
NGO	Non-Government Organisation
NZCP	New Zealand Communist Party
NZCT	New Zealand Council of Trade Unions
NZEI	New Zealand Educational Institute
NZFOL	New Zealand Federation of Labour
NZPD	New Zealand Parliamentary Debates
OECD	Organisation for Economic Co-operation and Development
PPC	Porirua City Council
PPTA	Post Primary Teachers Association
PSA	Public Service Association
SPOCTU	South Pacific and Oceanic Council of Trade Unions
SUP	Socialist Unity Party
TUEA	Trade Union Education Authority
TUF	Trade Union Federation
WCOB	Wellington College Old Boys
WDU	Wellington Drivers Union
WFTU	World Federation of Trade Unions
WTO	World Trade Organisation

Endnotes

INTRODUCTION

1. Through 2005 and early 2006, as its historical consultant, I worked closely with director Monique Oomen on the documentary *Ken Douglas — Traitor or Visionary?* which was shown on TV3 on 17 June 2006 (Topshelf Productions). My access to the voluminous unedited drafts of the interviewees' contributions to the documentary proved to be of immense value in this project.
2. Hazel Armstrong to Dr Warren Tucker, 27 November 2007; 23 July 2009; Tucker to Armstrong, 18 March 2008 (in possession of Ken Douglas). The first refusal to release information was in January 2005.
3. Tucker to Armstrong, 18 March 2008, op. cit.; 23 July 2009. Notes of meeting between Douglas, Armstrong, Tucker, Chris Rutledge and Alex (surname not disclosed for security reasons), 12 March 2010. In possession of Ken Douglas.

CHAPTER 1

4. Ken's grandmother was universally known to her sons as Carrie — an abbreviated version of Caroline, her birth name — or 'Jo'. The origin of Jo is obscure, although her granddaughter Terree Barrymore believes it might have come from the heroine of Louisa May Alcott's novel *Little Women* which was widely read during Carrie's youth.
5. Interview, Gwladys Robson, 29 March 2005.
6. Brian Fitzwater to author, 15 March 2005.
7. In my earlier publication, *On A Roll: A History of Gambling and Lotteries in New Zealand*, Wellington, 1993, I discuss the nature and spread of working-class gambling in this country. It was prolific, and often associated with the drinking of alcohol as an antidote to grim working lives.
8. Colin Browne to Ken Douglas, 10 July 1991; interview, Gwladys Robson, 29 March 2005.
9. Emma Dowthwaite was 72 when she died.

10. Fitzwater correspondence, 15 March 2005.
11. Another of Henry's habits was to purchase a favourite food — smoked herrings — which he would wrap up in his kerchief to take home. There they would sit, forgotten sometimes, until the smell gave them away, at which time Pop Douglas would remove them and dispatch them to the rubbish tin (interview, Ken Douglas, 10 March 2005). What happened to the Newtown house is not known (interview, Gwladys Robson, 29 March 2005; Browne to Douglas, 10 July 1991).
12. Kippenberger Military Archive and Research Library, Army Museum, Waiouru, and Commonwealth War Graves Commission website, www.cwgc.org.
13. Fitzwater correspondence, op. cit.
14. Brian Fitzwater correspondence, 25 May 2005. Ken's sister Terree Barrymore remembers Matthew constantly sniffing Boracure, a substance which removed the borer beetle from wood products.
15. One of Hilda and Walter's four children, Colin, was an acclaimed opera singer, winning many local contests before being successful in the Dominion Grand Opera contest in Wellington in 1935. This won him entry into the acclaimed Melbourne Sun Aria contest in 1936, where he was highly commended. He was 87 when he died in 1997. The Brownes were sometimes known as the Franklin-Brownes. The two varieties of surname seem to have been used interchangeably among the various family members (interview Gwladys Robson, 29 March 2005; Brian Fitzwater, correspondence, 22 May 2005).
16. Lillian and Ted's son James (Jim) lived for a period with his grandmother in Northland Rd, as well as being passed around among the other sisters to be raised. He married Stella and they had three children, Robyn, Lance and Edward. Robyn, who had cerebral palsy, became the star performer in Terree's family ballet 'productions' at Northland Rd. For years Lillian's house furniture was stored under the Douglas family home in Northland Rd, and it formed a great 'play' area for Terree and her cousin June Hoskin. Jim worked for Woolworths for 40 years, much of the time as manager of the produce department. He died in 1992. (Information on Ted Favell's war service gleaned from Kippenberger Military Archive, op. cit; Brian Fitzwater, correspondence, 22 April, 10 May 2005.)
17. Brian F O'Brien, *Kiwis With Gloves On: A History and Record Book of New Zealand Boxing*, Wellington, 1960, p. 201.
18. Terree Barrymore described Mary Dowthwaite as 'a woman locked inside a

woman' (interview, 29 May 2005).

19. Bert Dowthwaite's war service gleaned from Kippenberger Military Archive, op. cit.; see also W Wynne Mason, *Prisoners of War: Official History of New Zealand in the Second World War 1939–45*, Oxford University Press, London, 1954.

20. June Hoskin correspondence, 26 March 2005; Brian Fitzwater correspondence, op. cit; Gwladys Robson interview, op. cit; Gerald Dowthwaite, correspondence, 15 May 2005. It is possible that Bert Dowthwaite's post-war behaviour was an indication that he was suffering from post-traumatic stress disorder following his difficult wartime experiences. See Alison Parr, *Silent Casualties: New Zealand's Unspoken Legacy of the Second World War*, Auckland, 1995.

21. The Douglas family in Sydney established one of that city's first transport firms.

22. The Wireless Hill cottage still stands at the entrance to the reserve at the top of Orangi Kaupapa Rd.

23. The information on the front room as a 'garage' comes from Gary Fitzwater, whose father Keith also drove for Munt Cottrell.

24. June Hoskin correspondence, op. cit.

25. Interview, Terree Barrymore, 27 May 2005.

26. Interview Terree Barrymore, op. cit. While he was no scholar, George was well-read and had an affinity for mathematics. On arriving home from work he would demand of the child Ken what was '68 times 68'? When the answer was not forthcoming immediately he would berate Ken, albeit with a twinkle in his eye, 'Too bloody slow boy, too bloody slow!' By the time Ken, whose mathematical ability did not match that of his grandfather, had finally memorised the answer to 68 times 68, George arrived home and demanded of him what 72 times 72 was. 'He had a sixth sense at being able to catch me out,' Ken remembered (interview, 10 March 2005).

27. There is a rumour that George's mother came over from Sydney to help finance the property, but this has not been substantiated.

28. Gwladys also remembers her aunt as 'enormously generous', recalling one time when Carrie took her and her sister Kathy to the De Luxe Cinema to see Maurice Chevalier — her favourite actor — in a performance and then shouted them dinner at the Ritz afterwards.

29. Terree Barrymore, interview, 27 May 2005.

30. Ibid.

31. Kevin become an architect but he also died young, of a heart attack, in 1984; he

was just 43.

32. In the homophobic atmosphere of this time it was common for gay men to have girlfriends and marry. Terree Barrymore also 'did business' with her uncle Laurie, cleaning his shoes for 1/6d a week and also stitching up his coal sacks (Barrymore to author, op. cit). Laurie Douglas's unusual use of his bowls' case was the clear recollection of his cousin Maurice Fitzwater (Brian Fitzwater correspondence, 10 May 2005).

33. Betty described her years in the orphanage as happy ones: 'The matron was my special friend. She would often take me into her lounge and tell me wonderful stories.' Her son Earland was an Rh baby, being one of the first in Wellington Hospital to have blood transfusions to save his life (interview, Betty Walton, 13 August 2005).

34. Interview, Betty Walton, op. cit. Carrie even made Betty's wedding dress.

35. Terree Barrymore to author, 27 May 2005.

36. Earland's death probably could have been avoided. At the first-available stop he had staggered off the bus and lurched to the front door of the nearest house where he pleaded with the occupant to call an ambulance. Thinking the young man was drunk, the occupant shut the door in his face. Earland stumbled and fell into the gutter where he died, and when an ambulance did arrive it was too late to save him. After Earland's death, his widow remarried and took their daughter Donna, then aged three, to a different city. Betty never saw her granddaughter again. Earlier, Bryce and Betty had adopted a Maori boy, David, who had only been with them for a few months when Bryce died. So that he would not be returned to Social Welfare, Betty, Attie and Laurie looked after him in the house before he was passed on to Hannah and Lyndsay in Mangakino who officially adopted him. It was not a success; there were unresolved cultural difficulties in the adoption and David became an unrepentant alcoholic as an adult, dying at 40.

37. As a child, Eleanor Malligan's father Edward had migrated to Australia from Limerick in Ireland, becoming a seven-year-old orphan with his brother and sister after his parents both died when a plague swept the ship they were travelling on. A staunch Catholic, Edward worked as a farm labourer and then farmer at Wangaratta, dying at the age of 87. He was survived by his wife, the former Elizabeth Milne, and their six sons and five daughters, the third of whom was Eleanor, Mrs George Farrow. The spelling of Eleanor's name varies widely, and I have seen it spelt Elenor, Ellenor, Ellinor and Ellinora. I have used Eleanor as that is the name as it appears on Madge's

death certificate.

38. *On A Roll: A History of Gambling and Lotteries in New Zealand* includes an extended description of Chinese gambling in Haining Street, pp. 38, 72, 108, 144 and 247.

39. Interview, Ken Douglas, 15 November 2005. Terry Farrow anecdote gleaned from an interview undertaken for the Porirua Licensing Charitable Trust Oral History Project on 14 December 1997, stored in the Oral History Centre of the Alexander Turnbull Library, OH Coll-0961. George Farrow got on particularly well with Carrie Douglas, and accompanied her to Terree Barrymore's wedding in 1959. 'Those two should have been partners,' Terree commented in May 2005.

40. Lillian and Frank's son John trained as an accountant and spent 40 years working for the Wellington Harbour Board. Their daughter Lesley, born in 1934, married Norman Elvy at 19 and raised six children. Among all the cousins, Lesley was the closest to Ken Douglas, sharing a keen interest in politics and sport. She was also a family historian. Lesley died suddenly when she suffered an aneurysm on the concourse of the Westpac Stadium on 15 October 2004 (interview with her daughter Kieran Elvy, 4 June 2005). Frank had been a corporal in the New Zealand Army, guarding Japanese prisoners-of-war in the camp near Featherston during the Second World War.

41. Terree Barrymore recalls George Farrow handing over a bag containing his dirty washing to Mavis West and receiving a second bag with his clean washing in return (interview, op. cit.).

42. Ken Douglas had no idea of Susan Richards' existence until a documentary on his life was shown on television in 2006 and she contacted him in some excitement. Both Terree Barrymore and Kieran Elvy, Nell's daughter, confirm the validity of the story that Madge had two further illegitimate children. Terree believes it might even have been three (interviews 27 May, 8 June 2005).

43. Attie Douglas's war service gleaned from his Service Personnel File in the New Zealand Defence Force Archive and the Kippenberger Military Archive, op. cit. See also Laurie Brocklebank, Jayforce: *New Zealand and the Military Occupation of Japan 1945–48*, Oxford University Press, Auckland, 1997.

44. Interview, Ken Douglas, 10 March 2005.

45. Terree recalled that the falling men did everything in their power to avoid breaking the bottles they were holding, or which were in their pockets (interview, 28 May 2005).

46. Part of Madge's rehabilitation, as Ken recalled, was for there always to be alcohol in the house for her to 'resist' touching. The problem was greater when there was none around, tempting her to return to the pub.
47. Terree Barrymore interview, 28 May 2005.
48. Interview, Jackie and Alan Thomas, 25 June 2005.
49. Ken Douglas interview, 10 March 2005. When Terree was a child she enjoyed going out with her father on Sunday afternoons, often visiting relatives or friends. She was made to wear her Sunday best — new dress, kid gloves, patent leather shoes and smart hat — for these visits (interview, 27 May 2005).

CHAPTER 2

50. Interview, Betty Walton, 13 August 2005. HF Gabites was the principal of Northland Primary School when Ken arrived. He was replaced in 1942 by N Gilchrist, and CF Rockel followed in 1943. He lasted just a year and was replaced by EG Thomas who stayed until 1951 (L Stannard & AS Wickens [eds], *Northland School, Wellington: The First Fifty Years*, Wellington, 1954, p. 24).
51. Interview, Walton, op. cit.; Hoskin correspondence, 25 March 2005.
52. McLeod was secretary of the Wellington branch of the New Zealand Federated Seamen's Union from 1948 until 1962, and a close confidant of Fintan Patrick Walsh until they fell out towards the end of their careers.
53. Bob Goslin was featherweight boxing champion of New Zealand in 1946 and 1947 (O'Brien, op. cit., p. 258).
54. The Silvers later purchased Peter Fraser's house in Harbour View Road from the government.
55. The Northland Community Centre, next to St Anne's church, was built in the 1940s. The Douglas family was fully involved, with Attie, Bryce and Laurie all using their trucks to cart timber for the construction and for the collection of bottles which helped fund the project. Ken recalls one particular home — 43 Garden Road — where a whole truckload of bottles was sacked, lugged down from the basement of the house to the truck, to be deposited at ABC Bottlers in Lorne Street.
56. The following year Hogben fell out with his Board of Governors and hurriedly resigned. He was succeeded by HA Heron.

57. The information for this and the succeeding three paragraphs is gleaned from lists of classes and student progress accessed at the archives of Wellington College. The author acknowledges the generosity of the college archivist, Paddianne Neely, in providing access to this information and more pertaining to Ken Douglas's time at the school.
58. Hannah Douglas interview.
59. John McCormick correspondence, 14 May 2005. McCormick was a champion boxer at the college and in 1952 won the Hales Prizes for Sport and Sportsmanship.
60. HA Heron, *The Centennial History of Wellington College 1867–1967*, Wellington, 1967, p. 132.
61. Interview, 26 March 2005. The 'Callie' was the Caledonian Hotel, situated adjacent to the Basin Reserve.
62. The team's biggest wins were 15-0 and 13-0 against University and Karori respectively (*The Wellingtonian: The Magazine of Wellington College New Zealand*, Vol. 62, 1952, p. 42).
63. Sam Perry to author, 18 June 2005. Perry is now a Wellington lawyer.
64. At this time a young Ron Trotter was a salesman at Wright Stephensons. Their paths crossed, and Douglas recalled their conversation as friendly.
65. New Zealand Army, Statement of Service, Douglas, Kenneth George, Service No 712862, September 1954–March 1965. In the possession of Ken Douglas.
66. Information relating to Ted Thompson is from 'On the Wharf After '51' in *The Big Blue*, David Grant (ed.), Christchurch, 2004, p. 132. Bell, a former policeman, had been a member of the force that shot and killed the unarmed high chief, Tupua Tamasese Lealofi III, as he called for peace during a Mau independence protest march in Apia, Samoa, on 28 December 1929. Former Wellington seaman and wharfie Tom Gregory recalled that the diminishing numbers of post-lockout 'new union' men became known as the 'Ngaio' gangs and worked solely on Anchor Company coasters (Gregory to Rod Prosser, 13 November 2003, Maritime Union of New Zealand Archives).
67. Murphy was one of New Zealand's most successful boxers. He was New Zealand professional welterweight champion for a number of years and British Empire middleweight champion in 1948. Between 1944 and 1951, he fought 51 fights at home and abroad for 30 wins, 19 losses, 1 draw and 1 no contest (O'Brien, op. cit., pp. 221–3).
68. Interview, 26 March 2005. The information on the *Hororata* comes from IG

Stewart, *The Ships That Serve New Zealand*, Wellington, 1964, pp. 31, 128–9.
69. See Anna Green, 'The Shipping Companies and '51', in *The Big Blue: Snapshots of the 1951 Waterfront Lockout*, Christchurch, 2004, pp. 112–3. Gerry Evans describes some of his experience working as an Auckland watersider in the 1960s and early 1970s in *Where Giants Dwell, A Sailor's Tale*, David Ling, Auckland, 1999, pp. 58–9.
70. Later, when working as a truck driver, Douglas delivered coal to Ned Fitzgerald's house, lugging sacks up 70 steps to the cellar in his Highbury home.
71. Gerry Evans, who worked on the wharf at the time, recalls Thompson as 'a giant' in the close-quarter combat of industrial negotiation. A caring man, Thompson never involved himself in the rancorous backstabbing common in the New Zealand union movement (Evans, *Where Giants Dwell*, op. cit., pp. 53–4). Terry Farrow also commented on Thompson's skills in a 1996 interview (OH Coll-0961, ATL, op. cit.).
72. The All Blacks won the match, 17–10.
73. Ken bought the Morris off his school friend Don Baker.

CHAPTER 3

74. Interview with Alan Thomas, 25 June 2005. Alan Thomas, Harold's grandson and Ken Thomas' son, managed HW Thomas during the last five years of its existence before it was sold in 1980. Before that he had worked for many years as a driver and in the office.
75. Interview with Alan Thomas, op. cit.
76. Douglas, interview, 7 July 2005.
77. Not long before Douglas began working with the cement bags they were made of jute, which required the handler to use both gloves and bale hooks to prevent the skin being torn off his hands.
78. Interview, Alan Thomas, op. cit.; Ken Douglas, 8 July 2005.
79. Because Harold Thomas died suddenly without making provision for distributing his shares among his sons (his daughter Dulcie got his Eastbourne house and all the antiques in it), and huge death duties had to be paid, Ken Thomas had to start from scratch when he took over in 1956, having to raise money to gather sufficient equity. Alan Thomas took over the running of the firm after his father's death in 1975; later, when other members of the family wanted their share of the money out of the firm,

he found the financial burden too much to bear, and he sold the firm to Capital Wood and Coal in 1980.
80. To Ken Douglas's knowledge the letters QED represented nothing formal although as an acronym it could have stood for 'quite easily delivered'.

CHAPTER 4

81. In 1907, Parlane became president of the Wellington Trades Council. The bulk of the information on the first 50 years of this union is gleaned from Rob Campbell, *The Only Weapon: The History of the Wellington Drivers' Union*, Wellington, 1976, pp. 13–62 passim. From the period of the 1951 waterfront lockout until 1975 this information has been supplemented with material from the full set of Minute Books and Scrapbooks of the Wellington Drivers' Union, held in the archives of the Wellington Central Amalgamated Drivers' Union in Willis St, Wellington. The author is grateful to Richie Gillespie, assistant secretary of this union, for access to this material.
82. Minutes, Wellington Road Transport and Motor and Horse Drivers' and their Assistants' Industrial Union of Workers, 23 September 1947; 22 February, 28 September 1948; 22 March, 28 June 1949; 15 November 1952; 4 December 1953.
83. T Magee, Secretary, Wellington Road Transport and Motor and Horse Drivers' and their Assistants' Industrial Union of Workers to Secretary, NZFOL, 12 July 1960, NZFOL Ms 4,100, Folder 20/22/2, ATL. In April 1950, the Drivers' Federation had walked out of the FOL and helped form the Trade Union Congress (TUC). In July, the union's AC Melville became the TUC's provisional secretary. Unions represented at the first conference of the TUC in August 1950 were the New Zealand Waterside Workers' Union, New Zealand Carpenters' and Joiners' Union, Auckland Drivers' Union, Hawke's Bay Drivers' Union, Auckland General Labourers' Union, Otago General Labourers' Union, Christchurch Biscuit Workers' Union, Wellington Painters' Union, Christchurch Painters' Union, Stockton Miners' Union, Millerton Miners' Union, Runanga Miners' Union, Grey Valley Miners' Union, Brunnerton Miners' Union, Blackball Miners' Union, Waikato Miners' Strike Committee, Wellington Drivers' Union, New Zealand Drivers' Federation, NZ Freezing Workers' Association, Christchurch Rubber Workers' Union, Dunedin Tramways' Union, Auckland Hotel Workers' Union, Wellington Watersiders' Union, NZ Workers' Union (Mangakino),

Auckland TUC. Cited Michael Bassett, *Confrontation 51: The 1951 Waterfront Dispute*, Wellington, 1972, p. 233.

84. One consequence of this reunification meeting was that the union adopted a new name. No longer the Wellington Road Transport and Motor and Horse Drivers' and their Assistants' Industrial Union of Workers (Deregistered), it now became the Wellington Motor Truck and Horse Drivers' and their Assistants' Industrial Union of Workers. Even this name was outdated, however, and informally, and most commonly, it was called the Wellington Drivers' Union.

85. In December 1953 the union had purchased a second car, a Ford Prefect, principally to be used by the organiser. In September 1954, the executive concluded that the Prefect car was too small and it was traded in for a new Ford Zephyr. By June 1955, the reliable Ford 10 had gone, replaced by a second-hand Vauxhall Velox. Both cars were later ditched for two Volkswagens (Minutes, WDU, 16 December 1953; 14 September 1954; 1 June, 6 November 1955).

86. Ken Douglas notes that there has 'often been trouble' between union leaders and money. His view is that the men themselves are not intuitively dishonest but become crooks because of deficiencies in the integrity of the systems for handling money. It is easy, he says, for union leaders with large amounts of cash at their disposal to 'fail to account' for it through the sloppiness of the financial systems in place, and the lack of accountability in the process. When he was in charge of both the Wellington Drivers' Union and later the FOL and the CTU he was scrupulous in his handling of the finances, knowing this area was a weak point for antagonists to exploit if they could, as well as being fair and honest to all the members (interview, 9 July 2005).

87. Minutes, WDU, 7 August 1955. A vote to prosecute Magee through the court system failed by 15 votes to 6 at a quarterly meeting on 6 September 1955.

88. In the vote on 3 August, 213 members voted for Bailey, 142 for Jane, and 96 for Small. It was a disappointing turnout; more than 1580 members had been issued with ballot papers (WJ Welsh, Returning Officer, New Zealand Road Transport and Motor and Horse Drivers' and their Assistants' Industrial Association of Workers, to Chairman, Executive Council, WDU, 3 August 1955, cit. Minutes, WDU).

89. WDU Executive Committee Report, December 1955.

90. A third presidential candidate, W Reardon, scored 118 votes. Janes secured 143 votes for his place on the executive, Douglas 110. Joining these two from Wellington were Edward Hollis and Reardon. They joined R Garner and V O'Sullivan from the

Hutt Valley, AW Bensemann and W Sutherland from the Manawatu, RV Flaws from the Wairarapa, and HT Harley from the South Wairarapa. Turnout was poor. The total number of votes received for all positions — 837 — represented 24.45 per cent of eligible members. The percentage was higher in Wellington alone, where 214 voted out of 787, representing a 38.61 per cent take (WJ Welch, Returning Officers' Report, Election of Officers 1956/57, n.d., Minutes, WDU). Chip Bailey remained secretary, unopposed. The following year, 1958/59, Douglas also polled second to Jane. He did not stand for the presidency.

91. Douglas made these comments about Walsh during an interview for the *NZ Listener* on 16 July 1983.

92. Minutes, Annual Quarterly Meeting, WDU, 21 November 1956. 'Chip' Bailey had been a member of the WDU since he transferred from the Electrical Workers' Union in January 1948. By this time the FOL comprised 207 unions covering 215,000 workers (FOL Circular, 'New Zealand Federation of Labour Calls All Trade Unionists', K Baxter, secretary NZFOL, November 1956, cit. NZFOL Ms 4100, Folder 20/22/2, ATL).

93. At this time there were 12 drivers' unions throughout the country, all affiliated to the New Zealand Drivers' Federation. They were the Northern, Gisborne, Hawke's Bay, Taranaki , Wanganui, Wellington, Blenheim, Nelson, Westland, Canterbury, Otago and Southland Drivers' Unions. No unions represented drivers in Waikato and the Bay of Plenty.

94. The figures were Wellington 17 for, 9 against; Hutt Valley 9 for, 23 against; Palmerston North 11 for, 0 against; Levin 4 for, 3 against; Masterton, 3 for, 18 against; Martinborough 0 for, 9 against (Minutes, Quarterly Meeting, WDU, 5 September 1957). A government threat to deregister the union was not carried out, but it is likely that the concern it caused persuaded a number of members to change their minds and support reaffiliation to the FOL (Minutes, Executive Meeting, WDU, 14 May 1957).

95. Both unions had also been upset by the government's increasing use of the penal provisions of the Industrial Conciliation and Arbitration Act.

96. Minutes, Special Executive Meeting, WDU, 14 September 1958. RS Parkin (president); C Bailey (secretary), 'WDU Circular re Affiliation to FOL,' n.d., cit. NZFOL, MS 4100; Folder 20/22/3, ATL.; Bailey to Ken Baxter, secretary, NZFOL, 3 March 1959; Baxter to Bailey, 17 March 1959; Folder 20/22/3, op. cit. Not all drivers were affiliated

to the FOL, however. In July 1960, of 15,523 members of all the provincial unions, just 9945 representing six unions were affiliated; the rest, belonging to the other six unions — Taranaki, Gisborne, Hawke's Bay, Wanganui, Nelson and Canterbury — remained outside. Notably there were many stock-truck drivers in these unions; these men tended to be uninterested or opposed to the union and its activities Baxter to secretaries, Drivers' Unions, 11 July 1960, op. cit.

97. It was significant that in 1962, both the Wellington Drivers' Union and the Drivers' Federation closeted with Walsh and a leading FOL negotiator. Walsh now regarded the transport workers as 'key' to all disputes, as 'without their support the FOL could have been defeated in a number of disputes we have been called upon to handle in the last two years'.

98. Minutes, Quarterly Meeting, WDU, 25 March 1958; Minutes WDU executive council meeting, 10 August 1958.

99. Campbell, op. cit., p. 99.

100. Union rules allowed the executive to make an appointment for any expired portion of an elected officer's term of office.

101. Interview, 10 March 2005; *NZ Listener*, 16 July 1983.

CHAPTER 5

102. Two hundred and twenty delegates representing 143 unions with a card voting strength of 351 participated in the 1959 FOL conference. It took years for some of the other drivers' unions to join or rejoin the FOL. The Hawke's Bay union, for example, waited until February 1966 to affiliate. In November 1959, Douglas would relinquish the presidency of the Wellington Drivers' Union in favour of Andy Thomsen, because he felt he was not doing justice to it alongside working voluntarily as the union's city organiser — which he would continue to do until 1963 — as well as continuing to try to make a living as a full-time truck driver.

103. Minutes, Special Executive Meeting, WDU, 1 March 1959; Executive Council's Report, WDU, May 1959.

104. Minutes, Quarterly Meeting, WDU, 26 May 1959.

105. Cited in the *Evening Post*, 5 November 1987.

106. Interview, Ken Douglas, 10 July 2005.

107. Interview, op. cit.

108. Interview, Richie Gillespie, 24 July 2005. The irony was that Douglas and O'Brien knew each other outside of working hours, both playing rugby for the Wellington College Old Boys Club.

109. Karl du Fresne, 'Hard Labour', *Evening Post*, 30 October 1999. Hancox later went to jail after he defrauded the Sports Foundation, of which he was chief executive, of hundreds of thousands of dollars.

110. Ken Douglas recalls many of the ship-repair men at Cables being humorous Heelermen, Scouses and Glaswegians who, during industrial disputes, would take the plates off a ship when it was in dry-dock so it could not put back to sea. Once when he was president of the FOL, he had to intervene on behalf of the United States government to get the men to work on an ice-breaker of the US Coast Guard so that it could return to McMurdo Station (interview 10 July 2005).

111. Shand's comments cited in the *Dominion*, 17 September 1962. Others angry at the strike put in their pound's worth as well. AP O'Shea, general secretary of Federated Farmers, described New Zealand's system of law and order as under direct challenge from selfish trade unionists, and PJ Luxford, secretary of the New Zealand Employers' Association, questioned whether 'combined trade union militancy is to be tolerated and allowed to obtain its demands by the force of illegal tactics' (*Evening Post*, 14 September 1962).

112. *New Zealand Truth*, 18 September 1962.

113. Bailey, who had been experiencing health problems, took leave for five weeks without pay from 18 September for his trip to China. Since 1960, the Federation of Labour had been urging the government to officially recognise the government of China as legitimate, instead of the government of Taiwan. It needs to be stated that this had been passed at successive FOL conferences by simple majorities that were often close. Many delegates argued for the status quo.

114. The Cable dispute hogged newspaper headlines during the last two weeks of September 1962.

115. *Evening Post*, 20, 22 September 1962.

116. *Dominion*, 26 September 1962.

117. Ibid., 30 September, 4 October 1962.

118. Campbell, op. cit., pp. 88–89.

119. Minutes of Special Meeting of WDU, 28 October 1962.

120. For a long time Scotson was site delegate for the union at HW Thomas. WT Ward, who seconded his motion, was another Palmerston North driver (Minutes 28 October 1962, op. cit.; Campbell, op. cit., pp. 100–101).
121. 'Death of Chip Bailey', *Drum: Special Edition*, May 1963, cited in FOL MS 20/27/6, ATL; Peter Franks, 'Chip Bailey', *The Dictionary of New Zealand Biography, Volume Five 1941–1960*, Auckland University Press, 2000, pp. 28–29. Bailey's death occurred just weeks before that of Fintan Patrick Walsh on 16 May 1963.
122. *Wheels*, vol. 4, no. 9, May 1963, pp. 1, 7, 16; *Drum: Special Edition*, May 1963; Franks, op cit.
123. Interview, 10 July 2005. In his union leadership Douglas always kept apartheid issues at the forefront. In February 1964 he was responsible for writing and distributing a Drivers' Union leaflet protesting against the South African cricket tour of New Zealand, highlighting the persecution of African and coloured workers and trade unionists in that country. He tried to get the FOL and other unions to cover the expense of the leaflet but failed, receiving only endorsements for its content (WDU Circular, 'Trade Unions Oppose Racism', Douglas to Ken Baxter, secretary FOL, 17 February 1964, cited in NZFOL MS 4100, Folder 20/22/3, ATL).
124. Executive Report, WDU Quarterly Meeting, 26 November 1963. *Wheels*, vol. 4, no. 10, August 1963, 9. Interview, Ken Douglas, 10 July 2005. Pat Kelly replaced Douglas as city organiser until union elections took place in November.
125. In November 1963, the Wellington and Hutt Valley job and area delegates on the WDU were — Barton Ginger: Dave Jackson; B.A.L.M.: John Campbell; Belwoods: Pat Warbrick; Cables: Ted Metcale; Camerons: Bill Tahiwi; Certified Concrete (Wellington): Pat Kelly; Certified Concrete (Hutt): Harry Whiteman; Coutts and Hare: Bill Reardon; JJ Curtis: Bill Thompson; Denhard Bakeries: Eddie Corcoran; Downers: Jim Hunter; Drapers: Sam Westerby; Fords: Ted Sexton; Garth Tiles: K McRandall; General Motors (Petone): Jim Morgan; General Motors (Upper Hutt): Ken Orr; Griffins: Bill Wilkinson; Golden Bay: Mike Turner; RM Griffiths: Brian Carey; Billy Higgs: Dave Bennett; Hutt County (Mangaroa): Peter Douglas; Hutt County (Paraparaumu): Tom Cameron; Hygienic Laundry: Clive Chandler; Ivory's: Tangi Pahina; Jax Pies: Arthur Hagar; Lower Hutt City Council (Yard): Dave Johnstone; Lower Hutt City Council (Reserves): Bill Durning; Lever Brothers: Darby Munroe; Marris and Campbell: Ray Jones; Magnet (Paraparaumu): Frank

Brixton; Munt, Cottrell: Don Taylor; Morrisons Taxis: Barney Ruscoe; McGowan and Magee: Bill Slattery; Napier-Wellington: Claude Hanson; New Zealand Breweries: Johnny Hiroti; Petone Borough Council: Joe Colquhoun; Purity Bread: Eric Leyland; Tawa Borough Council: Bernie Brown; HW Thomas: Doug Scotson; Todd Motors: Chalky Love; Upper Hutt Borough Council: Harry Smith; Wellington City Council (Motor Transport): Eric Finucame; WCC (Electricity): Ted Coster; WCC (Machine Operators): Neville Collins and Johnny Neho; WCC (Johnsonville): Roy Harford; WCC (Reserves): Wally Hapi; WCC (Street Cleaning): Frank Drury; WCC (Drainage): Jack Brockie; WCC (Refuse): Chappy Smith; Wilkins and Davies: Jimmy Smith; Wellington Free Ambulance: Graham Whitaker and Ray Hunt; WD and HO Wills: Frank McHardy (*Wheels*, vol. 4, no. 8, November 1963, p. 11).

126. From 1949, the Federation communicated to its constituents through its quarterly publication *Wheels*.

127. From largest to smallest, the provincial totals were Southland, 950; Taranaki, 760; Hawke's Bay, 709; Nelson, 530; Wanganui, 470; Gisborne, 310; Blenheim, 300, and Westland, 298. Numbers were growing (*Wheels*, vol. 5, no. 11, March 1968, p. 2). The Wellington district included Manawatu, Horowhenua and the Wairarapa.

128. Minutes, AGM, New Zealand Drivers' Federation, 2–5 April 1968, pp. 22–23. Douglas defeated Southland delegate TE Harris in a ballot to become vice-president. (At the time he was a non-attendee, being in hospital with a cracked neck vertebra suffered in a rugby game.) Minutes, AGM, NZDF, 29 April–2 May, 1969, 1, 15; Distribution Workers of New Zealand MSY-6104, ATL. Blenheim was now the smallest of the driver unions, with 262 members through the 1968 financial year.

129. Walsh was succeeded by Stuart McCaffley, an organiser with the Northern Union. A political activist, McCaffley would become senior vice-president of the Labour Party and chairperson of its Industrial Affiliates Council in 1978.

130. Douglas to author, op. cit.

131. Interview, 10 July 2005.

132. The bulk of the material on the Curtis dispute is taken from Campbell, *The Only Weapon*, pp. 91–94, supplemented with information gleaned from the union's minute books, and from Ken Douglas's memory.

133. Shand's remarks were quoted in the *Dominion* of 7 August.

134. Douglas's comments cited in Campbell, p. 93.

CHAPTER 6

135. Douglas's activities in the New Zealand Communist Party and the Socialist Unity Party are dealt with in Chapter 7.

136. Cit RE Gillespie (president), D Crowley (vice-president), KG Douglas (secretary), 'Report of 15th Annual Job Delegates Conference, Wellington, 16 October 1973', 3, FOL MS 4100, Folder 20/27/08, p. 3. For some years the union had been running a Special Assistance Fund whereby 10 cents from each annual subscription went to provide financial assistance (generally up to $20) in cases of hardship for injury or sickness to members and/or their families. In 1967, the union established a Travel and Education Fund on the same 10-cent basis to provide financial assistance to enable any rank-and-filer to represent the union at an international trade union conference, or to assist the funding of an international conference in New Zealand. For decades also, the union had had a disputes fund to provide emergency hardship funding for members disadvantaged in industrial disputes (Douglas, 'Report of Financial Position Special Sub-Committee Job Delegates', Wellington Road Transport and Related Industries Motor and Horse Drivers' and their Assistants' Industrial Union of Workers, 25 March 1972, cited in FOL MS 4100, Folder 20/27/08, pp. 4–5).

137. This was a favoured ploy of the Storemen and Packers' Union as well.

138. Northern had 15 votes, Wellington 5, and Otago 4. Of those opposed to the motion, Canterbury had 7 votes while the smaller provincial unions had one and two among them (*Wheels*, vol. 4, no. 27, February 1968, pp. 1–2, 4, 28; May 1968, 24).

139. Skinner's anger was exacerbated by Holyoake's further decision to increase the size of his Cabinet (*Evening Post*, 13 February 1967). On 23 February, CARP established a branch in Wellington as a direct result of the increases (ibid., 24 February 1967).

140. *Dominion*, 13 February 1967.

141. *New Zealand Herald*, 14 March 1967. Further protest meetings were held in Dunedin's Market Reserve on 14 March; in Christchurch's Latimer Square on 15 March, and in Wellington's Town Hall and Concert Chamber on 17 March.

142. *Evening Post*, 10 March 1967.

143. Campbell, pp. 96–97.

144. *Wheels*, vol. 4, no. 29, August 1968, pp. 8–9.

145. Ibid.

146. Ibid.

147. There was a catch to this agreement, however. The Court directed that the increase be restricted to the first $40 earned by adult male workers, the first $30 earned by adult female workers and the first $25 earned by junior workers. It was of the opinion, naive of course, that when a worker had spent $40, any price increase would have no impact on the balance, if any, that he had left.

148. Douglas and Richie Gillespie, 'Report of 14th Annual Job Delegates Conference', Wellington Drivers' Union, 10 May 1974, 2. See Chapter 16 of my book *Jagged Seas: The Story of the New Zealand Seamen's/Seafarers' Union 1880–2003* for a full account of the 1971 deregistration of the Seamen's Union.

149. Ken Douglas interview, 22 February 2010.

150. Interview, 7 July 2005.

151. *New Zealand Herald*, 29, 31 July 1974.

152. *Dominion*, 20 September, 3 October 1974.

153. *Auckland Star*, 18, 19, 21 October 1974; *New Zealand Parliamentary Debates*, 18, 24 October 1974.

154. Andrews was an interesting character. A man of considerable girth, he had arrived in New Zealand some years earlier under an assumed name after undisclosed bother with police in his home country of Australia. He interspersed his driving career with appearances in the professional wrestling ring as the bucolic 'Farmer Andrews' in the Steve Rickard circus that was popular at the time.

155. Interview, Jane Douglas, 26 December 2009.

156. Interviews, Douglas, 10 October 2005; 15 January 2010.

157. The information in this and the following paragraph is gleaned from reports in the *New Zealand Herald*, *Auckland Star* and *Dominion* as the dispute unfolded through May and June of 1978.

158. Information in this and the following paragraph is gleaned from extensive newspaper reports collated in Roth MS 94-106-36/09, ATL.

159. The newspaper was the *Press*, 18 September 1979. The national strike was the lead story in most newspapers.

160. While numbers were falling, the Federation still represented close to 15,000 drivers.

161. Lesley had been earning £4/2/6d as a primary school teacher at Eastbourne and later Mt Cook Primary School, but was now a full-time mother to baby Jane.

162. Interview, 15 January 2010.

163. The author interviewed Helen, Peter and Jane Douglas on 26 December 2009, and John Douglas on 22 January 2010. All of them, except Peter, were also interviewed by Monique Oomen for a television documentary *Ken Douglas — Traitor or Visionary?*; Helen on 1 November 2005 and Jane and John on 13 November 2005. Unless otherwise stated all the information here is gleaned from these sources.
164. Gwen's commitment to her grandchildren and their mother was unconditional. She lived in Trentham, travelled by train to Wellington, caught another to Porirua and then a bus to Titahi Bay and Opapa Street before making the return trip in the evening.
165. Jane returned to work when her son Anthony was 11 months old.
166. In November 1986, Helen, aged 22, represented the SUP at the 12th Assembly of the World Federation of Democratic Youth in Budapest, Hungary. The assembly was attended by 700 delegates, and guests included two other New Zealanders — Stephanie Haworth from the New Zealand University Students Association, and another from the Nelson Polytechnic (NZSUP, 'Report to the Central Committee on the 12th Assembly of the World Federation of Democratic Youth attended by Helen Douglas', 27 February 1987; Douglas MS 1619, Folder 9960-029 ATL).
167. Interview, Jane Tucker, 12 March 2010.
168. Dai Hayward, *Follow Up: Wellington College Old Boys Rugby Football Club, 1989–1998*, Wellington, 1998, pp. 19–20; 75.
169. David Grant, *Drivers, Divots and Dongas: The Story of Titahi Golf Club 1958–2008*, Wellington, 2008, pp. 24–25.
170. Ibid., p. 28.

CHAPTER 7

171 Bryce was a particularly 'stable' influence since not only did he remain a long-term office-holder in the party, but also because the other Northland Rd adults — Ken's father Attie and uncles Laurie and Lyndsay — while keen Labourites, only lived in the house at times.
172. Groucho Marx anecdote from the *NZ Listener*, 16 July 1983.
173. Glen Hurley, 'The Heavy-Duty Labours of Ken Douglas', *Management*, March 1989, pp. 37–38.

174. Interview, 10 July 2005.

175. Initially the Communist Party established its headquarters in Wellington. In 1926 it transferred to Blackball (where it became affiliated to the Communist International in 1927) before returning to Wellington in 1928. In 1939 the headquarters moved to Auckland.

176. Interview, Douglas, 21 March 2010.

177. Drennan, a Scotsman, was born in December 1899. As well as being active early in the NZCP he was a leader of the Unemployed Workers' Movement between 1929 and 1935 and a foundation member of the Friends of the Soviet Union. Joining the Waterside Workers' Union in 1936, he became president of the Auckland branch in 1951 before the lockout. He made a number of trips to Russia, attending, among other events, the Lenin Centenary celebrations in 1970. He died in November 1971. Other key early members of the SUP were Frank McNulty, Ernie Hunter and Jack Marston.

178. 9 February 1966. The press statement read, 'We resign after nearly 120 years of active Party membership not to abandon the struggle for socialism in New Zealand, nor to take up "safe" posts in the present structure of society but to undertake with new vigour the formulation and application of real Marxist-Leninist policies.' Cited in Socialist Unity Party, *Communism in New Zealand: An Illustrated History*, Auckland, 1986, p. 33. This booklet was produced to commemorate then 65th anniversary of the founding of the Communist Party of New Zealand and the 20th anniversary of the Socialist Unity Party.

179. Interview with Tony Reid, *New Zealand Herald*, 25 June 1983.

180. Douglas to Monique Oomen, 12 December 2005; videotaped interview for *Ken Douglas — Traitor or Visionary?*

181. *Communism in New Zealand: An Illustrated History*, p. 35. The number of people in the SUP is an educated guess, because for security reasons the party never released membership figures or the identities of its members.

182. FOL, 'Minutes and Report of the Proceedings of the Thirty-Second Annual Conference, Trades Hall, Wellington, 15–18 April 1969', pp. 58–59.

183. Ibid., p. 59. Wally Molineux of the Carpenters' Union seconded Douglas's motion.

184. Of the other SUP candidates, Bill Andersen, who stood against Robert Muldoon in the Tamaki electorate, received 108, the highest number of votes. AJ Cox received

68 in Christchurch Central, and Jack Marston 105 in Dunedin Central (*New Zealand Official Year Book*, Department of Statistics, Wellington, 197; Douglas to Monique Oomen, 1 September 2005, op. cit.).

185. In 1975 the other candidates and their results were: John Lindsay (Dunedin Central) 32 votes; Ron O'Brien (Sydenham) 37; Les Taylor (Stratford) 21; Grahame Roberts (Franklin) 21; Bill Andersen (Tamaki) 39; Ella Ayo (Mangere) 14; John Willis (Otahuhu) 26; Bruce Skilton (Grey Lynn) 30; George Jackson (Mt Roskill) 17; Jim Thomson (Henderson) 35; Leslie Bravery (Mt Albert) 28; Peter Cross (New Lynn) 25 and Alan Marston (Manukau) 17 (*New Zealand Official Year Book*, 1976).

186. In 1981, the other SUP candidates were Ella Ayo (Otahuhu), Sonya Perrott (Waikato) and Ray Stewart (New Lynn) (*New Zealand Official Year Book*, 1979, 1982).

187. In 1979, the National Committee comprised Dave Arthur, Bill Andersen, Ken Douglas, Richie Gillespie, George Jackson, Jack Marston, Doug McCallum, Bernie O'Brien, Marilyn Tucker and Alan Ware. Throughout its life *The Tribune* was of the utmost importance to the SUP as it was the only way it could spread its message publicly and attract new members. Each branch was required to make a fortnightly statistical return noting where the newsletter was distributed and how many copies had been sold. For example, on 19 March 1983, the Dunedin branch reported that it had sold 51 copies (more than usual) — 28 at the Hillside workshops, three on the wharf, six at the university and 14 private sales. The return also required branches to report similar information on leaflets, pamphlets, programmes and public meetings (where held, attendance numbers, results, decisions), study (subject, attendance, where held), and other activities such as fundraising or recreational (including number attending, where held, description).

188. Some of this material was gleaned from Warwick Roger's article 'Battle for the Mind . . . Through the Socialist Unity Party', in the *Auckland Star Weekender*, 18 February 1978.

189. Statement from FE Bailey, Chairman, Auckland Branch of the Post Office Association, 20 September 1977, cited in Roth MS 94 Folder 106-70/18.

190. The judge was Mr Justice Wilson and he made the comment in an address to the Otago Branch of the New Zealand Legal Association on 14 November 1977.

191. 'Oasis Newsheet', n.d., cited in Roth MS 94, Folder 106-70/18. In Jackson's view Muldoon was simply trying to draw attention away from the measure by focusing the public and the media's attention on these 'dangerous communists'.

'Counterpunching and smear diversions are no substitute for reason. The continuing widespread opposition to this Bill is clear evidence of this. It will grow and the SUP will continue to play a legitimate part in that movement' (Jackson, 'Statement on SIS Amendment Bill submitted for publication by the New Zealand Socialist Unity Party', 17 October 1977, cited in Douglas MS 1619, Folder 8860-013).

192. Farrow's comments cited in OHColl-0961, Porirua Licensing Trust Oral History Project, Oral History Centre, ATL.

193. *New Zealand Herald*, 25 January 1980. It was not the first time Russian diplomatic officials had been expelled. On 13 July 1962, Prime Minister Keith Holyoake expelled VS Andreev, a commercial counsellor, and Mr NI (Nick) Shytov, second secretary, on suspicion of spying. They were given 48 hours to leave the country. The SIS asserted the men had been attempting to bribe 'well-placed' New Zealanders with gifts and money to part with information 'for which they were not entitled' concerning New Zealand's defence and external relations. Andreev and Shytov's expulsion caused shockwaves in Parliament when it was announced, and caused a sensation in the press.

194. Later, Sofinsky alleged that the United States and other Western forces had used Muldoon to have him expelled from New Zealand.

195. Knox's report was presented after Tony Neary had earlier led a resolution that the conference 'express its horror at the continuation of the widespread violation of human rights by the Ethiopian regime' (*Evening Post*, 2 May 1978).

196. *New Zealand Herald*, 3 May 1978; *Truth*, 9 May 1978; both cited in Roth MS 94-106-55/05, ATL.

197. Roger, op. cit.

198. *New Zealand Herald*, 25 January 1980.

199. Roth MS 'FOL Records and Research Notes,' MS 94-106-55/11, ATL. In Auckland, Andersen and Mike Jackson were also rebuffed by the majority of affiliates to the Auckland Trades Council over their publicly expressed support for the Russian invasion of Afghanistan. *New Zealand Herald*, 23 February 1980.

200. *New Zealand Herald*, 21 January 1980.

201. 'To that end,' the FOL's statement continued, 'the executive calls on the Russians to withdraw their troops, will afford all possible assistance to Afghan trade unions, calls upon the New Zealand government to exert pressure to secure Soviet

withdrawal both through its own offices and the United Nations, calls upon the UN to make every effort to continue to resolve the dispute peacefully, condemns the use of an Olympic boycott as such tactics should be a consideration when the composition of competing teams is influenced by racial policies and deplores the tactics of employers and sections of the news media who use this issue to try to split and divide the trade union movement and divert attention from efforts being made by the FOL to protect workers' interests and combat employer and government attacks upon New Zealanders' living standards.' Information on the FOL's stance on Afghanistan is gleaned from 'NZFOL Minutes and Report of the Proceedings of the Forty-Third Annual Conference held in Town Hall, Wellington on May 6, 7, 8, 9, 1980, pp. 114-5, MS X 2404, ATL.

202. Cable cited in 'Circulars 1979-1980', FOL MS 95-050, ATL; *Auckland Star*, 20 August 1980; *New Zealand Herald*, 23, 25 August 1980.

203. 'The Struggle for Peace and the Crisis of Capitalism in the Area of Transition from Capitalism to Socialism', in 'Draft Resolution for the 6th National Conference Socialist Unity Party of New Zealand', pp. 18-20, October 1982. Douglas MS Group 1619, Folder 8960-015.

204. The Oceania Region of the ICFTU comprised Australia, New Zealand and many Pacific Islands.

205. *Dominion*, 7, 8, 9, 11, 18 January 1981.

206. Douglas to Affiliates/District Councils, Trade Union Committees, 22 October 1982 (Roth MS 94-106-56/09, ATL).

207. The names of the 32 alleged members of the SUP (with their principal union affiliations in brackets) were: Gordon (Bill) Andersen (secretary, Northern Drivers' Union); John Andrews (vice-president, Wellington Drivers' Union); David Arthur (shop steward, NZR Hillside workshops); Ian Brown (organiser, Auckland Storemen and Packers); John Buckley (vice-president, Northern Drivers); Robert Campbell (Industrial Officer, NZ Drivers' Federation); Herrold Raymond Corrin (organiser, Wellington Carpenters); Peter Cross (delegate, Auckland Tramways); Richard Davis (organiser, Auckland Storemen and Packers); Ken Douglas (secretary FOL; president, NZ Drivers' Federation); Tom Downey (organiser, Northern Drivers); Jan Farr (secretary, NZ Writers' Guild); Bruce Fowler (organiser, Auckland Storemen and Packers); Richard Gillespie (organiser, Wellington Drivers); Michael Jackson (secretary, Auckland Storemen and Packers); Ken Johnson (member, Printing

Trades); Stuart Kennedy (organiser, Wellington Drivers); Robert Masefield (vice-president, Auckland Tramways); Thomas McLintock (president, Auckland Brewery Workers); Francis McNulty (secretary, Wellington Ice Cream Workers; national councillor, FOL); Kenneth Perrott (chairman, Ruakura PSA delegates' committee); Stephen Reilly (organiser, Auckland Labourers); Wayne Rickit (organiser, Porirua Labourers); James Ritchie (secretary, Auckland Saddlers, Sugar Workers and Meat Workers); Joseph Roberts (organiser, Northern Drivers); Albert Shipp (secretary, Wellington Branch, Railway Tradesmen's Association); Arthur Sims (secretary, Northern/Taranaki Labourers); Bruce Skilton (president, Auckland Watchmen's section, NZ Seamen); Jackson Smith (secretary, Wellington Drivers); Frederick Smitheram (president, Otago Trades Council); James Thomson (ex-executive member, Auckland Engine Drivers), and Alan Ware (advocate for nine unions at Huntly Power Station site). Comments from the 18 members cited in *New Zealand Herald*, 19 March 1980.

208. *Press*, 19 March 1980.

209. *Auckland Star, Nelson Evening Mail*, 17 March 1980; *New Zealand Herald*, 18, 19, 20 March 1980.

210. The *Star* poll showed that while 46 per cent believed the SUP was 'bad' for the country, 6 per cent thought it was 'good', while the rest, 48 per cent, believed it had little or no effect (*Auckland Star*, 29 April 1980).

211. *NZ Listener*, 16 July 1983.

212. Ibid., pp. 38–39. The party did better in local body elections. In 1983, it nominated candidates for the Auckland City Council, Waitemata City Council and Porirua City Council. Bill Andersen and Peter Devlin won 2025 and 1256 votes respectively, representing 11.7 and 7.3 per cent of the top vote. Ray Stewart won 245 votes, representing 11.3 per cent of the top vote, and John van der Ven 159 votes, representing 15.2 per cent of the top vote (*Tribune*, 17 October 1973).

213. Information from the report of the 'Credentials Committee', in 'Post-Conference Discussion Bulletin No 1', November 1982, pp. 1–3 (Douglas ms, op. cit.). The main players in 1982 were: Marilyn Tucker, pharmacist, national executive (and by now working in the national office two days a week); Ken Douglas, national committee; Bill Andersen, union official, national president, executive FOL; Jack Marsden, retired boilermaker, national committee; Bruce Skilton, retired seaman, national executive; George Jackson, retired fitter, national secretary; Ella Ayo, party worker,

vice-president; Ken Perrott, scientist, national committee, and Angus McConnell, dairy worker, branch chairman, executive Dairy Workers' Union.

214. *New Zealand Herald*, 13 April 1983. Douglas to Leuchars, 29 May 1985. Douglas Papers, 43/198, possession of Ken Douglas.

215. *New Zealand Herald*, 14 April 1983.

216. In November 1987, Tucker and George Jackson attended celebrations to commemorate the 70th birthday of the Communist Party of the Soviet Union in Moscow.

217. Jackson was elected president of the SUP, a largely ceremonial post. 'SUP Central Committee Report', February 1989. Douglas MS 1619, Folder 8860-059. Douglas, 'Report on Moscow Symposium, Future of the Working Class, the May Day Tradition and the 2nd International', 18 August 1989, Folder 8860-060. In 1988, for the first time, the SUP Congress hosted, in New Zealand, a three-person delegation from the Communist Party of the Soviet Union; the members of the delegation were Alexander Selenev, secretary of the Kursk Region; Svetlana Oukhtina, and Valery Koudinov.

218. Douglas, 'Cadre Development and Party Leadership', August 1985 (Douglas MS 1619, Folder 8860-048).

219. Andersen to the central executive, 4 February 1987 (Douglas MS 1619, Folder 8860-104). Soon afterwards two founding members, Ella Ayo and Bruce Skilton, stood down from the National Committee. Members who remained on this committee were Douglas, Andersen, George Jackson, Dave Arthur, Richie Gillespie, Jack Marston, Frank McNulty, Doug McCallum, Bernie O'Brien, Joe Tonner, Marilyn Tucker and Alan Ware. A Central Control Commission of Skilton and Johnny Mitchell looked after discipline, and a Finance Commission comprising Douglas, Skilton and Ware controlled SUP finances.

220. Interview, 22 February 2010.

221. 'Contribution by Comrade GH Andersen to Central Committee re Our Party's approach to the 1990 General Elections', 4 March 1990, cited in 'SUP Discussion Bulletin 90/1', pp. 6–8 passim (Douglas MS 1619, Folder 8860-019).

222. An associated gripe from Andersen was that the SUP had not come to terms with new pro-democracy moves in Eastern Europe. Communists, he said, had been slow to realise the need for more democracy. Marxist principles were based on 'democratic centralism', but the 'democratic' aspect had not been developed, he believed.

223. Andersen to Joe Tonner, Assistant Secretary, NZSUP, 28 June 1990. Douglas MS 1619, Folder 8860-107. Minutes of SUP Central Committee, 29, 30 June 1990. Folder 8860-052.

224. NZSUP '9th Annual Conference File', Douglas MS 1619, Folder 8860-019.

225. *Auckland Star*, 4 July 1990; *New Zealand Herald*, 5 July 1990; Minutes of SUP Central Committee, 29, 30 June; Douglas MS Folder 8860-053. Andersen became president of the new party, Doug McCallum its secretary, and Alec Morgan (president of the Stores Division of the NDU and well known for his role in the Nissan strike to try to defeat the 'Nissan Way') and Stan Stanford (Cleaners' and Caretakers' delegate to the Auckland CTU) were on its committee.

226. Jackson was still the party's president, Douglas its chairperson, Tucker its secretary, and Joe Tonner assistant secretary. Later Tucker became a vice-chairperson, with Alan Ware succeeding her as secretary.

227. Campbell, Harris and Reid to Monique Oomen,17, 28 and 9 November 2005; videotaped interviews for *Ken Douglas — Traitor or Visionary?*

228. Douglas talking to Pauline Swain, *Dominion*, 20 April 1992, p. 6.

229. Much of the information in this and succeeding chapters was gleaned from an interview Douglas did with John Goulter for the *Evening Post*, 1 May 1993.

230. Interview with Tony Reid, *New Zealand Herald*, 25 June, 1983.

231. NZSUP report, 20 August 1995, author not identified; Douglas MS 8860, Folder 8860-050.

CHAPTER 8

232. Douglas, D Crowley, RE Gillespie, 'Report of Proceedings of 15th Annual Job Delegates Conference', Wellington Drivers' Union, 16 October 1973, FOL MS 4100, Folder 20/27/09, p. 12. At the time the Wellington Drivers' Union was in a seemingly intractable dispute with the Storemen and Packers' Union over whose responsibility it was to cover forklift and shop-delivery van drivers, and its national body, the Drivers' Federation, was in a protracted dispute with the Timber Workers' Union over coverage of timber-mill drivers in the central North Island.

233. Douglas to Knox, 13 June; Knox to Douglas, 25 June 1974; FOL MS 4100, Folder 20/27/10.

234. In 1968, Jim Knox, from the Woollen Workers' Union (with 346 votes), Molineaux (300), Hadley (222) and Thorn (214 on a second ballot) were elected to the executive. Knox replaced Ken Baxter as secretary-treasurer the following year after Baxter retired. Seamen's Union president Pincher Martin was elected to the executive in Knox's place.

235. Hadley had now retired. These statistics are gleaned from the Minutes and Report of Proceedings of the various annual conferences of the FOL between 1968 and 1978. Sonja Davies won election to the executive in 1978 on her fourth try, the first woman to do so.

236. Ted Thompson, secretary of the Waterside Workers' Federation, persistently topped the poll in FOL executive elections during the late 1970s. He did not stand for the presidency on Skinner's retirement; it is likely that had he stood he would have run Knox very close.

237. Douglas needed the agreement of the Wellington Drivers' Union to stand for the executive. It was readily given.

238. Interview, Douglas, 22 February 2010. Russ, Thorn and Davies were all elected to the executive.

239. The confirmation of these 'special powers' is confirmed by Ken Douglas.

240. *NZFOL Bulletin*, No. 20, August 1979, p. 3. By this time there was a continuing and significant decline in the number of unions. In 1951, 411 unions served 272,843 workers; by 1976, 292 unions served 464,453 workers. The total number of unions had decreased by close to 30 per cent, while worker numbers had increased by 52.9 per cent. Membership of the unions ranged from seven in the Canterbury Coal Mine Workers' Union to 44,404 in the New Zealand Engineers' and Coach Builders' Union. In 1951, 56 per cent of unions had between 100 and 200 members; by 1976 this had dropped to 39 per cent. Despite the large number of unions, the 20 biggest unions accounted for 56 per cent of total union membership in 1976. In the same year, 224 secretaries looked after 292 unions; 101, or 45 per cent, were part-time, 53.6 per cent were full-time and 1.3 per cent were 'retired' people. Forty-three (19 per cent) of them had multiple secretaryships.

241. *New Zealand Herald*, 28 July 1979.

242. *Evening Post*, 15 May 1979; *New Zealand Herald*, 16 May 1979.

243. *New Zealand Herald*, Press, 20 September 1979.

244. Ibid., 21 September 1979; *Auckland Star*, 19, 22 September 1979.

245. *NZFOL Bulletin*, no. 22, September 1980, p. 1. The rallies were replicated not only in cities throughout New Zealand but also in small towns such as Taumarunui, Te Kuiti and Morrinsville, which were farming centres primarily and where trade unionism traditionally had little support.

246. Suspended workers were eligible for social welfare benefits so their plight was not so desperate.

247. Douglas to 'All Unions Involved in the Pulp and Paper Industry', 23 December 1980, FOL MS 95-050, ATL.

248. NZFOL, 'Minutes and Report of the Proceedings of the Forty-Fourth Annual Conference held in the Town Hall, Wellington on May 5, 6, 7 and 8, 1981', pp. 61–62, MS X 2405, ATL.

249. This information is gleaned from a series of news reports through the period.

250. One of the main FOL initiatives in 1981 was the August Unemployment Conference. The total registered unemployed in September 1974 was 1052; by September 1977 it had risen to 8075; three years later it had increased to a massive 42,549, the highest figure since the 1930s Depression. It continued to rise. By December 1981, after the conference had finished, it was 50,237 — still rising and seemingly out of control. Douglas as secretary took a leading role in organising the conference, which was held to determine working-class strategies in the fight for full employment. It followed a government-sponsored employment conference in late 1980 which in the view of the FOL and Combined State Unions failed to address the growing unemployment problem. The FOL conference was attended by a broad range of workers from both the private and the public sector, union officials and members, workers on 'PEP' schemes (who had work guaranteed for only six months and at minimum rates, subsidised by the government) and unemployed workers, including organisers in regional unemployment groups, students and other beneficiaries. (Unemployment figures from Alf Kirk, FOL economist, 'Economic News: Statistical Data', 6/1/3, Table 1: 1, n.d.; FOL MS 4100, Folder 53/3/10.)

251. *New Zealand Herald*, 14 April 1981.

252. FOL conferences through the 1970s and 1980s were huge affairs which ran for four days. Every year there was not only an extensive address by the president highlighting the FOL's year's work and future plans but also a rundown on the country's economy, balance of payments, unemployment, legislation, its wages and prices policies, health and safety issues, the impact of new technology, reports of all

the various FOL sub-committees, and a reading by the secretary of the year's annual report. The latter was often divided into sections such as, in 1983 for example, national executive and national council, national office, alternative economic strategy, wage policy working party, industrial law reform and implications, disputes in industry, unemployment, NZCTU progress, international affairs and financial statements. There were reports from the Credentials Committee, returning officers for elections, the Women's Advisory Committee, the Maori and Pacific Islands Advisory Committee, the Constitution, Organisation and Administration Committee, the Taxation and Legislation Committee, the Social Affairs Committee and the Early Childhood Education Working Party.

253. *New Zealand Herald*, 10, 11 June 1981.

254. *Auckland Star*, 11 June 1981.

255. Douglas, 'Address to the Commissioned Officers' Course at the New Zealand Police College, Porirua,' 1 November 1982, FOL MS 4100, Folder 45/3. The freeze also covered rents, dividends, and interest rates.

256. *Auckland Star*, 23 June 1982.

257. In the Auckland protest the Polynesian band Herbs entertained marchers in Aotea Square before speeches from Knox, Andersen, Labour Party president Jim Anderton and PSA president David Thorp. There were rallies in city suburbs as well In Wellington, for example, between 21 October and 8 November (before the main rally) there were nine — in Stokes Valley, Wainuiomata, Porirua/Plimmerton, Petone West, Tawa, Paraparaumu, Wellington North, Wellington Central and Wellington East.

258. *Seamen's Journal: Official Organ of the NZ Seamen's Union*, vol. 15, no. 6, December 1982, p. 1.

259. Ibid., pp. 24–28 passim; Douglas, secretary FOL, Tucker secretary CSU to Muldoon, 22 April 1983. Minutes FOL Forty-Sixth Annual Conference 3–6 May 1983, pp. 47–50. MS X 2407. Earlier, on 19 April 1983, Knox had said that a continuation of the wage freeze 'was simply not on'. (*New Zealand Herald*, 19 April 1983). Through all of this Muldoon had support from the Employers Federation, which agitated for the freeze to continue and further called for a nil wage order in 1983.

260. The newspaper in question was the *Dominion*, 6 May 1983; see also *Auckland Star*, 27 June 1983.

261. *Auckland Star*, 4 June 1983.

262. *NZ Listener*, 16 July 1983.

263. *New Zealand Herald*, 12 July 1983; *Auckland Star*, 3 November 1983.

264. It needs to be acknowledged that the number of days lost did increase markedly in Muldoon's time in response to his raft of anti-worker laws. In 1975, for example, the last year of the third Labour government, there were 208 working days lost whereas during the following year, the first year of the Muldoon government, the figure had more than doubled to 468. 'FOL Submission to Industrial Law Reform Bill', op. cit., October 1983, Appendices 4, 5 and 6. Those opting out of union membership were a very small minority. In 1982, for example, just 266 workers — from a total of some 453,000 private-sector trade unionists — applied for exemption, 191 of them being suc-cessful. Minutes NZFOL Special Meeting of Union Representatives and National Council, 10 October 1984; 'FOL Circulars', FOL 95-050, ATL;. *New Zealand Herald*, 18, 19 October 1983.

265. *New Zealand Herald*, 2 December 1983. Unemployment figures from *PSA Journal*, February 1984.

266. 'Report of Executive Committee of ICFTU on New Zealand Industrial Reform, 85EB/9 (c), (ii),' 24–5 May 1984, Annex 2 in 'Submissions to the Parliamentary Select Committee Union Membership Bill, February 1985'. FOL MS 4100, Folder 40/1/9, ATL. *New Zealand Herald*, 4 October 1984.

267. NZFOL, 'Minutes and Report of the Proceedings of the Forty-Seventh Annual Conference held in the Town Hall, Wellington on May 8, 9, 10, 11 1984, pp. 70–71. MS X 2408, ATL.

268. *Auckland Star*, 27 June 1984.

269. Interview Douglas, 21 March 2010.

270. Ibid.

271. *New Zealand Herald*, 11 May 1984.

CHAPTER 9

272. Neary had been instrumental in forming an ad hoc grouping of 10 unions outside the FOL, called the Administrative, Technical, Professional, Semi-Professional and Other Workers' Organisation. Its members were the Northern

Local Government Officers' Union, the Wellington Local Government Officers' Union, the Airline Pilots' Association, the Merchant Service Guild, the Institute of Marine and Power Engineers, the Police Association, the Nurses' Union, the New Zealand Storemen's Federation and the Society of Technicians, Administrators, Managers and Supervisors. It had no impact on the broader spread of trade union activity and influence.

273. There were 95 delegates altogether, with another 61 observers including Don Brash, then executive director of the Kiwifruit Authority.

274. *PSA Journal*, October 1984, p. 2.

275. Ken and Roger Douglas were not related. Both men were guest speakers at a Futures Trust Seminar in Wellington in May 1989, and after Roger had spoken first, raving about the advantages of a market-led economy and warning of the dangers of government intervention, the chairman asked whether the two men shared a common ancestry. Ken strode to the microphone and quickly set the record straight. Not only were they not related, he intoned, Scottish clan records showed that there were two sides to the Douglas clan — the red Douglases and the black Douglases. Although he did not identify which side he belonged to, the 200-strong audience quickly made their own assumptions (*Dominion Sunday Times*, 21 May 1989).

276. Ironically, Robert Muldoon believed that a 27 per cent rise was justified based on the real growth that the economy had experienced from 1982.

277. *Evening Post*, 6, 10 December 1984.

278. The companies and their profits were: Fletcher Challenge ($131 million), Forest Products ($75 million), Wattie's ($19.5 million after six months), AHI ($38 million), Carter Holt ($24.5 million), Goodman's ($23 million), UEB ($19 million), NZ Steel ($18.5 million), Lion Breweries ($18.5 million) and Fisher & Paykel ($18 million). The value of the top 50 companies was close to $448 million. As the FOL pointed out, that was a rise of $83.60 in untaxed income for every wage and salary earner every week. The FOL was claiming $15 for every worker each week.

279. *New Zealand Herald*, 29 April 1985.

280. Ken Douglas interview with Sharon Crosbie, *Dominion Sunday Times*, 21 August 1988, p. 16.

281. The principal finding of a Heylen Poll conducted on 27 October 1984 was that 24 per cent of 1000 respondents aged 15 and over randomly selected from

population centres of 2500 or more supported compulsory unionism, whereas 67 per cent believed people should not be made to join a union (Roth MS 94-106-57/14, ATL). The FOL wanted $208 as the minimum pay rate; the employers $145.

282. *New Zealand Herald*, 9 May 1985.

283. Ibid.

284. Ibid., 17 September 1985.

285. Ibid., 8 May 1986. Yet it was noteworthy that more than any preceding administration, this government was appointing FOL personnel to a raft of statutory bodies. Knox became a member of the board of the Railways Corporation and of the Marketing Development Board, while Douglas was appointed to the Industrial Development Steering Committee, the Employers' Training Association board, the Industrial Relations Foundation board, the Industrial Relations Syllabus Committee, the National Advisory Committee on the Transition from School to Working Life, the board of the Institute of Policy Studies, the board of the Standard Press and the Employers' Association Training Board. They were not alone. More than 70 trade unionists were Labour appointees to a wide range of boards, councils, commissions and committees, some with little or no relevance to industrial issues.

286. Through the FOL, New Zealand unions and members sent a total of close to $59,000 to the British Miners' Strike Appeal in 1984 and 1985. The New Zealand Seamen's Union sent directly through its British counterpart a sum of $83,737.38, with $26,000 in the form of a container of lamb, and the balance being sent in cash. 'NZFOL Minutes and Report of the Proceedings of the Forty-Ninth Annual Conference Held in the Town Hall, Wellington on May 6, 7, 8, 9 1986', pp. 93–96. MS X 2409, ATL.

287. Campbell was also appointed to a New Zealand Post Review Committee which recommended turning it into a state-owned enterprise.

288. *Auckland Star*, 25 August 1986; *New Zealand Herald*, 26 August 1986. Campbell was a media favourite, being quoted as often as Knox and Douglas, and wrote a weekly column for the *New Zealand Times*. Ironically, he was replaced on the FOL executive by Bill Andersen, his ideological opposite. Trevor Farmer, for whom Campbell later worked, was then a member of the Business Roundtable as head of Freightways.

289. Within days of his resignation Campbell was re-elected to the Labour Party executive.

290. Three other unionists served on the Labour Party executive. Stewart McCaffley retained his post as senior vice-president; the others were Engineers' Union delegate Fred Anderson and PPTA field officer Maryan Street, currently a Labour MP.

291. *New Zealand Herald*, 7 May 1986.

292. Script of Douglas on *Years of Change*, broadcast on TVI in August 1996, p. 11.

293. Ibid.

294. Information from Patricia Herbert, 'What About the Unions?' in *NZ Listener*, 13 August 1988, p. 31.

295. *NZ Listener*, 20 September 1986.

296. As well as government MPs, Robert Muldoon and Jim Bolger, now Leader of the Opposition, attended Neary's book launch. In December 1986, the FOL comprised 145 affiliated unions representing 454,000 workers. Along with Knox and Douglas it employed three research workers and eight support staff. It owned premises in Wellington, and was sustained by a $2-a-head levy on all members of its affiliated unions.

297. *NZ Listener*, 14 February 1987.

298. Ibid.

299. Douglas's whimsical side loved to make analogous comparisons. He told Reid that there was a simplistic view that labour and capital were equals: like two 35-stone Japanese wrestlers having an arm wrestle. 'You know that one wrestler will win one time and the other, the next. But the labour representative is now a 9-stone weakling that can't afford to go to Charles Atlas's gym. We're flat on our back. At this time, to remove traditional State support is really delivering trade unions up on a silver salver and giving the big monopolies a carving knife.' (Ibid.)

300. Douglas's comments cited in Herbert, 'What About the Unions?', op. cit.

301. Ibid.

302. For Ken Douglas, highlights of the 1987 conference were the historic march to the Appeal Court in support of Maori people's concern at further loss of their land; the reminiscences of union stalwarts such as Jock Barnes, John Mitchell, Jim Richards and Ted Thompson, demonstrating the qualities of their outstanding leadership, and the outstanding reception giving to retiring vice-president Sonja Davies who went to represent Labour in Parliament for Pencarrow; *New Zealand Tribune*, 16 March 1987.

CHAPTER 10

303. Representing the FOL at these meetings were Knox, Douglas and Ted Thompson, while David Thorp (chairman), Bruce Webster (vice-chairman) and Barry Tucker (secretary) represented the Combined State Unions.

304. Minutes, FOL Forty-Sixth Annual Conference, 3–6 May 1983, pp. 52–53, MS X 2408.

305. CM Clark, Secretary to the Working Party, 'Progress Report on the Proposal for a NZ Council of Trade Unions', to Secretary NZFOL, Secretary CSU, Affiliated and Non-Affiliated Unions, 15 November 1982; 'NZFOL Circulars', FOL MS 95-050 ATL.

306. See 'Proposed NZ Council of Trade Unions: Preliminary Conference, 18–19 February 1985', Folder 14/2/2, MS 4100, ATL.

307. Ibid.; 'Minutes, FOL Forty-Seventh Annual Conference', 8–11 May 1984, pp. 81–82, MS X 2408.

308. Other union leaders saw a more sophisticated body emerging which would bring trade union communication to radio stations and buy TV time to air trade union views. Bill Andersen was one of these. He regarded radio and TV time as essential to counteract the anti-union forces that controlled the media. Andersen also foresaw the organisation developing medical schemes, credit unions and discount services for members. Ibid.

309. *Evening Post*, 31 July 1985.

310. *Seamen's Journal*, vol. 21, no. 1, February 1988, p. 11.

311. Jennings was elected secretary, Goodfellow president and Morgan vice-president of the new organisation. Others to stay outside the new organisation were the Electrical Workers' Union, the United Food and Chemical Workers' Union, the Printers' Union, the Carpenters' Union and the Freezing Industry Clerical Workers' Union. Some of these took a 'wait and see' approach. Others cited cost, and unwieldy structure.

312. 'Working Party on Proposed NZ Council of Trade Unions: Final Progress Report'; FOL, 'Minutes Forty-Ninth Annual Conference, 6–9 May 1986, pp. 49–55 passim; MS X 2409.

313. See David Grant, *Those Who Can Teach: A History of Secondary Teaching In New Zealand from the Union Perspective*, Wellington, 2003, especially Chapters 16, 18 and 21, for a record of teachers' industrial militancy in recent years.

314. Jones replaced Ernie Ball as secretary of the Engineers' Union when Ball was appointed a workers' representative on the Arbitration Court.

315. 'New Zealand Council of Trade Union', FOL Minutes Fiftieth Annual Conference, 5–8 May 1987, pp. 24–25, MS X 2410. A three-day working conference the following March voted for biennial conferences and narrowly allowed for the establishment of women and Maori trade union committees in the new organisation's national and regional structures by 265,463 votes to 265,187, a majority of just 276.

316. Foulkes to Shaun Ryan, Trade Union History Project's Union Leaders Oral History Project, 19 October 1999, OH99/34, ATL.

CHAPTER 11

317. The most stirring speech at this conference was delivered by Ken Capstick, a visiting official of the British Miners' Union, then engaged in its deep and brutal battle for survival with Margaret Thatcher's Conservative government. It was Capstick — not Knox, nor David Lange (who received a muted albeit polite reception) nor Ken Douglas — who inspired the most rousing response from the crowd.

318. In Patricia Herbert, 'What About the Unions?' *NZ Listener*, p. 31, 13 August 1988. The FOL's 'hairy arm and mallet' had its origin in symbols used by De Leonite socialists, who were part of the original American Wobbly industrial revolutionaries. The 'arm' depicted the role of workers as the builders of society; the 'mallet' or 'hammer' depicted power as represented by an engineer, steel worker or riveter in his work.

319. Trotter's comments gleaned from the rushes of his interview with Monique Oomen for the documentary *Ken Douglas — Traitor or Visionary?*

320. Glen Hurley, 'The Heavy-Duty Labours of Ken Douglas', *Management*, March 1989, p. 38.

321. Under this arrangement, the workforce was divided into teams with leaders who briefed them. The 'Nissan Way' was a success story for both worker and management. Within three years Nissan was able to carry an extended warranty on its cars, and through increased market share created 70 new assembly jobs. Because pay increases were linked to performance and skills acquisition these

workers enjoyed the best rates of any car assembly workers in the country. For a full, albeit uncritical, description of the new industrial arrangements at the Wiri plant see Alan Williams, Bruce Owen and Alan Emerson, *The Nissan Way*, Auckland, 1991.

322. Herbert, 'What About the Unions?' op. cit., p. 30.

323. 'A Message from the President,' NZCTU pamphlet, July 1988, cited in Roth, op. cit. By this time, Douglas, Foulkes, Burgess and often Harris and other officers had settled into a work routine where they met weekly on Monday mornings to plan the work, both collectively and individually, for the week ahead. Kate Clark, who coordinated these meetings, acted as minutes secretary. Linda Sissons, a highly qualified academic who had been Douglas's executive assistant in the FOL for a period, would be appointed to lead the Trade Union Education Authority, the CTU's first reform. Its offices were also in the Tasman Hotel.

324. The new Labour Court saw the judges (currently Jack Horn, NP Williamson and DS Castle) stay on from the previous Arbitration Court, but workers' (Ernie Ball and Dave Jacobs) and employers' representatives (Phil Oldham and Terry Weir) gone. The new Court sat in Auckland, Wellington and Christchurch. Two lay advisors had voting rights.

325. NZCTU pamphlet, August 1988, cited in Roth, MS 94, Folder 106-59/02, ATL.

326. *New Zealand Herald*, 7 October 1989; unemployment statistics from *NZPD*, 10/10/89, cited in Roth MS 94, Folder 59/10.

327. *New Zealand Herald*, 21 November, 22 December 1988.

328. Interview, 12 March 2010.

329. The district councils were Auckland, Bay of Plenty, Buller, Canterbury, Gisborne, Hawke's Bay, Kaimai, Manawatu, Mangonui, Marlborough, Nelson, Oamaru, Otago, Southland, Taranaki, Thames, Timaru, Tokoroa, Waikato, Wairarapa, Wanganui, Wellington, West Coast and Whangarei. There were four further district sub-committees: Eastern Bay of Plenty, Horowhenua, Ohakune and Wairoa.

330. *New Zealand Herald*, 8 September 1989.

331. See Chris Trotter, 'The Big Deal', *NZ Listener*, 9 September 1989, p. 17.

332. Ibid., 26 November 1987.

333. In every issue through 1989 and the early months of 1990 the *People's Voice* printed lists of organisations and the names of those — usually left-wing union

or Communist Party activists or budding New Labour politicians — who were opposed to the compact. Sometimes discussion on this issue dominated the publication's pages.

334. *New Zealand Herald*, 16 September 1987.

335. Krasin was a charismatic teacher who gave lectures to political researchers from all around the world.

336. In giving the responsibility to Moore, Lange was sidelining Labour Minister Stan Rodger because of his earlier opposition to such a deal. The CTU Compact Working Group comprised Mark Gosche and Lianne Dalziell (Hotel Workers' Union), Allen Pascoe (Post Office Union), Maryan Street (Post Primary Teachers' Association), Ros Noonan (New Zealand Education Institute), Allan Ware (Pulp and Paper Workers' Union), Owen Harvey (Distribution Workers' Union), John Fisher (Electrical Workers' Union), Chris Eichbaum (Engineers' Union), Ray Potroz (Dairy Workers' Union), Calvin Fisher (Labourers' Union), Ross Wilson (Harbour Board Workers' Union), Pat Kelly (Cleaners' and Caretakers' Union) and Belinda Kitchen (Clerical Workers' Union). Also taking part were Ken Douglas, Peter Harris and Kate Clark from the CTU and Graeme Whimp from the Trade Union Education Authority (Roth MS 94, Folder 106-59/05).

337. Douglas, address to NZ Pulp and Paper Workers' Federation, 10 February, CTU Paper (Roth MS 106-59/ 13).

338. Ibid.

339. *New Zealand Herald*, 2 August 1989.

340. Stan Rodger forsook the labour portfolio, complaining that his workload was too high. He remained the Minister for 17 State-owned Enterprises, State Services and Railways.

341. 'The Compact: Statement by the Government and the New Zealand Council of Trade Unions', December 1989 (Roth MS 94 Folder 59/10).

342. The Compact Statement, op. cit.; *Auckland Star*, 3 January 1990.

343. NZCTU, 'Minutes of the Special Proceedings of the Special Conference', Wellington Town Hall, 3 April, 4 April 1990. It was a testy meeting, with Douglas and other pro-compact speakers being heckled from the floor. Security guards removed the two most vociferous anti-compact interjectors. Douglas told the conference at one stage that he did not care what people thought about him, 'but I have huge respect for this organisation and the people who lead it'.

344. *Sunday-Star*, 1 May 1990.

345. In Patricia Herbert, 'Opening the Industrial Gates', *Sunday Star-Times*, 26 June 1990.

346. *People's Voice*, 2 August 1990.

347. Moore paid weekly $4.50 dues by direct credit to the Canterbury-Westland branch of the Printers' Union.

348. *The New Zealand Herald*, 23 September 1990.

349. *The New Zealand Herald*, 20 October 1990.

350. Ibid., 29 October 1990.

351. Douglas, 'The Basics of Unity', address to 1990 Labour Party Conference, 9 November 1990 (Roth MS 94, op. cit.).

352. Ibid.

CHAPTER 12

353. Meat industry statistics from Tim Fulton, *Straight Off the Tussock*, Masterton, 2005, p. 135. See chapter five of David Grant, *Bulls, Bears and Elephants: A History of the New Zealand Stock Exchange*, Wellington, 1996, for a description and analysis of the 1987 stockmarket crash and its impact on the political, economic and social life of New Zealanders and their leaders. Roger Douglas's unemployment comments quoted in the *Dominion*, 9 February 1989.

354. However, Bolger was unable to hold to the wage restraint trade-off which was part of the Agreement, primarily because the government's sudden and expensive $620 million bail-out of the Bank of New Zealand had forced it to resume a programme of stock tendering which pushed interest rates to their highest levels within two years.

355. Cited in *People's Voice*, 26 November 1990, p. 2.

356. *New Zealand Herald*, 14 December 1990.

357. Department of Labour, 'The Employment Contracts Bill: A Backgrounder', December 1990 (Roth MS 94, Folder 106-60/04). NZCTU circular, 'Update on Employment Contracts Act, No 1: What's Happened: The Ideology', 24 January 1991 (Roth MS 94, Folder 106, 60/95). A precursor to this new hard line had come earlier when Minister of Finance Ruth Richardson savagely cut social welfare

benefits and instituted budgetary reviews in health, education and other areas of social service.

358. Business concerns cited in the *New Zealand Herald*, 10 April 1991.

359. *Auckland Star*, 24 December 1990.

360. Ibid.

361. Gordon Campbell, 'Act of Faith', *NZ Listener*, 27 May 1991, pp. 15–16 passim.

362. The Department of Labour report was requested by the select committee studying the Employment Contracts Bill to see how it could be ratified by the ILO. Department of Labour Report, Employment Contracts Bill: International Labour Organisation Obligations. Graeme Buchanan for Secretary of Labour to Chairman, Labour Select Committee, Parliament Buildings, Wellington, 3 April 1991, p. 2. cit. NZCTU Ms 2003 Folder 361-01/1. ICFTU comment cited *Tribune*, 30 April 1993.

363. NZCTU, 'Circular to Affiliates from President', No. 1990/150, 20 December 1990 (Roth MS 94, op. cit.). Employers' Federation president Steve Marshall foreshadowed the Bill, stating he was looking forward to 'hardline industrial reform'.

364. The National caucus had its mavericks, and not all members supported the legislation — chief among the dissenters were Hamish McIntyre, Grahame Thorne and Gilbert Myles.

365. NZCTU, 'Minutes of Meeting of Affiliates, Wellington, 21 February 1991' (Roth, MS 94, Folder 106-60/08). There were three National MPs on the Select Committee and two Labour. Max Bradford, National's Tarawera MP and former executive director of the Bankers' Association, was the chair; the other members were National MPs Ian Revell (Birkenhead) and Bruce Cliffe (North Shore), and Labour's Ross Robertson (Papatoetoe) and Koro Wetere (Western Maori.) The Select Committee received more than 400 written submissions on the Bill, one of the largest numbers ever in the country's history. On 18 April, five days before it was due to report back to Parliament, Bradford reported that he had heard 203 oral submissions and listened to 502 witnesses over 153 hours of sitting in the previous 10 weeks. Most submissions were opposed to the Bill.

366. 'Notes for an Address by Ken Douglas to Annual Conference of New Zealand Meatworkers' Union', 26 February 1991 (Roth MS 94, Folder 106-60/05). *People's Voice*, 25 February 1991, p. 18.

367. This was Bolger's 'state of the nation' address. Birch's comment quoted in the

New Zealand Herald, 19 March 1991.

368. Douglas's comments quoted in the *New Zealand Herald*, 9 March 1991.

369. Anglican views cited in *Auckland Star*, 17 April 1991.

370. Provincial divisions of the Employers' Federation also began campaigns of their own, taking out half- and full-page newspaper advertisements extolling the virtues of the forthcoming legislation.

371. *PSA Journal*, April 1991, p. 11.

372. *Harbourside*, journal of the New Zealand Harbour Workers' Union, April–May 1991, p. 3.

373. The next three paragraphs are gleaned from *People's Voice*, 17 April 1991, pp. 49–52.

374. At this time Kelly was the secretary of the Cleaners', Caretakers' and Security Officers' Union. The select committee had already received 62 submissions on the Bill and would hear 830 more, making it the most examined piece of legislation in New Zealand's history.

375. The executive resolution was seconded by Gay Williams of the Nurses' Association; NZCTU, 'Minutes of Special Meeting of Affiliates, Wellington, 18 April 1991', pp. 7–10 passim (Roth MS 94, Folder 106-60/07).

376. Ibid., pp. 13–14.

377. Ibid., pp. 14–15.

378. Ibid, p. 15; *New Zealand Herald*, 19 April 1991.

379. In Auckland large numbers also cheered and clapped from the footpath, vastly outnumbering those who jeered. There were also marches on 30 April in Thames (50), Hamilton (400), Tokoroa (300), Rotorua (100), Kawerau (where Tasman pulp and paper and timber workers walked off the job), Tauranga (100), Napier (1000), Hastings (100), New Plymouth (500), Wanganui (300), Palmerston North (2000), Nelson (2000), Kaiapoi (100), Christchurch (7500), Timaru (600), Oamaru (where factory workers went on strike), Westport (500), Greymouth (500), Dunedin (2000), Gore (workers at Flemings Cremoata Mill walked off the job for 24 hours, the first-ever strike in the company's 100-year history) and Invercargill (3000).

380. Auckland's May Day rally attracted 2000 unionists and supporters and became another 'de facto' protest against the Bill.

381. *NZPD*, vol. 5: 2, 23 April 1991, p. 1425.

382. *Auckland Star*, 15 May 1991; *New Zealand Herald*, 22, 23 May 1991.
383. Gordon Campbell, 'Leading from the Rear', *NZ Listener*, 3 June 1991, pp. 30–31.
384. The most common version of this nursery rhyme goes as follows:

'The Grand Old Duke of York
He had ten thousand men
He marched them up to the top of the hill
And he marched them down again
And when they were up they were up
And when they were down they were down
And when they were only halfway up
They were neither up nor down.'

385. Douglas's 1997 comment reported in the *New Zealand Herald*, 28 October 1997. Despite the impression often given by the press coverage, which was nearly always antagonistic, strikes in New Zealand tended to be short and sharp and based on parochial industrial matters. This was in stark contrast to the kind of militancy and determination shown in Great Britain during the first onslaught of Thatcherism where miners and nurses were on strike for months and, in the case of the former, their action was at times brutally repelled by police on horseback wielding batons and releasing dogs on the protesting miners and their families. In 1991, one local industrial relations commentator called New Zealand trade unionism 'a tame dog. It very rarely barks, let alone bites.'
386. Campbell, p. 33.
387. In 1988 the PSA had aggressively protested against the State Sector Bill. The failure of that campaign led them to take a more cautious approach in response to the Employment Contracts Bill.
388. *Sunday Star*, 28 April 1991.
389. Ibid.
390. Interview, Stansfield, 22 July 2005.
391. Galt to Rod Prosser, 5 May 2004, in possession of the Maritime Union of New Zealand.
392. Trotter's comments reported in the *Dominion*, 24 October 1997.
393. *PSA Journal*, June 1991.

CHAPTER 13

394. The biggest bargaining agent was Teesdale Meuli and Co. Teesdale was a former personnel manager with New Zealand Forest Products, Wilkins and Davies, and industrial relations manager for the State 11 extension of the Glenbrook steel mill. By the end of March 1992, his company had negotiated around 300 collective contracts and more individual contracts. There was no set fee for advocates' services, and they did not come cheap. Some set an upfront fee, such as 25 per cent of clients' settlement money. Others charged a standard rate — around $1000 was common for an average mediation, or $3000 to $4000 for an all-day hearing. Union advocates were generally cheaper. 1992/93 figures from NZCTU *Biennial Report* 1993, p. 14.
395. Douglas blames the current 'leaky homes' debacle on the lack of properly trained builders in New Zealand which occurred after the abandonment of the apprenticeship system and consequent destruction of a viable skills base in house construction. The removal of quality standards, regulatory compliances, environmental contamination, and recent untrammelled property speculation have all played a part as well.
396. The Northern and Southern groups later joined the Trade Union Federation, while the Central union remained within the CTU fold; loyalty to Ken Douglas was a key factor in its decision.
397. *New Zealand Herald*, 3, 5 October 1991.
398. This conference coincided with news that New Zealand and New Zealanders were worse off after the economic and labour reforms introduced by Roger Douglas and Bill Birch. According to OECD figures, between 1985 and 1990 gross domestic product per person had fallen by 0.7 per cent, whereas in Japan it had risen by 23 per cent and in Australia by 8.5 per cent. Moreover, the declining national wealth had been unevenly distributed. Statistics Department figures showed that over the previous 10 years the top 20 per cent of full-time workers had received an 8.1 per cent rise in real disposable income while the rest of the country's workers had lost. Since the reforms began jobs had fallen by 5.3 per cent. In contrast, over the same period in Australia they had grown by 13 per cent.
399. *NZ Listener*, 28 October 1991, p. 36.
400. The driving force behind the 'unionisation' of the Post Office Association was Ivan Reddish, Burgess's predecessor as head of the POA — which became the Post

Office Union at his urging at the end of his time in office — and the CSSO. Reddish also headed the international Post Office organisation for a period.

401. Previous to 1990, executive members were nominated from within six electoral colleges of related unions.

402. 'New Zealand Experiences with Deunionisation and Labour Market Deregulation', 15th World Congress of the International Confederation of the Free Trade Unions, 17–24 March 1992 (Roth MS 94, Folder 106-60/11).

403. Ibid. Earlier, in February 1992, Douglas was giving much the same message to 180 delegates who attended the second conference of the South Pacific and Oceanic Council of Trade Unions (SPOCTU) in Wellington. This conference was funded by the International Labour Organisation (ILO), the Asian Pacific Regional Organisation of the International Confederation of Free Trade Unions (ICFTU-APRO) as well as a substantial donation from the CTU.

404. *New Zealand Herald*, 18 January, 30 April 1992. The contracts the Department of Labour analysed covered 212,980 employees or about 14 per cent of the total labour force of 1,482,100; *New Zealand Herald*, 4 May 1993.

405. ICFTU comment cited in NZCTU *Biennial Report 1993*, p. 24. The Business Roundtable, incensed by the CTU's action, hired a 'friendly' lawyer, Dr Colin Howard, professor of law at Melbourne University. Howard proclaimed he was 'highly critical' of the procedure followed by the ILO in examining the complaint. 'The organization is clearly ignorant of New Zealand's system of law and government and has selectively disregarded or misstated information supplied to it.' He also pointed out that the ILO should not have even received a complaint which was 'merely a trade union political disagreement, motivated by self interest with laws properly enacted by a freely elected parliamentary democracy. For anyone to accuse New Zealand of "serious violation" of rights to associate, organize and bargain collectively as CTU president Ken Douglas does in his covering letter to the complaint, is a manifest absurdity and should have been treated by the ILO.' 'Resources and research material for CTU submission to ILO Contact Mission', NZCTU MS 2003, Folder 361-01/1.

406. 'ILO Complaint: A Summary of the Final Report of the Governing Body of the ILO on the Complaint by the NZCTU that the Employment Contracts Act Breached ILO Conventions on Freedom of Association and Collective Bargaining' (NZCTU MS 2003, Folder 361-04/2).

407. *NZPD*, 17 November 1994, pp. 4891–4 passim. Bolger's comments cited by John

Hughes, senior lecturer in labour law at the University of Canterbury who analysed the ILO's initial findings and the government's reactions to it in an article published in the *Press*, 18 April 1994. For a clear analysis of all the issues after the ILO's findings were made public see Ewan Paton, University of Nottingham, 'Case No 1698, ILO Committee on Freedom of Association: Complaint by the NZCTU Against the New Zealand Government', *Industrial Law Journal*, vol. 23, no. 3, 20 September 1994, pp. 256–61. Doug Kidd had replaced Maurice McTigue as Minister of Labour after McTigue lost his seat in the 1993 election.

408. *New Zealand Herald*, 14 May 1992.

409. These reports were gleaned from the 'case studies' section of the September 1993 'Report of the Labour Select Committee on the Effects of the Employment Contracts Act on the New Zealand Labour Market', pp. 53–90 passim. Members of the committee were Max Bradford (chairman), Helen Clark, Bruce Cliffe (until 5 April 1993), Ian Revell, Larry Sutherland and Grant Thomas (from 5 April 1993). Elizabeth Tennent replaced Helen Clark for much of the inquiry when Clark, now leader of the Labour Party, was absent on other business. While the Select Committee's 1993 report concluded, in general terms, that the Act was working successfully, two Labour members, Helen Clark and Larry Sutherland, produced a 'Minority Report' arguing that the Act had to be repealed. They believed that there were five fundamental areas where the Act fell short: it failed to provide fair and equitable working conditions; it failed to provide a bargaining system that protected the choice of parties about representation and conditions; it failed to improve living standards for working people of New Zealand; it failed to protect collective bargaining, and the institutions established by the Act were badly designed and stretched to breaking point ('Report of the Minority of the Labour Select Committee into the Effects of the Employment Contracts Act on the New Zealand Labour Market', 21 September 1993, p. 2). Both reports cited in NZCTU MS 2003, Folder 361-01/1.

410. Reported in *Harbourside/ Seamen's Journal*, March/April 1993, p. 9.

411. Ibid., pp. 91–107 passim. Pay rates had gone down, drastically in some cases. Before the ECA the hourly rate for a child-care worker was $7.16; in 1993 the going rate was $4 for those under 20 ('Minority Report of Select Committee', op. cit., p. 3).

412. Cit. Ross Wilson address, p. 4, op. cit. Criticisms were not restricted to workers and their unions. Allied Personnel of Auckland was one of the biggest firms of bargaining agents negotiating employment contracts and conducting advocacy

for worker clients at the Employment Tribunal. While supportive of the legislation, it acknowledged that some employers did not treat their employees fairly. Allied identified a number of serious problems with the Act. These included a lack of recognition of bargaining agents by some employers; a lack of some contracts being in writing so that rights were able to be enforced by litigation; the need for compulsion to vary a contract because the current provisions were too difficult to enforce; lack of personal grievance information given to employers, particularly small employers who did not have ready access to this information; the habit of issuing lockout notices causing logistical problems as some employees did not receive these notices; and long delays at the Employment Tribunal, especially when complainants were using lawyers. 'Report of the Select Committee', op. cit., p. 91.

413. Heylen Survey cited in 'Minority Report', op. cit., p. 9.

414. Reported in *New Zealand Herald*, 1 October 1992.

415. Ibid.; Douglas to author, 10 May 2010.

416. Clark's comments in *NZPD*, 1 October 1992, p. 11380. Linda Sissons, director of the TUEA, joined the New Zealand Qualifications Authority, as did TUEA staffer Joe Tepania, an SUP activist, who became Maori Liaison Officer at the NZQA. National replaced the TUEA with a contestable fund for educational projects on industrial-type issues. This year also saw the closing of the CTU's health and safety centres, which had been established in 1987 to promote good health and safety work practices among its members by providing training, advice, specialist services and resources for workers and their unions. They had been funded by the Accident Compensation Commission, but following the government's savage tightening of the criteria for funding, which henceforth restricted it to projects that directly reduced employer premiums, ACC withdrew its funding for the centres and they were forced to close.

417. Ibid., *New Zealand Herald*, 17 May 1992.

418. Despite the downturn in numbers the CTU was still a big organisation. In September 1992 it had a national executive of 18 including the three office-holders, Douglas, Foulkes and Wilson; a head office in Wellington; 14 District Councils (Auckland, Bay of Plenty, Canterbury, Gisborne, Hawke's Bay, Manawatu/Wanganui, Nelson/Marlborough, Northland, Otago, Southland, Taranaki, Waikato, Wellington, West Coast); two Health and Safety Centres, in Auckland and Wellington; 14 Trade Union Centres (Whangarei, Auckland, Hamilton, Rotorua, Mt Maunganui, Tokoroa, Gisborne, Hawke's Bay, Wanganui, Palmerston North, Christchurch, Nelson, Dunedin,

Timaru) and 37 affiliates, many of whom were a combination of smaller unions still operating locally and/or different organisations in different regions. These were the Flight Attendants and Related Services Association; Combined Early Childhood Union of Aotearoa; Clerical Workers' Unions; Communication and Energy Workers' Union; Community Services Union; Distribution Workers' Union; Distribution and General Workers' Union; Workers' Union (Amalgamated); Northern Drug and Chemical Workers' Union; New Zealand Educational Institute; New Zealand Engineering and Related Trades Union; Finsec; Professional Firefighters' Union; Food and Textile Workers' Union; Freezing Workers' Union — Auckland/Tomoana; Harbour Workers' Union; Hotel, Hospital and Restaurant Unions; Journalists' and Graphic Process Union (JAGPRO); Local Government Officers' Unions; Meat Workers' and Related Trades Union; Medical Specialists' (Salaried) Association; New Zealand Nurses' Association; Nurses' Union; New Zealand Police Association; Post Primary Teachers' Association; Public Service Association; Wood Industries Union of Aotearoa; New Zealand Combined Union of Railway Employees (CURE); Transport and General Workers' Union; Service Workers' Unions; Association of Staff in Tertiary Education (ASTE); Tertiary Institutes Allied Staff Association (TIASA); Tramways Employees' Union; University Staff Association; Waterfront Workers' Union and the Writers' Guild.

Unions outside the CTU were the Chartered Accountants Employees' Unions; Airline Pilots' Association; Air New Zealand Pilots' Association; Liquor, Food and Allied Workers' Union; APEX; Northern Apparel and Related Trades' Union; Aviation Industry Officers' Union; Baking Trades Employees' Union; Building Trades' Union; Clothing Trade Employees' Union; Clothing and Related Trades' Union; Cool and Cold Stores' Employees Branch Union; Southern Drivers' Union; Equine Workers' Association; International Flight Planners' Society; Food and Chemical Workers' Union; Footwear Workers' Union; Freezing Works Clerical Officers' Union; Furniture and Allied Industries' Union (except Northern); Furniture and Related Trades' Union (Northern); Manufacturing and Construction Workers' Union; Marine, Aviation and Power Engineers' Association; Medical Laboratory Workers' Union; Merchant Service Guild; Pharmacy Employees' Association; Plumbers' and Gasfitters' Union; Polytechnics Student Union of Aotearoa; Printing and Related Trades' Union; National Union of Railway Workers; Resident Doctors' Association, Rubber Workers' Union (Christchurch); Seafarers' Union; Store and Warehouse Employees' Union;

Totalisator and Allied Employees' Association; TradeSec; University Students' Association and Amalgamated Workers' Union. Amalgamation between or 'takeover' of smaller unions by bigger continued through this time. Bigger CTU-affiliated unions such as the Service Workers' Union had now absorbed the Cleaners', Caretakers' and Security Officers' Union; the Southland Clerical Workers' Union; Compass (the Commercial and Professional Administrative Secretarial Staff Union); the Hotel, Hospital and Restaurant Union (Northern, Wellington and Southern), and the Laundry Workers' Union (Southern). The Communication and Energy Workers' Union now included the Post Office Workers' Union. The Distribution Workers' Union now absorbed the Hotel Workers' Union in Nelson, Marlborough and Westland; the Engine Drivers', Firemen and Greasers' Union; and the Equity and Entertainment Union. The Workers' Union (Amalgamated) included the Drivers' Union (Taranaki and Wellington); the Labourers Local Bodies and the Labourers and Related Trades' Unions and the Mine Workers' United Union. The Transport and General Workers' Union included the Road Transport Workers' Union (Canterbury and Westland). The Wood Industries' Union, Aotearoa included the Timber Workers' Union and the Pulp and Paper Workers' Union (Northern, Wellington, Otago and Southland). In 1993, the NZ Nurses' Association and NZ Nurses' Union merged to form the NZ Nurses' Organisation. The Central and Invercargill Local Government Officers, Northern Local Government Officers' Association and the Public Service Association combined to become the NZ Public Service Association.

419. The margin represented just 7000 workers in a card vote representing more than 320,000 members. There were 69 delegates at this meeting, three officers, nine observers and eight staff. *New Zealand Herald*, 29 July 1992. NZCTU, 'Minutes of Special Meeting of Affiliates', Wellington, 28 July 1992 (Roth MS 94, Folder 106-60/13).

420. NZCTU, 'Workplace Reform: A Union Guide', September 1992 (Roth MS 94, Folder 106-60/13).

421. The CTU later rationalised the 'new way' into six basic principles — a national minimum code of basic rights and protections; the right to organise; the right to bargain collectively; multi-employer bargaining over key industry codes and standards; a tripartite process for developing industry, and a tripartite process for developing economic and social policies.

422. Douglas, 'Address to the Labour Party Conference', 5 September 1992 (Roth MS

94, Folder 106-60-13).

423. *NZPD*, 29 June 1994, p. 2452.

424. Ibid.

425. Kidd's comment, ibid., p. 2455.

426. *Workers' Voice*, 28 July 1992. It later said that the CTU was 'well-hated' inside the working class because of the 'jump into bed with the bosses' line promoted by Douglas and Foulkes (12 August 1982).

427. Playwright Dean Parker, an Auckland-based official of the Writers' Guild — and a perceptive political commentator — argued in a letter to the *Workers' Voice* that left-wing militants who chose to leave the main body of unionists were left isolated and without a voice in the wider more powerful group. To reinforce his argument Parker pointed to the short life of the last breakaway group, the Trade Union Congress, which had split from the Federation of Labour in 1950. This wisdom went unheeded. 1 May 1993, p. 22.

428. The 17 unions represented in the TUF were the Administrative and General Workers' Union, the Amalgamated Workers' Union, Building Trades' Union, Engine Drivers' Union, Furniture Workers' Union, Liquor, Food and Allied Workers' Union, Manufacturing and Construction Workers' Union (and their three affiliates the Pulp and Paper Council, South Pacific Tyre Rubber Workers' Union and the Wellington Branch of the Footwear Workers' Union), North and South Island Clothing Workers' Unions, Seafarers' Union, United Food and Chemical Workers' Union, Food and Textile Workers' Union and Northern Chemical Workers' Union. The last three named were affiliated to the CTU.

429. *Evening Post*, 14 October 1995.

430. Minutes, CTU National Executive Meeting, 10 May 1994, pp. 3–5 passim (NZCTU MS 2008, Folder 119-03/2). In an earlier, 1989 Seamen's Union dispute, when its assets were seized by sequestration after a pay hiatus, Douglas asked the Labour Court to lift the sequestration order which, he said, had the effect of encouraging the employer to make unilateral decisions about workers without consulting them, which had happened in this case. His request was denied. See David Grant, *Jagged Seas: The Story of the New Zealand Seamen's/Seafarers' Unions, 1879–2003*, in press, Chapters 20 and 21 for more information on these disputes.

431. The conference was originally designed for 350 participants but was scaled up because of the demand for places (*New Zealand Herald*, 26 September 1992). Other key

conference organisers were Pru Dryburgh, assistant conference coordinator; Paul Tolich, CTU union educator; Hel Loader, research officer for the Engineers' Union; Trevor Laurence, general manager of the Experimental Training Company; Roberta Hill of the Institute for Social Research and Development, and David Moloney, production manager for Interlock Industries.

432. In March 1993 the CTU still had a membership approaching 360,000, 10 times more than the TUF. White-collar unions — the PSA (60,488), NZEI (19,485), PPTA (13,302) and Finsec (22,350) —were holding their ground or increasing their numbers slightly as they were not affected by job losses. Both teacher unions were engaged in their own battles, the PPTA aggressively fighting government plans to bulk fund secondary schools, a fight which they eventually won. The Communication and Energy Workers' Union, an amalgamated group, was also healthy, its numbers increasing from 26,937 in 1991/92 to 31,657 in 1992/93.

433. *NZ Listener*, 6 October 1992.

434. NZCTU, 'Opening Address by Ken Douglas', President, Biennial Conference of the NZCTU, 20 September 1993 (Roth MS 94, Folder 106, op. cit., p. 2). In this address he also praised women in the movement and acknowledged that their role was not an easy one in a movement dominated by men. 'You fought hard for an equal say. You did it in a constructive and democratic way, in a spirit of unity and in recognition of the contribution you could make, not the benefit you could extract. Let me extend to the sprinkling of union and working class women who have been awarded the commemorative Suffrage Medal sincere congratulations. The pity is that there are so few, and I do feel a sense of resentment at the bypassing of so many who worked untiringly, and for so long. Women such as Nellie Bell, Margaret Long, Connie Birchfield, Ella Ayo, Mavis Drennan, Rona Bailey, Cath Kelly, and to them I apologise and say thank you, and the hundreds who stand behind you, for your work.' (Ibid., pp. 2–3).

435. The information in this and the succeeding five paragraphs comes from an interview with Douglas on 21 March 2010, an interview with Meo on 7 May 2010, and a 1999 CTU publication, 'A Trade Unionists' Guide to the New Zealand Business Roundtable'.

436. NZCTU, 'A Trade Unionists' Guide to the New Zealand Business Roundtable', op. cit., p. 6.

437. Rosanne Meo resume, May 2010; in possession of the author.

CHAPTER 14

438. Comments from Douglas's opening address to the 5th Biennial Conference of the NZCTU, 20 October 1995, CTU MS 2008, Folder 199-01/4.

439. Only in energy and utility services was employment up, from 11,129 to 12,791, an increase of 15 per cent.

440. Quoted in the *Evening Post*, 15 July 1995.

441. Ibid.

442. Secretary's Report, CTU Biennial Conference, September 1995, pp. 7–9 passim.

443. The information in this and the following three paragraphs has been gleaned from this report, pp. 10–20 passim.

444. The CTU employed Margaret Hanlon to run the workplace reform project and Stephanie Doyle to run the skills development. It also became actively involved in coordinating work on industry training, facilitating union representation on industry training organisations.

445. Earlier Douglas had been a member of the Prince Philip Trust, which funded Commonwealth Fellowships, some of which were won by trade unionists. He had also succeeded Jim Knox on the Administration Board of the Todd Foundation, a philanthropic organisation particularly aimed at helping young people. The Trade and Development Board had earlier evolved out of TRADENZ, a Mike Moore initiative to promote New Zealand trade overseas. Douglas had been a Labour government appointee to that board.

446. Interview, 26 April 2010.

447. In 1993 he also addressed an executive council meeting of the American Federation of Labour and Congress of Industrial Organisations (AFL-CIO) in Chicago, speaking on employment contract issues.

448. Ken Douglas, 'Unions in the Global Economy', speech to the CTU's 1995 Biennial Conference (Conference Minutes, pp. 41–42).

449. Nicola Shepheard wrote an excellent assessment of Little, the man and his work, in *North and South*, May 2005, pp. 80–90.

450. The information in this and the following six paragraphs is taken from a speech Douglas gave to an industrial relations conference on 19 March 1996, called 'The Future Shape of Employment Relations and the ECA: The View from the CTU' (NZCTU, MS 2003, Folder 361-10/2).

451. Bryan Philpott, 'A Note on Recent Trends in Labour Productivity Growth', Research Project on Economic Planning Paper 281, Victoria University of Wellington, October 1996, passim.

452. Quoted in the *Independent*, 12 April 1996.

453. *Independent*, 17 May 1996.

454. Ibid., p. 9; *Dominion*, 27 June 1995.

455. *Dominion*, 27 November 1996.

456. 'Introduction: Draft Bill to Replace/Amend Employment Contracts Act', NZCTU, Folder 2003; Folder 261-10/2, op. cit. Anderson is now professor of commercial law at Victoria University.

457. Points on the proposed Bill in this and subsequent paragraphs are gleaned from a speech by Angela Foulkes titled 'Partnership and Confrontation: The Challenge for Business', delivered to an Enterprise Horowhenua breakfast meeting in Levin on 25 November 1998 (NZCTU MS 2003, Folder 361-18/03, ATL). See also Gordon Anderson, 'The Workplace Relations Bill: A Way Forward or a Sellout?' address given to the 'Workers' Rights Are Human Rights' seminar organised by the NZCTU and the International Centre for Trade Union Rights, Te Papa Tongarewa, Wellington, 13 October 1998 (NZCTU MS 2003, Folder 361-18/06).

458. Anderson, 'The Workplace Relations Bill: A Way Forward or a Sell-out?' p. 3. The Bill did not meet the approval of all of New Zealand's trade unionists. The TUF was openly critical of it, basically arguing instead that revamped industrial legislation should be based on union rather than worker rights, and envisaging a return to pre-1991 bureaucracy of compulsion that provided for an enforcement function. The TUF wrote a paper outlining its criticism of the CTU Bill called 'The New Zealand Employment Law: A Contract of Labour Rights Approach'. Left-wing commentator Chris Trotter was also critical of the Workplace Employment Bill in *The Independent* of 30 September 1998.

459. Anderson's address, 13 October 1998, op. cit., pp. 5–8 passim.

460. 'Minutes, CTU National Affiliates Council Meeting', 8 September 1998, p. 5 (NZCTU MS 2008, Folder 119-04/2).

461. Ibid.

462. *Dominion*, 26 September 1995.

463. Ibid, 30 September 1995. Interview, Douglas, 21 March 2010. Bill Andersen died on 19 January 2005, two days short of his 81st birthday. He was still president of the

National Distribution Union.

464. CTU Review Committee, 'The Review of the New Zealand Council of Trade Unions', 1998, p. 13; NZCTU MS 2003, Folder 361-03/1. The members of the Review Committee were Douglas, Foulkes and Wilson, as well as members of the national executive: Joanna Beresford (NZEI), Paul Tolich (Engineering, Printing and Manufacturing Union), Lindsay Rea (Finsec and CTU Women's Committee), David Thorp (PSA), Darien Fenton (Service and Food Workers' Union) and Lawrence Tukaki-Millianta (CTU Runanga).

465. Douglas to affiliate secretaries, 12 August 1998 (NZCTU MS 2008, Folder 119-03/2). Despite the changes, some unions including the largest private sector union, the EPMU, were still unhappy. In December 1998 the EPMU complained that within the organisation there were conflicting priorities, a misallocation of resources, a wrong skill set among the mix of staff currently employed, and a failure to assist affiliates to straddle the various industrial agendas being raised by major corporates or public service organisations. The union believed that the CTU should campaign on the public profile of unionism that related to the average working person; encourage workers to identify with unions, collective issues and activity; and contest the public and economic agenda on a range of issues beyond that of work. It wanted the CTU to employ a lobbyist to assist in the media presentation of CTU positions and another person who could handle the agenda of pay systems design, skill-based pay options and performance pay-related issues (summary of letter from EPMU to president, CTU, 12 December 1998, CTU MS Folder 119-04/2).

466. Members of the CTU's International Committee were Douglas, Joanna Beresford (NZEI), Jane Kelsey or Rob Crozier (AUS), Paul Goulter (Finsec), John Ryall (SFWU), Sue Shone (CTU Women's Committee), Paul Tolich (EPMU), and Joe Tonner or Paul Cochrane (PSA). Delegates from other affiliated unions attended meetings from time to time.

467. Memo, Douglas to Affiliates and District Councils, 15 December 1997, NZCTU MS 2008, Folder 119-02/4. The APEC group comprised Australia, Canada, the People's Republic of China, Indonesia, Korea, Mexico, Papua New Guinea, Singapore, Chinese Taipei, Brunei, Chile, Hong Kong, Japan, Malaysia, New Zealand, the Philippines, Thailand and the United States, and from 1999, Peru, Russia and Vietnam.

468. The APLN was established in 1995 to support and promote the work of trade

unions in the APEC region in their dialogue with governments, business and other groups involved in the APEC process. It consisted of affiliates of the ICFTU in Chile, Mexico, the United States, Canada, Papua New Guinea, Singapore, Malaysia, the Philippines, Thailand, Hong Kong, Chinese Taipei, the Republic of Korea, Japan, Australia and New Zealand, and associated unions grouped in the International Trade Secretariats. 'Statement by the NZ Council of Trade Unions on Apec', September 1998, NZCTU MS 2008, Folder 119-02/4.

469. 'APEC's Role In Achieving Global Recovery from the Asian Financial and Economic Crisis', Trade Union Statement to the 1998 APEC Leaders Meeting adopted by the Fourth Conference of the ICFTU Asia Pacific Labour Network, Kuala Lumpur, 28–30 September 1998. NZCTU MS 2008, Folder 119-0214.

470. Shipley to Foulkes, 6 October 1998; MS 2008, Folder 119-02/4. It certainly was a representative body. Others invited to become members were a mix of politicians and business people, which might have been expected, but also writer Alan Duff and sportspeople Susan Devoy and Sean Fitzpatrick.

471. Fenton to Foulkes, 31 March 1999; Kelsey to Foulkes, 9 April 1999 (NZCTU MS 2008, Folder 2008-02/4).

472. Minutes, 'NZCTU International Committee Meeting', 13 April 1999 (NZCTU MS 2008, Folder 119-02/4). It was noteworthy that Foulkes could not have been accused of being 'bought off' and there was no remuneration attached to her appointment to the committee.

473. Memo, CTU Reunionisation Committee to National Affiliate Council, 31 August 1998 (NZCTU MS 2008, Folder 119-04/2). The APLN had presented to APEC leaders at their 1997 meeting in Vancouver a document that affirmed that APEC needed to develop a social dimension which included commitment to the internationally recognised fundamental human rights set out in the ILO's conventions on freedom of association and effective recognition of the right to collective bargaining, the elimination of all forms of forced or compulsory labour, the effective abolition of child labour and the elimination of discrimination in respect of employment and occupation (op. cit.). Also in 1998, an Asia Pacific People's Assembly (APPA) was organised in Kuala Lumpur alongside an APEC Leaders Summit in November, highlighting concerns about the 'free market, free trade' model of trade and investment liberalisation that APEC promoted. APLA was an umbrella grouping of non-government and people's organisations including SPOCTU and the CTU.

474. Bradford, media releases, 'Industrial Relations Package' and 'Industrial Relations Papers Released,' 23, 29 July 1998 (NZCTU MS 2003, Folder 361-15/1).

475. These and other unionists were also prominent in local Labour electorate committees. CTU 1999 Biennial Report, pp. 17–18; CTU 'Election Campaign Information Sheets', NZCTU MS 2003, Folder 361-19/10.

476. 'Minutes National Affiliate Council', 5 October 1999, p. 10 (NZCTU MS 2008, Folder 119-01/2).

477. 28 July 1999, p. 16.

478. Ibid., pp. 16–17.

479. Parsloe's comments quoted in 'Minutes, New Zealand Seafarers' Union, National Council Meeting', 1–17 October 2000, pp. 6–7 (Maritime Union of New Zealand Archives).

480. PP O'Shea, Clerk of the Executive Council, to Douglas, 27 September 1990; Douglas to Mike Moore, 5 October 1990; Catherine Tizard, Governor-General to Douglas, n.d. In possession of Ken Douglas. Prominent Maori carver and artist Cliff Whiting was awarded the Order of New Zealand at the same ceremony. Douglas followed Sonja Davies and Jim Knox as members of the Order. Earlier the Drivers' Union had persuaded the Federation of Labour to work for a change in the honours system to allow for a more indigenous recognition.

481. *Dominion*, 31 December 1998.

482. The Honorary Degrees Committee comprised a range of academic leaders and council members led by Chancellor Douglas White QC; the committee's membership and deliberations are confidential. Close to 50 years earlier Douglas had scored 4 per cent in his second attempt at School Certificate mathematics.

483. Citation of Kenneth George Douglas for the degree of Doctor of Laws, Victoria University of Wellington, 15 April 1999. In possession of Ken Douglas. The Doctor of Laws is a 'catch-all award' for recipients of such honours who do not fit into the other categories — Music, Science and Arts — the latter reserved for literary achievers (Christine Turner to author, 15 March 2010).

484. Sonja Davies served three years as MP for Pencarrow, and was an early recipient of the Order of New Zealand after turning down the offer to become a dame four times because it was not egalitarian. She wrote two best-selling memoirs, *Bread and Roses* (1984) and *Marching On* (1997). Her achievements, her books and Gaylene Preston's film based on *Bread and Roses* have ensured her place in New Zealand

feminist and trade union history. She died on 14 June 2005, aged 81.

485. Foulkes refused to be interviewed for this project.

486. Douglas interview, 21 March 2010.

487. Comments on both Douglas's and Wilson's speeches taken from *Evening Post*, 1 November 1999 and *New Zealand Herald*, 4 November 1999. The Dylan quote is from his song 'The Times They Are a-Changing'.

488. *Evening Post*, 30 October, 1 November 1999.

489. Douglas had fulfilled a similar role at the WTO conference in Singapore in 1995. Specifically the WTO deals with the opening up of trade between participating countries, provides a framework for negotiating and formalising trade agreements and runs a dispute resolution process aimed at enforcing participants' adherence to WTO agreements which are signed by representatives of member governments and ratified by their parliaments. Most current trade issues the WTO focuses on arise from previous trade negotiations, notably the Uruguay Round (1986-1994). Currently the Doha Round, begun in 2001, has been dogged by disagreement between developed and third world countries. The WTO's 153 members represent 97 per cent of the world's trade. Its headquarters, like the ILO, are in Geneva, Switzerland.

490. Douglas's comments quoted in the *New Zealand Herald*, 7 December 1999.

491. The surgery was to repair an ancient rugby injury.

CHAPTER 15

492. In 2007, Parliament passed a Bill sponsored by Sue Bradford which replaced youth pay rates with adult pay rates for 16- and 17-year-olds.

493. There have been some successes. Through the government's Trade and Enterprise Board — on which Douglas also sat — the trust provided a $2 million grant to Peter Jackson to enable him to use Telecom's broadband to send raw rushes of film to the United States overnight and have it returned the following day. That has enabled Jackson to expand his Miramar operation, creating more jobs, and more wealth for Wellington's economy. Interview, Douglas, 26 April 2010; Blakeley to author, 22 May 2010.

494. *Dominion*, 3 March 2003. Until August 2002, the Remuneration Authority

was known as the Higher Salaries Commission.

495. Blakeley to author, op. cit.

496. Ibid. Todd Motors employed 1200 workers at its peak.

497. Ibid.

498. Quoted in the *New Zealand Herald*, 7 April 2006.

499. In 2009, the three golfers chosen were Larissa Eruera of Auckland, Ben Campbell of Masterton and Peter Spearman-Burn of Wellington. It was through Michael Campbell that Douglas also became a trustee of Ronald McDonald House — a charitable trust run by a board of trustees, a small number of paid staff and lots of volunteers — of which Campbell became a patron in 2004 after it housed a close relative whose son was receiving treatment for cancer at Wellington Hospital.

500. Douglas had been approached by Beattie's brother John to chair this board. John Beattie had been active in the Employers' Federation and had known and respected Douglas's work as a trade union leader. Well-known 'green' businessman Rob Fenwick was also on the board.

501. Andrew Butcher, 'The Asia New Zealand Foundation and its Research Programme,' *New Zealand Sociology*, vol. 24, no. 2, 2009, p. 104. Butcher is the director of Policy and Research at the Asia New Zealand Foundation.

502. The other board members are Professor Manying Ip of Auckland University, Ruth de Douza of AUT and Gavin Ellis, formerly *New Zealand Herald* editor and now a member of the University of Auckland's politics department.

503. Interview, 26 April 2010.

504. Burdon to author, 19 May 2010.

505. Interview, 26 April 2010.

506. Palmer to author, 21 May 2010. Meo was a member of the AMP board.

507. Palmer to author, op. cit.

508. Ibid.

509. Healthcare also hired Ray Lind, Annette King's husband, as its chief operating officer after Lind left a similar post at the Hawke's Bay District Health Board.

510. A colleague of Douglas's on the FOL staff was very concerned about the possible implications of this statement and reported it to Douglas. He laughed and told her not to worry; 'He just wants a headline,' he said. Catley to author, 4 June 2010; Douglas to author, 10 June 2010.

511. *Dominion Post*, 11 June 2007.
512. Ibid., 9 November 2009. Douglas to author, 26 August.
513. Douglas to Ryall, 16 October 2009; in possession of Ken Douglas.
514. Allen to author, 2 June 2010.
515. Interview, 26 April 2010.
516. Between August 2007 and October 1999, Douglas also chaired the NZ Post Superannuation Plan Trust.
517. Allen to author, op. cit.
518. Tew to author, 26 May 2010.
519. Hobbs to author, 26 May 2010.
520. *Dominion Post*, 12 April 2007; *NZ Listener*, 8 October 2005, 1 December 2007.
521. *Dominion Post*, op. cit. Douglas also had a hip replaced in March 2010.

CHAPTER 16

522. Blakeley to author, 22 May 2010, op. cit.
523. Palmer to author, 21 May 2010, op. cit.
524. Burdon to author, 19 May 2010. Campbell to Monique Oomen, 17 November 2005. Videotaped interview for *Ken Douglas — Traitor or Visionary?* Burgess to Oomen, 29 November 2005, *Traitor or Visionary?*
525. Allen to author, 2 June 2010.
526. Tew to author, 26 May 2010.
527. Interview, 9 June 2010.
528. Ibid.
529. Ibid.
530. The *Evening Post* editorial of 2 November 1999 was one of a number which assessed the impact of Douglas's working life in positive terms.
531. Douglas, 'Speech Given to New Zealand Labour Party Congress', Quality Hotel, Willis St, Wellington, 25 May 1996, pp. 1-3 passim (NZCTU MS 2003, Folder 361-09/2).
532. According to Dalziel, between 1978 and 1984 the real gross domestic product paths between Australia and New Zealand were virtually identical, but after 1984 they diverged sharply with New Zealand's remaining static while Australia's grew

at 3 per cent per annum. 'While New Zealand's recovered between 1992 and 1998 to around 3.3 per cent it was still a percentage point below Australia's 4.2 per cent rate.' Over the entire period the output gap amounted to $215 million, equal to more than two years of output in New Zealand. These were huge numbers and represented an enormous sacrifice of lost economic development. (Dr Paul Dalziel, '"Third Way Economics": What This Might Mean in New Zealand', Research Paper, cited in NZCTU MS 2008-119-04/1, pp. 1, 3-4). Dalziel is now Professor of Economics at Lincoln University. Professor Chatterjee's figures are cited in Dalziel, p. 5.

533. Douglas, 'Congress Address . . .', op. cit., pp. 3, 6 (NZCTU MS 2003-361-09/2).

534. Kerr to Monique Oomen, 14 November 2005, videotaped interview for *Ken Douglas — Traitor or Visionary?*

535. O'Connell to author, 2 June 2010.

536. Ibid.

537. Ibid.

538. Tom Scott to author, 25 May 2010. This anecdote comes from an interview Scott conducted with Douglas as part of his television documentary on David Lange.

539. Harris to Monique Oomen, 28 November 2005; videotaped interview for *Ken Douglas — Traitor or Visionary?*

540. *Dominion Post*, 27 September 2007.

541. Max Bradford recalled that when he had just been appointed to lead the Employers' Association and he first met Douglas in his dingy Drivers' Federation office — in which he had a bust of Vladimir Lenin — Douglas gave him a series of texts by Marx and Engels. (Bradford to Oomen, 28 November 2005, *Ken Douglas — Traitor or Visionary?*)

542. Citation for Kenneth George Douglas for the degree of Doctor of Laws, Victoria University of Wellington, 15 April 1999, p. 3.

Index